GREEN TRANSITIONAL JUSTICE

This book rethinks the boundaries of transitional justice, urging scholars and practitioners to confront the often-overlooked nexus between mass violence and ecological harm.

Through an in-depth analysis of the field's limitations – such as its anthropocentric legalism, neocolonial practices, and alignment with neoliberalism – the book critiques the historical marginalisation of Nature in transitional justice discourse and practice. It argues that ignoring environmental harm not only undermines the possibility of holistic justice but also perpetuates structural violence and inequality. In response, the book sketches a 'greener' transitional justice, integrating principles from environmental justice, Indigenous knowledge systems, and ecocentric perspectives. It explores the possibilities of recognising Nature as a victim of mass violence, adapting existing mechanisms to incorporate environmental harm, and fostering transformative approaches premised on the interdependence of human and ecological well-being.

This book is written for students, researchers, and practitioners of transitional justice and fields related to conflict transformation, peacebuilding, environmental protection, and development.

Rachel Killean is a Senior Lecturer in the University of Sydney Law School.

Lauren Dempster is a Senior Lecturer in the School of Law at Queen's University Belfast.

Part of the TRANSITIONAL JUSTICE series

Series editor
Kieran McEvoy, *Queen's University Belfast, UK*

for information about the series and details of previous and forthcoming titles, see https://www.routledge.com/Transitional-Justice/book-series/TRANJ

GREEN TRANSITIONAL JUSTICE

Rachel Killean and Lauren Dempster

Routledge
Taylor & Francis Group
a GlassHouse Book

Designed cover image: rrodrickbeiler/iStock/Getty Images

First published 2025
by Routledge
4 Park Square, Milton Park, Abingdon, Oxon OX14 4RN

and by Routledge
605 Third Avenue, New York, NY 10158

Routledge is an imprint of the Taylor & Francis Group, an informa business

British Library Cataloguing-in-Publication Data
A catalogue record for this book is available from the British Library

Library of Congress Cataloging-in-Publication Data
Names: Killean, Rachel, author. | Dempster, Lauren, author.
Title: Green transitional justice / Rachel Killean and Lauren Dempster.
Description: Abingdon, Oxon [UK] ; New York, NY : Routledge, 2025. |
Series: Transitional justice | Includes bibliographical references and index.
Identifiers: LCCN 2025000826 (print) | LCCN 2025000827 (ebook) |
ISBN 9781032206219 (hardback) | ISBN 9781032206202 (paperback) |
ISBN 9781003264446 (ebook)
Subjects: LCSH: Liability for environmental damages. | Offenses against the environment–Law and legislation. | Environmental justice. |
Transitional justice. | Global environmental change. |
Climatic changes–Law and legislation.
Classification: LCC K955 .K53 2025 (print) | LCC K955 (ebook) |
DDC 344.04/6–dc23/eng/20250114
LC record available at https://lccn.loc.gov/2025000826
LC ebook record available at https://lccn.loc.gov/2025000827

ISBN: 9781032206219 (hbk)
ISBN: 9781032206202 (pbk)
ISBN: 9781003264446 (ebk)

DOI: 10.4324/9781003264446

Typeset in Sabon
by Deanta Global Publishing Services, Chennai, India

CONTENTS

ACKNOWLEDGEMENTS

Through nobody's fault but our own, this book took a lot longer to complete than we envisioned. As a result, we may have forgotten someone who helped us along this journey. If we have, know that we were grateful at the time and no doubt remembered that we should have included you shortly after the proofs were finalised.

Thanks go to our excellent colleagues in the School of Law; Transitional Justice Cluster; Institute for Criminology and Criminal Justice; Human Rights Centre; Senator George J. Mitchell Institute for Global Peace, Security and Justice; and McClay Library at Queen's University Belfast (QUB), and to Rachel's new colleagues at the Institute for Criminology, Sydney Southeast Asia Centre, Australian Centre for Climate and Environmental Law, and Law School at the University of Sydney. Both Sydney Law School and the Mitchell Institute provided funding which helped this project along, so our additional thanks for this. For their patience and encouragement, we thank the team at Routledge, particularly Colin and Naomi.

We presented various versions of this project at the following events and are grateful for the feedback we received there: the annual meetings of the Law & Society Association (a special shout-out goes to 2018 Conference in Toronto and Andrew Woolford and Wanda Hounslow's inspiring work on genocide and the destruction of buffalo in what is now the United States); the 2022 European Society of Criminology Conference; the 2022 Australia and New Zealand Society of Criminology conference; the 8th Annual Australian International Criminal Law Workshop; the annual meeting of the Socio-Legal Studies Association; the British Society of Criminology's Green Criminology Research Network (Twitter conference); various iterations of the International Association of Genocide Scholars conference; the Journal of Human Rights and the Environment Symposium in Cardiff; QUB's Senator George J. Mitchell Institute's Fireside Chat series; the 2022 Environmental Crimes and Protection Conference in Jersey; and the Irish North–South Criminology Conference.

For providing insightful feedback and guidance, we thank Elisa Arcioni, Peter Doran, Rosemary Grey, Kevin Hearty, Amanda Kramer, Louise Mallinder, Alice Panepinto, and Christoph Sperfeldt. Any mistakes that slipped past the eyes of these incredible scholars are ours alone. For helpful research assistance, we thank Victoria Bonilla-Baez, Monesa Mahdawi, Eamonn Murphy, Libby Newton, Sarah Oh, and Daniela Suarez-Vargas.

We received crucial support and good vibes from Nisan Aliči, Anna Bryson, Beatrice Canossi, Jason Chin, Oscar Dempster, Mark Drumbl, Matthew Evans, Gavin Gallagher, Kathryn Greenman, Amanda Kramer, Clyde Killean, Louise Mallinder, Peter Manning, Juliette Marchant, Anne-Marie McAlinden, Darryl Robinson, Ntina Tzouvala, and our families.

This book is dedicated to our niblings, in the hope that they don't grow up to live in a complete wasteland.

1

TRANSITIONAL JUSTICE AND NATURE

Scoping the Field

1.1 Introduction

Harms against Nature are deeply interlinked with periods of conflict, atrocity crimes, authoritarianism, and violent repression. For instance, the unequal exploitation of natural resources can motivate conflict; deliberate environmental destruction has been adopted as a tactic against targeted groups;[1] and authoritarian regimes can practice harmful policies of resource extraction alongside related human rights abuses.[2] The environmental impacts of methods of mass violence can be severe; periods of conflict have 'scorched the earth, eradicated species, destroyed entire ecosystems and rendered large swathes of land uninhabitable.'[3] Processes of transition can in turn bring their own harms,[4] including new resource conflicts in areas that might have

1 Ines Peterson, "The Natural Environment in Times of Armed Conflict: A Concern for International War Crimes Law?" *Leiden Journal of International Law* 22(2) (2009): 325–343.

2 Margarita Alario, "Environmental Policy Enactment Under the Military: Some Generalities Between Brazil and Chile," *International Journal of Comparative Sociology* 34(3–4) (1993): 222–230; Miles Kenney-Lazar, "Neoliberalizing Authoritarian Environmental Governance in (Post) Socialist Laos," *Annals of the American Association of Geographers* 109(2) (2019): 338–348.

3 Avi Brisman and Nigel South, "Resource Wealth, Power, Crime and Conflict," *Emerging Issues in Green Criminology: Exploring Power, Justice and Harm*, ed Reece Walters et al., (Palgrave, 2013), 64.

4 Bill McClanahan et al., "Conflict, Environment and Transition: Colombia, Ecology and Tourism after Demobilisation," *International Journal for Crime, Justice and Social Democracy* 8(3) (2019): 74–88.

DOI: 10.4324/9781003264446-1

been inaccessible due to armed violence.[5] These harms can be long-term and wide-ranging and can 'rupture' the ecological connectivity and interdependencies that exist within ecosystems and between humans and their natural environment.[6]

This nexus between what we have collectively termed 'mass violence' and Nature has received international recognition. In law, this has emerged through efforts to protect Nature during conflict. For instance, in 1994, the International Committee of the Red Cross (ICRC) produced the first *Guidelines for Military Manuals and Instructions on the Protection of the Environment in Times of Armed Conflict*, drawn from existing international humanitarian principles. These were updated in 2020 and now include recommendations that parties to a conflict can adopt to reduce the environmental effects of armed conflict.[7] Since 2013, the International Law Commission (ILC) has included the 'Protection of the Environment in Relation to Armed Conflicts' in its work.[8] In 2019, a United Nations (UN) Environment Assembly resolution acknowledged geoengineering's possible use as a weapon and related future security risks.[9]

There is also increased recognition of the need to protect Nature in the context of *jus post bellum* (postwar justice).[10] In February 2024, the Office of the Prosecutor at the International Criminal Court (ICC) commenced a consultation regarding how crimes against the environment can be effectively investigated and prosecuted as international crimes.[11] Calls for a new crime of ecocide also continue to gather momentum at an international, regional,

5 Andres Suarez et al., "Environmental Sustainability in Post-Conflict Countries: Insights for Rural Colombia," *Environment, Development and Sustainability* 20 (2018): 997–1015.

6 Janine Natalya Clark, "The COVID-19 Pandemic and Ecological Connectivity: Implications for International Criminal Law and Transitional Justice," *Journal of International Criminal Justice* 18(5) (2020): 1045–1068.

7 ICRC, Guidelines on Protection of Natural Environment in Armed Conflict, 2020. https://www.icrc.org/en/document/guidelines-protection-natural-environment-armed-conflict-rules-and-recommendations-relating%20/. See Helen Obregón Gieseken and Vanessa Murphy, "The Protection of the Natural Environment under International Humanitarian Law: The ICRC's 2020 Guidelines," *International Review of the Red Cross* 105(924) (2023): 1180–1207 for analysis.

8 ILC, Summaries of the Work of the International Law Commission: Protection of the Environment in Relation to Armed Conflicts. 2021. https://legal.un.org/ilc/guide/8_7.shtml

9 Gabriela Kolpak, "From ENMOD to Geoengineering: The Environment as a Weapon of War," *Conflict and Environment Observatory,* April 7, 2020, *https://ceobs.org/from-enmod-to-geoengineering-the-environment-as-a-weapon-of-war/*

10 Carsten Stahn et al., eds., *Environmental Protection and Transitions from Conflict to Peace: Clarifying Norms, Principles, and Practices* (OUP, 2017).

11 "The Office of the Prosecutor Launches Public Consultation on a New Policy Initiative to Advance Accountability for Environmental Crimes under the Rome Statute," Statement, *ICC Website*, February 16, 2024. https://www.icc-cpi.int/news/office-prosecutor-launches-public-consultation-new-policy-initiative-advance-accountability-0.

and domestic level.[12] Outside these legal contexts, the growth of environmental peacebuilding as a distinct body of scholarship and practice has further highlighted the environmental consequences of war, as well as the links between post-conflict peacebuilding and natural resource management.[13]

Against this backdrop, it is notable that the impact of mass violence on Nature has historically been under-theorised and under-explored in the field of transitional justice.[14] By 'transitional justice,' we mean the field of scholarship and practice centred around the question of how to respond to 'periods of conflict, civil strife and repression.'[15] Commonly used mechanisms include trials, truth recovery processes, reparations, memorialisation, reconciliation projects, and guarantees of non-recurrence. As we unpack below, the last decade has seen the emergence of a multidisciplinary literature characterised by a willingness to recognise Nature as a subject of concern for transitional justice, yet this has rarely been mirrored in practice.

To the extent that harms to Nature have been addressed, they have predominantly been framed in profoundly anthropocentric ways, whether as violations of property rights or as the means of perpetrating physical harms against human beings.[16] By way of example (others are explored in subsequent chapters): the UN War Crimes Commission, established to assist in the prosecution of war crimes committed by the Axis powers during World War II, framed the 'wilful felling' of Polish forests as the war crime of 'pillaging public property.'[17] Similarly, extractive crimes associated with the

12 Rachel Killean and Damien Short, *Scoping a Domestic Legal Framework for Ecocide in Scotland* (ECRS, 2024), https://www.ercs.scot/wp/wp-content/uploads/2024/04/Scoping-a-Domestic-Legal-Framework-for-Ecocide-in-Scotland_April24_online.pdf.

13 Tobias Ide et al., "The Past and Future(s) of Environmental Peacebuilding," *International Affairs* 97(1) (2021): 1–16; Anaïs Dresse et al., "Environmental Peacebuilding: Towards a Theoretical Framework," *Cooperation and Conflict* 54(1) (2019): 99-119. On the relationship between transitional justice and peacebuilding see Catherine Baker and Jelena Obradovic-Wochnik, "Mapping the Nexus of Transitional Justice and Peacebuilding," *Journal of Intervention and Statebuilding* 10(3) (2016): 281–301.

14 Janine Natalya Clark, "Are There 'Greener' Ways" of Doing Transitional Justice? Some Reflections on Srebrenica, Nature and Memorialisation," *International Journal of Human Rights* 20(8) (2016): 1199–1218; Lieselotte Viaene et al., "Editorial Special Section: 'Transitional Justice and Nature: A Curious Silence,'" *International Journal of Transitional Justice* 17(1) (2023): 1–14.

15 Naomi Roht-Arriaza, "The New Landscape of Transitional Justice," *Transitional Justice in the Twenty-First Century* ed Naomi Roht-Arriaza and Javier Mariezcurrena (CUP, 2012), 1–16.

16 See e.g. Mark A Drumbl, *Accountability for Property Crimes and Environmental War Crimes: Prosecution, Litigation, and Development* (ICTJ, 2009), https://www.ictj.org/sites/default/files/ICTJ-Development-PropertyCrimes-FullPaper-2009-English.pdf

17 UNWCC, 'Destruction of Polish Forests as a War Crime' Examination of Cases and Listing of War Criminals, 1948 History of the United Nations War Crimes Commission and the Development of the Laws of War, 496.

Liberian conflict were classed as 'economic crime' by the Republic of Liberia Truth and Reconciliation Commission.[18] In Guatemala, the 'scorched earth policies' identified in the 'Memory of Silence' Truth Commission report were primarily understood as the destruction of the Mayan people's property ('villages, makeshift homes, and crops') and a means of engineering displacement.[19] We argue in this book that this focus on property both simplifies the nature of the harm and fails to capture its full extent.[20]

In other instances, environmental harm has been framed as a method of inflicting suffering on human populations. For example, the Report of the Timor-Leste Commission for Reception, Truth and Reconciliation details the devastating impacts of herbicides on civilians,[21] and the 2009 Report of the South Korean Truth and Reconciliation Commission notes scorched-earth policies to the extent that they resulted in the death of civilians.[22] This sole focus on physical harm is not necessarily shared by victims themselves. At the ICC, witnesses have spoken of the 'ecological trauma' associated with seeing scorched-earth practices unfold,[23] but to date courts and tribunals have struggled to acknowledge and obtain accountability for such harms.[24]

We argue that a transitional justice that fails to account for harms against Nature is delivering incomplete justice. Excluding consideration of Nature can decontextualise periods of mass violence from their historic or structural

18 Republic of Liberia Truth and Reconciliation Commission, Volume Three: Appendices, Title III: Economic Crimes and the Conflict, Exploitation and Abuse, 164. See Eliana Cusato, "Back to the Future? Confronting the Role (s) of Natural Resources in Armed Conflict Through the Lenses of Truth and Reconciliation Commissions," *International Community Law Review* 19(4–5) (2017): 373–400.

19 Memory of Silence: Report of the Commission for Historical Clarification Conclusions and Recommendations, February 2019, xxxi. A similar reference to scorched earth can be found in Per Memoriam ad Spem: The Final Report of the Commission of Truth and Friendship Indonesia – Timor-Leste (2008) and CAVR, *Chega! The Final Report of the Timor-Leste Commission for Reception, Truth and Reconciliation (CAVR)* (KPG in cooperation with STP-CAVR, 2013).

20 Ryan Gilman, "Expanding Environmental Justice after War: The Need for Universal Jurisdiction over Environmental War Crimes," *Colorado Journal of International Environmental Law and Policy* 22(3) (2011): 447–471.

21 Chega!, 19, Chapter 7.5: Violations of the laws of War. See also, ICC, *Situation in Darfur, The Sudan, Summary of Prosecution's Application under Article 58*, ICC- 02/ 05- 152, 14 July 2008.

22 Truth and Reconciliation Commission, Republic of Korea, Activities of the Past Three Years, 2009, at 68.

23 ICC, *The Prosecutor v Dominic Ongwen*, ICC-02/04-01/15, Witness UGA-PCV-0003, Open Session, 23 May 2028, https://www.icc-cpi.int/sites/default/files/Transcripts/CR2018_02682.PDF, 81.

24 Pereira Ricardo, "After the ICC Office of the Prosecutor's 2016 Policy Paper on Case Selection and Prioritisation: Towards an International Crime of Ecocide?" *Criminal Law Forum* 31(2) (2020):179–224.

origins,[25] impede realistic assessments of the full range of harms experienced by humans, preclude the recognition of other-than-human victims,[26] reduce the chances of meaningfully addressing the drivers and legacies of violence, and create incomplete narratives about the past.[27] In turn, these limitations may inhibit the chances of creating meaningful, long-term, positive peace.[28] These risks are not equally distributed. Rather, they reinforce the material inequalities of the international system, placing the heaviest burdens of environmental degradation on the most vulnerable populations.[29] Moreover, they fail to recognise the intrinsic value of Nature, replicating anthropocentric assumptions that enable future harms against Nature to take place.

Taking this argument as our starting point, in this book we probe and challenge the marginalisation of Nature in dominant transitional justice scholarship and practice. This involves i) interrogating the limitations of dominant approaches to transitional justice as a means of responding to harm against Nature, ii) exposing the factors and contexts that have created those limitations, and iii) engaging with diverse theories of justice (e.g. environmental, Indigenous, transformative) to consider the possibilities of a 'green' transitional justice, meaning an approach which better recognises and responds to harms against Nature.[30]

This introductory chapter continues as follows. In Part 2, we establish what we mean by 'transitional justice' and 'Nature.' We also further unpack the relationship between mass violence and harms against Nature, providing the context to our subsequent discussions. In Part 3, we review the growing literature characterised by a willingness to frame Nature as a subject of concern for transitional justice. In Part 4, we outline the approach adopted in this book and summarise the chapters that follow.

25 Hugo van der Merwe and M. Brinton Lykes, "Transitional Justice and Corporate Accountability: Introducing New Players and New Theoretical Challenges," *International Journal of Transitional Justice* 16(3) (2022): 291–297.

26 Including the interrelationship between environmental harm and other harms, such as gender-based violence. See e.g. Natalia Urzola and María Paula González, "Gender-Based Environmental Violence in Colombia: Problematising Dominant Notions of Gender-Based Violence During Peacebuilding," *Australian Feminist Law Journal* 48(2) (2022): 245–264.

27 Zinaida Miller, "Effects of Invisibility: In Search of the 'Economic' in Transitional Justice," *International Journal of Transitional Justice* 2(3) (2008): 266–267.

28 Carl Bruch, "Considerations in Framing the Environmental Dimensions of Ius Post Bellum," in *Environmental Protection and Transitions from Conflict to Peace*, ed Carsten Stahn et al. (OUP, 2017).

29 Rob Nixon, *Slow Violence and the Environmentalism of the Poor* (Harvard University Press, 2011).

30 The phrase 'green transitional justice' was first used by Janine Natalya Clark in her article "Are There 'Greener' Ways."

1.2 Conceptualising Transitional Justice, Nature, and the Mass Violence–Nature Nexus

1.2.1 Transitional Justice

The emergence of 'transitional justice' as a field of scholarship, policy, and practice is attributable to sustained debate amongst activists, scholars, lawyers, policy makers, donors, and others on the question of how to respond to past harms in the context of 'exceptionally precarious political situations.'[31] This debate emerged out of a perceived need to redress the harms of the past in order to move towards a 'more hopeful' future, generally involving a shift towards democratic rule.[32] As such, the concept of 'transitional justice' contains both backward-looking aspects in the form of responses to past abuses, and forward-looking aspects involving the creation of conditions that might facilitate a more peaceful society. Although the term 'transitional justice' has retrospectively been applied to legal responses to World War II,[33] it was first used to describe responses to grave human rights violations in the 1980s and 1990s,[34] primarily in the context of regime change across Latin America, Eastern Europe, and South Africa.[35] Thus, its emergence coincided with the end of the Cold War and the associated optimism about free market ideology and political liberalisation.[36]

Over time, this new 'field' began to crystallise around a range of organisations, including specific civil society organisations, universities, and international institutions.[37] By the early 2000s, transitional justice was becoming the dominant framework for addressing questions about how to deal with the impacts and legacies of mass violence.[38] It was defined by the UN in 2004 as comprising:

31 Paige Arthur, "How 'Transitions' Reshaped Human Rights: A Conceptual History of Transitional Justice," *Human Rights Quarterly* 31 (2009): 322, citing the New Yorker writer Lawrence Weschler.

32 Makau Mutua, "What is the Future of Transitional Justice," *International Journal of Human Rights* 9(1) (2015): 1–9.

33 Ruti G. Teitel, "Transitional Justice Genealogy," *Havard Human Rights Journal* 16 (2003): 69–94.

34 Briony Jones, "The Performance and Persistence of Transitional Justice and Its Ways of Knowing Atrocity," *Cooperation and Conflict* 56(2) (2021): 163–180.

35 Arthur, "Transitions," noting the influence of Neil Kritz's four-volume compendium *Transitional Justice: How Emerging Democracies Reckon with Former Regimes* (United States Institute of Peace Press, 1995), in popularising the term.

36 Mutua, "What is the Future."

37 Arthur, "Transitions."

38 Rosalind Shaw et al., eds., *Localizing Transitional Justice: Intervention sand Priorities After Mass Violence* (Stanford University Press, 2010).

> the full range of processes and mechanisms associated with a society's attempts to come to terms with a legacy of large-scale past abuses, in order to ensure accountability, serve justice and achieve reconciliation. These may include both judicial and non-judicial mechanisms, with differing levels of international involvement (or none at all) and individual prosecutions, reparations, truth-seeking, institutional reform, vetting and dismissals, or a combination thereof.[39]

A 'standardised' form of transitional justice began to coalesce around certain state-led and/or internationalised mechanisms. This 'standardised' field continued to become more formally institutionalised through international organisations such as the UN,[40] by regional bodies such as the African and European Unions, and by national legislatures around the world.[41] Beyond these formal institutions, a global community of actors, including 'advocates, funders, policy makers, practitioners, scholars, and victims,' engaged and invested in the field.[42]

Transitional justice's institutionalisation was accompanied by the development of critical voices in academia and elsewhere, who critiqued the field's depoliticisation,[43] increasingly technocratic character,[44] and inattention to socioeconomic and cultural rights violations,[45] and structural and 'slow' violence.[46] As institutionalised transitional justice became increasingly accepted as the preferred choice of redress for societies grappling with legacies of violence,[47] concern grew that transitional justice was raising expectations but failing to deliver, disappointing victimised communities.[48] This critique

39 UN Secretary-General, *The Rule of Law and Transitional Justice in Conflict and Post-Conflict Societies,* UN Doc. S/2004/616, 23 August 2004, 8.

40 UN Secretary-General, *The Rule of Law and Transitional Justice.*

41 See e.g. the African Union, *Transitional Justice Policy*, February 2019 and the EU's *Policy Framework on Support to Transitional Justice*, 2015.

42 Laurel E. Fletcher and Harvey M. Weinstein, "How Power Dynamics Influence the North–South Gap in Transitional Justice," *Berkeley Journal of International Law* 37(1) (2018): 1–28.

43 See e.g. Bronwyn Anne Leebaw, "The Irreconcilable Goals of Transitional Justice," *Human Rights Quarterly* 30(1) (2008): 95–118.

44 See e.g. Shaw, Waldorf, and Hazan, *Localizing.*

45 See e.g., Louise Arbour, "Economic and Social Justice for Societies in Transition," *N.Y.U. Journal of International Law and Politics* 40(1) (2007): 1–26.

46 See e.g. Dustin N. Sharp. "Addressing Economic Violence in Times of Transition: Toward a Positive-Peace Paradigm for Transitional Justice," *Fordham International Law Journal* 35(3) (2012): 780–814 at 782–783; Randle C. DeFalco, "Time and the Visibility of Slow Atrocity Violence," *International Criminal Law Review* 21(5) (2021): 905–934.

47 Jelena Subotić, "The Transformation of International Transitional Justice Advocacy," *International Journal of Transitional Justice* 6(1) (2012): 106–125.

48 Lars Waldorf, "Anticipating the Past: Transitional Justice and Socio-Economic Wrongs," *Social & Legal Studies* 21(2) (2012): 171–186.

has been sustained over time, with the field described as 'all too often' failing to reach its potential.[49]

Despite these critiques, transitional justice has continued to expand as a field of practice in terms of the scenarios to which it applies, the agents involved, and the approaches adopted.[50] For example, transitional justice, as suggested by the name, traditionally required a 'transition,' historically from authoritarianism to democracy, or latterly from armed conflict to peace.[51] However, the field has become less stringent about the form and length of the transition,[52] enabling it to encompass both ongoing conflicts and attempts to redress long-term and ongoing legacies of colonisation.[53]

These 'aparadigmatic cases'[54] have been accompanied by an expansion of the actors engaged in transitional justice work. Social movements and victim groups increasingly challenge state-centric or 'top-down' approaches to transition,[55] turning towards less institutionalised, more informal mechanisms.[56] As a field designed to right wrongs, strong arguments have been made that transitional justice should be whatever victims want it to be.[57] Yet there is also a willingness among some actors, including victim groups,

49 M. Brinton Lykes and Colleen Murphy, "Decolonizing Transitional Justice: Soft, Radical or Beyond Reform," *International Journal of Transitional Justice* 17(3) (2023): 361–369.

50 Marcos Zunino, *Justice Framed: A Genealogy of Transitional Justice* (CUP, 2019).

51 Arthur, "Transitions"; Joanna R. Quinn, "Whither the 'Transition' of Transitional Justice?" *Interdisciplinary Journal of Human Rights* 8, (2014): 63–79; Stephen Winter, "Towards a Unified Theory of Transitional Justice," *International Journal of Transitional Justice* 7(2) (2013): 224–244.

52 Ray Nickson and John Braithwaite, "Deeper, Broader, Longer Transitional Justice," *European Journal of Criminology* 11(4) (2014): 445–463; Dustin N. Sharp, "Emancipating Transitional Justice from the Bonds of the Paradigmatic Transition," *International Journal of Transitional Justice* 9(1) (2015): 150–169; Winter, "Towards a Unified Theory."

53 Harry Hobbs, "Locating the Logic of Transitional Justice in Liberal Democracies: Native Title in Australia," *The University of New South Wales Law Journal* 39(2) (2016): 512–552.

54 Sarah Kerremans and Tine Destrooper. "Exploring the Nexus between Transitional Justice and Ecoterritorial Conflict Resolution: Time for an Ecoterritorial Turn in Transformative Transitional Justice?" *International Journal of Transitional Justice* 17(1) (2023): 54–70.

55 Kieran McEvoy and Lorna McGregor, *Transitional Justice from Below: Grassroots Activism and the Struggle for Change* (Hart Publishing, 2008).

56 Brigitte Herremans and Tine Destrooper, "Moving Beyond Formal Truth Practices and Forensic Truth in the Syrian Conflict: How Informal Truth Practices Contribute to Thicker Understandings of Truth," *Journal of Social & Legal Studies* 32(4) (2022): 1–21.

57 Simon Robins, "Whose Voices? Understanding Victims' Needs in Transition: Nepali Voices: Perceptions of Truth, Justice, Reconciliation, Reparations and the Transition in Nepal by the International Centre for Transitional Justice and the Advocacy Forum, March 2008," *Journal of Human Rights Practice* 1(2) (2009): 320–331; Lieselotte Viaene and Eva Brems, "Transitional Justice and Cultural Contexts: Learning from the Universality Debate," *Netherlands Quarterly of Human Rights* 28(2) (2010): 199–224.

to move beyond redress and connect the field to broader justice agendas.[58] There is now a multidisciplinary body of scholarship which envisions a 'broader and more holistic project'[59] for transitional justice.

In this book, we are predominantly critiquing the blind spots and limitations of the 'institutionalised' forms of transitional justice that continue to dominate the field. However, we recognise that important initiatives have developed at grassroots levels that are particularly relevant to our argument in favour of greater engagement with Nature. We note examples of these initiatives throughout the book and return to the importance of grassroots initiatives at several points.

1.2.2 Nature

We have chosen to use the terms 'Nature' and 'natural world' throughout this book. We use these terms to refer to the natural living space in which we live as well as humans' multifaceted (e.g. physical, cultural, spiritual) relationships with it. By 'harms against Nature,' we therefore mean harms such as the pollution of air, land, and water; the killing of other-than-human species; and the extreme degradation of ecosystems (such as forests or lakes). To be clear, we recognise that we are living in the Anthropocene and that all human activity has an environmental footprint of some kind.[60] We are not arguing that all such harms can or should necessarily attract a call for 'justice.'[61] In this book, we are focusing on severe, widespread, and/or long-term harm. We explore the harms that form the particular focus of this book further below when discussing the mass violence–Nature nexus.

We believe that the term 'Nature' is helpful to our work, as it encompasses a more holistic understanding of the natural environment than that implied by terms such as 'the environment' or 'natural resources.' Although

58 Jennifer Balint et al., "Rethinking Transitional Justice, Redressing Indigenous Harm: A New Conceptual Approach," *International Journal of Transitional Justice* 8(2) (2014): 194–216; Rosemary Nagy, "Transformative justice in a Settler Colonial Transition: Implementing the UN Declaration on the Rights of Indigenous Peoples in Canada," *International Journal of Human Rights* 26(2) (2022): 191–216; Natalia Szablewska and Sascha-Dominik Bachmann, "Current Issues and Future Challenges in Transitional Justice," *Current Issues in Transitional Justice: Towards a More Holistic Approach*, ed. Natalia Szablewska and Sascha-Dominik Bachmann (Springer, 2015), 339–361.

59 Dustin N. Sharp, "What Would Satisfy Us? Taking Stock of Critical Approaches to Transitional Justice," *International Journal of Transitional Justice* 13(3) (2019): 571. For a critique of 'holistic' transitional justice, see Mariam Salehi, "Trying Just Enough or Promising Too Much? The Problem-Capacity-Nexus in Tunisia's Transitional Justice Process," *Journal of Intervention and Statebuilding* 16(1) (2021): 98–116.

60 Simon L. Lewis and Mark A. Maslin, "Defining the Anthropocene," *Nature* 519 (2015): 171–180.

61 Our thanks go to Dr Peter Szigeti for pushing us to make this point.

there is no agreed upon legal definition of 'the environment,'[62] this term tends to invoke environmental law, and to suggest a 'pure' notion of public wildlife and ecosystems.[63] The term 'natural resources,' on the other hand, understands Nature primarily as a resource to be exploited, valued only to the extent that it is useful for production. Both terms frame Nature as something separate and external to humans and primarily objects of human governance.[64] Following the work of Usha Natarajan, Julia Dehm, and others,[65] we believe that identifying ways to meaningfully protect and repair the natural world requires engagement with worldviews that are more attuned to our inseparability from the world around us. Our terminology is designed to be more encompassing of these worldviews and less tied to the language of dominant Western-centric legal frameworks. Of course, when we are discussing those frameworks in the book, we engage with and use the terminology that they employ.

1.2.3 Mass Violence–Nature Nexus

The nexus between mass violence and Nature is multifaceted. Nature can be a source, means, and victim of mass violence, while responses to periods of mass violence can bring their own environmental harms.[66] Here we briefly discuss each of these aspects and interconnections.

Since 'time immemorable,' issues of access to and distribution of natural resources have been 'at the root of violent conflict.'[67] Over 40% of intra-state and internal conflicts over the last half century have related to natural resource exploitation.[68] Climate change and its consequences are increasingly

62 Cymie R. Payne, "Defining the Environment: Environmental Integrity," in *Environmental Protection and Transitions from Conflict to Peace,* ed Carsten Stahn et al. (CUP, 2017).

63 Payne, "Defining the Environment."

64 Usha Natarajan and Julia Dehm, "Where is the Environment? Locating Nature in International Law," *TWAILR Reflections* 3, August 30, 2019. https://twailr.com/where-is-the-environment-locating-nature-in-international-law/.

65 Usha Natarajan and Julia Dehm, eds. *Locating Nature: Making and Unmaking International Law* (CUP, 2022).

66 This classification follows UNEP, From Conflict to Peacebuilding: The Role of Natural Resources and the Environment, U.N. Doc. DEP/1079/GE, U.N. Sales No. 09.III.D.14 (2009); see also Luisa Gómez-Betancur, "The Rights of Nature in the Colombian Amazon: Examining Challenges and Opportunities in a Transitional Justice Setting," *UCLA Journal of International Law and Foreign Affairs* 25(1) (2020): 41–48.

67 Eliana Cusato, "International Law, the Paradox of Plenty and the Making of Resource-Driven Conflict," *Leiden Journal of International Law* 33(3) (2020): 649–666. See also Philippe Le Billon, "The Political Ecology of War: Natural Resources and Armed Conflict," *Political Geography* 20(5) (2001): 561–584.

68 UN Security Council, 8372nd Meeting, SC/13540, 16 October 2018; UNEP, *Protecting the Environment During Armed Conflict: An Inventory and Analysis of International Law* (UNEP, 2009). See also Le Billon. "The Political Ecology of War."

accepted as a trigger for conflict and a long-term security risk,[69] and internal displacement is associated with natural disasters.[70] The risk of conflict – and more prolonged conflict – is higher in countries with particularly desirable resources.[71] This dynamic has been referred to as the *resource curse*, defined as 'the adverse effects of a country's natural resource wealth on its economic, social or political well-being.'[72] The resource curse has been problematised for its erasure of the historical and structural drivers of global inequality. However, the theory continues to be used by some scholars, international organisations, and civil society[73] to at least partially explain the connections between natural resource wealth and increased economic and political instability, corruption, civil strife, armed conflict, and authoritarian rule.[74] The dynamics of resource exploitation can also cause conflict, for example between local populations, extractive corporations, and the state forces that protect extractive processes.[75] Although a less direct cause, the profits earned from natural resource exploitation can fuel and fund conflict, enabling its prolonged continuation.[76] While these causes obviously intersect with other social, political, and cultural factors, it is clear that violence is 'tightly interwoven with resource extraction.'[77]

The destruction of Nature can also be a deliberate strategy during periods of mass violence. Nature can be targeted to further a range of goals – including exposure of the enemy, reducing the amount of habitable land,

69 "Conflict and Climate," *United Nations Climate Change*, July 12, 2022, https://unfccc.int/news/conflict-and-climate#:~:text=The%20evidence%20is%20clear%20that,climate%20change%20into%20conflict%20risks.

70 See e.g. Internal Displacement Monitoring Centre, *Grid 2023: Internal Displacement and Food Security* (Norwegian Refugee Council, 2023).

71 Paivi Lujala and Siri Aas Rustad, "High-value Natural Resources: A Blessing or a Curse for Peace?" *Sustainable Development Law & Policy* 12(1) (2011): 19–22.

72 Michael L. Ross, "What Have We Learned About the Resource Curse?" *Annual Review of Political Science* 18 (2015): 239–256.

73 Cusato, "Paradox of Plenty."

74 Cusato, "Paradox of Plenty." Le Billon, "The Political Ecology of War"; Lujala and Aas Rustad, "High-value Natural Resources."

75 UNSC, *Final Report of the Panel of Experts on the Illegal Exploitation of Natural Resources and Other Forms of Wealth of the Democratic Republic of Congo*, S/2002/1, 16 October 2002.

76 Clementine Burnley, "Natural Resources Conflict in the Democratic Republic of Congo: A Question of Governance?" *Sustainable Development Law & Policy* 12(1) (2011): 7–11; Thor Hanson et al., "Warfare in Biodiversity Hotspots," *Conservation Biology* 23(3) (2009): 578–587; Ana Maria Ibañez, "Forced Displacement in Colombia: Magnitude and Causes," *The Economics of Peace and Security Journal*, 4(1) (2009): 47–54; UNSC, *Final Report* S/2002/11.

77 Eoghan Darbyshire "Deforestation in Conflict Areas in 2020" *Conflict Environment and Observatory*, April 2021, *https://ceobs.org/assessment-of-recent-forest-loss-in-conflict-areas/*

or removing the resources that groups use to fund their activities. Probably the most cited example of deliberate environmental destruction is the use of Agent Orange by the United States of America (USA) during the Vietnam War,[78] a strategy that has caused long-term, continuing harm to human populations and Nature alike across Southeast Asia.[79] Natural resources may also be targeted to remove resources that are in demand by parties to the conflict. For example, the deliberate destruction of tree cover and agricultural crops has been alleged in a range of conflicts, including Nagorno-Karabakh, Sudan, Syria, and El Salvador.[80] Targeting resources can lead to knock-on, long-term environmental damage. For example, the targeting of oil infrastructure during the Gulf War led to the pollution of the Persian Gulf, as well as the soil and air of numerous states.[81]

Nature is frequently a victim of mass violence, whether directly targeted or not. While it is difficult to measure the full impact of mass violence on Nature,[82] there is no doubt that the impacts are 'overwhelmingly deleterious.'[83] Indiscriminate weapons such as landmines can damage, destabilise, and contaminate ecosystems, whether detonated or not.[84] They can also impact biodiversity by destroying vegetation and killing animals heavy enough to activate the mine.[85] Weapons and armoured vehicles can similarly release hazardous substances, contaminating land, air, and water and reducing biodiversity for decades after the fact.[86] This continues after the cessation of violence: metallic items, fuel, unexploded ordinance, depleted uranium weapons, and nerve agents can survive in the soil for a long time,

78 See e.g. Matthias Baumann and Tobias Kuemmerle, "The Impacts of Warfare and Armed Conflict on Land Systems," *Journal of Land Use Science* 11(6) (2016): 672–688.

79 Giacomo Certini et al., "The Impact of Warfare on the Soil Environment," *Earth-Science Review* 127 (2013): 1–15.

80 Ken Conca and Jennifer Wallace, "Environment and Peacebuilding in War-Torn Societies: Lessons from the UN Environment Programme's Experience with Postconflict Assessment," *Global Governance* 15(4) (2009): 485–504; Darbyshire, "Deforestation in Conflict Areas"; Commission on the Truth for El Salvador, *From Madness to Hope: the 12-Year War in El Salvador: Report of the Commission on the Truth for El Salvador,* https://www.usip.org/sites/default/files/file/ElSalvador-Report.pdf.

81 Cusato, "Paradox of Plenty."

82 Anwesha Dutta and Trishant Simlai, "If the Army Cuts Trees, Why Can't We? Resource Extraction, Hunting and the impacts of Militaries on Biodiversity Conservation," *Enforcing Ecocide Power, Policing & Planetary Militarization*, eds. Alexander Dunlap and Andera Brock (Palgrave, 2022), 199--225.

83 Michael J. Lawrence et al., "The Effects of Modern War and Military Activities on Biodiversity and the Environment," *Environmental Review,* 23(4) (2015): 453.

84 Asmeret Asefaw Berhe, "The Contribution of Landmines to Land Degradation," *Land Degradation and Development* 18(1) (2007): 1–15; Certini et al., "The Impact of Warfare."

85 Berhe, "The Contribution of Landmines"; Lawrence et al.. "The Effects of Modern War."

86 Lawrence et al.. "The Effects of Modern War."

causing ongoing contamination.[87] Beyond contamination, military aircraft and ships may result in the introduction of invasive species, leading to the extinction of some endemic species.[88] In addition to being at risk of injury and death from weapons use, wildlife can face threats from the use of their habitats by armed groups and displaced populations, increased hunting for consumption and trade, and disruption from the noise pollution associated with weapon use.[89] More broadly, mass violence is often accompanied by weak law enforcement, rising corruption, and, in some instances, the failure of the state, leading to increased and unregulated exploitation of natural resources.[90]

Phases of peace-making and transitioning from conflict can raise equally important environmental challenges. These can include the ongoing impacts of weak law enforcement, reduced administrative capacity, and the significant resource needs associated with societal reconstruction.[91] Access to Nature may become easier and safer, as armed groups may have previously rendered certain land inaccessible.[92] An increase in accessibility,[93] combined with an influx of international aid and attempts at economic, political, and social reforms, can lead tonatural resource exploitation;[94] deforestation often increases sharply in countries emerging from conflict.[95] As well as posing environmental risks, this growth in natural resource exploitation can complicate peacebuilding and risk a return to conflict.[96] For example, re-opening or developing mines can 'intensify' the 'fragility' of post-conflict

87 Certini et al.. "The Impact of Warfare"; Conca and Wallace, "Environment and Peacebuilding"; Lawrence et al., "The Effects of Modern War."

88 Lawrence et al., "The Effects of Modern War."

89 Dirk Draulans and Ellen Van Krunkelsven, "The Impact of War on Forest Areas in the Democratic Republic of Congo," *Onyx* 36(1) (2002): 35–40; Kaitlyn M. Gaynor et al., "War and Wildlife: Linking Armed Conflict to Conservation," *Frontiers in Ecology and the Environment* 14(10) (2016): 533–542; Hanson et al., "Warfare in Biodiversity Hotspots"; Lawrence et al., "The Effects of Modern War."

90 Baumann and Kuemmerle "The Impacts of Warfare"; Conca and Wallace, "Environment and Peacebuilding"; Dutta and Simlai, "If the Army Cuts Trees."

91 Conca and Wallace, "Environment and Peacebuilding."

92 Paulo J. Murillo-Sandoval et al., "The End of Gunpoint Conservation: Forest Disturbance after the Colombian Peace Agreement," *Environmental Research Letters* 15(3) (2020): 034033.

93 Brigitte Baptiste et al., "Greening Peace in Colombia," *Nature, Ecology and Evolution* 1 (2017): article no. 0102.

94 Conca and Wallace, "Environment and Peacebuilding."

95 Darbyshire, "Deforestation in Conflict Areas."

96 Conca and Wallace, "Environment and Peacebuilding."

settings,[97] while post-conflict natural resource governance can facilitate a return to pre-existing patterns of corruption and exploitation.[98]

Harms to Nature are deeply intertwined with harms experienced by human populations. Interlinked harms can include mass refugee movements and related impacts on the natural world,[99] depleted natural resources available for social reconstruction,[100] increased risk of zoonotic disease through the destruction of natural habitat,[101] and – in the long term – toxic remnants of war that can both deplete soil health for generations and exacerbate the climate crisis.[102] These harms are not limited to the loss of resources, but can also disrupt the spiritual and cultural relationships that human communities can have with their territories and the other-than-human species that share those territories.[103] Thus, while this book centres itself around harms to Nature, we do not consider this to detract from or conflict with the consideration of how best to respond to human harm. Rather, we understand the pursuit of a 'greener' transitional justice to be the pursuit of a more holistic response to the impacts of mass violence on human *and* other-than-human life.[104]

1.3 Scoping the Field

Before moving onto our own arguments, it is valuable to set out the state of the field at the time of writing. In what follows, we consider whether and to what extent transitional justice literature has engaged with the mass violence–Nature nexus. To do so, we borrow from the methodology on scoping reviews: 'a form of knowledge synthesis that addresses an exploratory

97 Volker Boege and Daniel Franks, "Reopening and Developing Mines in Post-conflict Settings: The Challenge of Company-Community Relations," *High-Value Natural Resources and Peacebuilding*, eds. Päivi Lujala and Siri Aas Rustad (Routledge, 2012), 87–120.

98 Michael D. Beevers, "Forest Governance and Post-Conflict Peace in Liberia: Emerging Contestation and Opportunities for Change," *The Extractive Industries and Society* 3(2) (2016): 320–328.

99 Mohammad Pizuar Hossain, "The Rohingya Refugee Crisis: Analysing the International Law Implications of its Environmental Impacts on Bangladesh," *International Journal of Human Rights* 27(2) (2023): 238–257.

100 Sandra S. Nichols, "Reimagining Transitional Justice for an Enduring Peace: Accounting for Natural Resources in Conflict," *Justice and Economic Violence in Transition*, ed. Dustin Sharp (Springer, 2014), 203–231.

101 Clark, "The COVID-19 Pandemic."

102 Caitlin E. Werrell and Francesco Femia, "Climate Change Raises Conflict Concerns," *The UNESCO Courier*, March 29, 2018, https://en.unesco.org/courier/2018-2/climate-change-raises-conflict-concerns.

103 Jérémie Gilbert and Kanyinke Sena, "Litigating Indigenous Peoples' Cultural Rights: Comparative Analysis of Kenya and Uganda," *African Studies* 77(2) (2018): 204–222.

104 Clark, "The COVID-19 Pandemic."

research question aimed at mapping key concepts, types of evidence, and gaps in research related to a defined area or field by systematically searching, selecting, and synthesizing existing knowledge.'[105] What follows is the result of a structured literature search, drawing on our pre-existing research on this topic and preliminary review of the literature.[106] Search terms were designed to identify scholarship concerning harm to Nature as a means or result of conflict,[107] Nature as a victim of conflict,[108] and/or Nature as a recipient, component, or focus of justice.[109] We used 'transitional justice' as a consistent search term throughout.

In recognition of transitional justice's interdisciplinary nature, we searched all the legal, social science, and humanities databases that we were able to access through our institutions.[110] The structured search was then supplemented using citation tracing to draw in other relevant papers. Academic databases are biased towards the Global North, so we made efforts to include papers written by Indigenous scholars and scholars from the Global South (where identifiable). The search was limited to English language sources; we acknowledge that there may be important literature that we were unable to include here. We also acknowledge that there is rich literature in related fields of scholarship, such as the literature examining environmental concerns in the context of peacebuilding, *jus post bellum,* and international criminal law. This literature is not included here but is part of the scholarship that we draw upon to inform our analysis throughout the rest of the book. Our purpose here is to specifically map the *transitional justice* academic discourse.

105 Heather L. Colquhoun et al., "Scoping Reviews: Time for Clarity in Definition, Methods and Reporting," *Journal of Clinical Epidemiology* 67(12) (2014): 1291–1294.

106 Rachel Killean and Lauren Dempster, "'Greening' Transitional justice?" *Beyond Transitional Justice: Transformative Justice and the State of the Field (or Non-field),* ed. Matthew Evans (Routledge, 2022); Rachel Killean and Lauren Dempster, "Mass Violence, Environmental Harm and the Limits of Transitional Justice," *Genocide Studies and Prevention* 16(1) (2022): 11–39.

107 Search terms included: Harm to/against Nature; Crimes against Nature; Natural resource exploitation; Environmental destruction; Environmental harm; Environmental degradation; Ecocide; Ecological harm; Ecological destruction.

108 Search terms included: Other-than-human victims; More-than-human victims; Non-human victims; Environmental victimhood; Green victimology.

109 Search terms included: Rights of Nature; Environmental justice; Ecological justice; Multispecies justice; Ecocentrism/ecocentric; Eco-justice; Species justice; Earth jurisprudence; Wild law.

110 Anthropology Plus; AustLII; Cambridge Journals via Cambridge Core; Elgar Online; Google Scholar, HeinOnline Law Journal Library; INFORMIT; JSTOR; Kluwer Law Online; Legal Source via Ebscohost; Lexis Advance; Oxford Scholarship Online; Routledge Handbooks Online; Social Science Database; SpringerLink; Westlaw (International), and Wiley Online Library.

When conducting the literature search in June 2024, we found that the field had expanded significantly since we started our research in 2020.[111] A notable indicator of a 'green' shift was the 2023 special issue on 'Transitional Justice and Nature: A Curious Silence' in the field's leading journal, the *International Journal of Transitional Justice*.[112] The editors of this collection shared our disquiet over the lack of engagement with 'environmental and ecological issues in the transitional justice field,'[113] and our belief that engagement with this silence could form a meaningful contribution to a 'critically reflexive transitional justice practice.'[114] The special issue touched on several themes that are reflected in the broader literature on transitional justice and Nature. We have grouped these themes as follows.

1.3.1 'Greening' Existing Approaches

A considerable component of the literature explores how the existing transitional justice toolkit – including prosecutions, truth-seeking, memorials, reparations, and institutional reform – could be adapted to offer more holistic and/or ecocentric understandings of harm. Initial work in this space often focused on the exploitation of natural resources as a root cause of conflict or a means of either funding or attacking armed groups. Carl Bruch and Avika Fishman's 2011 exploration of 'the future of natural resources in transitional justice' adopts such a framing, while providing an early discussion as to how international law might inform future transitional justice practice. Examining the experience of the UN Compensation Commission in determining reparations for environmental damage caused by Iraq's invasion of Kuwait, they argue that any future tribunals should adopt a 'broad and flexible definition of "environmental and natural resource damage" to ensure accountability for conflict-related environmental crimes.'[115] The ongoing failure of tribunals to account for environmental crimes in the years since this article was published is reflected in the wide-ranging literature on the environment and international criminal law (see Chapters 3 and 4).

Turning to truth commissions, Sandra Nichols draws on her work in Liberia to argue that transitional justice mechanisms can and should engage

111 Killean and Dempster, "'Greening' Transitional Justice?"
112 Viaene et al., 'Transitional Justice and Nature."
113 Viaene et al., 'Transitional Justice and Nature," 1.
114 M. Brinton Lykes and Hugo van der Merwe, "Critical Reflexivity and Transitional Justice Praxis: Solidarity, Accompaniment and Intermediarity," *International Journal of Transitional Justice* 13(3) (2019): 411–416.
115 Carl Bruch and Akiva Fishman, "Institutionalizing Peacebuilding: The UNCC, Conflict Resources, and the Future of Natural Resources in Transitional Justice," *Gulf War Reparations and the UN Compensation Commission: Environmental Liability*, eds. Cymie R. Payne and Peter H. Sand (OUP, 2011), 240.

with natural resource exploitation as a rights violation and a root cause of conflict.[116] In doing so, she builds on existing literature that argues for transitional justice to better address social, economic, and cultural rights violations,[117] including, more recently, environmental rights.[118] Nichols examines the Truth Commissions in Liberia, Sierra Leone, and Timor Leste to highlight how some transitional justice mechanisms have acknowledged natural resource extraction as having a nexus to conflict, while arguing that efforts could go much further. Eliana Cusato's analysis of the Liberian and Sierra Leonian Truth Commissions is similar in both its praise and critique, noting that despite the limitations of existing practice, truth commissions may offer advantages over trials as a way of interrogating the relationship between natural resources and conflict, due to their ability to provide 'over-reaching narrative[s] of historical injustices and institutional failures.'[119]

Other scholars have adopted approaches to 'greening' existing mechanisms which look beyond natural resource exploitation as a cause or means of conflict. For some, incorporating Nature into the design of transitional justice mechanisms offers pathways to more holistic responses to harm. For example, Janine Natalya Clark has argued that incorporating Nature into memorialisation (e.g. through memorial parks) might offer more authentic recognition of the 'ecological connections' violated by atrocity.[120] Sofía N. González-Ayala and Alejandro Camargo also explore Nature and memorialisation, examining depictions of water in an exhibition about the Colombian conflict and arguing 'for a more comprehensive discussion about the implications of deeming non-human beings … victims of the armed conflict and subjects of reparations.'[121] One of us has also previously engaged with the concept of Nature as victim, exploring the possibility of environmental reparations and restorative justice, both in theory and through the case study of the Niger Delta.[122]

116 Nichols, "Reimagining Transitional Justice."

117 See e.g. Karen Hulme, "Using a Framework of Human Rights and Transitional Justice for Post-Conflict Environmental Protection and Remediation," *Environmental Protection and Transition from Conflict to Peace,* eds Carsten Stahn et al. (OUP, 2017).

118 Amar Jibi Ghimire, "Articulating the Linkages between Human Rights and Environmental Rights: The Perspective of Transitional Justice," *NJA Law Journal* 5(1) (2011): 85–106.

119 Cusato, "Back to the Future?"

120 Clark, "Are There 'Greener' Ways"; Clark, "The COVID-19 Pandemic."

121 Sofía N. González-Ayala and Alejandro Camargo, "Voices of Water and Violence: Exhibition Making and the Blue Humanities for Transitional Justice," *Curator: The Museum Journal* 64(10) (2021): 201.

122 Rachel Killean, "Environmental Restorative Justice in Transitional Settings," *The Palgrave Handbook of Environmental Restorative Justice*, ed. Brunilda Pali et al. (Palgrave, 2022); Rachel Killean, "From Ecocide to Eco-sensitivity: 'Greening' Reparations at the International Criminal Court," *International Journal of Human Rights* 25(2) (2021): 323–347; Rachel Killean and Damien Short, "The Prosecutor v

Others have drawn on 'green' theories of justice, such as 'environmental justice' (the non-discriminatory protection from environmental toxins and hazards)[123] and 'wild law' (a theoretical approach to law and governance based on principles of ecology)[124] to explore new directions for transitional justice. This exploration has theoretical and practical examples. In relation to the former, Alessandro Pelizzon has explored the possibility of 'cross-pollination' between transitional justice, wild law, and what he terms 'ecological jurisprudence.' He argues that such engagement could facilitate the 'reimagining' of how law and justice are conceived in the aftermath of unrest.[125] In relation to the latter, David M. Ong has argued that notions of environmental justice might helpfully be incorporated into the reconstruction of the rule of law in Kosovo, thereby countering an unmitigated focus on economic development at the risk of furthering ethnic and social divisions.[126] We explore similar themes in Chapter 6.

Taken together, these examples provide pathways towards 'greener' transitional justice measures, with Nature framed as both a beneficiary and constituent of transitional justice. Despite these innovative suggestions, it is clear from the literature that transitional justice practice has for the most part failed to take up calls for more Nature-inclusive approaches.[127]

1.3.2 Expanding Transitional Justice

Others have sought to expand the principles or mechanisms of transitional justice beyond the usual contexts to which transitional justice paradigmatically applies.[128] Danielle Celermajer and Anne Therese O'Brien adopt a broad approach to this exploration, seeking to unpack how the ideas of transitional justice can be 'put to work' to address harms against other-than-human

Shell: Imagining Reparations for Ecocide," *The UK Earth Judgments Project*, eds. Helen Dancer et al. (Hart, 2024).

123 See e.g. Leslie London et al., "Environmental Justice: An International Perspective," *The Encyclopaedia of Environmental Health*, ed. J. O. Nriagu (Elsevier, 2011), 441–448.

124 See e.g. Cormac Cullinan, *Wild Law: A Manifesto for Earth Justice* (Bloomsbury, 2002).

125 Alessandro Pelizzon, "Transitional Justice and Ecological Jurisprudence in the Midst of an Ever-Changing Climate," *Current Issues in Transitional Justice*, ed. Natalia Szablewska and Sacha-Dominik Bachmann (Springer, 2015).

126 David M. Ong, "Prospects for Transitional Environmental Justice in the Socio-economic Reconstruction of Kosovo," *Tulane Environmental Law Journal* 30(2) (2017): 217–272.

127 For a deconstruction of one such failure, see Montserrat Abad Castelos, "Towards a Holistic Consideration of Crimes Against Nature Committed in Times of Armed Conflict: A Critical Approach to the Case of Iraq," *International Journal for Crime, Justice and Social Democracy* 12(3) (2023): 77–92.

128 Sharp, "Emancipating."

beings.[129] Others have looked at more specific examples, such as natural disasters,[130] extractive practices,[131] and, most extensively, climate change.[132] As this area of scholarship moves further away from our own focus on more 'paradigmatic' cases of transitional justice, we do not explore this scholarship in depth here.

However, in several cases, these explorations retain, build on, or flow from a nexus to paradigmatic cases. For example, John G. Ikubaje and Usani Odum argue that the African Union's transitional justice policies should be adapted to suit both climate-induced conflicts and the broader harms that result from climate's impacts on the continent.[133] Elsewhere, Manuel Rodeiro highlights the nexus between environmental destruction and genocide before arguing for a 'modest expansion' of transitional justice to encompass ecocide that results in cultural rather than physical destruction.[134]

This body of scholarship is more normative than empirical; there are very few real-life examples in the literature. However, Sarah Kerremans and Tine Destrooper highlight how Indigenous communities and others have used

129 Danielle Celermajer and Anne Therese O'Brien, "Alter-transitional Justice: Transforming Unjust Relations with the More-Than-Human," *Journal of Human Rights and the Environment* 12, Special Issue (2021): 125–147. See also Danielle Celermajer et al., "Justice Through a Multispecies Lens," *Contemporary Political Theory* 19(3) (2020): 475–512; Veronica Strang, "Justice for All: Inconvenient Truths and Reconciliation in Human–Non-Human Relations," *Routledge Handbook of Environmental Anthropology*, eds. Helen Kopnina and Eleanor Shoreman-Ouimet (Routledge, 2016).

130 Megan Bradley, "More Than Misfortune: Recognizing Natural Disasters as a Concern for Transitional Justice," *International Journal of Transitional Justice* 11(3) (2017): 400–420.

131 Nathaniel Umukoro, "Human Rights Violations and Transitional Justice in Nigeria's Niger Delta during Civilian Rule," *Journal of Global South Studies* 35(1) (2018): 87–103.

132 See e.g. Sonja Klinsky and Jasmina Brankovic, *The Global Climate Regime and Transitional Justice* (Routledge, 2018); Sonja Klinsky, "Transitional Justice for Climate Change: Transformation Through Solidarity," *Research Handbook on Transitional Justice*, eds. Cheryl Lawther et al. (Elgar, 2023); Jasmina Brankovic, "Transitional and Climate Justice: New Opportunities for Justice in Transition," *International Journal of Transitional Justice* 17(2) (2023): 185–191; Werner Scholtz and Gerrit Ferreira, "Climate Change Negotiations and Transitional Justice: The Advent of a Carbon Truth Reconciliation Commission," *Comparative and International Law Journal of Southern Africa* 48(1) (2015): 42–88; Birsha Ohdedar, "Loss and Damage from the Impacts of Climate Change: A Framework for Implementation," *Nordic Journal of International Law* 85(1) (2016): 1–36; Szablewska, and Bachmann, "Current Issues and Future Challenges"; Usha Natarajan, "Climate, Conflict, and International Law in the Middle East and Beyond," *Proceedings of the ASIL Annual Meeting*, 114 (2020): 160–164.

133 John G. Ikubaje and Usani Odum, "Envisioning a Transitional Justice-Based Approach to Climate-Induced Conflicts in Africa," *Horn of Africa Bulletin*, February 14, 2023, https://life-peace.org/hab-bulletin/envisioning-a-transitional-justice-based-approach-to-climate-induced-Conflicts-in-Africa/.

134 Manuel Rodeiro, "Responding to Ecocide Through Transitional Justice," *Dialogo* 55(113) (2024). 47–79.

'bottom-up' approaches to transitional justice to draw attention to territorial disputes and the impacts of oil extraction on their communities and ecosystems. As they argue, it may be that these communities have drawn inspiration from Peru's earlier experiences of using transitional justice mechanisms to address political internal conflict.[135] This literature therefore both raises and interrogates questions around how transitional justice mechanisms can be adapted to new challenges.

1.3.3 Mass Violence, Nature, and Indigenous Peoples

The final, substantial, strand of scholarship relates to the connections between mass violence, Nature, and Indigenous peoples. This scholarship builds on established critiques of transitional justice's need to meaningfully address land dispossession,[136] as well as the growing literature on transitional justice's applicability to colonial harms.[137] We identified three overlapping arguments woven through this scholarship.

The first argument is that transitional justice should better account for the nexus between harms against Nature and Indigenous peoples' experiences of mass violence.[138] The literature includes theoretical framings for better understanding this nexus; for example, the concept of 'body-territory' or 'land-body-territory' is used in Latin American contexts to

135 Kerremans and Destrooper, "Exploring the Nexus."

136 Andrew Dusek, "Ill Fares the Land: Reparations for Housing, Land, and Property Rights Violations in Myanmar," *Harvard Human Rights Journal* 30 (2017): 129–164; Matthew Evans, "Land and the Limits of Liberal Legalism: Property, Transitional Justice and Non-Reformist Reforms in Post-Apartheid South Africa," *Review of African Political Economy* 48(170) (2021): 646–655; Phanuel Kaapama, "The Enduring Colonial Legacies of Land Dispossessions and the Evolving Property Rights Legal Discourse: Whither Transitional Justice," *Human Rights & International Legal Discourse* 11(1) (2017): 108–119; Khanyisela Moyo, "Mimicry, Transitional Justice and the Land Question in Racially Divided Former Settler Colonies," *International Journal of Transitional Justice* 9(1) (2015): 70–89; Omwanza Ombati, "Repossession of Illegally Acquired Public Land in Kenya: Limits of Law and the Prospects for Transnational Justice in Redress," *The East African Journal of Human Rights & Democracy* 2(3) (2004): 46–57; Jon D. Unruh and Musa Adam Abdul-Jalil, "Housing, Land and Property Rights in Transitional Justice," *International Journal of Transitional Justice* 15(1) (2021): 1–6.

137 Jennifer Balint and Julie Evans, "The Australian and New Zealand Critical Criminology Conference 2010 Proceedings: Transitional Justice and Settler States" (2011); Balint et al., "Rethinking"; Nagy, "Transformative Justice"; Bill Rolston and Fionnuala Ní Aoláin, "Colonialism, Redress and Transitional Justice: Ireland and Beyond," *State Crime Journal* 7(2) (2018): 329–348.

138 Kerremans and Destrooper, "Exploring the Nexus"; Colin Luoma, "Reckoning with Conservation Violence on Indigenous Territories: Possibilities and Limitations of a Transitional Justice Response," *International Journal of Transitional Justice* 17(1) (2023): 89–106.

articulate the connection between harms against territory and physical violence experienced by Indigenous women.[139] The literature also interrogates why Indigenous people's experiences of territorial violations are overlooked. Mark Evenhuis's account of state–corporate crime in Bougainville draws attention to how the pursuit of economic development can lead to Indigenous peoples' justice claims being sidelined at 'critical moments of transition.'[140] This sidelining of justice in the pursuit of economic development is arguably reflective of transitional justice's 'sympathy for capitalism,'[141] a theme we explore in Chapter 6.

The second argument is that greater recognition of Nature as a victim of harm may assist in the 'decolonising' of transitional justice.[142] Belkis Izquierdo Torres and Lieselotte Viaene have argued that Indigenous 'norms and practices concerning justice, reparation and reconciliation' challenge anthropocentric approaches to transitional justice, and require the recognition of other-than-human beings as victims deserving of redress.[143] Similarly, M. Brinton Lykes and Colleen Murphy draw on Mayan scholars and Indigenous feminist activists to argue for a transitional justice that recognises the land-body-territory,[144] and in doing so shifts away from understanding territory as an object or resource, 'recentring it as living' and 'recognising its rights.'[145]

The third argument is that Indigenous understandings of justice can be used to enhance responses to natural resource–driven conflicts. Examples

139 Angela Santamaria et al., "To Pay, Heal, and Repair Mother Earth in the Sierra Nevada de Santa Marta: Experiences of Indigenous Women's Reparation in the Implementation of the Colombian Peace Accord," *International Review of Victimology* 29(2) (2023): 170–198. See also Diana Gómez Correal et al., "Feminist trajectories from Peru to Colombia: Taking Violence Experienced by Women into Account in Truth Commissions," *International Feminist Journal of Politics* 25(3) (2023): 482–505.

140 Mark Evenhuis, "Developmental Faith, Sacrifice and the Betrayal of Transitional Justice: A Bougainvillean Case Study," *State Crime Journal* 6(1) (2017): 102–131.

141 Zunino, *Justice Framed*, 53.

142 E.g. Abdullahi Ahmed An-Na'im, "Editorial Note: From the Neocolonial 'Transitional' to Indigenous Formations of Justice," *International Journal of Transitional Justice* 7(2) (2013): 197–204; Gómez-Betancur, "The Rights of Nature." On the call for decolonisation, see e.g. Jennifer Matsunaga, "Two Faces of Transitional Justice: Theorizing the Incommensurability of Transitional Justice and Decolonization in Canada," *Decolonization: Indigeneity, Education & Society* 5(1) (2016): 24–44; Augustine S.J. Park, "Settler Colonialism, Decolonization and Radicalizing Transitional Justice," *International Journal of Transitional Justice* 14(2) (2020): 260–279; Mohamed Sesay, "Decolonization of Postcolonial Africa: A Structural Justice Project More Radical than Transitional Justice," *International Journal of Transitional Justice* 16(2) (2022): 254–271.

143 Belkis Izquierdo and Lieselotte Viaene, "Decolonizing Transitional Justice from Indigenous Territories," *Peace in Progress* 34 (2018): 11–19.

144 Lykes and Murphy, "Decolonizing."

145 Lykes and Murphy, "Decolonizing."

are drawn from Indigenous justice practices around the world to demonstrate how this might be done.[146] These include conflict-resolution techniques common in pre-colonial Africa (with similarities to Western concepts of mediation), which Abe Oyeniyi argues could be adapted to address resource-driven conflicts by establishing 'relationships based on trust, social cohesion and confidence within the communities.'[147] Other examples draw links between Indigenous forms of justice and more recent legal developments. For example, Annika Reynolds links First Law in Australia with Rights of Nature movements,[148] arguing that healing the human and other-than-human harms of colonialism requires settlers to recognise Indigenous stewardship over land and engage in collective caring for Country.[149]

It is in the context of Indigenous justice that the most discernible progress has been made in practice, particularly through the jurisprudence of the Colombian *Jurisdicción Especial para la Paz* (JEP). The JEP was established as part of Colombia's attempt to deal with decades of armed conflict, a conflict where Nature has been a source, means, and victim of armed violence.[150] Since 2019, JEP has issued a series of resolutions which recognise the victimhood of the territories of the Awá,[151] Nasa,[152] Wiwa,[153] and Eparara Siapidara[154] peoples and of the Black communities of Tumaco,[155] as

146 Carlos Arturo Gutiérrez-Rodríguez, "Beyond Liberal Justice? Decolonising Colombian Transitional Justice through Victims' Participation and Indigenous Rights," *International Journal of Human Rights* (2024): 1–23; Izquierdo and Viaene, "Decolonizing Transitional Justice"; Kristina Lyons, "'Nature' and Territories as Victims: Decolonizing Colombia's Transitional Justice Process," *American Anthropologist* 125(1) (2023): 63–76; Esme G. Murdock, "Storied with Land: 'Transitional Justice' on Indigenous Lands," *Journal of Global Ethics* 14(2) (2018): 232–239.

147 Abe Oyeniyi, "Conflict Resolution in the Extractives: A Consideration of Traditional Conflict Resolution Paradigms in Post-Colonial Africa," *Willamette Journal of International Law and Dispute Resolution* 25(1) (2017): 56–77.

148 For a critical exploration of the links between Rights of Nature and Indigenous justice, see e.g. Lieselotte Viaene, "Can Rights of Nature Save us From the Anthropocene Catastrophe? Some Critical Reflections from the Field," *Asian Journal of Law and Society* 9(2) (2022): 187–206.

149 Annika Reynolds, "A Coloniser's View: On Healing and Native Title Reform," *Alternative Law Journal* 47(4) (2022): 291–295. Of course, as we will explore in subsequent chapters, tensions can also arise between Indigenous claims and 'environmental' initiatives.

150 Isabella Ariza-Buitrago and Luisa Gómez-Betancur, "Nature in Focus: The Invisibility and Re-Emergence of Rivers, Land and Animals in Colombia's Transitional Justice System," *International Journal of Transitional Justice* 17(1) (2023): 71–88; Gómez-Betancur, "The Rights of Nature."

151 JEP, Caso 002, Auto SRVBIT 079, 12 November 2019.

152 JEP, Caso 005, Auto 002, 17 January 2020.

153 JEP, Caso 009, Ruling SRVBIT-XCBM-NNHC-JJCP-ACHP- 01, 11 July 2024.

154 JEP, Caso 002, Auto 094, 10 June 2020, 94.

155 JEP, Caso 002, Resolución SRVBIT, Auto 018, 24 January 2020.

well as the Cauca River.[156] This recognition has been described as 'pushing transitional justice into new terrain'[157] and has been attributed to Indigenous and Afro-Colombian activism,[158] the increased judicial recognition of the rights of Nature,[159] and the 'multicultural politics' of Colombia.[160]

Colombia's transitional justice process has been praised as a novel example of how Indigenous communities' worldviews can be incorporated into transitional justice processes,[161] and how a mechanism can acknowledge other-than-human harms.[162] Hopes are expressed that the JEP will continue to develop its practice through prosecutions of crimes against Nature[163] and the awarding of reparations that address interconnected human and other-than-human harms.[164] However, critiques and cautionary notes are also evident in the literature. Alexandra Huneeus and Pablo Rueda Sáiz warn against the 'exploitative' extraction of Indigenous justice concepts for application in other contexts,[165] invoking the literature advocating for context-specific approaches to transitional justice.[166] Others have drawn attention to ongoing ecoterritorial disputes that have emerged or continued after formal peace was declared, highlighting transitional justice measures' limitations as a means of addressing continuums of environmental conflict.[167]

156 JEP, Caso 005, Auto SRVR 226, 11 July 2023.

157 Alexandra Huneeus and Pablo Rueda Sáiz, "Territory as a Victim of Armed Conflict," *International Journal of Transitional Justice* 15(1) (2021): 210–229.

158 Daniel Ruiz-Serna, "Transitional Justice Beyond the Human: Indigenous Cosmopolitics and the Realm of Law in Colombia," *Cultural Politics* 19(1) (2023): 57–76.

159 Luis López Zamora, "The Recognition of the Rights of Nature in Latin America – The Lost Linkage with the Rights of Future Generations," *Representing the Absent*, eds. Hélène Ruiz Fabri et al., (Nomos Verlag, 2023): 463–496.

160 Lyons, "'Nature."

161 Gutiérrez-Rodríguez, "Beyond Liberal Justice?"; Daniel Ruiz Serna, "Territory as Victim. Political Ontology and the Laws for Victims of Indigenous and Afrodescendant Communities in Colombia," *Revista Colombiana de Antropología* 53(2) (2017). 85–113.

162 Janine Natalya Clark, "Harm, Relationality and More-Than-Human Worlds: Developing the Field of Transitional Justice in New Posthumanist Directions," *International Journal of Transitional Justice* 17(1) (2023): 15–31; Ruiz-Serna, "Transitional Justice Beyond."

163 Camilo Ramirez Gutierrez and A. Sebastian Saavedra Eslava, "Protection of the Natural Environment Under International Humanitarian Law and International Criminal Law," *UCLA Journal of International Law and Foreign Affairs* 25(1) (2020): 123–158.

164 Huneeus and Rueda Sáiz, "Territory as a Victim"; Santamaria et al., "To Pay, Heal, and Repair"; Urzola and González, "Gender-Based Environmental Violence."

165 Huneeus and Rueda Sáiz, "Territory as a Victim."

166 For a cautionary approach see Dustin N. Sharp, "Transitional Justice and 'Local' Justice," *Research Handbook on Transitional Justice*, ed. Cheryl Lawther et al. (Elgar, 2023), 142–158.

167 Gutiérrez-Rodríguez "Beyond Liberal Justice?"; McClanahan et al., "Conflict, Environment and Transition"; María Carolina Olarte-Olarte, "From Territorial Peace to Territorial Pacification: Anti-riot Police Powers and Socio-environmental Dissent in the Implementation of Colombia's Peace Agreement," *Revista de Estudios Sociales* 67

Centring and respecting Indigenous justice is understood as crucial not only to the projects of decolonising transitional justice and redressing harms experienced by Indigenous peoples, but also to the long-term protection of Nature. As Colin Luoma notes, 'Indigenous peoples' custodianship and traditional knowledge have positively shaped their territories for millennia,'[168] and 'biodiversity loss cannot be adequately stemmed without increasing Indigenous governance, participation, and consent in nature conservation.'[169] Thus, transitional justice is framed as more than a corrective. Rather, it offers a means of facilitating transition to more environmentally sustainable ways of being, as well as a response to past injustice.

1.3.4 Towards a 'Greener' Transitional Justice?

This review demonstrates that our previous claim that harms against Nature constitute a 'blind spot'[170] in the field no longer holds true, at least theoretically. There is a growing, multidisciplinary scholarship that draws on multijurisdictional examples to interrogate the connections that make up the mass violence–Nature nexus. Yet, a recurrent argument throughout even the more recent literature is that environmental concerns are far from integrated into the 'mainstream' of transitional justice discourse. At the same time, there are gaps in this growing scholarship. There is a need for a deeper analysis of the reasons for transitional justice's frequent failure to address harms against Nature – that is, what are the underlying assumptions, entrenched structures, normative frameworks, and intellectual traditions that have facilitated this exclusion, and can they be upended? Relatedly, there is more in-depth work to be done on whether, how, and to what extent other areas of scholarship and practice might assist in developing a 'greener' approach to transitional justice. Building on and engaging with the above literature, this book addresses these gaps in scholarship.

1.4 Our Approach and Chapter Summaries

We engage with the prospects and limitations of a 'green' transitional justice in three ways. We interrogate the limitations of dominant approaches

(2019): 26–39. For a discussion on grassroots alternatives, see e.g. Patrical M. Rodriguez, "Charting a New Human Rights Discourse 'From the Territories': Social Movements and Peace in Cauca, Colombia", Rapoport Center Human Rights Working Paper Series, 5/2018.

168 Erle C. Ellis et al., "People have Shaped Most of Terrestrial Nature for at Least 12000 Years," *Proceedings of the National Academy of Sciences* 118(17) (2021): 1–8.

169 Luoma, "Reckoning."

170 Killean, and Dempster, "'Greening' Transitional Justice?"

to transitional justice as a means of responding to environmental harms; we excavate the reasons for those limitations; and we engage with diverse theories of 'justice' to consider the possibilities of an approach which better recognises and responds to harms against Nature.

To do so, we situate the literature outlined above against a broader critical and interdisciplinary transitional justice scholarship, characterised by a willingness to interrogate transitional justice's 'foundational limitations.'[171] While this scholarship may not explicitly engage with Nature, we have found certain critiques to be valuable tools for understanding the relative invisibility of Nature in the transitional justice field. Four such critiques are used to structure this book's analysis: First, that knowledge production in the field of 'institutionalised' transitional justice is neocolonial and predominantly shaped by Eurocentric and 'Global North' voices;[172] second, that transitional justice is characterised by a 'dominance of legalism' which has resulted in anthropocentric understandings of harm and victimhood and a focus on violations of civil and political rights over other forms of harm;[173] third, that transitional justice often leaves intact structural inequalities that precede and succeed periods of mass violence;[174] and fourth, that the field is shaped by 'taken-for-granted assumptions' that political and economic (neo) liberalisation offer the best methods for restructuring societies after conflict, atrocity, and repression.[175]

We argue that these critiques help to illuminate the limitations of transitional justice as a response to harms against Nature. While recognising the entrenched nature of these limitations, we nonetheless argue that there may be 'greener' ways of doing transitional justice. To make these arguments and suggestions, we bring this critical transitional justice scholarship into conversation with multidisciplinary literature that engages with harms against Nature in different ways. This includes green criminology and victimology, environmental justice and environmental restorative justice literature, critical legal theory, and Indigenous scholarship from around the world. While cautious of overclaiming what transitional justice can achieve, we argue that drawing lessons from more inclusive, multispecies approaches to justice might enable transitional justice to better address the mass violence–Nature nexus.

171 Sharp, "What Would Satisfy."
172 An-Na'im, "Editorial Note"; Hobbs, "Locating the Logic."
173 Kieran McEvoy, "Beyond Legalism: Towards a Thicker Understanding of Transitional Justice," *Journal of Law and Society* 34(4) (2007): 411–440.
174 Susan Marks, *The Riddle of All Constitutions. International Law, Democracy and The Critique of Ideology* (OUP, 2000), 70–74.
175 Fletcher and Weinstein, "How Power Dynamics"; Park, "Settler Colonialism."

The book proceeds as follows. Chapter 2 interrogates how knowledge is produced and reproduced in transitional justice. It begins by introducing the relationship between knowledge and power in general terms, demonstrating how power–knowledge dynamics have been used to enforce gendered, racial, and Eurocentric hierarchies. It then explores how power-knowledge manifests in transitional justice, beginning with an overview of the emergence of the field, before turning to the rise of transitional justice 'expertise.' It highlights how, for some, transitional justice represents a site of epistemic injustice. It then turns to an analysis of how power–knowledge dynamics have shaped the field's response to harms against Nature, through the entrenching of anthropocentric perspectives and the ability of powerful actors to place parameters around the types of situations that the field responds to. Finally, it considers alternative approaches to knowledge production, drawing from feminist epistemology and decolonisation literature to imagine pathways to a more environmentally inclusive transitional justice. The themes explored in the final section lay the foundations for the chapters that follow.

In Chapter 3, we turn to the 'dominance of legalism' in transitional justice. This critique is used as a lens to examine which harms and victims are recognised, and the implications of this for transitional justice's ability to 'see' harms against Nature. We examine the anthropocentricity of dominant legal frameworks (human rights and criminal law), how this anthropocentrism manifests in transitional justice, and the implications of this for the recognition of other-than-human harm. For example, we explore how civil and political rights are prioritised over social, economic, cultural, and environmental rights, and how a 'crime-driven lens'[176] has further excluded harms against Nature from consideration.

Chapter 4 continues the theme of legalism, examining the construction of victimhood and harm in transitional justice. We explore the rise of 'ecocentric' legal movements around the world, characterised by a willingness to move beyond the anthropocentric legalism identified in the previous chapter. We consider initiatives that seek to recognise Nature as an entity protected by criminal law, as a rights-bearer, and as a victim deserving of redress. Drawing on these movements, we interrogate the possibilities of a more expansive conceptualisation of victimhood in transitional justice, one that extends to the other-than-human. While we highlight the potential benefits of such an approach, we also acknowledge and explore the risks and limitations to using more law to address law's own blind spots. This theme is unpacked further in the following chapters.

176 Aldo Zammit Borda, "History in International Criminal Trials: The 'Crime-driven Lens' and Its Blind Spots," *Journal of International Criminal Justice* 18(3) (2020): 543–566.

Chapter 5 turns to the critique that transitional justice can overlook and leave intact structural inequalities and forms of 'slow violence'[177] that may precede and survive periods of conflict, atrocity, and repression, in part due 'implied temporal parameters' of the field.[178] By prioritising episodic harm, the field often overlooks the interconnectedness of human and ecological violence and fails to account for harm caused by structural forces and state–corporate partnerships. The chapter highlights how these exclusions perpetuate injustices and engages with justice frameworks that might challenge these exclusions. These include literature on crimes of the powerful and transformative justice,[179] which we argue might assist in identifying overlooked structural harms. We then turn to environmental justice,[180] and Nancy Fraser's trivalent justice framework of redistribution, recognition, and representation to explore the possibilities of an environmentally transformative approach to transitional justice.[181]

Chapter 6 then considers transitional justice's forward-looking dimensions. It considers the critique that transitional justice is grounded in the 'taken-for-granted assumption' that political and economic liberalisation offer the best methods for restructuring societies after violence.[182] We engage with claims that the field has overlooked the role of market forces in causing conflict, continued to offer support for environmentally unsustainable economic reforms, and produced scholarship that 'naturalises capitalism.'[183] Drawing from our previous chapters' analyses, we consider arguments that transitional justice's focus on individual harm, exclusion of structural harms, and alignment with particular ideas concerning economic development might 'prefigure and support processes of neoliberalisation,'[184]

177 Nixon, *Slow Violence.*

178 Cynthia M. Horne, "Transitional Justice and Temporal Parameters: Built-in Expiration Dates?" *International Journal of Transitional Justice* 14(3) (2021): 544–565.

179 Matthew Evans, "Structural Violence, Socioeconomic Rights, and Transformative Justice," *Journal of Human Rights* 15(1) (2016): 1–20; Paul Gready and Simon Robins, *From Transitional to Transformative Justice* (CUP, 2019).

180 Robert Bullard, ed., *The Quest for Environmental Justice: Human Rights and the Politics of Pollution* (Sierra Club Books, 2005); David N. Pellow, "Toward a Critical Environmental Justice Studies," *Du Bois Review: Social Science Research on Race* 13(2) (2016): 221–236.

181 Nancy Fraser "From Redistribution to Recognition? Dilemmas of Justice in a 'Post-Socialist' Age," *New Left Review*, 1(212) (1995): 68–93; Nancy Fraser, *Scales of Justice: Reimagining Political Space in a Globalizing World* (Columbia University Press, 2009).

182 Park, "Settler Colonialism."

183 Mark. A Drumbl, "Justice Framed: A Genealogy of Transitional Justice," *European Journal of International Law* 30(4) (2019): 1447–1463, discussing Zunino, *Justice Framed.*

184 Josh Bowsher, "'Omnus et Singulatim': Establishing the Relationship between Transitional Justice and Neoliberalism," *Law Critique* 29(1) (2018): 83.

precluding calls for redistributive justice and delegitimising other more environmentally sustainable futures. We explore what it might mean to ground transitional justice in alternative world visions, such as *Buen Vivir*, *Ubuntu* and *Ecological Swaraj*, which each, in different ways, embrace the interconnections between humans, other-than-humans, and the natural world.

In the final chapter, we draw together the threads of our analysis to offer some concluding thoughts on what 'greening' transitional justice might entail. We acknowledge that transitional justice does not operate in a vacuum, and therefore cannot fundamentally redress and transform human relationships to Nature without broader accompanying changes. However, we believe that it is possible to push for reform while remaining cognisant of the need for more radical change. Moreover, while transitional justice continues to be the preferred method of responding to mass violence, it remains worthwhile to consider how it might better redress harms against Nature. To that end, we suggest that what is required is a fundamental shift in how we think about and 'do' transitional justice, before offering six principles that we think might usefully inform such a shift. While acknowledging the limits of transitional justice as a means of transforming society, we argue that it is worth considering whether these moments of rupture may present a nexus of opportunity for progressive change with regards to the governance of and relationship with the natural world.

2

KNOWLEDGE PRODUCTION IN TRANSITIONAL JUSTICE

2.1 Introduction

In this chapter, we interrogate the production of knowledge in transitional justice discourse. By 'knowledge production' we mean the creation and sharing of accepted knowledge within an identified field of discourse and/or practice, with a particular focus on the actors, mechanisms, structures, and geographies with the power to influence those processes.[1] By 'discourse' we mean the views of those who engage with and shape transitional justice, such as scholars, practitioners, and activists, as evidenced by academic publications, judicial and legal documents, policy or organisational reports, and media coverage. As this chapter explores, the dynamics of knowledge production influence the situations and issues that this discourse prioritises, the victims whose harms are acknowledged, the mechanisms that are deployed, and the concepts of justice that inform the field.[2] This, in turn, has profound implications for the field's conceptualisation of and engagement with Nature. As such, this chapter forms the foundation on which later chapters are built by highlighting how transitional justice has been shaped by particular worldviews and agendas. Subsequent chapters take a closer look at how this has manifested in the legal developments that have proven most influential to transitional justice (Chapters 3 and 4), in the exclusion of structural

1 Raewyn Connell, *Southern Theory: The Global Dynamics of Knowledge in Social Science* (Routledge, 2020).

2 For a description of transitional justice's discourse or 'discursive space' see Marcos Zunino, *Justice Framed: A Genealogy of Transitional Justice* (CUP, 2019), Chapter 2.

DOI: 10.4324/9781003264446-2

and slow violence (Chapter 5), and through the links between transitional justice and (neo)liberalism (Chapter 6).

Before proceeding, it is important for us to reflect on our positionality as authors who benefit from a privileged position within academia.[3] This is a chapter about the dominance of certain voices within the transitional justice field, particularly those from the Global North. These arguments are echoed at various points throughout the book. As two researchers from the Global North, based in wealthy academic institutions, publishing in English in the field of transitional justice, we are aware that we are critiquing a system that benefits us. We agree with Fionnuala Ní Aoláin's emphasis on the importance of 'seeing one's own position in the project of moulding the field'[4] and are aware that the arguments adopted in this chapter cannot be divorced from our own subjectivity. Through this chapter, we seek to interrogate the ways in which the dynamics of knowledge production have granted people like us privileged space, and to identify pathways to undoing some of those dynamics. Our goal is never to assume knowledge on behalf of those who have historically found their voices marginalised. Rather, following Aziz Choudry, we hope to 'recognise lineages of ideas, concepts, debates and theories,'[5] and to engage in citation practice which acknowledges sources of ideas that emerge from outside the dominant discourse. We acknowledge that there are limits to the extent to which we have done this. A notable limitation is our necessary focus on English-language sources, a focus that does little to challenge the dominance of English in academic communication.[6] This chapter (and book) should be read with these limitations in mind.

This chapter proceeds as follows. In Part 2, we introduce the intersection of power and knowledge production, or 'power–knowledge.'[7] We highlight how dominant knowledge production processes represent one way in which the broader reproduction of gendered, racialised, classist, and Eurocentric

3 Michelle Daigle and Margaret Marietta Ramírez, "Decolonial Geographies," in *Keywords in Radical Geography: Antipode at 50*, ed. T. Jazeel et al., (Antipode, 2019).

4 Fionnuala Ní Aoláin, "Advancing Feminist Positioning in the Field of Transitional Justice," *International Journal of Transitional Justice* 6(2) (2012): 210. See also M. Brinton Lykes and Hugo van der Merwe, "Critical Reflexivity and Transitional Justice: Solidarity, Accompaniment and Intermediarity," *International Journal of Transitional Justice* 13(3) (2019): 411–416; Selbi Durdiyeva, "Towards Decolonial Agenda for Transitional Justice: 'The Old is Dying and the New Cannot Be Born,'" in *The Wretched of the Global South. International Law and the Global South*, eds. Thamil Venthan Ananthavinayagan and Amritha Viswanath Shenoy (Springer, 2024).

5 Aziz Choudry, "Reflections on Academia, Activism, and the Politics of Knowledge and Learning," *The International Journal of Human Rights* 24(1) (2020): 28.

6 Janina Brutt-Griffler, "Intellectual Culture and Cultural Imperialism: Implications for the Growing Dominance of English in Academia," in *English in Academia: Catalyst or Barrier?* ed. Claus Gnutzmann (Verlag, 2008).

7 Michel Foucault, *Discipline and Punish: The Birth of the Prison* (Penguin, 1977), 27–28.

hegemonies is maintained. In Part 3, we turn to the dynamics of knowledge production in transitional justice, examining the field's origins, the disproportionate influence of Global North voices and institutions, and critiques that transitional justice perpetrates epistemic injustice through the silencing and exclusion of subaltern voices. In Part 4, we consider the effects of these overlapping power dynamics on the field's ability to recognise and respond to the environmental impacts of mass violence. We highlight the prioritisation of anthropocentric world views, and the ability of powerful actors to set parameters on the field's scope, as effects that play a particularly silencing role with regards to harm against Nature. In Part 5, we consider how knowledge production in transitional justice could be re-imagined to better capture and respond to harms against Nature. Drawing on feminist epistemology and decolonising scholarship, we identify several principles that could contribute to 'greening' knowledge production in transitional justice, including a shift towards more embedded, interconnected, and ecocentric understandings of harm and justice. We argue that a rethinking of relationships to, and understandings of, Nature is a prerequisite for any transitional justice approach that seeks to comprehensively respond to environmental harm. These ideas are expanded further in the chapters that follow.

2.2 Introducing Power and Knowledge Production

In this section, we introduce and explore the relationship between power and knowledge production. While acknowledging that 'power' is an 'essentially contested' concept,[8] we use it here to mean the ability and opportunity to act in a way that effects change or influences others.[9] In what follows, we discuss the relationship between power and knowledge production in general terms, before focusing on the particular influences of gender, race, and Eurocentrism on this relationship.

2.2.1 Power and Knowledge Production

It is well established that power and knowledge production are interconnected, and that to study knowledge is 'not a simple apolitical study of

8 Meaning it cannot be settled empirically. See Steven Lukes, *Power: A Radical View* (MacMillan, 1974).

9 For an overview of some of power's multiple meanings, see Stewart R. Clegg and Mark Haugaard, *The SAGE Handbook of Power* (SAGE, 2009).

truth.'[10] Michel Foucault's oft-cited adage, 'knowledge is always a form of power,' sums this up:[11]

> Power produces knowledge ... power and knowledge directly imply one another ...there is no power relation without the correlative constitution of a field of knowledge, nor any knowledge that does not presuppose and constitute at the same time power relations ... it is not the activity of the subject of knowledge that produces a corpus of knowledge, useful or resistant to power, but power–knowledge, the processes and struggles that traverse it and of which it is made up, that determines the forms and possible domains of knowledge.[12]

Foucault thereby argues that knowledge and power are mutually reinforcing.[13] As such, it does not make sense to discuss one in the absence of the other, leading to the conjoined concept of power–knowledge. This concept can be understood as encompassing an expansive web of power relationships and knowledge systems, many of which are not commonly rendered visible within societies, institutions, or contexts.

The mutually reinforcing relationships of power–knowledge are manifest within academic institutions and in ideas regarding what constitutes science and scholarship.[14] While some consider knowledge to mirror an objective reality,[15] others have argued that 'mainstream epistemology' presents 'a mask of objectivity and value-neutrality' that disguises 'complex structures of vested interest, dominance, and subjugation.'[16] As Maria do Mar Pereira argues, ideas of what constitutes 'good' science or knowledge can 'normalize the epistemic and material domination of a narrow subset of epistemic agents and activities over others.'[17] As we explore in this chapter, the dominance of

10 Grada Kilomba, *Plantation Memories: Episodes of Everyday Racism* (Unrast Verlag, 2008), 301.

11 Stuart Hall, "Foucault," in *Discourse Theory and Practice: A Reader,* eds. Margaret Wetherell et al. (Sage, 2001), 76.

12 Foucault, *Discipline*, 27–28.

13 Michel Foucault, *Power/Knowledge: Selected Interviews and Other Writings, 1972–1977* (Doubleday Publishing Group, 1980), 52. See also Hall, "Foucault" and Joseph Rouse, "Power–knowledge," in *The Cambridge Companion to Foucault*, ed. Garry Gutting (CUP, 1994).

14 Pereira, drawing on Grada Kilomba, in Maria do Mar Pereira, *Power, Knowledge and Feminist Scholarship: An Ethnography of Academia* (Routledge, 2017), 46.

15 Kathleen Lennon and Margaret Whitford, "Introduction," in *Knowing the Difference: Feminist Perspectives in Epistemology*, eds. Kathleen Lennon and Margaret Whitford (Routledge, 1994), 2.

16 Lorraine Code, *What Can She Know? Feminist Theory and the Construction of Knowledge* (Cornell University Press, 1991), 208. See also Lennon and Whitford, "Introduction."

17 Pereira, *Power*, 46.

certain scientific approaches and forms of knowledge over others is one of the ways in which transitional justice is restricted in its ability to recognise harms against Nature.

To focus on *which* power relations are reproduced, Lorraine Code tells us that 'the structures of power-knowledge in Western societies ... are historically rooted in an ancient, taken-for-granted biological determinism.'[18] What this means, and as argued by Black, feminist, postcolonial, and other critical scholars, is that mainstream knowledge production processes are one manifestation of 'the broader, ongoing (re)production of gendered, racialized, classist and Eurocentric hegemonies.'[19] As a result, there is a close relationship between long-standing dynamics of power and exclusion and the perceived legitimacy of particular knowledge claims or forms of knowledge.[20] When we encounter knowledge, it is most likely that this will have emerged from those considered to be 'in a better position to have their claims to epistemic status accepted as true and justified.'[21] These dynamics of knowledge production, and the concomitant marginalisation or exclusion of those deemed 'less able to produce ... proper knowledge,'[22] lie at the heart of this chapter. Of these various dynamics,[23] we will focus on gender, race, and Eurocentrism, as these are relevant to our analysis of transitional justice discourse and its engagement with Nature.

2.2.2 Gender, Race, and Eurocentrism

First, we will look to the role of gender in knowledge production. As Lorraine Code argues, the 'knower' 'has long been tacitly assumed to be male.'[24] In particular, 'an adult (but not *old*), white, reasonably affluent (latterly middle-class) educated man of status, property, and publicly acceptable accomplishments.'[25] Consequently, both women's knowledge and their

18 Code, *What*, 181.
19 Pereira, *Power*, 47
20 Lennon and Whitford, "Introduction." See also Pereira, *Power* and Linda Tuhiwai Smith, *Decolonizing Methodologies: Research and Indigenous Peoples* (Zed Books, 1999).
21 Pereira, *Power*, 56.
22 Pereira, *Power*, 56.
23 See e.g. Linda Martin Alcoff and Eva Feder Kittay, eds., *The Blackwell Guide to Feminist Philosophy* (Blackwell Publishing, 2007); Code, *What*, for whom knowledge is a 'commodity of privilege,' 207; Connell, *Southern*; Pereira, *Power*; Grada Kilomba, "Africans in Academia – Diversity in Adversity," essay extracted from Grada Kilomba, *Plantation Memories: Episodes of Everyday Racism* (Unrast Verlag, 2008); Kathleen Lennon and Margaret Whitford, eds., *Knowing the Difference: Feminist Perspectives in Epistemology* (Routledge, 1994).
24 Code, *What*, 8. See also Lennon and Whitford, "Introduction."
25 Code, *What*, 8.

claims to be knowers are frequently dismissed.[26] This gendering of knowledge production has been argued to have several associated characteristics. One is a fetishisation of objectivity (associated with masculinity) as both possible and the basis of valid knowledge.[27] Another is a related universalism which 'overlooks the fact of difference in human experience,'[28] and the exclusion or devaluing of knowledges not considered to be 'scientific.'[29] Another is the focus on individualism and individuals as agents of change, and the marginalisation of more collective ways of thinking, organising, and being.[30] This gendered hierarchy brings with it other hierarchies, such as value dualisms (false dichotomies or 'either/or' ways of thinking)[31] and – importantly for our arguments – the logic of patriarchal domination over both women and Nature.[32]

The second power–knowledge hierarchy we wish to highlight relates to racism. The racialised nature of knowledge production is an area that has received significant attention from Black, decolonial, and critical feminist scholars. From these perspectives, and as articulated by Grada Kilomba, 'structures of knowledge validation, which define what true and valid scholarship is, are controlled by *white* scholars.'[33] Similarly, knowledge production has been framed as a 'systematic way through which the West reaffirms its power as a centre of legitimate knowledge.'[34] This racial hierarchy has significant impacts, as explored by Achille Joseph Mbembe,

26 Code, *What*, 4.

27 Oshadi Mangena, "Against Fragmentation: The Need for Holism" in *Knowing the Difference: Feminist Perspectives in Epistemology*, eds. Kathleen Lennon and Margaret Whitford (Routledge, 1994).

28 Mangena, "Against," 275. See also Linda Martín Alcoff and Eva Feder Kittay, "Defining Feminist Philosophy" in *The Blackwell Guide to Feminist Philosophy*, eds. Linda Martín Alcoff and Eva Feder Kittay (Blackwell Publishing, 2007); Anita Silvers, "Feminism and Disability," in *The Blackwell Guide to Feminist Philosophy*, eds. Linda Martín Alcoff and Eva Feder Kittay (Blackwell Publishing, 2007).

29 Code, *What*; Pereira, *Power*; Laura Nader, *Naked Science: Anthropological Inquiry into Boundaries, Power, and Knowledge* (Routledge, 1996).

30 Code, *What*; Marilyn Freidman and Angela Bolte, "Ethics and Feminism" in *The Blackwell Guide to Feminist Philosophy*, eds. Linda Martín Alcoff and Eva Feder Kittay (Blackwell Publishing, 2007), 93; Nancy J. Hirschmann, "Feminist Political Philosophy" in *The Blackwell Guide to Feminist Philosophy*, eds. Linda Martín Alcoff and Eva Feder Kittay (Blackwell Publishing, 2007).

31 Code, *What*; Lorraine Code, "Feminist Epistemologies and Women's Lives" in *The Blackwell Guide to Feminist Philosophy*, eds. Linda Martín Alcoff and Eva Feder Kittay (Blackwell Publishing, 2007).

32 Karen J. Warren, "The Power and Promise of Ecological Feminism," *Environmental Ethics*, 12(2) (1990): 125–146.

33 Kilomba, "Africans."

34 Shastry Njeru and Tyanai Masiya, "The Politics of Knowledge in the Emergence of the Transitional Justice Industry in Zimbabwe: The Case of the 'Taking Transitional Justice to the People Programme', 2009–10," in *Knowledge for Peace: Transitional Justice and the*

Kilomba, and others.[35] For example, scholars from the African continent have often been marginalised within academic discourse, including in discourse concerning the African continent.[36] Another example relates to Indigenous peoples: Linda Tuhiwai Smith asserts that the racialised nature of knowledge production has resulted in a 'positional superiority' of the West over the 'knowledge, language and culture' of many Indigenous peoples.[37] What emerges is an 'ethnocentrism' that 'runs deep,'[38] leading to the overlooking of subaltern ideas and the prioritisation of predominantly 'white' perspectives.[39]

The third, and related, dynamic is that of Eurocentrism – a hierarchy that has been criticised for decades by Southern scholars and their allies.[40] The racialised nature of knowledge production has resulted in a 'Eurocentric canon ... that attributes truth only to the Western way of knowledge production' and 'disregards other epistemic traditions.'[41] As Raewyn Connell summarises under the label of 'Northern theory,' 'modern social science embeds the viewpoints, perspectives and problems of metropolitan society, while presenting itself as universal knowledge.'[42]

As a result of these power–knowledge dynamics, the knowledge we encounter in academia 'is not an objective scientific truth ... but rather the result of unequal power relations.'[43] Within transitional justice discourse, knowledge production must be understood in light of these power

Politics of Knowledge in Theory and Practice, eds. Briony Jones and Ulrike Lühe (Elgar, 2021), 135, drawing on Smith, *Decolonizing.*

35 See e.g. Connell, *Southern*; Kilomba, "Africans"; Achille Joseph Mbembe, "Decolonizing the University: New Directions," *Arts and Humanities in Higher Education* 15(1) (2016): 29–45; Nader, *Naked Science.*

36 Kilomba, "Africans."

37 Smith, *Decolonizing*, 67. See also Sandra Harding and Brent Mendoza, "Latin American Decolonial Feminist Philosophy of Knowledge Production" in *The Routledge Handbook of Feminist Philosophy of Science*, eds. Sharon Crasnow and Kristen Intemann (Routledge, 2021).

38 Nader, "Anthropological," 3.

39 See e.g. Annie Hikido and Susan B. Murray, "Whitened Rainbows: How White College Students Protect Whiteness Through Diversity Discourses," *Race, Ethnicity and Education*, 19(2) (2016): 389–411; Kai Linke, "Keeping Academia White: A Case Study," in *Who Can Speak and Who Is Heard/Hurt? Facing Problems of Race, Racism, and Ethnic Diversity in the Humanities in Germany*, eds. Mahmoud Arghavan et al., (Verlag, 2019); Tsedale M. Melaku and Angie Beeman, "Academia Isn't a Safe Haven for Conversations About Race and Racism," *Harvard Business Review*, June 25, 2020, https://hbr.org/2020/06/academia-isnt-a-safe-haven-for-conversations-about-race-and-racism.

40 Lennon and Whitford, "Introduction"; Harding and Mendoza, "Latin American."

41 Mbembe, "Decolonizing," 32.

42 Connell, *Southern*, vi–vii.

43 Kilomba, "Africans."

relations, particularly those between the Global North and the Global South.[44] Gendered and racial hierarchies also overlap and intersect in ways that render certain perspectives particularly marginalised.[45] For example, white feminist scholars from the Global North have gained access to increased voice and power. Yet, Black, Indigenous, and Global South women continue to experience silencing due to their gender, ethnic identities, and location, or can experience 'gender washing,' whereby their experiences are subsumed into ideas about 'universal' gendered experiences.[46] As will be examined in the next section, we see these power relations play out in the field of transitional justice, alongside additional dynamics particular to the field.

2.3 The Dynamics of Knowledge Production in Transitional Justice

Transitional justice has 'a rich and complex knowledge landscape.'[47] However, reflecting the above discussion, this 'landscape' is shaped by hierarchies regarding 'whose knowledge counts, whose knowledge is acted upon, and what is even considered to be knowledge.'[48] These hierarchies have practical implications, as transitional justice discourse can play a crucial role in determining '*who* is accountable for *what* and *when*.'[49] In such a context, those 'who can speak' are in a powerful position to influence how the past is understood and responded to. In this section, we will examine how the field has shaped 'who can speak' by tracing transitional justice's epistemic, historical, and geographic origins; its development into a professionalised industry; and its resulting role in perpetrating 'epistemic injustice' against voices from the Global South and of Indigenous peoples.

44 Briony Jones and Ulrike Lühe, "Knowledge for Peace: Transitional Justice and the Politics of Knowledge in Theory and Practice," in *Knowledge for Peace: Transitional Justice and the Politics of Knowledge in Theory and Practice*, eds. Briony Jones and Ulrike Lühe (Elgar, 2021), 4.

45 Kimberlé Crenshaw, *On Intersectionality: Essential Writings* (The New Press, 2014).

46 Laura Rodríguez Castro, *Decolonial Feminisms, Power and Place: Sentipensando with Rural Women in Colombia* (Palgrave, 2021); Benita Roth, "Second Wave Black Feminism in the African Diaspora: News from New Scholarship," *Agenda: Empowering Women for Gender Equity* 58 (2003): 46–58.

47 Jones and Lühe, "Knowledge," 3.

48 Jones and Lühe, "Knowledge," 3.

49 Rosemary Nagy, "Transitional Justice as Global Project: Critical Reflections," *Third World Quarterly* 29(2) (2008): 286.

2.3.1 The Origins of a Field

As Michel Foucault asserts, when thinking about the power–knowledge relationship, it is important to consider the 'epistemic context within which ... bodies of knowledge become intelligible and authoritative.'[50] In this section, we will examine the epistemic context from which transitional justice emerged as a discursive space.

There are different ways to tell this history. If we focus on the geographical contexts from which 'transitional justice' first emerged, we see a relatively multicultural origin story. While the term 'transitional justice' has been retrospectively applied to post-World War II criminal justice,[51] the term, and many of the mechanisms that we now associate with the field, emerged in the context of transitions to democracy across Latin America, Eastern Europe, and South Africa.[52] Argentina was a particular 'trailblazer' in transitional justice, being the first in a series of democratic transitions in Latin America to attempt two of the key accountability mechanisms in the field – truth commissions and trials.[53] Although transitional justice discourse did not immediately emerge from its transition, Argentina became a 'regular point of reference,' and its truth commission model was replicated across numerous contexts.[54] Ellen Lutz and Kathryn Sikkink's work on 'the justice cascade'[55] demonstrates that Latin America more generally has

50 Rouse, "Power–knowledge," 93.

51 Susanne Karstedt, "From Absence to Presence, From Silence to Voice: Victims in International and Transitional Justice Since the Nuremberg Trials," *International Review of Victimology* 17(9) (2010): 9–30; Bronwyn Leebaw, "The Irreconcilable Goals of Transitional Justice," *Human Rights Quarterly* 30(1) (2008): 95–118; Zinaida Miller, "Embedded Ambivalence: Ungoverning Global Justice," *Transnational Legal Theory* 11(3) (2020): 353–381. While efforts to confront the legacies of war are not new (see e.g. Jon Elster, *Closing the Books: Transitional Justice in Historical Perspective* (CUP, 2004)), Nuremberg remains dominant in the literature as the key juncture in recent history in the development of the field.

52 Leebaw, "Irreconcilable"; Pablo de Greiff, "The Future of the Past: Reflections on the Present State and Prospects of Transitional Justice," *International Journal of Transitional Justice* 14(2) (2020): 251–259; Diane Orentlicher, "'Settling Accounts' Revisited: Reconciling Global Norms with Local Agency," *International Journal of Transitional Justice* 1(1) (2007): 10–22; Jens Iverson, "Transitional Justice, *Jus Post Bellum* and International Criminal Law: Differentiating the Usages, History and Dynamics," *International Journal of Transitional Justice* 7(3) (2013): 413–433; Phil Clark and Nicola Palmer, "Challenging Transitional Justice" in *Critical Perspectives in Transitional Justice,* eds. Nicola Palmer et al. (Intersentia, 2012), 15.

53 Kathryn Sikkink and Carrie Booth Walling, "Argentina's Contribution to Global Trends in Transitional Justice," in *Transitional Justice in the Twenty-First Century*, eds. Naomi Roht-Arriaza and Javier Mariezcurrena (CUP, 2006), 313.

54 Zunino, *Justice*, 72.

55 Ellen Lutz and Kathryn Sikkink, "The Justice Cascade: The Evolution and Impact of Foreign Human Rights Trials in Latin America," *Chicago Journal of International Law* 2(1) (2001): Article 3.

been central to the emergence and global spread of accountability norms and practices.[56] In addition, Iosif Kovras has highlighted the emergence and dispersion of 'forensic truth recovery' in and from Latin America in the context of efforts to recover the disappeared.[57] Latin America has remained an important site of developments in the field, including in relation to harms against Nature.[58]

The abrupt end of the Cold War and the commencement of transitions from communism to democratic governance across Eastern Europe 'reinvigorated and transformed' the transitional justice movement. [59] The idea that transitional justice was capable of comparative study and crosscultural applicability began to gain traction, and scholars and policy makers sought to learn and apply lessons from Latin America to the post-communist context.[60] Yet, rather than following in Latin America's footsteps, new approaches were emerging from Europe, most notably truth-telling through the disclosure of secret files, the vetting of public officials (known as lustration), and the restitution of private property.[61] While many considered the post-communist transitions to be disappointing, these methods were incorporated into transitional justice's list of practices, feeding the evolution of field-specific 'concepts, objects and actors.'[62]

The African continent has been another important site of the field's development.[63] The UN's establishment of the International Criminal Tribunal for Rwanda in 1994[64] and South Africa's innovative Truth and Reconciliation

56 Sikkink and Walling, "Argentina's." See also Kathryn Sikkink, "Latin American Countries as Norm Protagonists of the Idea of International Human Rights," *Global Governance* 20(3) (2014): 389–404.

57 Iosif Kovras, *Grassroots Activism and the Evolution of Transitional Justice: The Families of the Disappeared* (CUP, 2017), 84; 94.

58 Alexandra Huneeus and Pablo Rueda Sáiz, "Territory as a Victim of Armed Conflict," *International Journal of Transitional Justice* 15(1) (2021): 210–229; Laura Ordóñez-Vargas et al., "An Ecocentric Turn in the Transitional Restorative Justice Process in Colombia," *International Journal of Transitional Justice* 17(1) (2023): 107–122; Isabella Ariza-Buitrago and Luisa Gómez-Betancur, "Nature in Focus: The Invisibility and Re-Emergence of Rivers, Land and Animals in Colombia's Transitional Justice System," *International Journal of Transitional Justice* 17(1) (2023): 71–88.

59 Zunino, *Justice*, 79.

60 Zunino, *Justice*, 83.

61 Lavinia Stan, "Transitional justice in Central and Eastern Europe," *Research Handbook on Transitional Justice*, eds. Cheryl Lawther et al. (Elgar, 2017).

62 Zunino, *Justice*, 79.

63 Jones and Lühe, "Knowledge."

64 UN Security Council, *Statute of the International Criminal Tribunal for the Prosecution of Persons Responsible for Genocide and Other Serious Violations of International Humanitarian Law Committed in the Territory of Rwanda and Rwandan Citizens Responsible for Genocide and Other Such Violations Committed in the Territory of*

Commission (SATRC)[65] the following year are two high-profile examples of the range of transitional justice mechanisms adopted across the continent.[66] While the former can be understood as part of the turn towards international criminal law in transitional justice (see Chapter 3), the latter attracted multidisciplinary, international attention due its inclusion of redemption, healing, and reconciliation.[67] As Marcos Zunino outlines, those responsible for establishing the SATRC consciously examined other examples of transitional justice, helping 'to consolidate the transitional justice narrative linking the Latin American, Eastern European and South African transitions' and creating a 'pool' of transitional justice experiences.[68]

However, this geographical diversity is not reflected in the 'profession' that has grown around the increasingly institutionalised field of practice, as explored in the following section.

2.3.2 Expertise and Professionalisation

Over the second half of the twentieth century, transitional justice became 'an increasingly professionalised industry.'[69] As the 'field' of transitional justice emerged,[70] those involved in its creation and reproduction formed 'an epistemic community'[71] in which the theories and practices of transitional justice could be shared through particular disciplines and professions.[72] Through this process of professionalisation, certain forms of knowledge

---

Neighbouring States, between 1 January 1994 and 31 December 1994, UNSC Res. 955 (1994), 8 November 1994.

65 South Africa, Promotion of National Unity and Reconciliation Act 1995.

66 Zunino, *Justice*, 60–61. See also the African Union's Transitional Justice Policy, adopted February 2019.

67 Zunino, *Justice*, 117.

68 Zunino, *Justice*, 119.

69 Astrid Jamar, "The Crusade of Transitional Justice: Tracing the Journeys of Hegemonic Claims," *Violence and Democracy* (The British Academy, September 2019): 53, https://www.thebritishacademy.ac.uk/documents/242/Violence-and-Democracy.pdf

70 Christine Bell, "Transitional Justice, Interdisciplinarity and the State of the 'Field' or 'Non-field,'" *International Journal of Transitional Justice* 3(1) (2009): 5–27.

71 Lutz and Sikkink, "Justice Cascade." An epistemic community is a community of individuals connected by the creation, learning, and sharing of knowledge, who often use this knowledge to respond to complex and uncertain situations (see e.g. Emanuel Adler and Peter Haas, "Conclusion: Epistemic Communities, World Order, and the Creation of a Reflective Research Programme," *International Organization* 46(1) (1992): 367–390; Mai'a K. Davis Cross, "Rethinking Epistemically Communities Twenty Years Later," *Review of International Studies* 39(1) (2013): 137–160; Peter Haas, "Introduction: Epistemic Communities and International Policy Co-ordination," *International Organization* 46(1) (1992): 1–35.

72 Vasuki Nesiah, "Theories of Transitional Justice: Cashing in the Blue Chips," in *The Oxford Handbook of the Theory of International Law*, eds. Anne Orford and Florian Hoffman (OUP, 2016), 781–782.

came to be recognised as 'expertise,'[73] thereby (re)producing respectability, influence, and power for certain 'knowers.'[74] In this section, we consider *who* has been able to obtain recognition for their expertise.

Reflecting the above discussion on power–knowledge, to have one's expertise recognised requires more than knowledge. Rather, experts are often those with 'professional power,' meaning the ability 'to display or access valued professional resources.'[75] This access to 'professional power' is not distributed equally. Instead, a disproportionate amount of contemporary transitional justice knowledge has been and continues to be created by those educated in 'the language of the Global North.'[76] Thus, actors with expertise in what has been described as 'EuroUnitedStatesian human rights practices'[77] are more readily recognised as 'authoritative.'[78] While the role of Latin America complicates the picture of Global North hegemony somewhat, there is nonetheless a general consensus that the Global North remains dominant in both scholarship and practice.[79]

As the field has developed, it has become more centred around 'internationally mobile and privileged experts,'[80] coalescing around a range of organisations, universities, and institutions.[81] By the early 2000s, transitional justice's 'epistemic community' could be found in organs of the UN,[82] international non-governmental organisations such as the International

73 Code, *What*.
74 Pereira, *Power*, 47.
75 Pereira, *Power*, 56.
76 Jones and Lühe, "Knowledge," 5.
77 M. Brinton Lykes and Colleen Murphy, "Decolonizing Transitional Justice: Soft, Radical or Beyond Reform," *International Journal of Transitional Justice*, 17(3) (2023): 361–369.
78 Briony Jones et al., "Producing Knowledge on and for Transitional Justice: Reflections on a Collaborative Research Project," in *Knowledge for Peace: Transitional Justice and the Politics of Knowledge in Theory and Practice*, eds. Briony Jones and Ulrike Lühe (Elgar, 2021), 52.
79 See e.g. Abdullahi Ahmed An-Na'im, "Editorial Note: From the Neocolonial 'Transitional' to Indigenous Formations of Justice," *International Journal of Transitional Justice* 7(2) (2013): 197–204; John Braithwaite, "Criminology, Peacebuilding and Transitional Justice: Lessons from the Global South," in *The Palgrave Handbook of Criminology and the Global South*, eds. Kerry Carrington et al. (Palgrave, 2018); Jones and Lühe, "Knowledge"; Mohamed Sesay, "Decolonization of Postcolonial Africa: A Structural Justice Project More Radical than Transitional Justice," *International Journal of Transitional Justice* 16(2) (2022): 254–271; Hakeem O. Yusuf, "Colonialism and the Dilemmas of Transitional Justice in Nigeria," *International Journal of Transitional Justice* 12(2) (2018): 257–276.
80 Jones and Lühe, "Knowledge," 5. See also Kimberley Theidon, "Editorial Note," *The International Journal of Transitional Justice* 3(3) (2009): 295–300.
81 Paige Arthur, 'How "Transitions" Reshaped Human Rights: A Conceptual History of Transitional Justice," *Human Rights Quarterly* 31 (2009): 321–367.
82 UN Security Council, Report of the Secretary-General on the Rule of Law and Transitional Justice in Conflict and Post-Conflict Societies, UN Doc S/2004/616 (2004), 23 August 2004.

Center for Transitional Justice,[83] and dedicated research centres such as the Transitional Justice Institute in Northern Ireland.[84] In the 20 years since, the UN has cemented itself as a key player in transitional justice; the UN Human Rights website identifies Afghanistan, the Central African Republic, Colombia, the Democratic Republic of the Congo, El Salvador, the Gambia, Guatemala, Iraq, Lebanon, Liberia, Mali, Mexico, Nepal, South Sudan, Sri Lanka, the Sudan, the Syrian Arab Republic, Tunisia, and the Western Balkans, including Kosovo, as states where it is currently engaged in 'designing and implementing' transitional justice processes.[85]

This turn towards internationalised professionalism has been accompanied by a preference for 'technocratic and decontextualised solutions'[86] and an emphasis on 'universal' human rights norms.[87] This has had implications for local actors, including those with direct experience of the causes and effects of conflict, such as victims, communities, and local organisations,[88] who seek to exert influence over transitional justice processes in their own contexts.[89] Reduced to the status of non-experts,[90] local actors can see their perspectives 'channelled or streamlined'[91] by top-down understandings of

83 Priscilla Hayner, "International Center for Transitional Justice (ICTJ)," in *Encyclopedia of Human Rights,* ed David Forsythe (OUP, 2009).

84 Zunino, *Justice*, 60.

85 OHCHR, Transitional Justice and Human Rights, n.d., https://www.ohchr.org/en/transitional-justice.

86 Nagy, "Transitional," 275. See also Jennifer Matsunaga, "Two Faces of Transitional Justice: Theorizing the Immeasurability of Transitional Justice and Decolonization in Canada," *Decolonization: Indigeneity, Education and Society* 5(1) (2016): 24–44; Tshepo Madlingozi, "On Transitional Justice Entrepreneurs and the Production of Victims," *Journal of Human Rights Practice* 2(2) (2010): 208–228.

87 An-Na'im, "Editorial," 197. See also Jennifer Balint et al., "Rethinking Transitional Justice, Redressing Indigenous Harm: A New Conceptual Approach," *International Journal of Transitional Justice* 8(2) (2014): 194–216; Augustine S. J. Park, "Settler Colonialism, Decolonization and Radicalizing Transitional Justice," *International Journal of Transitional Justice* 14(2) (2020): 260–279; Hugo van der Merwe and M. Brinton Lykes, "Racism and Transitional Justice," *International Journal of Transitional Justice* 14(3) (2021): 415–422.

88 Serge-Alain Yao N'Da and Gilbert Fokou, "Knowledge Asymmetry and Transitional Justice in Côte d'Ivoire," in *Knowledge for Peace: Transitional Justice and the Politics of Knowledge in Theory and Practice*, eds. Briony Jones and Ulrike Lühe (Edward Elgar Publishing Ltd., 2021).

89 Everisto Benyera, ed., *Indigenous, Traditional, and Non-State Transitional Justice in Southern Africa: Zimbabwe and Namibia* (Lexington Books, 2019); Jamar, "The Crusade."

90 Mónica Acosta et al., "The Colombian Transitional Process: Comparative Perspectives on Violence Against Indigenous Women," *International Journal of Transitional Justice* 12(1) (2018): 108–125.

91 Nagy, "Transitional," 276.

how transitional justice should be done.[92] This emphasis on top-down solutions can mean that survivors are unlikely to have their calls for justice recognised if they are unaligned with international legal norms.[93] For instance, in her analysis of the role of the UN in the Burundian transitional justice process, Wendy Lambourne found that the UN failed to take 'local traditional or informal' justice models seriously, showing 'little recognition that other, more creative options might prove to be more appropriate in different cultural and conflict settings.'[94]

Similar hierarchies have emerged in academic contexts, where 'knowledge produced in contemporary and historical, social, political and environmental struggles' can be either overlooked entirely or 'overwritten by accounts by "experts."'[95] Although attempts have been made to 'localise' transitional justice research,[96] inequalities persist in relationships between international and local actors. Raewyn Connell explores these relationships using the model of a 'division of labor [sic],' highlighting that a tendency remains for 'lead theorists' from the Global North to develop approaches which are applied or tested by local partners or organisations in the South.[97] As captured by Fionnuala Ní Aoláin, in this regard transitional justice has become a 'form of discursive colonization in that its language and "tool box" codify knowledge in ways that exclude and produce hierarchies of value.'[98]

Of course, hierarchies emerge in local contexts too.[99] As Peter Manning, Jordan Tchilingirian, Somaly Kum, and Tudor Nedelcu explore through

92 See also Brigitte Piquard, "What Knowledge Counts? Local Humanitarian Knowledge Production in Protracted Conflicts. A Central African Republic Case Study," *Peacebuilding*, 10(1): 85–100 for a similar point regarding humanitarian knowledge.

93 Rosalind Shaw and Lars Waldorf, "Introduction," in *Localizing Transitional Justice: Interventions and Priorities After Mass Violence*, eds. Rosalind Shaw et al. (Stanford University Press, 2010), 4.

94 Wendy Lambourne, "Power Struggles and the Politics of Knowledge Production in the Burundian Transitional Justice Process," in *Knowledge for Peace: Transitional Justice and the Politics of Knowledge in Theory and Practice*, eds. Briony Jones and Ulrike Lühe (Edward Elgar Publishing Ltd., 2021), 102. See also Laura Arriaza and Naomi Roht-Arriaza, "Social Reconstruction as a Local Process," *International Journal of Transitional Justice*, 2(2) (2008): 152–172.

95 Choudry, "Reflections," 28. See also Victoria Openif'Oluwa Akoleowo, "Critical Pedagogy, Scholar Activism and Epistemic Decolonisation," *South African Journal of Philosophy* 40(4) (2022): 436–451.

96 Shaw, et al., *Localizing*.

97 Connell, *Southern*, cited in Braithwaite, "Criminology," 971.

98 Ní Aoláin "Advancing," 206.

99 Jelena Obradovic-Wochnik, "Hidden Politics of Power and Governmentality in Transitional Justice and Peacebuilding: The Problem of 'Bringing the Local Back In'," *Journal of International Relations and Development* 23 (2020): 117–138; Pamina Firchow and Yvette Selim, "Meaningful Engagement from the Bottom-Up? Taking Stock of Participation in Transitional Justice Processes," *International Journal of Transitional Justice* 16(2) (2022): 187–203.

their analysis of transitional justice networks in Cambodia, 'transitional justice networks tend ... to be characterised by hierarchy and inequalities within groups of both local and international actors.'[100] Senior roles within local organisations can end up occupied by individuals in positions of relative privilege, or can be allocated in tokenistic ways.[101] In this way, even 'localisation agendas can embed hierarchies of knowledge that reproduce racial and gender inequalities.'[102] These tensions reflect the risks of assuming the 'local' is singular, rather than its own site of power asymmetries.[103]

By neglecting and thereby reproducing these unequal power–knowledge dynamics, transitional justice professionals arguably continue to consolidate a normative framework that is, at best, contentious, and at worst, experienced as unjust.[104] This theme is continued in the following section, where we explore how these power–knowledge dynamics can be understood as a form of 'epistemic injustice'[105] through which certain voices are rendered not only marginal, but also 'unhearable' on their own terms.[106]

2.3.3 Transitional Justice as Epistemic Injustice

Decisions surrounding whose knowledge is accepted are deeply political.[107] The turn towards internationalised professionalism has enabled liberal democratic states (many of which are former colonisers) to exert influence over transitional justice discourse.[108] As a result, mainstream approaches to transitional justice can reflect the inequality 'and even violence of relations between the Global North and Global South.'[109] This continued inequality in terms of who can shape academic discourse has been described as the 'colonial matrix of power,'[110] whereby the legacies of colonisation continue to define relations and knowledge production long after the end of direct

100 Peter Manning et al., "Transitional Justice Networks and the Role of 'Local' Actors in Cambodia," *Journal of Peacebuilding & Development*, 18(2) (2023): 158–176.
101 Toni Haastrup and Jamie J. Hagen, "Racial Hierarchies of Knowledge Production in the Women, Peace and Security Agenda," *Critical Studies on Security*, 9(1) (2021), 27–30.
102 Manning et al., "Transitional."
103 Adam Kochanski, "The 'Local Turn' in Transitional Justice: Curb the Enthusiasm," *International Studies* Review, 22(1) (2020): 26–50.
104 Jamar, "The Crusade," 54.
105 Miranda Fricker, *Epistemic Injustice: Power and the Ethics of Knowing* (OUP, 2007).
106 Kiran Kaur Grewal, "The Epistemic Violence of Transitional Justice: A View from Sri Lanka," *International Journal of Transitional Justice*, 17(2) (2023): 322–338.
107 See e.g. Pereira, *Power*; Nader, *Naked*.
108 Yusuf, "Colonialism."
109 Jones and Lühe, "Knowledge," 5.
110 Sabelo J. Ndlovu-Gatsheni, *Coloniality of Power in Postcolonial Africa: Myths of Decolonization* (Conseil pour le Developpement de la Recherche Economique et Sociale en Afrique, 2013). See also Nelson Maldonado-Torres, "On the Coloniality of Being:

domination. As a result, academia has been described as a 'space of violence'[111] for scholars from the Global South.

These dynamics are visible in transitional justice discourse, where what Mohamed Sesay frames as a 'coloniality of knowledge' persists.[112] While much transitional justice research is conducted in Global South contexts and involves collaboration between researchers and practitioners in both the Global North and Global South, it is predominantly published by Global North institutions and scholars.[113] Collaborations can go unacknowledged, meaning the contribution of those from the Global South is hidden.[114] Decolonial scholars have drawn attention to the parallels between knowledge production and the division of labour in other spheres: the Global South is expected to produce the raw material, while the Global North produces the final product.[115] Meanwhile, theories emerging from the Global South continue to face marginalisation.[116] This pre-eminence of particular intellectual groups effectively silences 'other subaltern ways of knowing' and creates a field which appears 'unable or unwilling to envisage ways of knowing that surpass our own imagination.'[117]

Consequently, some have argued that transitional justice is a space of 'epistemic injustice,'[118] whereby Global South scholars and communities are wronged in their capacity as knowers.[119] For example, Maja Davidović and Catherine Turner analyse citation practices to demonstrate the colonial 'policing of the boundaries' of transitional justice, highlighting how 'othered' knowledge has been precluded from shaping the scholarship 'and by extension praxis' of the field.[120] Going further, Tshepo Madlingozi has argued

Contributions to the Development of a Concept," *Cultural Studies*, 21(2–3) (2007): 240–270.

111 Kilomba, "Africans."

112 Sesay, "Decolonization," 262.

113 Jones et al., "Producing," 52.

114 Jones and Lühe, "Knowledge," 5.

115 See e.g. Jeremiah O. Arowosegbe, "Decolonising the Social Sciences in the Global South: Claude Ake and the Praxis of Knowledge Production in Africa" (Working Paper 79/2008; Leiden, African Studies Centre, 2008).

116 Braithwaite, "Criminology," 971; Padraig McAuliffe, *Transformative Transitional Justice and the Malleability of Post-Conflict States* (Elgar, 2017), 82.

117 Stephanie Vieille, "Transitional Justice: A Colonizing Field?" *Amsterdam Law Forum* 4(3) (2012): 58–68.

118 Fricker, *Epistemic Injustice.*

119 For broader discussions on epistemic injustice in knowledge production see e.g. Pascah Mungwini, "'African Know Thyself': Epistemic Injustice and the Quest for Liberative Knowledge," *International Journal of African Renaissance Studies – Multi-, Inter- and Transdisciplinarity*, 12(2 (2017): 5–8.

120 Maja Davidović and Catherine Turner, "What Counts as Transitional Justice Scholarship? Citational Recognition and Disciplinary Hierarchies in Theory and Practice," *International Studies Quarterly* 67 (2023): sqad091.

that transitional justice can be considered a form of epistemicide, defining this as the 'killing of Indigenous knowledge, the killing of other people's way of understanding the world.'[121] Other scholars have similarly noted this 'neo-colonial' tendency,[122] whereby Indigenous conceptions of justice struggle to gain legitimacy in transitional justice discourse or are dismissed as out of step with the 'modernising' approach of the Global North.[123]

Epistemic injustice can be accompanied by 'the epistemology of ignorance,' whereby members of dominant groups are kept ignorant of harms experienced by non-dominant groups 'by virtue of their ethically bad knowledge practices.'[124] This can be the case even when marginalised groups have the knowledge, concepts, and language necessary to articulate their harms; dominant groups can refuse to acknowledge the marginalised group's epistemic tools or fail to regard the marginalised as a 'knower' in the first place.[125] As Kieran Kaur Grewal has explored in relation to Sri Lanka, reaching across this epistemology of ignorance can require victims and marginalised communities to use 'experts' who are deemed more 'acceptable' as a conduit. Grewal notes that the conversion of justice claims into transitional justice's 'technical language' is far from neutral. Rather, it 'gives power to those already versed in transitional justice's lexicon and logic.'[126] Thus, the turn towards professionalism can be understood as one of the ways in which epistemic injustice is reinforced.

In this section, we have sought to expose some of the interrelated dimensions of knowledge production in transitional justice. We have explored how foundational dimensions of power–knowledge such as race, gender, and Eurocentrism shape who is recognised as a 'knower' with the ability to influence transitional justice discourse. In the following section, we highlight the implications of the '*uneven possibilities* of establishing credibility and being heard'[127] for the recognition of harms against Nature.

121 Tshepo Madlingozi, "There is Neither Truth nor Reconciliation in So-Called 'South Africa'" (in conversation with Léopold Lambert). The Funambulist. 29 June 2020. https://thefunambulist.net/magazine/reparations/there-is-neither-truth-nor-reconciliation-in-so-called-south-africa-a-conversation-with-tshepo-madlingozi.

122 An-Na'im, "Editorial," 197. See also Balint et al., "Rethinking"; Briony Jones and Ulrike Lühe, *Knowledge for Peace: Transitional Justice and the Politics of Knowledge in Theory and Practice* (Elgar, 2021); Park, "Settler Colonialism"; van der Merwe and Brinton Lykes, "Racism."

123 An-Na'im, "Editorial," 197.

124 Rebecca Mason, "Two Kinds of Unknowing," *Hypatia* 26(2) (2011): 294–307.

125 Rachel McKinnon, "Epistemic Injustice," *Philosophy Compass* 11(8) (2016): 437–446.

126 Grewal, "Epistemic."

127 Pereira, *Power*, 51.

2.4 Knowledge Production and Harms against Nature

In this section, we argue that there are two facets of the power–knowledge relationship which have had an identifiable impact on the place of Nature within transitional justice discourse. The first is conceptual. We argue that power–knowledge dynamics have facilitated the dominance of anthropocentrism in the mainstream discourse, placing epistemological limitations on the visibility of harm to Nature. The second is ontological. We argue that power–knowledge dynamics have enabled those with greater influence to place certain additional parameters around the matters and harms which transitional justice will address.[128] Unpacked further in subsequent chapters, these arguments are introduced here to demonstrate their connections with knowledge production.

2.4.1 Entrenching Anthropocentrism

Our first argument is that the relative priority given to traditional, (white) male-dominated knowledge production has entrenched a 'logic of domination'[129] and a false 'value dualism' or dichotomy between humankind and Nature.[130] We further contend that the continued dominance of Global North voices and ideas in mainstream transitional justice discourse has hindered the possibility of correcting the field's resulting anthropocentrism. We will examine each of these points in turn.

As discussed, a central argument in the knowledge production scholarship is that 'mainstream' knowledge prioritises certain knowledge or 'knowers' over others. Mainstream science is argued to normalise 'the epistemic and material domination of a narrow subset of epistemic agents and activities over others.'[131] This 'logic of domination'[132] is both rooted in and justified by the persistence of 'dichotomous thinking,' a 'peculiar characteristic of malestream thought' that constructs distinctions as 'both hierarchical and polar.'[133] Hierarchically, such dichotomies preserve inequality, whereby (for instance) perceived objectivity supersedes subjectivity, male dominates

128 Zunino, *Justice*.

129 Warren, "Power and Promise."

130 Val Plumwood, "Beyond the Dualistic Assumptions of Women, Men, Nature," *The Ecologists* 22(1) (1992): 8–13.

131 Pereira, *Power*, 46.

132 Warren, "Power and Promise."

133 Code, *What*, 28. See also Judith Butler, *Frames of War: When is Life Grievable?* (Verso Books, 2016); Connell, *Southern*; Donna Haraway, *Simians, Cyborgs and Women* (Free Association Books, 1991); Warren, "Power and Promise." 'Malestream' means male-dominated and male-oriented sites of knowledge production (including academia). See e.g. Pamela Abbott et al., *An Introduction to Sociology: Feminist Perspectives* (Routledge, 2006) for engagement with the notion of the 'malestream.'

female, Judeo-Christian ideologies supersede other beliefs, and 'culture' or 'civilisation' dominates Nature.[134]

At the heart of narratives that reinforce man's domination over Nature lies the false binary opposition of *physis* (Nature) and *nomos* (law or custom).[135] A belief in the dichotomy of the two terms was a common feature of philosophical debates dating back to Ancient Greece and the fourth and fifth century BC. The terms were also used politically. For instance, *physis* was used both by the social and political elite to justify class differentiation as natural, and by those who sought to question the class hierarchy and argue that society should be democratic rather than oligarchic.[136] The relationship and perceived tension between these two concepts has preoccupied many scholars, who have repeatedly returned to these concepts to address legal and philosophical problems.[137] Indeed, similar themes around the separation of Nature from 'man' can be found in the evolution of Western philosophy. For example, the Cartesian philosophies of the Enlightenment period furthered ideas of separation from, fear of, and dominance over Nature, with an accompanying ethos of control underpinned by science, technology, and power–knowledge.[138]

In the twentieth century, the concept of *nomos* was explicitly applied to the concept of international law by Carl Schmitt, a prominent member of the Nazi party who glorified the age of European colonisation.[139] For Schmitt, European colonisation resulted in 'the first *nomos* of the earth,' bringing with it the partition and classification of land, and subsequently the first land appropriations.[140] Although Schmitt was explicit about not being a theologian, others have noted the ways in which his Christian faith influenced his

134 Colin Scott, "Science for the West, Myth for the Rest?" in *Naked Science: Anthropological inquiry into Boundaries, Power, and Knowledge*, ed. Laura Nader (Routledge, 1996), 69. See also Harding and Mendoza, "Latin American."

135 Angela Hobbs, "Physis and Nomos" in *The Routledge Encyclopaedia of Philosophy*, ed. Edward Craig (Routledge, 1998), 381–382; Val Plumwood, *Feminism and the Mastery of Nature* (Routledge, 1993).

136 Hobbs, "Physis and Nomos."

137 Lukas van ben Berge, "Ancient Greek Nomos and Modern Legal Theory: A Reappraisal" *Netherlands Journal of Legal Philosophy* 51(2) (2022): 264–276.

138 Peter Doran, *A Political Economy of Attention, Mindfulness and Consumerism* (Routledge, 2017), Ch. 3.

139 Carl Schmitt, *The Nomos of the Earth in the International Law of the Jus Publicum Europseum*, translated: G. L. Ulmen (Telos Press Publishing, 2003); Stuart Elden, "Reading Schmitt Geopolitically: Nomos, Territory and Großraum," in *Spatiality, Sovereignty and Carl Schmitt: Geographies of the Nomos*, ed. Stephen Legg (Routledge, 2011).

140 Schmitt, *Nomos*, 49. See also Stephanie Jones and Stewart Motha, "A New Nomos Offshore and Bodies as their Own Signs," *Law and Literature* 27(2) (2015): 253–278.

work.[141] The connections between his political theory and religious beliefs are relevant. Judeo-Christian faiths have been critiqued for being 'the most anthropocentric of religions' and for justifying the uncontrolled exploitation of natural resources, due to references in the Old Testament to man 'dominating' Nature.[142] While contemporary Judeo-Christian denominations include those who argue that 'dominion' should instead be interpreted as 'stewardship,' Christianity has been used to legitimise the colonial exploitation of Asia, Africa, and Latin America's people and resources (sometimes referred to as 'settler capitalism').[143]

While we can, following Julia Lossau in her critique of Schmitt's work, choose 'to think without Schmitt,'[144] it is important to observe that his account of the *nomos* reveals the logic of domination which underlay the colonising mindset writ large. Indigenous and decolonial scholars have catalogued and made explicit the impact of such a logic. Pre-colonial contexts were considered empty, lawless, and devoid of history, development, and culture, an understanding expressed through the mechanism of *terra nullius*.[145] The powers of colonisation were first made visible in efforts to 'map, cultivate, and order' this 'empty' space.[146] Achille Mbembe describes a 'colonial principle of rationality' which clearly differentiates 'between being and existing.' The coloniser exists, whereas Indigenous people and land 'belong to the *universe of immediate* things' – and are thus ripe for exploitation.[147] This 'thingification' is central to the colonial logic.[148] This speaks to what

141 György Geréby, "The Theology of Carl Schmitt," *Poiteja* 72 (2021): 21–49; Mika Ojakangas, "Carl Scmitt and the Sacred Origins of Law," *Telos* 147 (2009): 34–54.

142 Lynn White, "The Historical Roots of our Ecologic Crisis," *Science* (1967): 3767; Ph Bourdeau, "The Man–Nature Relationship and Environmental Ethics," *Journal of Environmental Radioactivity* 72(1) (2004): 9–15.

143 Kathleen Wellman, *Hijacking History: How the Christian Right Teaches History and Why it Matters* (OUP, 2019). On settler capitalism more broadly, see Nick Estes, *Our History Is the Future: Standing Rock versus Dacota Access Pipeline, and the Long Tradition of Indigenous Resistance* (Verso, 2019).

144 Julia Lossau, "Postcolonialism," in *Spatiality, Sovereignty and Carl Schmitt: Geographies of the Nomos*, ed. Stephen Legg (Routledge, 2011).

145 Irus Braverman, *Settling Nature: The Conservation Regime in Palestine-Israel* (University of Minnesotta Press, 2023); Irene Watson, "Re-Centring First Nations Knowledge and Places in a Terra Nullius Space," *AlterNative: An International Journal of Indigenous* Peoples 10(5) (2014): 508–520.

146 Achille Joseph Mbembe, *On the Postcolony* (University of California Press, 2001), 138. See also Alex Zukas, "Terra Incognita/Terra Nullius: Modern Imperalism, Maps, and Deception," in *Lived Topographies and Their Mediational Forces*, eds. Gary Backhaus and John Murungi (Lexington Books, 2005).

147 Mbembe, *Postcolony,* 147. See also Vandana Shiva, "Reductionism and Regeneration: A Crisis in Science," in *Ecofeminism*, eds. Maria Mies and Vandana Shiva (Zed Books, 2014).

148 Aimé Césaire, *Discourse on Colonialism* (Monthly Review Press, 1972), 21.

Mbembe contends is 'the Western tradition' according to which 'the human being can say "I" only if capable of positing himself/herself as a conscious subject, essentially different from nature.'[149] Such rationales enabled the suppression of Indigenous laws and claims to land, facilitating accumulative expansion.[150] Going further, as Eric Katz has argued in his comparison of the Nazis' genocidal violence and subsequent modern ecocides, human and other-than-human experiences of destruction 'may be linked together by an analysis of the concept of domination.'[151] Drawing from the Holocaust, Katz's work demonstrates how domination can be understood as something at the heart not only of policies of colonisation and genocide, but also policies centred around the management of Nature.[152]

A 'binary, dualist perspective' that distinguishes 'man' from the natural world[153] is key to understanding the legitimation of expansionist projects. Colonial powers were able to frame themselves as 'a culmination of a civilising trajectory from a state of nature' to a state of modernity or civilisation,[154] rather than perpetrators of capitalist expansion.[155] Capitalism and coloniality are 'inextricably linked.'[156] With the formation of capitalism, colonial powers focused on increasing production, including in their colonies, with little consideration given to 'the harmony of life.'[157] Today, the opposition of humans and Nature remains a key component of 'the commodifying logic of the modern capitalist world-ecology,'[158] and we continue to see genocides of Indigenous people and destruction of Indigenous lands in the pursuit of extractivist projects.[159] This Nature/culture binary thus continues to impact upon understandings of Nature, which is seen as a 'raw material'

149 Mbembe, *Postcolony*, 149.

150 See Ntina Tzouvala, *Capitalism as Civilisation: A History of International Law* (CUP, 2020), particularly her discussion around the 'logic of biology.'

151 Eric Katz, "Nature's Presence and the Technology of Death: Reflections on Healing and Domination," *Bulletin of Science, Technology and Society* 17(1) (1997): 3–7.

152 Katz, "Nature's."

153 Arturo Escobar, "Beyond the Third World: Imperial Globality, Global Coloniality and Anti-Globalisation Social Movements," *Third World Quarterly*, 25(1) (2004): 211.

154 Anibal Quijano, "Coloniality of Power, Eurocentrism and Latin America," *Nepantla: Views from South*, 1(3) (2011): 542.

155 Tzouvala, *Capitalism*, at 29.

156 Karsten A. Schulz, "Decolonising the Anthropocene: The Mytho-Politics of Human Mastery," in *Critical Epistemologies of Global Politics*, eds. Marc Woons and Sebastian Weber (E-International Relations Publishing, 2017), 46.

157 Walter D. Mignolo, "Epistemic Disobedience and the Decolonial Option: A Manifesto," *Transmodernity*, 1(2) (2011): 57. See also Jane Caputi, *Call Your "Mutha": A Deliberately Dirty-Minded Manifesto for the Earth Mother in the Anthropocene* (OUP, 2020).

158 Schulz, "Decolonising the Anthropocene," 47.

159 See e.g., Damien Short and Martin Crook, *The Genocide–Ecocide Nexus* (Routledge, 2022); Harding and Mendoza, "Latin American."

for exploitation, appropriation, and disposal.[160] As Irus Braverman argues, 'colonial projects ... have all been disastrous for local ecologies,'[161] with implications for humans and other-than-humans alike. Patrick Wolfe makes clear this fundamental connection: 'land is life – or, at least, land is necessary for life. Thus, contests for land can be – indeed, often are – contests for life.'[162] Under colonialism, natural resources are overexploited in the pursuit of capitalist expansion, and the connections between Indigenous peoples and the land destroyed.[163]

One problem with these 'Western epistemic traditions' is that they have become hegemonic, creating 'discursive scientific practices and ... interpretive frames that make it difficult to think outside of these frames.'[164] As a result, other understandings of Nature are repressed.[165] The marginalisation of Indigenous knowledge is a particularly acute example of this practice. As Colin Scott articulates, 'the historical disqualification and subjugation of [I]ndigenous knowledge is intimately linked to Western culture's domination of nature.'[166] Colonialism has been a process of replacing such world views with the 'logic of domination' and separation from Nature, a process that has disrupted, but not destroyed, 'Indigenous collective capacities' that 'are intricately enmeshed in socio-ecological relations, in land ... land as a system, or web of relations.'[167] Within academic research more broadly, Linda Tuhiwai Smith contends that 'most of the "traditional" disciplines are grounded in cultural world views which are either antagonistic to other belief systems or have no methodology for dealing with other knowledge systems.'[168] As a result, Indigenous ways of knowing are frequently excluded and marginalised.[169] Notably, while Indigenous peoples have continued to assert the value of their ontologies and resist extractivism on their land, this

160 Haraway, *Cyborgs*, 198; Shiva, "Reductionism and Regeneration."

161 Braverman, *Settling*, 34.

162 Patrick Wolfe, "Settler Colonialism and the Elimination of the Native," *Journal of Genocide Research* 8(4) (2006): 387.

163 David R. Goyes, Nigel South, Mireya Astroina Abaibra, Pablo Baigué, Angie Cuchimba, and Deisy Tatiana Ramos Ñeñetofe, "Genocide and Ecocide in Four Colombian Indigenous Communities: The Erosion of a Way of Life and Memory," *British Journal of Criminology* 61(4) (2021): 965–984.

164 Mbembe, "Decolonizing" 32–33.

165 It is of course important not to juxtapose 'science for "the West" to myth and magic for "the rest"'; as Scott argues, it is an 'artificial dichotomy that separates Western and non-Western forms of knowledge, simultaneously discrediting and romanticising the latter.' Scott, "Science for the West," 70.

166 Scott, "Science for the West," 85.

167 Esme G. Murdock, "Storied With Land: 'Transitional Justice' on Indigenous Lands," *Journal of Global Ethics* 14(2) (2018): 237.

168 Smith, *Decolonizing*; 68. See also Connell, *Southern*.

169 Smith, *Decolonizing*. See also Connell, *Southern*.

has come with the cost of increased physical violence perpetrated against their communities. This is evidenced by the targeting of land and environmental defenders, with over 2,000 murdered by governments, businesses, and other non-state actors between 2012 and 2023.[170]

This exclusion has significant implications for thinking about relationships with Nature. Without overly generalising, research suggests that Indigenous ways of 'knowing and seeing' the natural world have often led to more protective behaviours than those enabled by the domineering approach outlined above.[171] For many Indigenous peoples, the relationship between humans and Nature is interdependent rather than hierarchical, and disruptions of this relationship constitute violations requiring redress.[172] As Belkis Izquierdo Torres and Lieselotte Viaene describe, Indigenous ontologies often question or entirely reject the culture/Nature binary, recognising the natural world as sacred.[173] Thus, the exclusion of these perspectives silences ways of knowing that envision relationships with Nature very differently.[174] For transitional justice, this has implications for how harm is identified and how justice is conceptualised, a theme that is returned to throughout this book. For now, we turn to considering how power–knowledge dynamics have placed parameters around which situations are considered as falling within the remit of transitional justice.

170 Global Witness, *Missing Voices: The Violent Erasure of Land and Environmental Defenders* September 10, 2024, https://www.globalwitness.org/en/campaigns/environmental-activists/missing-voices/?gad_source=1&gclid=Cj0KCQiA88a5BhDPARIsAFj595iLuq8jdVD9ILms8nuF3-nyOJ8fxsYikOHbeJWLfgpo_fdhPHr1rToaAv4EEALw_wcB

171 David R. Goyes et al., "Genocide"; Elizabeth Macpherson et al., "Evolving Rights to (and of) Water in Chile: A Case for Relationship-Based Water Law and Governance," *The International Journal of Human Rights* (2023): 1–26.

172 Eduardo S. Brondízio et al., "Locally Based, Regionally Manifested, and Globally Relevant: Indigenous and Local Knowledge, Values, and Practices for Nature," *Annual Review of Environment and Resources* 46(1) (2021): 481–509; Belkis Izquierdo and Lieselotte Viaene "Decolonizing Transitional Justice from Indigenous Territories," *Peace in Progress* 34 (2018): 11–19; Val Plumwood, "Decolonizing Relationships with Nature," in *Decolonizing Nature*, eds. William M. Adams and Martin Mulligan (Routledge, 2012); Daniel Ruiz-Serna, *When Forests Run Amok: War and Its Afterlives in Indigenous and Afro-Colombian Territories* (Duke University Press, 2023).

173 Izquierdo and Viaene, "Decolonizing."

174 See e.g. Irene Watson, "Aboriginal Relationships to the Natural World: Colonial 'Protection' of Human Rights and the Environment," *Journal of Human Rights and the Environment* 9(2) (2018): 119–140; Vanessa Watts, "Indigenous Place-Thought & Agency Amongst Humans and Non-Humans (First Woman and Sky Woman go on a European World Tour!)" *Decolonization, Indigeneity, Education and Society* 2(1) (2013): 20–34.

2.4.2 Power and the Parameters of the Field

As transitional justice has become a 'global norm'[175] or 'global project'[176] it has become associated with and responsible for the spread of certain norms and priorities, playing a normalising and universalising role.[177] Despite calls to 'localise' the field and design measures reflective of local cultures and approaches,[178] transitional justice still 'has a tendency to implement processes through a top-down template-driven tool-box.'[179] As noted above, the field has been disproportionately impacted by voices from the Global North, while both the UN and international organisations such as the International Center for Transitional Justice are examples of the ways that large organisations can become involved in shaping the design and delivery of transitional justice.

In this section, we consider how the power–knowledge dynamics of transitional justice discourse enable powerful actors to set certain parameters around the field. We assert that 'agenda-setting power' in transitional justice is unequally distributed[180] and dominated by the Global North. We contend that this has implications for the 'objects that form the matters' transitional justice deals with.[181] We further argue that these exclusions have negative implications for the recognition of the relationship between mass violence and Nature. Each of the parameters introduced below is explored further in subsequent chapters. They are briefly introduced now to illustrate their connection to power-knowledge.

The first parameter we wish to highlight is an overt emphasis on the acts of individuals. Mainstream power–knowledge dynamics have prioritised the 'Western psychological 'self'' and Western understandings of relationships between individuals and groups, both of which are often framed

175 Jones and Lühe, "Knowledge," 4.

176 Nagy, "Transitional." See also Ruti Teitel, *Globalizing Transitional Justice: Contemporary Essays* (OUP, 2014).

177 Jones and Lühe, "Knowledge."

178 See e.g. Lia Kent, "Local Memory Practices in East Timor: Disrupting Transitional Justice Narratives," *International Journal of Transitional Justice* 5(3) (2011): 434–355; Kieran McEvoy and Lorna McGregor (ed), *Transitional Justice from Below: Grassroots Activism and the Struggle for Change* (Bloomsbury Publishing, 2008); Shaw et al., (eds.) *Localizing.*

179 Jones and Lühe, "Knowledge," 4. See also Line Engbo Gissel, "The Standardisation of Transitional Justice," *European Journal of International Relations* 28(4) (2022): 859–884.

180 Ulrike Lühe, "Developing the African Union Transitional Justice Policy: An Assemblage Perspective," in *Knowledge for Peace: Transitional Justice and the Politics of Knowledge in Theory and Practice*, eds. Briony Jones and Ulrike Lühe (Elgar, 2021), 168.

181 Zunino, *Justice.*

as 'highly individualized' notions.[182] This individualism, often contrasted with more 'collective' understandings present in Eastern,[183] African,[184] and Indigenous[185] societies,[186] manifests as a focus on individuals' actions,[187] individual rights,[188] and individualised responsibility rather than more collective framings of accountability.[189] Yet, environmental harm is a manifestation of mass violence that may require an international or even a global lens to be fully understood.[190] We revisit the implications of this in Chapter 3.

The second – and related – parameter relates to transitional justice's relationship to time. The individualised framing of justice narrows the field's gaze to individual people and individual events, excluding historical context and thus belying the reality that incidents of political violence happen within 'cycles of violence.'[191] Built into this temporality is the field's resistance to acknowledging and engaging with longer-term harms, such as the legacies

182 Smith, *Decolonizing*, 73. This has significant implications for the approach to justice that we see in transitional justice. See also e.g. Mahmood Mamdani, "Beyond Nuremberg: The Historical Significance of the Post-Apartheid Transition in South Africa," *Politics and Society* 43(1) (2015): 61–88.

183 Bee Chen Goh, "An Idea for a Better World: Human Rightsponsibility," *Scholarship, Practice and Education in Comparative Law: A Festschrift in Honour of Mary Hiscock* (2019): 69–80.

184 Kofi Quan-Baffour et al., "Ubuntu: A Dialogue on Connectedness, Environmental Protection and Education," in *Mixed Methods and Cross-Disciplinary Research*, eds. Janet McIntyre-Mills and Norma R. A. Romm (Springer, 2019).

185 Elizabeth Fast and Margaret Kovach, "Community Relationships within Indigenous Methodologies," *Applying Indigenous Research Methods: Storying with Peoples and Communities* 2 (2019): 21–36.

186 While a simplistic distinction between Western individualism and Eastern collectivism has been problematised (see e.g. Tim Lomas et al., "Complexifying Individualism versus Collectivism and West versus East: Exploring Global Diversity in Perspectives on Self and Other in the Gallup World Poll," *Journal of Cross-Cultural Psychology* 54(1) (2023): 61–89), this distinction has continued to influence understandings of culture and relationality.

187 On the colonial framing of individuals as criminally accountable, see e.g. George Pavlich, "Reframing Colonial Law's Criminally Accused Persons" in *Interrupting the Legal Person*, eds. Austin Sarat et al. (Emerald Publishing Limited, 2022).

188 Freidman and Bolte, "Ethics and Feminism," 93.

189 On the scapegoating of individuals to detract from state violence, see e.g. Richard Mailey, "The Role of the Person in Modern Constitutional Law: How State-inflicted Harms Become Personal," in *Interrupting the Legal Person*, eds. Austin Sarat et al. (Emerald Publishing Limited, 2022).

190 Christian Dorninger et al., "Global Patterns of Ecologically Unequal Exchange: Implications for Sustainability in the 21st Century," *Ecological Economics* 179 (2021): 106824; Jennifer E. Givens et al., "Ecologically Unequal Exchange: A Theory of Global Environmental Injustice," *Sociology Compass* 13(5) (2019): e12693.

191 Mamdani, "Beyond Nuremberg," 81.

of colonial violence,[192] structural harms, and slow violence.[193] These forms of violence are closely connected to mass violence but are often overlooked in what Tshepo Madlingozi has termed the 'miracle of transition,' whereby a narrative is created that distinguishes a previous period of acute violence from what has gone before, and what follows the transition.[194]

To illustrate, in Côte d'Ivoire, disputes over inequalities regarding rural land tenures were a 'driving factor' in the outbreak of violence but were overlooked by external transitional justice practitioners.[195] These land tenure conflicts were in turn rooted in the 'agricultural colonisation' of the country, which saw an expansion of cocoa and coffee plantations in particular areas, resulting in competition between incoming labourers and local inhabitants.[196] Overlooking this context therefore excluded a key environmental facet to the conflict. Similarly, a focus on the period of 'acute violence' can overlook slow, environmental harms that emerge in the aftermath, such as the long-term pollution and associated sickness caused by cluster bombs and depleted uranium weapons.[197] We explore the limits of transitional justice's temporal scope in Chapter 5.

The third parameter consists of the spatial limits on accountability. As Rosemary Nagy contends, there are forms of mass violence 'that liberal democracies fail to "see" as a result of their self-definition as human rights protectors.'[198] These 'epistemologies of ignorance' facilitate the framing of the Global North as 'an international saviour,' while the Global South is depicted

192 Bill Rolston and Fionnuala Ní Aoláin, "Colonialism, Redress and Transitional Justice: Ireland and Beyond," *State Crime Journal* 7(2) (2018): 329–348.

193 By 'structural violence' we mean violence that is not directly perpetrated by an individual actor against another, but rather a phenomenon by which institutional policies and practices negatively and disproportionately impact vulnerable populations (Johan Galtung, "Violence, Peace, and Peace Research," *Journal of Peace Research*, 6(3) (1969): 167–191. By 'slow violence' we mean induced environmental conditions that cause active harm in ways that are spread across space and time (Rob Nixon, *Slow Violence and the Environmentalism of the Poor* (Harvard University Press, 2011)). We revisit both concepts in Chapter Five.

194 Tshepo Madlingozi, "Social Justice in a Time of Neo-Apartheid Constitutionalism: Critiquing the Anti-Black Economy of Recognition, Incorporation and Distribution," *Stellenbosch Law Review* 28(1) (2017): 123–147.

195 Yao N'Da and Fokou, "Knowledge Asymmetry," 86.

196 Jean-Pierre Chauveau, "Question Foncière et Construction Nationale en Côte d'Ivoire. Les Enjeux Silencieux d'un coup d'Etat" *Politique Africaine* 78 (2000): 94–125. English translation available at: https://www.iied.org/sites/default/files/pdfs/migrate/X186IIED.pdf.

197 Nixon, *Slow Violence*, 210.

198 Rosemary Nagy, "Transformative Justice in a Settler Colonial Transition: Implementing the UN Declaration on the Rights of Indigenous Peoples in Canada," *The International Journal of Human Rights* 26(2) (2021): 194.

as the home of 'broken societies.'[199] These spatial limits are deeply connected to the field's temporal parameters. As Jennifer Balint, Julie Evans, and Nesam McMillan describe, transitional justice remains 'relatively presentist in its concerns'[200] and has largely failed to expand its gaze to the historical violations perpetrated during the Global North's colonial expansion. This is a significant oversight, as contemporary conflicts are often rooted in a past of 'genocidal, colonial violence.'[201] For example, in East Timor, transitional justice efforts focused on human rights violations that took place during Indonesia's occupation but failed to engage with the violence perpetrated during the Portuguese occupation.[202]

The creation of a false 'starting point' for conflicts and atrocities stymies the ability of the field to encompass interconnected harms that flow from colonial exploitation and extractivism.[203] Indeed, 'colonisation is not only a discussion of the past, but also of the present.'[204] For instance, in Canada, 'the relentless capitalist demand for energy sources' has led to continued and increasing exploitation of Indigenous lands for resource extraction, including logging, mineral exploration, and mining, accompanied by pollution of land and water and poisoning of wildlife.[205] These ongoing colonial effects can be understood as forms of 'slow violence' that are ongoing within Indigenous homes, families, bodies, and territories.[206] While some of these harms can therefore be gradual in their impacts, the continuation of colonial domination has arguably led to ever-more visible indicators of harm to people and Nature,[207] as

199 Jamar, "The Crusade," 59; Balint et al., "Rethinking," 194–195.
200 Balint et al., "Rethinking," 201.
201 Sarah Maddison and Laura J. Shepherd, "Peacebuilding and the Postcolonial Politics of Transitional Justice," *Peacebuilding* 2(3) (2014): 262.
202 Bill Rolston and Fionnuala Ní Aoláin, "Colonialism, Redress and Transitional Justice: Ireland and Beyond," *State Crime Journal* 7(2) (2018): 329–348.
203 See e.g. Jones and Lühe, *Knowledge*; Maddison and Shepherd, "Peacebuilding"; Zinaida Miller, "Transitional Justice Temporalities," *The Oxford Handbook of Transitional Justice*, eds. Jens Meierhenrich et al. (OUP, 2023).
204 Alexander Dunlap, "The 'Solution' is Now The 'Problem': Wind Energy, Colonisation and the 'Genocide–Ecocide Nexus' in the Isthmus of Tehuantepec, Oaxaca," *The International Journal of Human Rights* 22(4) (2018): 552.
205 Elizabeth Comack, "Corporate Colonialism and the 'Crimes of the Powerful' Committed Against the Indigenous Peoples of Canada," *Critical Criminology* 26(4) (2018): 467.
206 Leane Makey et al., "(Un)Heard Voices of Ecosystem Degradation: Stories from the Nexus of Settler-Colonialism and Slow Violence," *Sustainability* 14(22) (2022): 14672. See further in Chapter Five.
207 Michael Lynch, Averi Fegadel, and Michael Long, "Green Criminology and State–Corporate Crime: The Ecocide–Genocide Nexus with Examples from Nigeria," *Journal of Genocide Research* 23(2) (2021): 256.

modern industrial states have continued to grow beyond their ecological limits.[208]

To say that there has been no transitional justice response to colonial violence would be inaccurate. Both Belgium and Germany have engaged to some extent with their colonial harms, while Australia, Canada, and New Zealand have made limited recompense for the harms perpetrated against their Indigenous populations.[209] However, these are relatively limited examples, with little proportionality to the scale of harm perpetrated by the Global North.[210] Furthermore, the emphasis has been placed on specific episodes of violence rather than the prolonged periods of structural injustice and the unfair enrichment gained from the exploitation of peoples' territories, labour, and natural resources.[211] In Canada, Jennifer Matsunaga has critiqued a reductionist approach that 'muffles those Indigenous land-centred and resurgent voices that express anger or rage at colonial rule – past and present – by reducing these expressions to the effects of the residential schools legacy.'[212]

As John Braithwaite argues, 'Northern theory of transitional justice is ... complicit in the cover-up of insidious forms of Northern crime.'[213] Examples outside of colonialism include the failure to frame former presidents of the United States as war criminals, despite their responsibility for mass violence perpetrated in the Middle East.[214] Another frequently cited example is that of the ICC, a permanent international criminal tribunal that sits in The Netherlands and to date has placed only Africans on trial for atrocity crimes.[215] A field that stays oriented around 'non-Western, developing countries'[216] is limited in its capacity to engage with the most severe examples of the mass violence–Nature nexus. Taken together, the dominance of the Global North in shaping transitional justice, combined with those nations'

208 Tim Lindgren, "Ecocide, Genocide and the Disregard of Alternative Life-Systems," *The International Journal of Human Rights* 22(4) (2018): 525–549.
209 Durdiyeva, "Decolonial Agenda."
210 Jamar, "The Crusade," 59.
211 Carsten Stahn, "Confronting Colonial Amnesia: Towards New Relational Engagement with Colonial Injustice and Cultural Colonial Objects," *Journal of International Criminal Justice* 18(4) (2020): 793–824; Larissa van den Herik, "Historical Inquiry as a Form of Colonial Reparation?" *Harvard International Law Journal Online* 59 (2018) 1–5; Maddison and Shepherd, "Peacebuilding."
212 Matsunaga, "Two Faces," 26.
213 Braithwaite, "Criminology," 672.
214 Braithwaite, "Criminology," 672.
215 Kamara Maxine Clarke, "Negotiating Racial Injustice: How International Criminal Law Helps Entrench Structural Inequality," *Just Security*, 24 July 2020, https://www.justsecurity.org/71614/negotiating-racial-injustice-how-international-criminal-law-helps-entrench-structural-inequality/.
216 Nagy, "Transitional."

unwillingness to recognise their responsibility for causing harm, means the global forces that can underlie atrocity-related harms against Nature are frequently overlooked.

The final – and again, related – parameter relates to transitional justice's 'liberal imprint.'[217] The brief history outlined above demonstrates that transitional justice is rooted in the post-Cold War rise of liberal democracy. For Madlingozi, this means that transitional justice has been understood as doing "justice differently" for a short time[218] with the end goal being liberal democracy. For Nature, liberalism, and more pertinently the neoliberalism that has followed it, has an association with free-market capitalism and a related increase in privatisation and deregulation that render it a source of severe harm.[219] The culture/Nature binary entrenched and exploited during colonialism continues under capitalism,[220] and the global capitalist economy 'relies upon systemic modification and using up of the natural environment.'[221] As we will examine in Chapter 6, transitional justice can be critiqued as 'an agent of neoliberal globalisation,'[222] with the emerging dominance of neoliberalism only increasing the risks to Nature.[223]

The themes explored in this section demonstrate how the politics of knowledge production in transitional justice has implications for the harms that are recognised, the situations that are given precedence, and the forms of justice that are envisioned in policy and practice.[224] Transitional justice's embedding in Global North normativity serves to both extend hegemonic narratives regarding how the past should be addressed and silence certain debates about the past, sustaining the epistemic violence outlined above.[225] In the following section, we turn from this critique to consider those voices that have traditionally been marginalised by power–knowledge dynamics but that might offer ways to push past some of the field's limitations in this regard.

217 Zunino, *Justice*, 51.
218 Madlingozi, "There is."
219 Shahar Hameiri, *Regulating Statehood: State Building and the Transformation of the Global Order* (Springer, 2010); Chandra Lekha Sriram and Amy Ross, "Geographies of Crime and Justice: Contemporary Transitional Justice and the Creation of 'Zones of Impunity,'" *The International Journal of Transitional Justice* 1(1) (2007): 45–65.
220 Schulz, "Decolonising the Anthropocene."
221 Rob White, "Critical Green Criminology," in *Theorising Green Criminology: Selected Essays*, ed. Rob White (Routledge, 2022), 29.
222 Pierre Hazan, *Judging War, Judging History: Behind Truth and Reconciliation* (Stanford University Press, 2010), 151.
223 Pierre Dardot and Christian Laval, *The New Way of the World: On Neoliberal Society* (Verso Books, 2014).
224 Jones and Lühe, "Knowledge," 10.
225 Durdiyeva, "Decolonial Agenda."

2.5 'Greening' Knowledge Production

Atrocity-related environmental harms can be both severe and complex, increasing the risk of future conflicts and reducing the chances of long-term and/or positive peace. This situation will only become more pronounced in the future, as the climate crisis increases environmental pressures and conflict in turn exacerbates the climate crisis. Yet, the prevalence of particular viewpoints has facilitated a situation where we are, in the words of Mbembe, 'fighting battles of the present and the future with outdated tools.'[226]

In this section, we argue that if transitional justice is to meaningfully grapple with these realities – which we think it should – then there is a need to rethink the field's conceptualisation of and relationship to Nature. To do so requires a critical re-evaluation of how knowledge is produced in the field. In the following sections, we therefore re-imagine what knowledge production in transitional justice could look like by exploring how feminist epistemologies and decolonising approaches can contribute to a re-thinking of how we create transitional justice 'knowledge.'

2.5.1 Feminist Epistemologies

Feminist epistemology arguably presents a useful starting point for this exercise as it comprises scholarship focused on critically interrogating 'the nature of knowledge and our methods for attaining it.'[227] At its heart lies the need to question claims to objectivity, and the 'conviction that knowledge just *is* knowledge.'[228] Drawing on this scholarship, we argue that transitional justice scholarship can be enriched and strengthened by engaging with ways of knowing and thinking beyond those that have become accepted as mainstream in the field. In this section, we examine how feminist epistemology can contribute to 'greening' the field of transitional justice in two main ways: by breaking down false binaries, and by shifting away from individualism towards more relational forms of knowing. We conclude this section by noting the importance of intersectional approaches to feminism.

As examined above, binary oppositions are a feature of Western and male-dominated modes of knowledge production.[229] Feminist epistemologies encourage the breaking down of these binaries.[230] For thinking about

226 Mbembe, "Decolonizing," 37.

227 Lennon and Whitford, "Introduction," 13. See also Hirschmann, "Feminist Political Philosophy"; Haraway, *Cyborgs*.

228 Lorraine Code, "Ignorance, Injustice and the Politics of Knowledge," *Australian Feminist Studies* 29(80) (2014): 150.

229 See also Durdiyeva, "Decolonial Agenda."

230 Colleen Mack-Canty, "Third-Wave Feminism and the Need to Reweave the Nature/Culture Duality," *NWSA Journal* 16(3) (Autumn, 2004): 154–179.

harms against Nature, the unpacking of certain well-established binaries is particularly useful – for example, the political demarcation[231] between 'proper' science and 'non' science (which may encompass Indigenous practices of ecosystem management), or the distinction between 'real' law and customary laws.[232] While transitional justice scholarship has emphasised the importance of the 'local,'[233] certain voices and approaches continue to be given preference in ways that reflect these political demarcations.[234] A feminist epistemology perspective would embrace different forms of knowledge and knowledge producers, valuing their contributions more equitably.[235] There is emerging evidence that such an approach can be of benefit to the recognition of Nature in transitional justice processes, for example in Colombia, where engagement with Indigenous perspectives has 're-shaped' the meaning of territory in Colombia's transitional justice process.[236]

Feminist epistemology can also disrupt the physis/nomos or culture/Nature divide and its role in legitimising the patriarchal domination of women[237] and Nature.[238] While transitional justice has historically failed to meaningfully engage with the interconnectedness of these forms of domination,[239] feminist epistemology offers tools with which to name and resist these connections.[240] For example, Black, decolonial, and Indigenous communitarian feminisms, such as those found across Latin America, use the concept of *Cuerpo-Territorio* to collapse the binary between Nature and humans.[241] This concept (which translates as 'body-territory' or 'body-land')

231 Pereira, *Power*, 46; see also Nader, *Naked Science*; Code, "Ignorance."

232 Val Napoleon, "Thinking About Indigenous Legal Orders," in *Dialogues on Human Rights and Legal Pluralism. Ius Gentium: Comparative Perspectives on Law and Justice*, eds. René Provost and Colleen Sheppard (Springer, 2013).

233 Shaw and Waldorf, *Localising*.

234 See e.g. Valeria Vázquez Guevara, "Crafting the Lawful Truth: Chile's 1990 Truth Commission, International Human Rights and the Museum of Memory," *London Review of International Law* 7(2) (2019): 253–280, discussing the distinction between women's artistic accounts of everyday life under the Chilean dictatorship and the more 'lawful' truth-telling mechanisms. See also Roger MacGinty, "Indigenous Peace-Making Versus the Liberal Peace," *Cooperation and Conflict* 43 (2008): 139–163.

235 Angela Santamaría et al., "Decolonisation Sketches and Intercultural Approaches to Truth: Corporeal Experiences and Testimonies of Indigenous Women in Colombia," *International Journal of Transitional Law* 14(1) (2020): 56–79.

236 Huneeus and Rueda Saiz, "Territory," 219.

237 See e.g. Silvia Federici, *Caliban and the Witch: Women, the Body and Primitive Accumulation* (Penguin, 2004).

238 Shannon Sullivan, "Pragmatism," in *The Blackwell Guide to Feminist Philosophy*, eds. Linda Martín Alcoff and Eva Feder Kittay (Blackwell Publishing, 2007), 65.

239 Ariza-Buitrago and Gómez-Betancur, "Nature," 78.

240 Code, *What*, 270.

241 Rogerio Haesbaert, "Del Cuerpo-Territorio al Territorio-Cuerpo (de la Tierra): Contribuciones Decoloniales," *Cultura y Representaciones Sociales* 15(29) (2020):

understands the domination of territory and women's bodies as intwined harms, experienced on a cultural, spiritual, and physical level.[242] Also of relevance are the various branches of ecological or 'eco-feminism' which have emerged since the 1970s.[243] Following in the footsteps of Indigenous communitarian feminism, these bodies of work similarly draw parallels and interrogate the patriarchal suppression of women and Nature.[244] Taking such theorisations seriously offers a challenge to 'universalising' narratives around how harm is experienced,[245] and can legitimise communities' own narratives of their lived experience.[246]

Drawing from feminist epistemologies could also offer a counter narrative to 'malestream' thought's preoccupation with individualism.[247] Feminist epistemology scholarship is critical of an overemphasis on individualism,[248] instead foregrounding a knowledge production that is 'situated, plural, political and contested, reflexive and a product of engagement by feminist researchers, practitioners and activists.'[249] There is a greater role for 'interpersonal connections,'[250] 'knowledge-conveying exchanges between and among people in the real world,'[251] and an atmosphere of openness and interaction. The concept of 'relational autonomy,' for instance, incorporates a 'different understanding of what it meant to be a person: not separate and inherently distinct from all others, but connected through networks of

267–301. For an exploration of the applicability of this concept to transitional justice, see Brinton Lykes and Murphy, "Decolonizing."

242 See e.g. Marcela Tovar-Restrepo and Clara Irazábal, "Indigenous Women and Violence in Colombia: Agency, Autonomy, and Territoriality," *Latin American Perspectives* 41(1) (2014): 39–58; Elizabeth L. Sweet and Sara Ortiz Escalante, "Engaging Territorio Cuerpo-Tierra through Body and Community Mapping: A Methodology for Making Communities Safer," *Gender, Place & Culture* 24 (2017): 1–13.

243 Françoise D'Eaubonne, *Feminism or Death* (Verso, 2022); Maria Mies and Vandana Shiva, *Ecofeminism* (Zed Books, 1993); Carolyn Merchant, *Radical Ecology: The Search for a Livable World* (Routledge, 1992).

244 D'Eaubonne, *Feminism or Death*.

245 Daniela Suarez Vargas and Rachel Killean, "Women's Experiences of Environmental Harm in Colombia: Learning from Black, Decolonial and Indigenous Feminisms," in *Gendering Green Criminology*, eds. Emma Milne et al. (Bristol University Press, 2023).

246 Sofia Zaragocin and Martina Angela Caretta, "Cuerpo-Territorio: A Decolonial Feminist Geographical Method for the Study of Embodiment," *Annals of the American Association of Geographers* 111(5) (2020): 1503–1518.

247 See also Freidman and Bolte, "Ethics and Feminism."

248 Freidman and Bolte, "Ethics and Feminism"; Hirschmann, "Feminist Political Philosophy."

249 Pauline Cullen, Myra Marx Ferree, and Miele Verla, "Introduction to Special Issue: Gender, Knowledge Production and Knowledge Work," *Gender, Work and Organisations* 26 (2019): 765–771.

250 Freidman and Bolte, "Ethics and Feminism," 93.

251 Code, "Ignorance," 152.

relationships.'[252] This interrelatedness is not limited to humans. As Lorraine Code argues, feminist ways of knowing are associated with 'a readiness to listen perceptively and responsibly to a variety of "voices" in the environment, both animate and inanimate, manifested in a tolerance of diversity.'[253] Code encourages us to think about human beings as 'ecologically rather than individualistically positioned,' part of a network of 'mutual relations of organisms with one another and the relations between organisms and their environment.'[254] For Code, this 'environment' is not solely physical nor solely in the present, rather it comprises a more 'complex network of relations' that spans space and time.[255] These 'relational ontologies' have become ever more central to feminist epistemological work, with 'ecological thinking' now used as a way to describe the centring of 'epistemological, ontological, ethical, scientific, and political relationships' in the pursuit of making just and cohabitable lives.[256] Thus, feminist epistemology arguably captures an interrelatedness between beings that can help us to think differently about relationships with Nature.

It is essential that a feminist approach be intersectional. For many years, the 'most visible forms of feminist writing came from a restricted group of women, predominantly white, middle-class, living in colonizing or ex-colonizing countries.'[257] Such forms of feminism were criticised by Black, Global South, LGBTQ+, and other feminists, who drew attention to the ways in which their knowledge and experiences were ignored, marginalised, or silenced by white, middle-class, liberal feminism.[258] In addition to excluding the lived experience of women with intersecting marginalised identities, such approaches were considered to be inappropriately universalising and at risk of unwittingly reinforcing the power structures feminism was intended to challenge.[259] In transitional justice scholarship, liberal feminism has been critiqued for adopting too narrow a conceptualisation of harm and overlooking the cultural, material, and geopolitical sites in which transitional

252 Hirschmann, "Feminist Political Philosophy," 152.
253 Code, *What*, 13.
254 Code, *What*, 269. See also Haraway, *Cyborgs*.
255 Code, *What*, 269-270.
256 Andrea Doucet, "Shorelines, Seashells, and Seeds: Feminist Epistemologies, Ecological Thinking, and Relational Ontologies," in *The Palgrave Handbook of Relational Sociology*, ed. François Dépelteau (Palgrave, 2018).
257 Lennon and Whitford, "Introduction," 3.
258 Susan Strickland, "Feminism, Postmodernism and Difference," in *Knowing the Difference: Feminist Perspectives in Epistemology*, eds. Kathleen Lennon and Margaret Whitford (Routledge, 1994), 265.
259 Marina Lazreg, "Women's Experience and Feminist Epistemology," in *Knowing the Difference: Feminist Perspectives in Epistemology*, eds. Kathleen Lennon and Margaret Whitford (Routledge, 1994), 45.

justice practices have emerged.[260] There is increased recognition of the need for feminist theory to be more critically aware 'of its own situatedness'[261] and to 'include careful examination of the intersections of gender with race, ethnicity, nationality, class, sexuality, and other salient axes of lived experience.'[262] We take seriously the need to engage in what François Vergès describes as a 'struggle for epistemic justice ... a struggle that demands equality between knowledges and contests the order of knowledge imposed by the West.'[263] This is particularly crucial in the context of harms against Nature, where Black, decolonial, and Indigenous communitarian feminisms offer important ways of conceptualising such harms. The particular importance of decolonial perspectives is explored further in the following section.

2.6 'Decolonising' a Field

When it first emerged in the 1960s and 1970s, the concept of 'decolonisation' was primarily understood as 'part of a nation-building project' associated with the pursuit of post-colonial self-determination.[264] However, the term has broadened, and in recent years 'the idea of "decolonization" ... has become the rally cry for those trying to undo the racist legacies of the past.'[265] Despite several decades of decolonial advocacy, knowledge production remains characterised by 'stark asymmetries of power,'[266] and decolonial thought has emerged from Indigenous philosophies as well as African, Caribbean, and Latin American philosophies and contexts.[267]

260 Ní Aoláin, "Advancing."
261 Strickland, "Postmodernism and Difference," 265.
262 Sullivan, "Pragmatism," 75.
263 François Vergès, *A Decolonial Feminism* (Pluto Press, 2021), 13.
264 Mbembe, "Decolonizing," 33. Although not exclusively, see e.g. the work of Ghanian president and pan-Africanist leader Dr Kwame Nkrumah, in particular, his establishment of the Institute of African Studies and his work with W. E. B. Du Bois on the *Encyclopaedia Africana*. See e.g. Jean Allman, "Kwame Nkrumah, African Studies, and the Politics of Knowledge Production in the Black Star of Africa," *The International Journal of African Historical Studies* 46(2) (2013): 181–203.
265 Mbembe, "Decolonizing," 32.
266 Gordon Crawford et al., "Decolonising Knowledge Production on Africa: Why it's Still Necessary and What Can be Done," *Journal of the British Academy* 9(1) (2021): 21–46.
267 Elsa Koleth and Linda Peake, "Decolonising Feminist Knowledge," in *Doing Feminist Urban Research*, eds. Linda Peake et al. (Routledge, 2024). For an overview of the 'anti-colonial strategies and trajectories' that constitute decolonisation, see Folúké Adébísí, *Decolonisation and Legal Knowledge: Reflections on Power and Possibility* (Bristol University Press, 2024). Adébísí notes the critique of the mode of colonial thought emerging from the Latin American and Caribbean School that some scholars have 'co-opted and diluted indigenous thought' (p. 29). Cognisant of this critique, we have sought to draw on the work of decolonial scholars from a range of backgrounds in our analysis, including from Africa, Asia, and Latin America and members of Indigenous communities.

In the context of knowledge production, decolonial scholarship seeks to interrogate 'lingering structures of colonialism in power, ontology [and] epistemology'[268] and to draw attention to the 'lived and living voices and experiences of colonized subjects.'[269] As such, decolonising knowledge production has two aspects. One is a critique of 'Eurocentric' power–knowledge dynamics, sometimes referred to as 'epistemic coloniality' or 'epistemic injustice'.[270] This aspect seeks to push back against 'imperialism in the guise of scientific knowledge'[271] and the 'endless production of theories that are based on European traditions,'[272] and includes resistance to the dominance of colonial language itself.[273] The second aspect comprises attempts at 'imagining what the alternative to this model could look like' both in theory and in practice.[274] This section explores this second aspect's relevance to exploring the relationship between Nature and transitional justice.

The decolonisation of transitional justice requires recognition of the fact that 'all thinking is located,'[275] and 'it is often the ordinary people in struggles who create knowledge and ideas.'[276] These realities necessitate taking seriously the views of those who have experienced harm, rather than enabling the terms of justice to be dictated by external 'experts.'[277] Critical transitional justice scholarship has echoed calls in the decolonisation literature to renegotiate the terms of knowledge production.[278] As early as 2008, Kieran

268 Emma D. Velez and Nancy Tuana, "Toward Decolonial Feminisms: Tracing the Lineages of Decolonial Thinking through Latin American/Latinx Feminist Philosophy," *Hypatia* 35(3) (2020): 366–372.

269 Sarah de Leeuw and Sarah Hunt, "Unsettling Decolonizing Geographies," *Geography Compass* 12(7) (2018).

270 See Gayatri Chakravorty Spivak, "Can the Subaltern Speak?" in *Imperialism*, eds. Peter H. Cain and Mark Harrison (Routledge, 2004); Edward Said, "Orientalism," in *Colonial Discourse and Post-Colonial Theory: A Reader*, eds. Patrick Williams and Laura Chrisman (Harvester Wheatsheaf, 1994).

271 Claude Ake, *Social Science as Imperialism* (Ibadan University Press, 1982), xiii.

272 Mbembe, "Decolonizing," 36.

273 Ngũgĩ wa Thiong'o, *Decolonising the Mind: The Politics of Language in African Literature* (Heinemann Education, 1986); Abida Bano, "Hegemony and Decolonising Research Praxis: A Researcher's Journey in the Perepheries of Pakistan," in *Thinking with the South*, eds. Andrea Fleschenberg et al. (ZMO-Studien, 2024). Although see also Marlies Glasius, "Gramsci for the Twenty-First Century: Dialectics and Translatability," *International Studies Review* 14(4) (2012): 666–686 on the usefulness of English for facilitating cooperation and shared resistance across borders.

274 Mbembe, "Decolonizing," 36.

275 Mignolo, "Epistemic Disobedience," 52.

276 Choudry, "Reflections," 33.

277 Kwesi Yankah, "Displaced Academies and the Quest for a New World Academic Order," *Africa Today*, 42(3) (1995): 7–25.

278 Hana Horáková, "Knowledge Production in and on Africa: Knowledge Gatekeepers, De-colonization, Alternative Representations," in *Knowledge Production in and on Africa*, eds. Hanah Horáková and Katerina Werkman (Lit Verlag, 2016).

McEvoy and Lorna McGregor[279] and Patricia Lundy and Mark McGovern[280] argued for a transitional justice 'from below.' However, we argue that fully situating knowledge may require a further shift in how transitional justice knowledge producers approach their work. While much transitional justice research is based on interviews or focus groups with those affected by harm, this methodology is itself constitutive of power–knowledge dynamics and can be shaped by the preconceived ideas of the researchers.[281] There is an ongoing need for a shift from a 'logic of "discovery"' to a 'power-charged social relation of conversation.[282] Knowledge production that is more 'dialogical' or 'communicative'[283] may give greater space for those on-the-ground to actively contribute.

Briony Jones and Ulrike Lühe have suggested that although a more 'complex, interdependent and interactional' knowledge production dynamic is emerging in transitional justice scholarship,[284] 'this complex relationship … often remains invisible.'[285] Others have criticised efforts to decolonise the field as being extractive or superficial.[286] For example, Jennifer Matsunaga emphasises that 'efforts to incorporate decolonisation into transitional justice …foreground *conscientization* rather than decolonization' – '*conscientization*' being understood here as a concept that 'involves settlers treating decolonisation mainly as a process of changing one's thinking – of educating oneself and others or of becoming more conscientious.'[287] This critique demonstrates the importance of connecting knowledge production with its real-world impacts.[288] Without this, there is a risk that transitional justice may be presented as a model that is 'in need of tailoring' but still 'workable.' From such a perspective, it can continue to facilitate practices that overlook structural and slow violence and that fail to take seriously differing relationships to land.[289] Such an approach risks reinforcing harm rather than redressing it.[290]

279 McEvoy and McGregor, *Transitional.*
280 Patricia Lundy and Mark McGovern, "Whose Justice? Rethinking Transitional Justice from the Bottom Up," *Journal of Law and Society* 35(2) (2008): 265–292.
281 We have interrogated this in relation to our own research. See Cheryl Lawther et al., "Working with Others: Reflections on Fieldwork in Postconflict Societies," *International Journal of Transitional Justice*, 13(2) (2019): 387–397.
282 Haraway, *Cyborgs*, 198.
283 Freidman and Bolte, "Ethics and Feminism," 93.
284 Jones and Luhe, "Knowledge," 7.
285 Jones and Luhe, *Knowledge.*
286 Durdiyeva, "Decolonial Agenda."
287 Matsunaga, "Two Faces," 32.
288 Eve Tuck and K. Wayne Yang, "Decolonization is Not a Metaphor," *Decolonization: Indigeneity, Education & Society* 1(1) (2012): 1–40.
289 Matsunaga, "Two Faces," 32.
290 Matsunaga, "Two Faces," 39.

To avoid extractive practices in knowledge production, what is arguably needed is a more 'radicalised transitional justice', which engages with previously marginalised views from a place of respect[291] and seeks 'a change in the order of the world.'[292] Substantively, an important aspect of decolonisation is therefore the recognition of Indigenous laws and perspectives. There is an emerging recognition that transitional justice should be 'informed by [I]ndigenous worldviews.'[293] Of course, 'not all Indigenous experiences are the same,' and there is no monolith of Indigenous thought or law.[294] However, as Laura Nader argues, 'We need not idealise non-Western science to make the point that there are different types of knowledge that provide valid truths of use to human kind.'[295] While acknowledging substantial differences amongst Indigenous peoples, it is possible to identify themes such as ethics of environmental responsibility, relationality, and connectedness that have proven more elusive in 'Western' societies.[296] Moreover, and as explored in greater depth in Chapter 4, Indigenous laws and practices contain methods for engaging with the agency and interests of other-than-human species. Such methods may offer important lessons for how the transitional justice field might move beyond its anthropocentric limitations.

Māori scholar Linda Tuhiwai Smith makes clear that engagement with such perspectives may not come easy: 'the arguments of different [I]ndigenous peoples based on spiritual relationships to the universe, to the landscape and to stones, rocks, insects and other things, seen and unseen, have been difficult arguments for Western systems of knowledge to deal with or accept.'[297] While cognisant of the potential challenges, there is value in broadening understandings of the natural world by engaging with these perspectives.[298] As Augustine Park argues, a commitment to decoloniality encourages an associated honouring of 'longstanding relationships with the land and with one another.'[299] This brings us back to the idea of decolonisation as a process of imagining alternatives. For Ngũgĩ wa Thiong'o,

291 Park, "Settler Colonialism."
292 Tuck and Yang, "Not a Metaphor."
293 Balint et al., "Rethinking," 215.
294 Rob White, "The Four Ways of Eco-Global Criminology," *International Journal for Crime, Justice and Social Democracy* 6(1) (2017): 8–22.
295 Nader, *Naked Science*, 24.
296 Scott, "Science for the West," 85.
297 Smith, *Decolonizing*, 74
298 In so doing, it is essential to consider the knowledge production dynamics within such perspectives – for instance, Harding and Mendoza contend that contemporary Indigenous knowledge production is dominated by men and thus excludes or sidelines the knowledge of Indigenous women. Yet, women would have had a particularly important role pre-colonisation (Harding and Mendoza, "Latin American").
299 Park, "Settler Colonialism."

'decolonization is not an end point. It is the beginning of an entirely new struggle,' and this struggle 'is about defining clearly what the centre is.'[300] By redefining the centre of transitional justice efforts away from the Global North and creating space for previously marginalised voices, it may be that the field can start to combat some of its anthropocentric, gendered, and racialised presumptions.

2.7 Conclusion

In this chapter, we have laid the foundations for the analysis to come, examining how knowledge production has shaped transitional justice to the exclusion of harms against Nature and exploring how this might change. Our analysis demonstrates the need to foreground an ethics of knowledge production, in which there is a need to both 'rethink thinking'[301] and work towards knowing 'justly, responsibly and well.'[302] In this concluding section, we highlight points of connection across the feminist and decolonising scholarship that can provide foundational principles for the remainder of the book's discussion. In particular, we argue that a 'greener' approach towards transitional justice knowledge production must be i) willing and able to name the sources of harm, ii) embedded in lived experience, iii) interconnected, and iv) able to challenge the field's anthropocentrism.

Feminist (particularly eco and critical) and decolonising perspectives are united in drawing attention to the interconnected sources of harms against Nature – namely patriarchy and colonialism. For instance, Latin American decolonial feminists make explicit the role of patriarchy in colonisation with their slogan 'there is no decolonization without depatriarchalization,'[303] while Donna Haraway has argued that it is 'white, capitalist patriarchy … that turns everything into a resource for appropriation.'[304] These bodies of work therefore offer theoretical tools through which to better engage with the forms of slow and structural violence that can precede, accompany, and endure beyond periods of mass violence, as well as the intersectional forms of violence experienced by marginalised communities. As Augustine Park has argued, transitional justice must better orient itself not only around the 'decolonisation of the mind,' but also around the need to transform structural injustice.[305] At the same time, these bodies of scholarship offer

300 Mbembe, "Decolonizing," 35 citing Thiong'o, *Decolonizing the Mind.*
301 Sabelo J. Ndlovu-Gatsheni, *Epistemic Freedom in Africa: Deprovincialization and Decolonization* (Routledge, 2018).
302 Code, "Ignorance," 155.
303 Maria Galindo, cited in Harding and Mendoza, "Latin American," 110.
304 Haraway, *Cyborgs*, 197.
305 Park, "Settler Colonialism."

a critique of transitional justice's embeddedness in notions of a liberal (or neoliberal) transition.[306]

A second dominant theme in feminist epistemology and decolonisation scholarship is the importance of 'situatedness,'[307] or the need for knowledge production to be embedded in, and driven by, those living the experience under investigation.[308] A pragmatic philosophical approach could be useful in this regard. 'Pragmatist philosophy stresses the dynamic relationship between theory and practice and especially the value of each for transforming the other.'[309] Rather than being led by the paradigms and priorities of those who have come to dominate transitional justice scholarship, pragmatism encourages us to listen and learn from those closest to the harm.[310] Furthermore, this position requires engagement with perspectives located elsewhere; knowledge is thus co-constructed. Such an approach to knowledge production thereby challenges any notion of a 'universal' knowledge. This may require listening that extends beyond the human. Doing so may help us to uncover what Haraway describes as a 'more adequate, richer, better account' of the world in which we live.[311]

Third, feminist epistemological and decolonial scholars foreground forms of knowledge production that are collective and collaborative.[312] Code writes of 'multiplicity,'[313] and for Mbembe, there is a need for 'pluriversity ... a process of knowledge production that is open to epistemic diversity. It is a process that does not necessarily abandon the notion of universal knowledge for humanity, but which embraces it via a *horizontal strategy of openness to dialogue among different epistemic traditions*.'[314] This 'horizontal' approach is a significant challenge to the hierarchising dynamics of domination present within white, patriarchal understandings of knowledge production. Such an approach has a particular significance when thinking about Nature, encouraging us to consider human–Nature relationships 'as

306 Durdiyeva, "Decolonial Agenda."
307 The notion of 'situated knowledge' is perhaps most associated with Donna Haraway, for whom situated knowledge is a form of embodied and feminist objectivity in which the knower has a specific and limited location from which they see, and that location and its limitations are clearly acknowledged so that knowledge is recognised as 'partial' and 'locatable.' As Haraway captures, we are dealing with 'the view from a body' instead of a 'view from above.' Haraway, *Cyborgs*, 191–195.
308 Durdiyeva, "Decolonial Agenda."
309 Sullivan, "Pragmatism," 65.
310 Sullivan, "Pragmatism," 65.
311 Haraway, *Cyborgs*, 187
312 Zainab Batul Naqvi et al., "Back at the Kitchen Table: Reflections on Decolonising and Internationalising with the Global South Socio-legal Writing Workshops," *Feminist Legal Studies* 27 (2019): 123–137.
313 Code, "Ignorance."
314 Mbembe, "Decolonizing," 37.

genuinely social and actively relational.'[315] This is relevant not just for the present, but also for the future. Mbembe argues that we must 'rethink the human not from the perspective of its mastery of the Creation as we used to, but from the perspective of its finitude and possible extinction.'[316] This could involve thinking about future generations, but also understanding human history as 'entangled' with other species.[317] As Judith Butler contends, 'our very survival depends ... on recognising how we are bound up with others.'[318]

Finally, what is required is a 'new understanding' that 'can only be achieved by overcoming anthropocentrism and humanism, the split between nature and culture' and ultimately a 'decentering of the human.'[319] There is an emerging consensus among feminist and decolonial scholars alike that 'a dualistic understanding of humanity and nature as separate and monolithic entities is insufficient to describe the richness of relations "beyond the human" and the embeddedness of humans in the independent web of life.'[320] To this end, we argue that a more ecocentric approach to transitional justice is required, whereby Nature is valued for its own sake, rather than purely by virtue of its utilitarian value to humans.[321] As M. Brinton Lykes and Colleen Murphy argue, it is time to recognise that decolonising the land also involves recentring it as living and recognising its rights.[322]

These themes are taken forward in subsequent chapters. In Chapter 3, we explore the role of law in restricting transitional justice's ability to redress harms against Nature. This chapter picks up the theme of anthropocentrism and highlights how the power-knowledge dynamics explored in this chapter manifest in the legal regimes that have shaped transitional justice. Chapter 4 then considers how this anthropocentric legalism might be challenged, exploring examples of more ecocentric responses to harm. Chapter 5 then turns to the temporal limits placed on the field and the capacity of transitional justice to meaningfully engage with structural and slow violence. Finally, Chapter 6 digs deeper into the field's 'liberal imprints,' considering whether transitional justice can free itself of its sympathies for capitalism.

315 Haraway, *Cyborgs*, 3.
316 Mbembe, "Decolonizing," 42.
317 Mbembe, "Decolonizing," 42.
318 Butler, *Frames of War*, 52.
319 Mbembe, "Decolonizing," 42–43.
320 Schulz, "Decolonising the Anthropocene," 46.
321 Rob White, "Ecocentrism and Criminal Justice," *Theorising Green Criminology: Selected Essays*, ed. Rob White (Routledge, 2022), 40.
322 Brinton Lykes and Murphy, "Decolonizing."

3

ANTHROPOCENTRIC LEGALISM AND THE CONSTRUCTION OF VICTIMHOOD

3.1 Introduction

In Chapter 2, we explored transitional justice as a discursive space influenced by certain actors and forms of knowledge. We demonstrated how the dominance of Global North voices and the disregard for Global South, Indigenous, and other marginalised perspectives have created a discourse characterised by value binaries and power–knowledge differentials. One theme we highlighted was how these binaries and power dynamics have shapeda field grounded in the belief that humankind and Nature are separate, and that views Nature primarily through an instrumentalist lens. This theme is explored in greater detail throughout this chapter, which examineshow mainstream transitional justice discourse conceptualises harms and – more specifically – victimhood.

The construction of victimhood is particularly relevant to understanding transitional justice's systems of inclusion and exclusion. That victims are (purportedly at least) the raison d'être of transitional justice is well-established in the field's scholarship.[1] Transitional justice has been said to be about

1 See e.g., Jonathan Doak, "The Therapeutic Dimension of Transitional Justice: Emotional Repair and Victim Satisfaction in International Trials and Truth Commissions," *International Criminal Law Review* 11(2) (2011): 263–298; Michael Humphrey, "From Victim to Victimhood: Truth Commissions and Trials as Rituals of Political Transition and Individual Healing," *The Australian Journal of Anthropology* 14(2) (2003): 171–187; Susanne Karstedt, "From Absence to Presence, From Silence to Voice: Victims in International and Transitional Justice Since the Nuremberg Trials," *International Review of Victimology* 17(1) (2010): 9–30; Kieran McEvoy and Kirsten McConnachie, "Victimology

DOI: 10.4324/9781003264446-3

the recognition of and provision of 'a modicum of justice to' victims,[2] with victimhood the 'moral centre' of the field[3] – both legitimising its existence and driving its progress. However, there is no simple correlation between having been harmed and availing of transitional justice. Rather, those able to access transitional justice measures are those whose identities align with the legal, political, and social constructions of victimhood applicable to that context. Victim recognition can be tied to, for instance, the type of harm suffered, the community to which an alleged victim belongs, or the identity of the perpetrator of their harm.[4] Access to justice moreover requires that the victim is recognised as having a claim, or a right, to redress. As such, transitional justice plays an instrumental role not only in shaping societal understandings of victimhood but also in deciding who 'counts' as a victim for the purposes of participating in, or seeking support from, a particular justice mechanism.[5]

Defining victimhood has legal and political dimensions[6] and can be highly contentious.[7] A broad definition can be a source of tension, as it might include individuals or entities considered by some not to qualify as victims.[8] Hierarchisation can occur, with notions of who suffered 'most' driving competition over who can legitimately be considered a victim.[9] Perhaps what renders the process so contentious is that recognising victimhood shapes understandings of who is responsible for past violence, who is innocent, where blame can be placed, and who is entitled to recompense. These understandings in turn

in Transitional Justice: Victimhood, Innocence and Hierarchy," *European Journal of Criminology* 9(5) (2012): 527–538; Simon Robins, "Towards Victim-Centred Transitional Justice: Understanding the Needs of Families of the Disappeared in Postconflict Nepal," *International Journal of Transitional Justice* 5(1)(2011): 75–98.

2 Pablo de Greiff, "The Future of the Past: Reflections on the Present State and Prospects of Transitional Justice," *International Journal of Transitional Justice* 14(2) (2020): 252.

3 Kris Brown and Fionnuala Ní Aoláin, "Through the Looking Glass: Transitional Justice Futures through the Lens of Nationalism, Feminism and Transformative Change," *International Journal of Transitional Justice* 9(1) (2014): 140.

4 Brown and Ní Aoláin, "Through the Looking Glass."

5 See e.g., Vincent Druliolle and Roddy Brett, eds., *The Politics of Victimhood in Post-Conflict Societies* (Springer International Publishing, 2018).

6 E.g., Sarah Jankowitz, "The 'Hierarchy of Victims' in Northern Ireland: A Framework for Critical Analysis," *International Journal of Transitional Justice* 12(2) (2018): 216–236; Cheryl Lawther, "The Construction and Politicisation of Victimhood," *Victims of Terrorism: A Comparative and Interdisciplinary Study*, eds. Orla Lynch and Javier Argomaniz (Taylor and Francis, 2014); Jemima García-Godos, "Victim Reparations in the Peruvian Truth Commission and the Challenge of Historical Interpretation," *International Journal of Transitional Justice* 2(1)(2008): 63–82.

7 Jankowitz, "Hierarchy of Victims."

8 García-Godos, "Victim Reparations."

9 Jankowitz, "Hierarchy of Victims."

feed into the construction of community- or national-level narratives, collective memories of past violence, and visions of the future.[10]

Environmental destruction has been described as 'victim-full,' extending to 'ecosystems, streams, trees, plants, animals, biodiversity and water,'[11] as well as human individuals, communities, and future generations.[12] Yet, these victimisations have rarely been recognised in the mechanisms and practices of transitional justice. In this chapter, we argue that this lack of recognition can in part be attributed to the 'dominance of legalism'[13] in transitional justice – meaning a reliance on legal concepts, frameworks, mechanisms, and solutions to periods of mass violence. Law can be narrowly or broadly constructed, and in some instances can encompass a multitude of perspectives, including customary and/or Indigenous understandings of law. Our more specific focus is the role of Western legal theories and frameworks in precluding engagement with Nature. We interrogate two 'anthropocentric' legal frameworks: human rights and criminal law, which are formulated on understandings of personhood and victimhood that exclude human victims of environmental harms and harms against Nature itself.

This chapter proceeds as follows. In Part 2, we interrogate the concept of 'anthropocentric legalism.' To do so, we first introduce the argument that there is a dominance of legalism in transitional justice – a dominance that persists despite transitional justice being rooted in a recognition that legal mechanisms alone do not always provide the most appropriate or effective responses to past violence. We then explore the meaning of 'anthropocentrism' both as an ethical approach and as a mechanism of exclusion. In Part 3, we outline the interconnected histories of human rights and transitional justice before turning to two ways anthropocentrism manifests through this interconnection: first, through the entrenching of certain definitions of legal personhood and associated understandings of which entities can experience a rights violation; and second, through the replication of hierarchies of rights – with certain civil and political rights violations given greater emphasis that social, economic and cultural rights – which preclude greater consideration of harms against Nature, albeit through a human-centric lens. In Part 4, we turn to criminal law, with a particular emphasis on the emergence of international criminal law as a key framework for understanding atrocity crimes. We consider which interests are protected by international criminal law and

10 Pierre Hazan, *Judging War, Judging History: Behind Truth and Reconciliation* (Stanford University Press, 2010).

11 Mark Hamilton, *Environmental Crime and Restorative Justice: Justice as Meaningful Involvement* (Palgrave MacMillan, 2021), 127.

12 Femke Wijdekop, Restorative Justice Responses to Environmental Harm. An IUCN Report, Amsterdam, 2019, http://files.harmonywithnatureun.org/uploads/upload864.pdf.

13 Kieran McEvoy, "Beyond Legalism: Towards a Thicker Understanding of Transitional Justice," *Journal of Law and Society* 34(4) (2007): 411.

highlight how notions of legal personhood are reinforced by courts' and tribunals' understandings of victimhood. Part 5 concludes, reflecting on the ways in which these legal frameworks embed the belief that humans alone possess intrinsic value, with other entities (such as ecosystems and other living beings) existing as means to human ends.[14]

3.2 Anthropocentric Legalism

3.2.1 The Dominance of Legalism in Transitional Justice

Legalism has been described as the 'morality of rule following,'[15] or the placing of 'great faith in the power of law and legal institutions to solve problems.'[16] Attempts to define legalism have been described as 'hazardous' as it is a 'complicated and ambiguous concept.'[17] Here, we use the term 'legalism' to describe the prioritisation of, or belief in the pre-eminence of, legal rules, professionals, and institutions as tools for addressing problems and responding to harm. Building on the previous chapter, we focus on the dominance of laws predominantly constructed and informed by the Global North.

Transitional justice as a field of scholarship is interdisciplinary, with work by lawyers, criminologists, anthropologists, socio-legal scholars, political scientists, and others making up its literature. However, its practice has often remained dominated by legalism.[18] This dominance has continued to be a consistent focus of critique in the field.[19]

14 We acknowledge that all law is anthropocentric in so far as it is created, implemented, and interpreted by humans, but we consider this a rather ethically uninteresting argument. See e.g. Lissy Goralnik and Michael Nelson, "Anthropocentrism," *Encyclopedia of Applied Ethics*, ed. Ruth Chadwick (Academic Press, 2012), 145–155.

15 Judith Shklar, *Legalism* (Harvard University Press, 1964), 87.

16 Eric Posner, *The Perils of Global Legalism* (University of Chicago Press, 2009), 16.

17 Posner, *Global Legalism*, 19.

18 E.g. Kora Andrieu, "Confronting the Dictatorial Past in Tunisia: Human Rights and the Politics of Victimhood in Transitional Justice Discourses," *Human Rights Quarterly* 38(2) (2016): 261–293; Louise Arbour, "Economic and Social Justice for Societies in Transition," *New York University Journal of International Law and Politics* 40(1) (2007): 1–28; McEvoy, "Beyond Legalism"; Zinaida Miller, "Effects of Invisibility: In Search of the 'Economic' in Transitional Justice," *International Journal of Transitional Justice* 2(3) (2008); Rosemary Nagy, "Transitional Justice as Global Project: Critical Reflections," *Third World Quarterly* 29(2) (2008): 275–289; Susan Thomson and Rosemary Nagy, "Law, Power and Justice: What Legalism Fails to Address in the Functioning of Rwanda's Gacaca Courts," *International Journal of Transitional Justice* 5(1)(2011): 11–30; Catherine Turner, "Deconstructing Transitional Justice," *Law and Critique* 24(2) (2013): 193–209.

19 Matthew Evans, "Beyond Disciplines, Beyond Fields, Beyond Transitional Justice," *Beyond Transitional Justice: Transformative Justice and the State of the Field (or non-Field)*, ed. Matthew Evans (Routledge, 2022), 34–42; Briony Jones, "The Performance and Persistence of Transitional Justice and its Ways of Knowing Atrocity," *Cooperation and Conflict* 56(2) (2021): 163–180; Thomson and Nagy, "Law, Power and Justice"; Turner, "Deconstructing."

There is a certain inevitably to the dominant use of law as a vehicle for responding to violence. Legalism is pervasive, not only impacting upon our behaviour as individuals, but also expressing itself through 'philosophical thought ... political ideologies, and ... social institutions.'[20] Furthermore, the promises of legalism have proven particularly seductive during transitions from conflict, when 'claims that the "rule of law" speaks to values and working practices such as justice, objectivity, certainty, uniformity, universality, rationality, and so on' can become especially 'prized'[21] as a way of regulating between ethics, rights and politics.[22] The fact that legal reform does not necessarily lead to real-world improvements, and can in fact mask ongoing rights violations and violence, is reflected in Stanley Cohen's term 'magical legalism.'[23] Taking this notion further, Julieta Lemaitre has accused lawyers of engaging in 'legal fetishism,' whereby law becomes not the means to an end but an end in itself, regardless of real-world impacts.[24]

The dominance of legalism is evident in the origin stories commonly told about the field of transitional justice. Retrospectively understood as one of the key origin points of transitional justice,[25] the Allies' response to the crimes of the Nazi regime 'provided transitional justice's legitimacy, constructed its moral and legal arguments, and outlined what would become, decades later, the institutions, values, and practices of transitional justice.'[26] The Nuremberg trials promoted and reinforced 'legalistic values,'[27] with criminal justice playing 'an essential role'[28] (we return to this in Part 3). This sense that legalism can 'flourish' when politics fail[29] has meant that justice after conflict can become considered synonymous with legal morality and the use of courts and trials.[30]

20 Shklar, *Legalism*, 1.
21 McEvoy, "Beyond Legalism," 417.
22 Turner, "Deconstructing," 205.
23 Stanley Cohen, *States of Denial: Knowing about Atrocities and Suffering* (Polity Press, 2013), 108.
24 Julieta Lemaitre, "Legal Fetishism: Law, Violence, and Social Movements in Columbia," *Revista Juridica Universidad de Puerto Rico* 77(2) (2008): 331–344.
25 E.g., Ruti Teitel, "Transitional Justice: Postwar Legacies," *Cardozo Law Review* 27(4) (2005): 1615–1632; Brianne McGonigle Leyh, "Nuremberg's Legacy within Transitional Justice: Prosecutions Are Here to Stay," *Washington University Global Studies Law Review* 15(4) (2016): 559–574.
26 Hazan, *Judging War*, 13.
27 Shklar, *Legalism*, 146.
28 Hazan, *Judging War*, 14.
29 Posner, *Global Legalism*, 228.
30 Shklar, *Legalism*.

This perception has been further entrenched by the increased institutionalisation and professionalisation of transitional justice.[31] For many years, the notion of a 'toolbox' has been used to denote the various institutions and mechanisms of transitional justice, revealing the 'instrumental vision' that had come to dominate the field.[32] The reliance on 'a top-down template-driven tool-box approach' persists,[33] and particular legal frameworks have played central roles in shaping the norms relied upon by transitional justice institutions and professionals.[34]

Part of legalism's appeal is the idea that law is premised on 'neutral and impartial principles' and can therefore play a mediating role between victims' demands for justice and political realities in the aftermath (or in the midst) of conflict.[35] In another example of the value dualism explored in Chapter 2, there can be a tendency, particularly within Western culture, to assume that law is separate from its context.[36] The reality is that laws are far from neutral[37] and are by no means separate from the values, beliefs, perspectives, and politics of the context in which they are created, implemented, and enforced.[38] Rather, legal reforms and mechanisms can play a central role in shaping narratives, determining whose stories are told,[39] and creating 'subjects and truths which are blind to certain forms of injustice and harm.'[40] As Pierre Hazan remarked with regards to the post-World War II Nuremberg trials, 'to pretend that an absolute barrier was possible between law and politics was as absurd as to pretend to live without oxygen.'[41] Legalistic approaches to transitional justice will inevitably 'embody prevailing constellations of power.'[42] These power dynamics can play a central role in shaping legal definitions of 'victims,'[43] thereby influencing who can access rights and

31 Briony Jones and Ulrike Lühe, eds., *Knowledge for Peace: Transitional Justice and the Politics of Knowledge in Theory and Practice* (Elgar, 2021), 4.

32 Hazan, *Judging War*, 30.

33 Jones and Lühe, "Knowledge for Peace," 4.

34 Philipp Kastner, "A Resilience Approach to Transitional Justice?" *Journal of Intervention and Statebuilding* 14(3) (2020): 368–388.

35 Turner, "Deconstructing," 205.

36 Jana Norman, *Posthuman Legal Subjectivity: Reimagining the Human in the Anthropocene* (Routledge, 2022), 64.

37 Miller, "Effects of Invisibility," 266. See also Hazan, *Judging War.*

38 Norman, *Posthuman Legal Subjectivity*, 64.

39 Nagy, "Global Project"; Margaret Davies, *Law Unlimited: Materialism, Pluralism and Legal Theory* (Routledge, 2017).

40 Nagy, "Global Project," 276; Kevin Hearty, "Law, 'Presentist' Agendas, and the Making of 'Official' Memory after Collective Violence," *Journal of Law and Society* 49(3) (2022): 495–517.

41 Hazan, *Judging War.*

42 Thomson and Nagy, "Law, Power and Justice," 13.

43 Jemima García-Godos and Knut Andreas O. Lid, "Transitional Justice and Victims' Rights Before the End of a Conflict: The Unusual Case of Colombia," *Journal of Latin American Studies* 42(3) (2010): 500.

support,[44] who is able to contribute to transitional justice mechanisms,[45] whose harm will be acknowledged,[46] and what narratives will be told about past violence.[47]

With others,[48] we argue that this dominance of legalism impedes transitional justice scholarship and practice by narrowing its scope and excluding other forms of knowledge and ways of understanding harm and redress. Taking this further, we argue that the dominance of *anthropocentric* legalism has restricted the ability of transitional justice mechanisms to recognise and respond to harms against Nature. We demonstrate that this restriction plays out in two ways: through the linking of 'victimhood' with anthropocentric concepts of legal personhood, and through the prioritisation of physical violence and property-based harms.

3.2.2 Anthropocentric Legalism as a System of Exclusion

Anthropocentrism can be understood as an ethical approach that perceives humans as having intrinsic value and everything other than human as having only instrumental value. Such an approach therefore understands Nature as a resource to be used for human benefit.[49] Anthropocentric priorities such as the protection of private property rights (in the case of individuals and corporations), territorial sovereignty (in the case of nation-states),[50] and economic growth[51] underpin most legal systems. Anthropocentrism is a particularly dominant ideology in the Global North, where it finds its roots in the theories of human domination over Nature and the Nature/culture divide. This ideology has been linked to logics of colonial domination and

44 UN General Assembly, Declaration of Basic Principles of Justice for Victims of Crime and Abuse of Power, 29 November 1985, UNGA Res 40/34 (hereafter UN Basic Principles); UN General Assembly, Basic Principles and Guidelines on the Right to a Remedy and Reparation for Victims of Gross Violations of International Human Rights Law and Serious Violations of International Humanitarian Law, UNGA Res60/147, 16 December 2005 (hereafter Basic Principles and Guidelines).

45 García-Godos, "Victim Reparations," 66.

46 Frank Haldemann, "Another Kind of Justice," *Cornell International Law Journal* 41(3) (2008): 675–737.

47 Andrieu, "Dictatorial Past."

48 Arbour, "Economic and Social Justice"; McEvoy, "Beyond Legalism"; Miller, "Effects of Invisibility."

49 Suzanne Gagnon Thompson and Michelle Barton, "Ecocentric and Anthropocentric Attitudes Toward the Environment," *Journal of Environmental Psychology* 14(2) (1994): 149–157.

50 Klaus Bosselmann, "Earth Trusteeship and the Sovereign State," *The Palgrave Handbook of Environmental Restorative Justice*, eds. Miranda Forsyth et al. (Palgrave Macmillan, 2022), 131.

51 Michelle Maloney, "Earth Jurisprudence and Sustainable Consumption," *Southern Cross University Law Review* 14(1) (2011): 124.

racism and can be critiqued for being 'far removed from being a concern with humans in any rich and inclusive sense.'[52] Rather, it is an approach embedded in capitalist logics which, in practice, protect only certain human interests.

Anthropocentrism is reflected in a range of legal frameworks, but its influence extends beyond the structures of law, as law is more than a mirror to society – it helps shape dominant ways of thinking.[53] As Carsten Stahn notes, 'By deciding what comes within the ambit of law, legal proceedings, trials or reparations, justice institutions inevitably produce new social realities, structural relations and forms of power.'[54] Anthropocentrism is evident in the legal regimes that have proven preponderant in shaping transitional justice, namely 'human rights law, criminal law and international law of war.'[55] Environmental law is notably absent, having rarely been considered applicable to the field,[56] but it is worth noting that environmental law has also been critiqued for being primarily concerned with Nature as a consumable rather than a living entity.[57] This anthropocentrism is evident even in foundational international agreements to protect nature; the UN Conference on Environment and Development, for example, identifies human beings as 'the centre of concerns for sustainable development.'[58] The idea of environmental 'sustainability' in this context remains anthropocentric due to its framing of the environment as something 'other,' a resource to be protected in order to serve human interests.[59]

Vito de Lucia has described anthropocentrism as a 'mechanism of exclusion (epistemological as well as legal and material) through which certain humans and natural ecosystems are systematically disadvantaged by liberal,

52 Anna Grear, "Law's Entities: Complexity, Plasticity and Justice," *Jurisprudence* 4(1) (2013): 76.

53 Marie-Catherine Petersmann, "Narcissus' Reflection in the Lake: Untold Narratives in Environmental Law Beyond the Anthropocentric Frame," *Journal of Environmental Law* 30(7) 2018): 235–259.

54 Carsten Stahn, *A Critical Introduction to International Criminal Law* (CUP, 2018), 425.

55 Ruti Teitel, "Transitional Justice Genealogy," *Harvard Human Rights Journal* 16(4) (2003): 69–94.

56 David Ong, "Prospects for Transitional Environmental Justice in the Socio-Economic Reconstruction of Kosovo," *Tulane Environmental Law Journal* 30(2) (2017): 218.

57 Petersmann, "Narcissus"; Usha Natarajan and Kishan Khoday, "Locating Nature: Making and Unmaking International Law," *Leiden Journal of International Law* 27(3) (2014): 573–593.

58 UN Conference on Environment and Development, Rio de Janeiro, Brazil, 3–14 June 1992 (also known as the 'Earth Summit' or the 'Rio Conference').

59 Teea Kortetmäki, "Anthropocentrism versus Ecocentrism Revisited: Theoretical Confusions and Practical Conclusions," *SATS: Northern European Journal of Philosophy* 14(1) (2013): 21–37.

modern law.'[60] In the following subsections, we explore how these mechanisms of exclusion manifest in transitional justice's foundational legal regimes. We focus on human rights law and international criminal law, noting that the latter is itself based on human rights law, criminal law, and international humanitarian law. For each area of law, we offer a brief explanation of the area of law, outline its role in shaping transitional justice's evolution, and critique the features of the legal regime that serve to exclude environmental victimhood.

3.3 Human Rights, Personhood, and Hierarchies of Rights

Human rights law is a body of law which places obligations on states to act in certain ways or to refrain from certain acts, to promote and protect the human rights and fundamental freedoms of individuals and/or groups.[61] Its origins as a body of international (or at least multinational) law are debated.[62] However, some of its earliest articulations can be found in the work of the International Labour Organisation, an organisation explicitly established in the aftermath of World War I as a response to the perceived threat of socialism.[63] Thus, these early expressions of 'rights' have been connected to 'the triumph of liberal democracy' and the belief that the protection of rights, and the maintenance of peace, were necessary for the purposes of economic efficiency.[64]

The horrors of World War II created greater impetus for an international human rights framework. Foundational statements of international human rights include the 1948 Universal Declaration of Human Rights (UDHR),[65]

60 Vito De Lucia, "Competing Narratives and Complex Genealogies: The Ecosystem Approach in International Environmental Law," *Journal of Environmental Law* 27(1) (2015): 91–117.

61 Paul Gordon Lauren, *The Evolution of International Human Rights: Visions Seen* (University of Pennsylvania Press, 1998).

62 See e.g. Philip Alston, "Does the Past Matter: On the Origins of Human Rights," *Harvard Law Review* 126(7) (May 2013): 2043–2082; Jenny S. Martinez, "Human Rights and History," *Harvard Law Review* 126 (7–8) (2013): 221–240.

63 Thank you to Professor Louise Mallinder for flagging the ILO's history.

64 Olivia Liang, "Governing Globalization: Labour Economic Paradigms and International Labour Standards at the International Labour Organization, 1919–1998," Interactions: Regional Studies, Global Processes, and Historical Analysis, 28 February–3 March 2001, https://webdoc.sub.gwdg.de/ebook/p/2005/history_cooperative/www.historycooperative.org/proceedings/interactions/index.html. See also Albert Thomas, "The International Labour Organisation: Its Origins, Development and Future," *International Labour Review* vol. 135(34) (1996): 261–276.

65 UN General Assembly, *Universal Declaration of Human Rights*, A/RES/217(III), 10 December 1948.

the International Covenant on Civil and Political Rights (ICCPR),[66] and the International Covenant on Economic, Social and Cultural Rights (ICESCR),[67] collectively termed the International Bill of Human Rights. Additional human rights frameworks are now found in domestic laws and at regional levels, such as in the European,[68] Inter-American,[69] and African human rights conventions[70] and the Association of Southeast Asian Nations (ASEAN) human rights declaration.[71]

It is important to problematise the notion of 'universal' asserted by the UDHR. The initial creation of the international human rights frameworks was characterised by absences and exclusions that have ongoing repercussions for human rights' implementation. Human rights emerged at a time when much of the colonised world remained under direct occupation, limiting their ability to influence the development of early international documents.[72] Priority was given to English-language and Western sources during the drafting of the UDHR; drafters rejected suggestions that they engage with Asian philosophies, and only three African nations were involved in either drafting or voting for the final resolution.[73] When it came to drafting the International Covenants, Cold War disputes led to the differentiation of human rights into two categories: civil and political rights, which refer to the ability of persons to take part in the civil and political life of their community;[74] and economic, social, and cultural rights, which refer to the

66 UN General Assembly, *International Covenant on Civil and Political Rights*, United Nations Treaty Series, 999(171), 16 December 1966.
67 UN General Assembly, *International Covenant on Economic, Social and Cultural Rights*, United Nations Treaty Series, 993(3), 16 December 1966.
68 Council of Europe, *European Convention for the Protection of Human Rights and Fundamental Freedoms*, as amended by Protocols Nos. 11 and 14, ETS 5, 4 November 1950.
69 Organization of American States (OAS), *American Convention on Human Rights*, ("Pact of San Jose"), Costa Rica, 22 November 1969.
70 Organization of African Unity (OAU), *African Charter on Human and Peoples' Rights* ("Banjul Charter"), CAB/LEG/67/3 rev. 5, 21 I.L.M. 58 (1982), 27 June 1981.
71 Association of Southeast Asian Nations (ASEAN), *Human Rights Declaration*, 19 November 2012.
72 Although it is not a story of simple Global North inclusion/Global South exclusion. See e.g. Kathryn Sikkink, "Latin American Countries as Norm Protagonists of the Idea of International Human Rights," *Global Governance* 20(3) (2014): 389–404.
73 Asad Kiyani, "International Crime and the Politics of Criminal Theory: Voices and Conduct of Exclusion," *New York University Journal of International Law and Politics* 48(1) (2015): 178–180. See also Makau Mutua, "The Ideology of Human Rights," *Virginia Journal of International Law* 36(3) (1996): 603–607. It is notable in this context that the African Charter on Human and People's Rights contains several differences to other multinational human rights treaties, including the right to a generally acceptable environment, further problematising the notion of universalism.
74 See e.g. ICCPR.

ability of persons to prosper and take part in social and cultural activities.[75] While the ICCPR places immediate and unqualified commitments upon states, the ICESCR gives states greater latitude in determining the extent of implementation, reflecting Western fears that economic, social, and cultural rights would interfere with liberal, free market economies.[76] The implications of these exclusions and divisions for the recognition of harms against Nature emerge below.

3.3.1 Human Rights and the Foundations of Transitional Justice

The evolution of transitional justice and human rights are deeply intertwined. Initially a descriptor for transitions from authoritarian regimes to liberal democracies,[77] the concept of 'transitional justice' soon evolved into something more normative, characterised by the idea that transitions should be accompanied by justice for victims of certain human rights abuses.[78] The end of the Cold War and the accompanying rise of liberalism contributed to this shift[79] by enabling the 'resurgence of the idea of international human rights law'[80] and a move away from state responsibility towards individual criminal accountability for human rights abuses.[81] Transitional justice's emphasis on individual human rights has continued into the present; justice is often equated with the application of human rights law to past abuses and the protection of human rights moving forward.[82] As Ron Dudai states, the 'common purpose of transitional justice is to redefine some acts that were previously considered "normal" as human rights violations.'[83]

International human rights instruments and mechanisms have also shaped transitional justice. Key influencers include the 2005 *Basic Principles and Guidelines on the Right to a Remedy and Reparation for Victims of Gross*

75 See e.g. ICESCR.

76 Barbara Stark, "Economic Rights in the United States and International Human Rights Law: Toward an Entirely New Strategy," *The Hastings Law Journal* 44(1) (1992): 79–130.

77 Ruti Teitel, *Transitional Justice* (OUP, 2000), 5; Paige Arthur, "How 'Transitions' Reshaped Human Rights: A Conceptual History of Transitional Justice," *Human Rights Quarterly* 31 (2009) 321–367.

78 Turner, "Deconstructing," 196; Teitel, *Transitional Justice.*

79 Janine Natalya Clark, "Harm, Relationality and More-than-Human Worlds: Developing the Field of Transitional Justice in New Posthumanist Directions," *International Journal of Transitional Justice* 17(1) (2023): 15–31. See Chapter 6.

80 Turner, "Deconstructing," 194.

81 Joanna Quinn et al., "The Development of Transitional Justice," *Research Handbook on Transitional Justice*, eds. Cheryl Lawther et al. (Elgar, 2017).

82 Turner, "Deconstructing."

83 Ron Dudai, "Transitional Justice as Social Control: Political Transitions, Human Rights Norms and the Reclassification of the Past," *The British Journal of Sociology* 69(3) (2017): 691–711.

Violations of International Human Rights Law and Serious Violations of International Humanitarian Law ('UN Basic Principles').[84] These principles, which took several decades to develop,[85] detail victims' rights to remedies, access to justice, reparation for harm suffered, and access to relevant information.[86] The same year, the UN Commission on Human Rights endorsed the *Updated Set of Principles for the Protection and Promotion of Human Rights through Action to Combat Impunity*.[87] This link between human rights and criminal accountability has been further facilitated by findings of regional human rights courts, who have interpreted their constituent treaties to argue that gross violations of human rights require reparations and the investigation and prosecution of those responsible.[88] As we explore below, the link has only strengthened over time.[89]

We argue that there are two reasons an emphasis on human rights law has precluded greater recognition of harms against Nature in transitional justice. First, we argue that human rights are by definition anthropocentric, precluding the recognition of other-than-human victimhood. Second, we argue that while there are human rights frameworks that might facilitate greater recognition of environmental harm, albeit through an anthropocentric lens, these are rarely the focus of transitional justice measures. These are considered in turn.

3.3.2 Anthropocentrism, Legal Personhood, and Human Rights

Human rights are, on the face of it, the rights one has because one is human. As Jack Donnelly explains, 'one is or is not a human being, and therefore has the same human rights as everyone else (or none at all).'[90] But there is more to it than that. The idea that humans can hold rights is grounded in

84 Basic Principles and Guidelines.

85 Theo van Boven, "The United Nations Basic Principles and Guidelines on the Right to a Remedy and Reparation for Victims of Gross Violations of International Human Rights Law and Serious Violations of International Humanitarian Law," *United Nations Audiovisual Library of International Law*, United Nations, 2010.

86 Basic Principles and Guidelines.

87 Van Boven, 1.

88 See e.g. *Blake v. Guatemala*, Judgment (Merits), IACtHR, 24 January 1998, 96–97; *Velasquez-Rodriguez v. Honduras*, Judgment, IACtHR, 29 July 1988, 174; *Aydin v. Turkey*, Judgment, ECtHR, App. No. 23178/94, 25 September 1997; *Aksoy v. Turkey*, Judgment, ECtHR, App. No. 21987/93, 18 December 1996.

89 Karen Engle, "Anti-Impunity and the Turn to Criminal Law in Human Rights," *Cornell Law Review* 100(5) (2015): 1069–1128; Philip Alston, "Criminalizing Human Rights," *Journal of Human Rights Practice* 15(3) (2023): 660–677.

90 Jack Donnelly, "1. The Concept of Human Rights," *Universal Human Rights in Theory and Practice*, ed. Jack Donnelly (Cornell University Press, 2013), 10.

a foundational concept of Western law, that of 'legal personhood.'[91] This is explicitly acknowledged in the UDHR, which grants the right to 'recognition everywhere as a person before the law,'[92] thereby framing the right to legal personhood as a human right. It also creates a framework of rights described by legal theorist Visa A. J. Kurki as the 'incidents of legal personhood' – rights that can be asserted by 'all human beings.'[93] The recognition of personhood thereby enforces a legal distinction born of Continental European philosophy: the conceptual distinction between persons, or 'subjects', and non-persons, or 'objects.'[94] As Kurki further explains, one can understand the legal implications of this distinction in the following way: while legal persons can hold a range of different legal rights (and duties), legal objects or 'things' can be understood as being susceptible to being owned.[95]

The idea that humans (sometimes termed 'natural persons') are entitled to rights simply by dint of being human is rooted in the idea of humans' unique moral nature.[96] This idea is foundational to the German philosopher Immanuel Kant's idea that humans should not be treated as a means to an end, but as an end in themselves.[97] The concept of human dignity is central to this discourse, finding early legal expression in the UDHR and most international human rights documents produced since.[98] The concept assumes that humans have particular characteristics that justify the creation of specific rights and associated rights protections.[99] Related to the concept of human dignity is the idea that human rights should protect individuals against humiliation,[100] an experience that has often been considered unique to the human condition.[101]

91 Visa A. J. Kurki, *Legal Personhood* (CUP, 2023).
92 UDHR, Article 6.
93 Kurki, *Legal Personhood*, 35.
94 Kurki, *Legal Personhood*, 10.
95 Visa A. J. Kurki, "Animals, Slaves and Corporations: Analyzing Legal Thinghood," *German Law Journal* 18(5) (2017): 1069–1090.
96 Donnelly, "The Concept of Human Rights," 15.
97 Immanuel Kant, "Groundwork of the Metaphysics of Morals," *Practical Philosophy*, ed. Mary Gregor (CUP, 1996), 429.
98 Christopher McCrudden, "Human Dignity and Judicial Interpretation of Human Rights," *European Journal of International Law* 19(4) (2008): 655–724.
99 On the dignity of animals, see Rebekah Humphreys, "Dignity and its Violation Examined within the Context of Animal Ethics," *Ethics and the Environment* 21(2) (2016): 143–162.
100 Paulus Kaufmann et al., *Humiliation, Degradation, Dehumanization: Human Dignity Violated* (Springer, 2010); Evelin Gerda Lindner, "Humiliation and Human Rights: Mapping a Minefield," *Human Rights Review* 2(2) (2001): 46.
101 Although this understanding has been contested, see Stefanie Schindler, "The Animal's Dignity in Swiss Animal Welfare Legislation – Challenges and Opportunities," *European Journal of Pharmaceutics and Biopharmaceutics* 84(2) (2013): 251–254.

Not all humans have historically been recognised as legal persons; many have been relegated to what Franz Fanon termed the 'zone of non-being.'[102] For much of history, European jurisdictions and those influenced by them through colonisation understood the legal person as someone male, white, able-bodied, and often in possession of property.[103] Part of the human rights project has been to recognise and grant rights to a wider range of humans (e.g. enslaved people, women, minorities, Indigenous peoples, children, people with disabilities).[104] Despite this expansion, and in particular the evolution of 'third generation' collective rights of certain groups of people,[105] human rights have continued to 'foreground individualism,'[106] remaining predominantly focused on individuals as autonomous and independent legal subjects.[107] This understanding of the person has given primacy to rights premised on the role of the state as one of non-interference with the individual's freedoms rather than those geared towards more life-enhancing provisions.[108] A particular emphasis has been placed on the 'near-absoluteness of the right to property.'[109] We return to the dominance of certain human rights below.

The expansion of rights holders demonstrates law's constructive power. Michel Foucault explores this through his idea of 'subjectification,' arguing that the law does not only presuppose certain subjectivities (such as personhood) but also creates them.[110] Through such a lens, a 'person with human rights' is something 'drafted, recognised and created' through human rights

102 Franz Fanon, *Black Skins, White Masks* (Grove Books, 2008).

103 Ngaire Naffine, *Law's Meaning of Life: Philosophy, Religion, Darwin and the Legal Person* (Hart Publishing, 2009); Anna Arstein-Kerslake et al., "Relational Personhood: A Conception of Legal Personhood with Insights from Disability Rights and Environmental Law," *Griffith Law Review* 30(3) (2021): 530–555; Anna Grear, "The Closures of Legal Subjectivity: Why Examining 'Law's Person' is Critical to an Understanding of Injustice in an Age of Climate Crisis," *Research Handbook on Human Rights and the Environment*, ed. Anna Grear (Elgar, 2015).

104 Lynn Hunt, *Inventing Human Rights: A History* (W. W. Norton & Company, 2008).

105 Ingrid Nifosi-Sutton, *The Protection of Vulnerable Groups under International Human Rights Law* (Routledge, 2017).

106 Karen Morrow, "The Anthropocene and Human Rights: A New Context and the Need to Revisit Collective Human Concerns," *The Routledge Handbook of Law and the Anthropocene*, eds. Peter Burdon and James Martel (Routledge, 2023).

107 John Locke, *Two Treaties of Government, from the Works of John Locke* (Yale University Press, 2003), 1689.

108 Erin O'Donnell and Anna Arstein-Kerslake, "Recognising Personhood: The Evolving Relationship Between the Legal Person and the State," *Griffith Law Review* 30(3) (2021): 339–347.

109 Upendra Baxi, *The Future of Human Rights* (OUP, 2008).

110 Michel Foucault, *Discipline and Punish* (Penguin Books, 1977).

frameworks and their enforcement.[111] It is therefore possible to separate the notion of legal personhood from that of a human being. As Hans Kelsen notes, a 'person is a concept of jurisprudence, of the analysis of legal norms,' and 'legal personhood' is therefore the rights and duties ascribed to an entity, rather than the entity itself.[112]

Such an understanding of personhood leaves open the question as to who should 'count' as a person, enabling scholars, lawyers, activists, and policy makers to debate whether and which other-than-human entities should have personhood.[113] Notably, human rights have sometimes been claimed by the other historically accepted non-human legal person: the corporation.[114] Indeed, corporations gained personhood, and associated rights, before women and racialised peoples in many contexts.[115] The idea of corporations as artificial or juristic legal persons continues to be shared by all Western legal systems, although their specific status varies, and not all jurisdictions will accept human rights complaints on their behalf.[116] While it can be argued that corporations are reducible to human individuals, they have a separate existence, and the fact that this separate entity has rights further demonstrates the constructive force of law.[117] Taken together, these points highlight law's cultural specificity, its power to shape reality, and its malleability. These characteristics are in turn helpful for exploring how law can both restrain and enhance transitional justice's ability to respond to harms against Nature.

Returning to human rights law, notions of personhood have naturally shaped how 'victims' of human rights violations are defined and understood: being a 'person' (i.e. a rights-bearer) facilitates access to remedies when one's rights are violated. For example, the UN 1985 Basic Principles identify victims as 'persons who individually or collectively suffered harm,' which can in some cases extend to 'the immediate family or dependents of the direct victim and persons who have suffered harm in intervening to assist victims in distress.'[118] The UN 2005 Principles and Guidelines also require victims to be treated with 'humanity and respect for their dignity and human rights.'[119]

111 Susanna Lindroos-Hovinheimo, *Private Selves: Legal Personhood in European Privacy Protection* (CUP, 2021), 34, cited in Visa A. J. Kurki, *Legal Personhood* (CUP, 2023), 5.
112 Hans Kelsen, *General Theory of Law and State* (Transaction, 2006), 94.
113 Luis Chiesa, "Of Persons and the Criminal Law: (Second Tier) Personhood as a Prerequisite for Victimhood," *Pace Law Review* 28(4) (2008): 759–782.
114 Marius Emberland, *The Human Rights of Companies* (OUP, 2006); Stefanie Khoury and David Whyte, *Corporate Human Rights Violations* (Routledge, 2017).
115 Grear, "The Closures of Legal Subjectivity."
116 Kurki, *Legal Personhood*, 2.
117 Kurki, *Legal Personhood*, 26.
118 UN Basic Principles, Principle 1.
119 Principles and Guidelines, Principle 10.

At a regional level, the Inter-American Court of Human Rights defines a victim as a 'person whose rights have been violated, according to a judgment emitted by the Court,'[120] while the European Court of Human Rights recognises 'any person, non-governmental organisation or group of individuals' if they have been a victim of a violation under the European Charter on Human Rights.[121] Similar framings are evident in institutional definitions of transitional justice. For example, the International Center for Transitional Justice identifies transitional justice as being 'about victims,' focusing on 'their rights and dignity as citizens and human beings' and ensuring 'all citizens are included and everyone's rights are protected.'[122]

Anthropocentric understandings of who and what can experience a rights violation are a fundamental limitation on the utility of human rights as a framework for redressing harms against Nature. This limitation has been expressed through the charge of 'speciesism,' meaning the inappropriate prioritisation of human interests over other species.[123] Some have attempted to broaden the scope of personhood to species perceived to be close to humans, such as chimpanzees.[124] Others have argued for a different category altogether, in recognition of personhood's 'liberal humanist' limitations.[125] Still others have more foundationally problematised the dominance of Western ontologies in legal understandings of personhood and rights.[126] They have highlighted that for many Indigenous peoples, Nature and other-than-human species are endowed with interests and agency, rendering their exclusion from the category of rights-bearing legal person less tenable.[127] Indeed,

120 Inter-American Court of Human Rights, Rules of Procedure, Approved by the Court during its LXXXV Regular Period of Sessions, held 16–28 November 2009. For an analysis of the Court's approach, see Clara Sandoval-Villalba, "The Concepts of 'Injured Party' and 'Victim' of Gross Human Rights Violations in the Jurisprudence of the Inter-American Court of Human Rights: A Commentary on their Implications for Reparations," *Reparations for Victims of Genocide, War Crimes and Crimes against Humanity*, eds. Carla Ferstman and Mariana Goetz (Brill Nijhoff, 2009).

121 ECHR, Article 34.

122 'What is Transitional Justice?' ICTJ, n.d., https://www.ictj.org/what-transitional-justice. The language of 'citizen' is in itself problematic, excluding as it does refugees, foreign residents, and/or stateless persons.

123 See e.g. Peter Singer, *Animal Liberation Now* (Random House, 2023). For a response, see Heiner Bielefeldt, "Moving Beyond Anthropocentrism? Human Rights and the Charge of Speciesism," *Human Rights Quarterly* 43(3) (2021): 515–537.

124 See e.g. the work of the Nonhuman Rights Project; www.nonhumanrights.org.

125 Maneesha Deckha, *Animals as Legal Beings: Contesting Anthropocentric Legal Orders* (University of Toronto Press, 2021).

126 Norman, *Posthuman Legal Subjectivity.*

127 See e.g. Margaret Robinson, "Animal Personhood in Mi'kmaq Perspective," *Societies* 4(4) (2014): 672–688; Martuwarra RiverOfLife et al., "Yoongoorrookoo: The Emergence of Ancestral Personhood," *Griffith Law Review* 30(3) (2021) 505–529; Andrew Brighten, "Aboriginal Peoples and the Welfare of Animal Persons: Dissolving the

Indigenous laws and customs[128] have informed the rise of Rights of Nature movements, explored further in Chapter 4.[129] These developments highlight the fact that 'law' does not shape 'personhood' in an inevitable, pre-determined way but can instead be understood as reflecting and in turn shaping particular cultural framings.

While other-than-human entities are not recognised as having experienced harm in their own right, this exclusion does not entirely preclude the consideration of harms against Nature through the lens of human rights. In factthe links between human rights and the protection of Nature are increasingly receiving attention. In the following section, we explore this nexus in the context of transitional justice. However, we argue that hierarchies of rights in transitional justice practice have further impeded the use of human rights to recognise harms against Nature.

3.3.3 Hierarchies of Rights in Transitional Justice

The early international human rights conventions introduced in the aftermath of World War II contain no explicit reference to Nature, environmental rights, or environmental protection.[130] This is a notable omission, as the war had provided a stark demonstration of the interconnected nature of conflict,

---

Bill C-10B Conflict," *Indigenous Law Journal* 10(1) (2011): 39–72; Jacinta Ruru, "First Laws: Tikanga Māori in/and the Law," *Victoria University of Wellington Law Review* 49(2) (2018): 211–228; Guido Sprenger, "Buddhism and Coffee: The Transformation of Locality and Non-Human Personhood in Southern Laos," *Sojourn: Journal of Social Issues in Southeast Asia* 33(2) (2018): 265–290.

128 Note that while many Indigenous cultures do not draw the same distinction between social and legal status, it is now clear that oral traditions and customs can be understood as 'law.' See Hadley Friedland, "Waniska: Reimagining the Future with Indigenous Legal Traditions," *The Windsor Yearbook of Access to Justice* 33(1) (2016): 85–102; Hadley Friedland and Val Napoleon, "Gathering Threads: Developing a Methodology for Researching and Rebuilding Indigenous Legal Traditions," *Lakehead Law Journal* 1(1) (2015): 16–44; Mattias Ahren, "Indigenous Peoples' Culture, Customs, and Traditions and Customary Law – The Saami People's Perspective," *Arizona Journal of International and Comparative Law* 21(1) (2004): 63–112.

129 The specific cultural relationship between Indigenous peoples and their territories, as well as the right to the conservation and protection of the environment, is recognised in the UN General Assembly, *Declaration on the Rights of Indigenous Peoples*, A/RES/61/295, 2 October 2007. However, while this demonstrates a development in the human rights paradigm by recognising the interrelationship of Indigenous rights with access to territory, the Declaration reasserts state sovereignty and continues to emphasise individual human rights. It is also notable that the Declaration is soft law, further limiting its impact. See Karen Engle, "On Fragile Architecture: The UN Declaration on the Rights of Indigenous Peoples in the Context of Human Rights," *The European Journal of International Law* 22(1)(2021): 141–163.

130 Although there are indirect references, for example to the right to a standard of living adequate for health and well-being (UDHR, Article 25). See Susana Borràs,

environmental devastation, and human suffering.[131] However, connections between environmental pollution and human rights began to emerge in the 1960s, following several man-made environmental catastrophes.[132] The first explicit links between human rights and the environment followed in the 1972 Stockholm Declaration and solidified over the following decades.[133] Nowadays, it is arguable that various internationally recognised rights offer pathways to responding to environmental destruction.[134] These include the right to an adequate standard of living, the right to health (including the improvement of all aspects of environmental hygiene and the prevention of disease), the right to family and cultural life, the right to development, the right to freedom from displacement, Indigenous cultural rights, and the emerging right to a healthy environment.[135]

These links have had limited impact on transitional justice, where the rights that might facilitate engagement with harms against Nature – albeit through an anthropocentric lens – are often those that are overlooked. Instead, transitional justice measures have tended to stay oriented around violations of civil and political rights,[136] with social, economic, and cultural rights often framed as 'background' or 'context' rather than violations themselves.[137]

This emphasis is evident in the way 'violations' of human rights are frequently understood in transitional justice literature and practice. For

"New Transitions from Human Rights to the Environment to the Rights of Nature," *Transnational Environmental Law* 5(1) (2016): 113–143.

131 Petersmann, "Narcissus."

132 Petersmann, "Narcissus," 242.

133 See e.g. *African Charter on Human and Peoples' Rights*; *Additional Protocol to the American Convention on Human Rights in the Area of Economic, Social and Cultural Rights (Protocol of San Salvador)*, entered into force 16 November 1999 OAS Treaty Series No 69 (1988); League of Arab States, *Arab Charter on Human Rights*, adopted 22 May 2004, entered into force 15 March 2008; ASEAN Human Rights Declaration.

134 For an early example of this kind of argument, see Caroline Dommen, "Claiming Environmental Rights: Some Possibilities offered by the United Nations' Human Rights Mechanisms," *Georgetown International Environmental Law Review* 11(1) (1998): 1.

135 Cristy Clark and Beth Goldblatt, "The Right to a Healthy Environment and Social and Economic Rights – Responding to Climate Change in Australia," *Australian Journal of Human Rights* 23(1) (2023): 65–83; Karen Hulme, "Using a Framework of Human Rights and Transitional Justice for Post-Conflict Environmental Protection and Mediation," *Environmental Protection and Transitions from Conflict to Peace: Clarifying Norms, Principles, and Practices*, eds. Carsten Stahn et al. (OUP, 2017).

136 See, e.g. Arbour, "Economic and Social Justice"; Miller, "Effects of Invisibility."

137 Dustin Sharp, "Addressing Economic Violence in Times of Transition: Toward a Positive-Peace Paradigm for Transitional Justice," *Fordham International Law Journal* 35(3) (2012): 781–814; Sam Szoke-Burke, "Not Only Context: Why Transitional Justice Programs Can No Longer Ignore Violations of Economic and Social Rights," *Texas International Law Journal* 50(2-3) (2015): 465–494.

example, Tricia Olsen, Leigh Payne, and Andrew Reiter define transitional justice as being the processes designed to address human rights violations perpetrated during periods of conflict, political turmoil, or conflict, with 'human rights violations' defined as 'extrajudicial killings, disappearances, torture and arbitrary arrest and imprisonment.'[138] Similarly, as argued by Sally Engle Merry, 'physical injury and death' are considered to fall within the definition of a 'violation,' while 'economic violence, environmental degradation, or the violence of development' are not.[139]

Turning to examples in practice, the South African Truth and Reconciliation Commission limited the definition of 'victim' to those who 'suffered harm in the form of physical or mental injury, emotional suffering, pecuniary loss or substantial impairment of human right,' with violations of human rights defined as 'killing, abduction, torture or severe ill-treatment of any person.'[140] Numerous Latin American truth commissions have similarly focused on acts of physical violence, such as assassinations, disappearances, and the treatment of prisoners.[141] In Northern Ireland, criminal justice processes and investigatory mechanisms have primarily focused on victims of political violence.[142] This emphasis on civil and political rights across different contexts appears to contradict the wishes of victimised populations themselves, many of whom have repeatedly made clear that the social, economic, and cultural conditions of their lives are at least as significant, if not more significant, a concern as redress for violations of civil and political rights.[143]

While social, economic, and cultural rights violations tend to remain 'in the shadow of the political dimension of transitional justice,'[144] there

138 Tricia Olsen et al., *Transitional Justice in Balance – Comparing Processes, Weighing Efficacy* (US Institute of Peace Press, 2010), cited in Amanda Cahill-Ripley, "Foregrounding Socio-Economic Rights in Transitional Justice: Realising Justice for Violations of Economic and Social Rights," *Netherlands Quarterly of Human Rights* 32(2) (2014): 183–213.

139 Sally Engle Merry, "Introduction," *The Practice of Human Rights: Tracking Law Between the Global and the Local*, eds. Mark Goodale and Sally Engle Merry (CUP, 2007).

140 Promotion of National Unity and Reconciliation Act 34 of 1995 sec. 1(1)(xix)(a), 1(1)(ix), cited in Pablo de Greiff, "Introduction: Repairing the Past: Compensation for Victims of Human Rights Violations," *The Handbook of Reparations*, ed. Pablo de Greiff (OUP, 2006).

141 Szoke-Burke, "Not Only Context."

142 Luke Moffett et al., "Redressing Displacement in Northern Ireland: Identity, Land and Dealing with the Past," *Political Geography* 106(1) (2023): 102941.

143 Padraig McAuliffe, "Dividing the Spoils: The Impact of Power Sharing on Possibilities for Socioeconomic Transformation in Postconflict States," *International Journal of Transitional Justice* 11(2)(2017): 198.

144 Nicolas Lemay-Hébert and Rosa Freedman, "Appraising the Socio-Economic Turn in Reparations: Transitional Justice for Cholera Victims in Haiti," *International Journal of Transitional Justice* 15(3) (2021): 533–552.

are some exceptions. As Eliana Cusato explores, the Sierra Leonean and Liberian Truth and Reconciliation Commissions engaged with the exploitation of the natural world not only as background information, but as part of human rights abuses, 'economic crimes,' and associated injustices.[145] However, the practical implications of this recognition were relatively limited, and left intact the structural factors that facilitated environmental and associated human harms.[146] We return to the challenges of addressing structural violence in Chapter 5.

Multiple, overlapping explanations have been offered for transitional justice's prioritisation of civil and political rights violations. One is that this prioritisation mirrors human rights discourse and practice.[147] While the non-justiciability of social, economic, and cultural rights has been frequently rebutted, they are nonetheless often understood as 'directive principles of state policy', 'softer obligations,' or even 'secondary rights' rather than legally enforceable rights requiring remedy in the aftermath of a violation.[148] Zinaida Miller argues that transitional justice's tendency to 'almost uniformly' emphasise civil and political rights is a result of the field having 'imported' these biases from its 'parent' human rights movement.[149]

Another explanation is that transitional justice has historically emphasised 'negative peace' (the absence of conflict) rather than 'positive peace' (stability and lasting peace), enabling it to overlook more fundamental, structural rights violations.[150] It is worth acknowledging that there are pragmatic dimensions to this argument as well as political ones. Transitional justice mechanisms may choose to focus on the harms that they can address in a relatively short amount of time, rather than those that might require more

145 Eliana Cusato, "Back to the Future? Confronting the Role(s) of Natural Resources in Armed Conflict Through the Lenses of Truth and Reconciliation Commissions," *International Community Law Review* 19(4–5) (2017): 373–400.

146 Cusato, "Back to the Future?"

147 Cahill-Ripley, "Foregrounding Socio-Economic Rights"; Sharp, "Addressing Economic Violence"; Szoke-Burke, "Not Only Context."

148 Padraig McAuliffe, "Programmatic Approaches to Realising Socio-Economic Rights: Debates, Definitions and Trends," *Melbourne Journal of International Law* 22(1) (2021): 30–31.

149 Miller, "Effects of Invisibility"; a similar point is made by Lars Waldorf, "Anticipating the Past: Transitional Justice and Socio-Economic Wrongs," *Social & Legal Studies* 21(2) (2012): 173, noting human rights' 'longstanding legalistic bias towards civil and political rights.'

150 Hulme, "Post-Conflict Environmental Protection and Mediation," 122. Although there is a counter argument that social, economic, and cultural rights violations can be discrete as well as structural; see Evelyne Schmid and Aoife Nolan, "Do No Harm? Exploring the Scope of Economic and Social Rights in Transitional Justice," *International Journal of Transitional Justice* 8(3) (2014): 363.

systemic or long-term interventions.[151] Transitional justice mechanisms are also often the products of political negotiation and compromise; negotiators may feel less comfortable with measures that disrupt pre-existing structures than they are with responses to acute instances of physical violence.[152] However, this prioritisation can also be linked to the field's focus on liberal democratisation and free market logic, which might preclude consideration of rights violations which require more distributive justice outcomes. This focus can be encouraged or even required by international financial institutions such as the World Bank or International Monetary Fund, which may require structural reforms that reduce the role of the state and inhibit a recovering state from pursuing redistribution.[153]

Finally, it is possible that the prioritisation of certain rights over others is attributable to the emergence of transitional justice's emphasis on criminal justice as the appropriate response. As Louise Arbour argues, the field's neglect of economic, social, and cultural rights is 'merely symptomatic' of a similar and 'deeper ambivalence within justice systems.'[154] We return to the limitations posed by a focus on criminal justice solutions in the following section.

Over the last 20 years, calls for transitional justice to encompass a broader range of human rights concerns have become common in the literature, particularly amongst those drawing from more critical theoretical perspectives.[155] Scholars point to the indivisibility of human rights, the role of structural violence in causing human rights violations, and the importance of addressing social, economic, and cultural rights for preventing the recurrence of atrocity.[156] While part of the broader critical engagement with transitional justice, these calls are notable for remaining grounded in human rights frameworks. As Frank Haldemann and Rachelle Kouiassi note, this

151 Roger Duthie, "Transitional Justice, Development, and Economic Violence," *Justice and Economic Violence in Transition*, ed. Dustin Sharp (Springer, 2013), 172–173.

152 On transitional justice as compromise see Colleen Murphy, "On Principled Compromise: When does a Process of Transitional Justice Qualify as Just?" *Proceedings of the Aristotelian Society* 120(1) (2020): 47–70.

153 See for example the case of Tunisia, as explored in Saerom Han, "Transitional Justice for Whom? Contention over Human Rights and Justice in Tunisia," *Social Movement Studies* 21(6) (2022): 816–832.

154 Arbour, "Economic and Social Justice," 5.

155 See e.g. Laura Garciá Martín, "Challenging the Transitional Justice Paradigm: Addressing ESRs Violations in Transitional Justice Processes," *Anuario Espanol de Derecho Internacional* 35(4) (2019): 655–680; Rama Mani, *Beyond Retribution: Seeking Justice in the Shadow of War* (Polity Press, 2002); Tafadzwa Pasipanodya, "A Deeper Justice: Economic and Social Justice as Transitional Justice in Nepal," *International Journal of Transitional Justice* 2(3) (2008): 378–397; Schmid and Nolan, "Do No Harm?"

156 Ismael Muvingi, "Sitting on Powder Kegs: Socioeconomic Rights in Transitional Societies," *International Journal of Transitional Justice* 3(2) (2009): 163–182.

approach is understandable; human rights can be 'a powerful strategy for winning arguments and, perhaps, changing social realities.'[157] The 'aspirational and future focused' elements of human rights enable faith in their prospects to proliferate even in the absence of concrete improvements in social conditions.[158]

Yet, a continued emphasis on human rights frameworks keeps the debate grounded in anthropocentric assumptions. While accountability for environmental harms through human rights mechanisms has increased, and new possibilities are offered by the right to a healthy environment, they have remained centred around identifiable legal persons. As Usha Natarajan argues, the way human rights law distinguishes between who we are (the subjects of law) and where we are (the objects of law) only reinforces the false idea that human and environmental well-being are separable.[159] Similarly, Marie-Catherine Petersmann demonstrates how such a distinction limits the framing of the natural world to that of a 'material and commodified object' to be protected only to fulfil human interests.[160] This is notable in the examples cited above of the Liberian and Sierra Leonian Truth and Reconciliation Commissions – to the extent that harms against the environment were recognised, they were understood through the lens of enabling physical violations and economic crimes.[161] This approach limits the extent to which mechanisms can meaningfully respond to environmental harm and risks overlooking the complex relationships that exist between environmental and human interests in the aftermath of conflict.[162] Similar 'blind spots' emerge when we turn to the second of our legal frameworks: international criminal law.

3.4 The 'Crime-Driven Lens' of Transitional Justice

Criminal investigations and prosecutions form one of the main mechanisms of transitional justice. Retributive (or corrective) justice has had a profound

157 Frank Haldemann and Rachelle Kouassi, "Transitional Justice Without Economic, Social, and Cultural Rights?" *Economic, Social, and Cultural Rights in International Law: Contemporary Issues and Challenges*, eds. Eibe Riedel, Gilles Giacca, and Christophe Golay (OUP, 2014), 502.

158 Usha Natarajan, "Who Do We Think We Are? Human Rights in a Time of Ecological Change," *Locating Nature: Making and Unmaking International Law*, eds. Usha Natarajan and Julia Dehm (CUP, 2022).

159 Natarajan, "Who Do We Think We Are?"

160 Petersmann, "Narcissus," 250.

161 Cusato, "Back to the Future?"

162 Petersmann, "Narcissus."

influence on the development of the field,[163] and transitional justice has in turn influenced the increased connections drawn between human rights and criminal justice. This is evidenced by the intertwined evolution of transitional justice and the anti-impunity approach to human rights. Until the mid-1980s, human rights organisations had rarely called for prosecutions of grave human rights violations, as the power to do so was perceived to lie with the same actors who had perpetrated the violations.[164] The emergence of transitional justice challenged this perception; domestic prosecutions featured in many transitions from authoritarianism,[165] and criminal law grew in popularity as a method for pursuing accountability.[166]

It seems that in the beginning, there was relatively little debate as to whether human rights violations actually necessitated criminal accountability.[167] Rather, early debates centred questions regarding the tension between punishment and political stability.[168] This changed over time, as questions arose as to whether trials furthered the other goals of transitional justice (such as truth, reconciliation, and peace)[169] and as to whether criminal responses were even able to deliver on their own 'penalogical objectives' in the context of atrocity crimes.[170] Yet, the practice of prosecuting individuals

163 Patrick Lenta, "Transitional Justice and Retributive Justice," *Ethic Theory and Moral Practice* 22(2) (2019): 385–398.

164 Karen Engle, "A Genealogy of the Criminal Turn in Human Rights," *Anti-Impunity and the Human Rights Agenda*, ed. Karen Engle (CUP, 2016), 18–21.

165 Samuel Huntington, *The Third Wave: Democratization in the Late 20th Century* (University of Oklahoma Press, 1991).

166 Mattia Pinto, "Historical Trends of Human Rights Gone Criminal," *Human Rights Quarterly* 42(4) (2020): 729–761. See also Louise Mallinder and Kieran McEvoy, "Rethinking Amnesties: Atrocity, Accountability and Impunity in Post-Conflict Societies," *Contemporary Social Science* 6(1) (2011): 107–128 on the broader meanings of accountability.

167 Pinto, "Historical Trends," 744.

168 Louise Mallinder, "Can Amnesties and International Justice be Reconciled?" *International Journal of Transitional Justice* 1(2) (2007): 208–230.

169 See e.g. Devin Pendas, *Democracy, Nazi Trials, and Transitional Justice in Germany, 1945–1950* (CUP, 2020); Colleen Murphy, *The Conceptual Foundations of Transitional Justice* (CUP, 2017); Lillian Barria and Steven Roper, "How Effective are International Criminal Tribunals? An Analysis of the ICTY and ICTR," *International Journal of Human Rights* 9(3) (2005): 349–368; Laurel Fletcher and Harvey Weinstein, "Violence and Social Repair: Rethinking the Contribution of Justice to Reconciliation," *Human Rights Quarterly* 24(3) (2002): 573–639; David Mendeloff, "Trauma and Vengeance: Assessing the Psychological and Emotional Effects of Post-Conflict Justice," *Human Rights Quarterly* 31(3) (2009), 592–623; Jack Snyder and Leslie Vinjamuri, "Trials and Errors: Principle and Pragmatism in Strategies of International Justice," *International Security* 28(3) (2004): 5–44.

170 Mark Drumbl, *Atrocity, Punishment and International Law* (CUP, 2007), 181.

for grievous human rights violations quickly spread across the world.[171] As this practice became more normalised, the peace versus justice debate receded somewhat, and retribution for serious violations of human rights came to be understood as aligned with rather than in tension with other justice goals.[172] By the early twenty-first century, 'accountability' had come to be considered synonymous with prosecution and punishment.[173]

This entrenchment of transitional criminal justice was cemented by the evolution of international criminal law as a distinct body of law over the latter half of the twentieth century. Indeed, as noted above, one version of transitional justice's origin story links its emergence to the use of international tribunals after World War II.[174] The turn to tribunals as a response to atrocity crimes constituted a major shift in international norms,[175] offering a pathway to individual, rather than state, accountability for grave violations of human rights.[176] Although the Cold War precluded the level of international cooperation required to introduce international tribunals for several decades, the 1990s brought the International Criminal Tribunals for Rwanda[177] and the former Yugoslavia,[178] with the permanent International Criminal Court (ICC) following in 2002.[179] Hybrid institutions, featuring a mix of domestic and international law, procedures, and personnel, have also been introduced in multiple instances,[180] while universal jurisdiction (whereby a state extends its

171 Kathryn Sikkink, *The Justice Cascade: How Human Rights Prosecutions are Changing World Politics* (W. W. Norton, 2011).

172 Naomi Roht-Arriaza, "The New Landscape of Transitional Justice," *Transitional Justice in the Twenty-First Century: Beyond Truth Versus Justice*, eds. Naomi Roht-Arriaza and Javier Mariezcurrena (CUP, 2006).

173 Mallinder and McEvoy, "Rethinking Amnesties."

174 Marc Polizzi, "Transitional Justice," *Oxford Research Encyclopedia of International Studies*, ed. Nukhet Sandal (OUP, 2022). Note, there are also much earlier accounts of war crimes: see Gregory Gordon, "The Trial of Peter von Hagenbach: Reconciling History, Historiography and International Criminal Law," *The Hidden Histories of War Crimes Trials*, eds. Kevin Heller and Gerry Simpson (OUP, 2013).

175 See Drumbl, *Atrocity, Punishment* for a critique of the application of methods and assumptions of ordinary liberal criminal law to collective violence.

176 Alejandro Chehtman, "A Theory of International Crimes: Conceptual and Normative Issues," *The Oxford Handbook of International Criminal Law*, eds. Kevin Heller et al. (OUP, 2020).

177 Megan Westberg, "Rwanda's Use of Transitional Justice after Genocide: The Gacaca Courts and the ICTR," *University of Kansas Law Review* 59(2) (2010): 331.

178 Natasa Kandic, "The ICTY Trials and Transitional Justice in Former Yugoslavia," *Cornell International Law Journal* 38(3) (2005): 789–792.

179 Kai Ambos, "The Legal Framework of Transitional Justice: A Systematic Study with a Special Focus on the Role of the ICC," *Building a Future on Peace and Justice*, eds. Kai Ambos et al. (Springer, 2009).

180 Alberto Costi, "Hybrid Tribunals as a Viable Transitional Justice Mechanism to Combat Impunity in Post-Conflict Situations," *New Zealand Universities Law Review* 22(2) (2006): 213–239.

jurisdiction beyond its own territory and nationals) has facilitated the domestic prosecution of individuals for international crimes.[181]

International criminal mechanisms have been subject to a range of critiques, not least for their decontextualisation of atrocity[182] and selectivity in the perpetrators, harms, and victims they recognise.[183] Yet, trials for international crimes have become an embedded feature of transitional justice[184] and have normalised the application of a 'crime-driven lens'[185] to atrocities.[186] More specifically, there has been a tendency in some of the academic literature to frame transitional justice as requiring 'a fixed, almost invariable (ICC-centred) international criminal justice response to atrocities.'[187] This logic – an odd one given how few situations the ICC examines and how few perpetrators it indicts – has further cemented a 'transitional justice orthodoxy' grounded in penal logic.[188] While a range of other mechanisms are still used, such as truth commissions, reparation programs, and memorials, criminal accountability has been framed by international, regional, and local actors alike as 'the only legitimate option for addressing past atrocities.'[189]

An emphasis on criminal accountability has implications for the recognition of harms against Nature. It is not a generalisation to say that the

181 Luc Reydams, "The Rise and Fall of Universal Jurisdiction," *Routledge Handbook of International Criminal Law*, eds. William Schabas and Nadia Bernaz (Routledge, 2011), 337.

182 Martti Koskenniemi, "Between Impunity and Show Trials," *Max Planck Yearbook of United Nations Law* 6(1) (2002): 13; Engle, "Anti-Impunity."

183 Andre Armenian, "Selectivity in International Criminal Law: An Assessment of the 'Progress Narrative'," *International Criminal Law Review* 16(4) (2016): 642–672; Robert Cryer, *Prosecuting International Crimes: Selectivity and the International Criminal Law Regime* (CUP, 2005); Elies van Sliedregt, "One Rule for Them – Selectivity in International Criminal Law," *Leiden Journal of International Law* 34(2) (2021): 283–290.

184 See e.g. UN Security Council, *The Rule of Law and Transitional Justice in Conflict and Post-Conflict.*

Societies: Report of the Secretary General, S/2004/616, 23 August 2004. For a critique of this dominance, see Sarah Nouwen and Wouter Werner, "Monopolizing Global Justice: International Criminal Law as Challenge to Human Diversity," *Journal of International Criminal Justice* 13(1) (2015): 157–176.

185 Aldo Zammit Borda, "History in International Criminal Trials: The 'Crime-driven Lens' and Its Blind Spots," *Journal of International Criminal Justice* 18(3) (2020): 543–566.

186 Alston, "Criminalizing Human Rights"; César Rodríguez-Garavito, "The Future of Human Rights: From Gatekeeping to Symbiosis," *Sur: International Journal on Human Rights* 11(2) (2014): 499.

187 Obiora Chinedu Okafor and Uchechukwu Ngwaba, "The International Criminal Court as a 'Transitional Justice' Mechanism in Africa: Some Critical Reflections," *International Journal of Transitional Justice* 9(1) (2015): 90–108.

188 Okafor and Ngwaba, "Critical Reflections."

189 Pinto, "Historical Trends." See also Drumbl, *Atrocity, Punishment*; Engle, "Anti-Impunity."

construction of criminal law in most states is strongly influenced by anthropocentric perspectives.[190] As Rob White argues, 'human victims of environmental harm are not widely recognised as victims of "crime".'[191] Moreover, within the category 'victim', the non-human environmental victim is seldom considered worthy of attention.[192] Anthropocentrism is thereby embedded in assumptions regarding whose interests are protected by criminal law and who counts as a victim of a crime. The implications of these assumptions for transitional justice are explored in the following sections.

3.4.1 Who are the 'Protectees' of International Criminal Law?

The concept of a 'protectee' refers to an entity whose interests are protected through the criminalisation of certain forms of conduct or failures to act.[193] This concept is broader than that of a legally recognised 'victim' of crime.[194] The latter tends to be more prescribed, as it is linked to associated benefits and/or rights, including compensation and, in some instances, participation in criminal proceedings.[195] Thus, while Nature has not been widely accepted as a victim of crime, many jurisdictions do criminalise certain harms against Nature (e.g. environmental pollution)[196] as well as other-than-human species.[197] In some jurisdictions, other-than-human entities including dogs,[198]

190 Ted Benton, "Rights and Justice on a Shared Planet: More Rights or New Relations?" *Theoretical Criminology* 2(2) (1998): 149–175.

191 Rob White, "Green Victimology and Non-human Victims," *International Review of Victimology* 24(2) (2018): 239–255.

192 Matthew Hall, "Environmental Harm and Environmental Victims: Scoping out a 'Green Victimology'," *International Review of Victimology* 20(1) (2013): 129–143.

193 Kurki, *Legal Personhood*, 18.

194 See e.g. Brian Preston, "The Use of Restorative Justice for Environmental Crime," a paper presented to EPA Victoria Seminar on Restorative Environmental Justice, 22 March 2011, https://lec.nsw.gov.au/documents/speeches-and-papers/preston_use%20of%20restorative%20justice%20for%20environmental%20crime.pdf.

195 See e.g. Tyrone Kirchengast, *Victimology and Victim Rights: International Comparative Perspectives* (Routledge, 2017).

196 Environmental criminal law emerged across many jurisdictions from the 1970s onwards: see e.g. Michael Faure, "The Development of Environmental Criminal Law in the EU and its Member States," *Review of European, Comparative & International Environmental Law* 26(2) (2017): 139–146; David Uhlmann, "Environmental Crime Comes of Age: The Evolution of Criminal Enforcement in the Environmental Regulatory Ccheme," *Utah Law Review* 4 (2009): 1223.

197 Animal cruelty laws have a much longer history. See David Favre and Vivien Tsang, "The Development of Anti-Cruelty Laws during the 1800s," *Detroit College of Law Review* 1(1)(1993): 1–35.

198 Luis Chiesa, "Of Persons and the Criminal Law: (Second Tier) Personhood as a Prerequisite for Victimhood," *Pace Law Review* 28(4) (2008): 759–782.

waterways,[199] and trees[200] have been the beneficiaries of reparative measures following domestic criminal proceedings, even in the absence of explicit victim recognition. These examples, we argue, demonstrate a willingness to recognise other-than-human natural entities as protectees of the criminal law. Against this backdrop, this section considers who (or what) constitutes the protectees of international criminal law.

At the heart of international criminal law lies an assumption that there is an international community that shares certain values concerning what conduct deserves condemnation through criminalisation.[201] This is reflected in the Rome Statute of the ICC – currently the only permanent international criminal tribunal. The Statute's Preamble identifies the 'peace, security and wellbeing of the world' as its protected interest, describes 'all peoples' as 'united by common bonds,' and establishes a court 'for the sake of present and future generations.'[202] This language frames humanity itself as the protectee of international crimes,[203] and human peace and security as the justification for pursuing prosecution. This emphasis on 'humanity,' David Luban argues, forms the normative ideal on which international criminal law is based.[204] It also, as we will explore below, manifests in the specific framings of international crimes.

However, it is worth noting how the crimes that threaten the 'peace, security and wellbeing of the world' have been shaped by specific interests, rather than those of 'all peoples.' In the immediate aftermath of World War II, the UN established an International Law Commission (ILC) to formulate the principles of international law recognised by the Nuremberg

199 Auckland District Court, *Waikato Regional Council v. Huntly Quarries Ltd*, McElrea DCJ, 30 July 2003 and 28 October 2003; Auckland District Court, *Canterbury Regional Council v. Interflow (NZ) Ltd*, McElrea DCJ, 2 March 2006.

200 Auckland District Court, *Auckland City Council v. 12 Carlton Gore Road Ltd and Mary-Anne Catherine McKay Lowe*, McElrea DCJ, 11 April 2005; Auckland District Court, *Rodney District Council v. Sam Wong and Josh Topou,* JP Doogue DCJ, 28 February 2005.

201 Immi Tallgren, "The Voice of the International: Who is Speaking?" *Journal of International Criminal Justice* 13(1) (2015): 135–155.

202 UN General Assembly, *Rome Statute of the International Criminal Court* (last amended 2010), ISBN No. 92-9227-227-6, 17 July 1998, Preamble.

203 Merle Kooijman, "From Anthropos to Oikos in International Criminal Law: A Critical-Theoretical Exploration of Ecocide as an 'Ecocentric' Amendment to the Rome Statute," *Netherlands Yearbook of International Law 2021: A Greener International Law – International Legal Responses to the Global Environmental Crisis*, eds. Daniëlla Dam-de Jong and Fabian Amtenbrink (TMC Asser Press, 2023).

204 David Luban, "The Enemy of All Humanity," *The Oxford Handbook of International Criminal Law*, eds. Kevin Heller et al. (OUP, 2020), 558–582. See also Kai Ambos, "Punishment Without a Sovereign? The Ius Puniendi Issue of International Criminal Law: A First Contribution Towards a Consistent Theory of International Criminal Law," *Oxford Journal of Legal Studies* 33(2) (2013). 308.

Tribunal, and to prepare a draft code of offenses 'against the peace and security of mankind.'[205] During its early stages, the ILC had conceptualised crimes against peace and security as those that breached 'obligations intended to protect the most fundamental interests of mankind,' including not only peace and the protection of fundamental human rights but also the human environment and the right to self-determination.[206] However, the ILC faced serious pressure from a small group of Western states – most notably the United States, the United Kingdom, and the Netherlands – to limit the scope of criminality.[207] By the 1990s (the process took decades), this sustained pressure had caused the ILC to scale back to a narrower list of defined crimes.[208] These 'core crimes'[209] were cemented through the creation of the Rome Statute of the ICC,[210] and international criminal law is now generally understood as comprising war crimes (derived from international humanitarian law or *jus in bello*), crimes against humanity, genocide, and the crime of aggression. As such, the core crimes can be understood as protecting victims of a relatively narrow set of human rights priorities,[211] which were substantially shaped by the interests of powerful states.

The more specific intended protectees of atrocity crimes can be adduced from the crimes' definitions. Genocide is defined under the Rome Statute (Article 6) as acts that are 'committed with the intent to destroy, in whole or in part, a national, ethnical, racial or religious group, as such.' Although the 'group' is not explicitly defined as 'human,' victims of genocide are clearly understood as human.[212] As Andrew Woolford and Wanda Hounslow argue, 'genocide law has failed to fully consider the role of other-than-human

205 UN General Assembly, *Formulation of the Principles Recognized in the Charter of the Nürnberg Tribunal and in the Judgment of the Tribunal,* UNGA Res. 177 (II), U.N. Doc. A/CN.4/4, 21 November 1947 at 9.

206 Representative of the International Law Commission, 37th Session, 6 May–26 July 1985, UN Doc. A/40/10.

207 There was resistance to apartheid and colonialism's inclusion. See Comments and Observations received from Governments, International Law Commission, UN Doc. A/ CN.4/448 (Mar. 1, 1993) and Add. 1 (May 19, 1993), reprinted in *Yearbook of the International Law Commission* 59(2) (1993) UN Doc. A/ CN.4/SER.A/1993/Add.1 (Part 1).

208 Kiyani, "Politics of Criminal Theory."

209 Christine Schwöbel-Patel, "The Core Crimes of International Criminal Law," *The Oxford Handbook of International Criminal Law*, eds. Kevin Heller et al. (OUP, 2020).

210 Roy Lee, *The International Criminal Court: The Making of the Rome Statute* (Kluwer Law International, 1999).

211 Kiyani, "Politics of Criminal Theory," 184.

212 Andrew Woolford and Wanda Hounslow, "Symbiotic Victimisation and Destruction: Law and Human/Other-than-Human Relationality in Genocide," *Genocide and Victimology*, ed. Yarin Eski (Routledge, 2020).

actors in the constitution of group life.'[213] The relationships between humans and other-than-humans are acknowledged only to the extent that natural resources are deemed necessary for the existence of the group. For example, 'deliberately inflicting on the group conditions of life calculated to bring about its physical destruction in whole or in part' (Article 6(c)) has been interpreted to include environmental destruction.[214] We return to attacks on Nature as a means of perpetrating atrocity crime in a moment.

Whilst genocide is premised on the protection of specific groups, crimes against humanity protect any civilian population, in times of war or peace, from 'widespread or systematic attacks' (Article 7 of the Rome Statute). Again, the protectees are explicitly identified as human beings, through the naming of the crime itself, the reference to 'civilian population,' and references to the protection of identifiable groups from persecution. As in the case of genocide, no consideration has been given to the extension of 'groups' or 'populations' beyond the human.

The crime of aggression is somewhat different, as it seeks to criminalise 'the use of armed force by a State against the sovereignty, territorial integrity or political independence of another State' which 'by its character, gravity and scale, constitutes a manifest violation' of the UN Charter (Article 8*bis*). While a state naturally encompasses Nature within its territory, the protectee in this instance is the sovereign state as a political entity, rather than the territory itself. While the framings of these crimes do not in themselves preclude all possibility of their being used to prosecute attacks on Nature (discussed below), the protectees identified here clearly centre around humans and human groups.

War crimes are the sole context in which Nature is explicitly recognised as a protectee of international criminal law. War crimes protect 'persons or property protected under the provisions of the relevant Geneva Convention' (Article 8 of the Rome Statute), including the sick and wounded, prisoners of war, civilians, and civilian objects. Based on pre-existing international humanitarian law,[215] Article 8(2)(b)(iv) of the Rome Statute criminalises 'intentionally launching an attack in the knowledge that such attack will cause ... widespread, long-term and severe damage to the natural environment which would be clearly excessive in relation to the concrete and direct

213 Woolford and Hounslow, "Symbiotic Victimisation," 86.

214 Matthew Gillett, "Eco-Struggles – Using International Criminal Law to Protect the Environment During and After Non-International Armed Conflict," *Environmental Protection and Transitions from Conflict to Peace: Clarifying Norms, Principles, and Practices*, eds. Carsten Stahn et al. (OUP, 2017).

215 *Convention on the Prohibition of Military or Any Other Hostile Use of Environmental Modification Techniques, ENMOD Convention*, 10 December 1976; Additional Protocol I, Articles 35(4) and 55.

overall military advantage anticipated.'[216] To some extent, this represents an 'ecocentric' provision, in that it recognises Nature as a protectee independent from human interests.[217] However, human interests are re-asserted through the subjective proportionality requirement and high threshold of damage, which allows the 'military advantage anticipated' to trump all but the most excessive, widespread, long-term, and severe environmental damage.[218] This test, which is more restrictive than the international humanitarian law on which the crime is based, entrenches a 'warfare pragmatism which is centred around human interests'[219] and has been described as a 'huge leap backwards' in accountability for environmental war crimes.[220] At the time of writing, there have been no successful prosecutions (or even indictments) of this war crime, either in the ICC or in other courts with international criminal jurisdiction.[221]

It has been comprehensively argued by many scholars that while the core crimes place a strong emphasis on harms to people and property,[222] attacks on Nature can be recognised as either a means or a result of atrocity crimes.[223] In addition to being a means of 'bringing about the destruc-

216 ICC Rome Statute, Article 8(2)(b)(iv).
217 Jessica Lawrence and Kevin Heller, "The First Ecocentric Environmental War Crime: The Limits of Article 8 (2)(b)(Iv) of the Rome Statute," *Georgetown International Environmental Law Review* 20(1)(2007): 61.
218 Eliana Cusato, "Beyond Symbolism: Problems and Prospects with Prosecuting Environmental Destruction before the ICC," *Journal of International Criminal Justice* 15(3) (2017): 491–507.
219 Kooijman, "From Anthropos to Oikos," 116.
220 Mark Drumbl, "Accountability for Property Crimes and Environmental War Crimes: Prosecution, Litigation and Development," International Center for Transitional Justice, 2009, https://www.ictj.org/sites/default/files/ICTJ-Development-PropertyCrimes-FullPaper-2009-English.pdf.
221 See Caitlyn Johnson, "The ICC and Environmental Protection: Prosecuting Environmental War Crimes in Ukraine," *Journal of National Security Law and Policy* 14(2) (2023): 287–311; Shah Maruf, "Environmental Damage in Ukraine as Environmental War Crime under the Rome Statute: The Kakhovka Dam Breach in Context," *Journal of International Criminal Justice* 22(1) (2024): 99–126; Richard Rogers et al., "No Longer the Silent Victim: How Ukrainian Prosecutors are Revitalising Environmental War Crime Law," *Just Security*, 23 January 2024, https://www.justsecurity.org/91357/no-longer-the-silent-victim-how-ukrainian-prosecutors-are-revitalizing-environmental-war-crime-law/ for discussions on the potential application of Article 8(2)(b)(iv) to the situation in Ukraine.
222 Nagy, "Global Project," 284.
223 See e.g. Donald Anton, "Adding a Green Focus: The Office of the Prosecutor of the International Criminal Court Highlights the 'Environment' in Case Selection and Prioritisation," *Griffith Law School Research Paper* 17(3) (2016): 1–13; Steven Freeland, "Human Rights, the Environment and Conflict: Addressing Crimes Against the Environment," *International Journal on Human Rights* 2(2) (2005): 113–141; Pauline Martini and Maud Sarliève, "Fighting Deforestation in Non-International Armed Conflicts: The Relevance of the Rome Statute for Rosewood Trafficking in Senegal,"

tion of a group' (genocide), attacks on Nature could constitute a means of exterminating or persecuting a civilian population, or another 'inhumane act' (crimes against humanity). Attacks on Nature could also be the result of attacks on civilian targets, pillaging or the use of indiscriminate weapons (war crimes), or the bombardment of a state's territory (aggression). Some have even argued that international criminal law could recognise the harms associated with violations of the right to a healthy environment as a crime against humanity.[224] Yet, despite a wide range of inventive arguments regarding how environmental harms might be recognised subject to the 'anthropocentric values' of international criminal law,[225] no tribunal since Nuremberg has prosecuted individuals for atrocity-related damage to Nature.[226] There are signs that this might change, and that a more environmentally inclusive approach to atrocity prosecutions is gaining support. This is illustrated, for example, by the ICC Office of the Prosecutor's 2024 public consultation on advancing accountability for environmental crimes, which aims to better 'address crimes within the Court's jurisdiction committed by means of, or that result in, environmental damage.'[227] Russia's invasion of Ukraine has also sparked academic commentary as to whether it might result in the first prosecutions of environmental war crimes.[228] However, to date, international criminal law has tended to prioritise the prosecution of crimes that harm humans and human property 'from a very anthropocentric and economic perspective.'[229]

Transnational Environmental Law 11(1) (2021): 95–117; Alessandra Mistura, "Is There Space for Environmental Crimes under International Criminal Law? The Impact of the Office of the Prosecutor Policy Paper on Case Selection and Prioritisation on the Current Legal Framework," *Colombian Journal of Environmental Law* 43(1)(2018): 181–225; Regine Paulose, *Green Crimes and International Criminal Law* (Vernon Press, 2021); Tara Weinstein, "Prosecuting Attacks that Destroy the Environment: Environmental Crimes or Humanitarian Atrocities," *Georgetown International Environmental Law Review* 17(4) (2005): 697–721.

224 Pauline Martini et al., "Mass Deforestation as a Crime against Humanity," *The International and Comparative Law Quarterly* 72(4) (2023): 1013–1046.

225 Gillett, "Eco-Struggles."

226 United Nations War Crimes Commission, *1948 History of the United Nations War Crimes Commission and the Development of the Laws of War* (Commission No. 7150), 486.

227 The Office of the Prosecutor Launches Public Consultation on a New Policy Initiative to Advance Accountability for Environmental Crimes under the Rome Statute, *ICC Website*, 16 February 2024, https://www.icc-cpi.int/news/office-prosecutor-launches-public-consultation-new-policy-initiative-advance-accountability-0

228 Johnson, "The ICC and Environmental Protection"; Maruf, "Environmental Damage in Ukraine."

229 Reece Walters et al., *Emerging Issues in Green Criminology* (Palgrave MacMillan, 2013), 7.

It is important to recognise the pragmatic challenges of prosecuting crimes against Nature. As Eliana Cusato points out, the lack of use of Article 8(2)(b)(iv) may not only be an issue of a narrow definition but an indicator of the challenges (perceived or real) of proving environmental crimes to a criminal standard.[230] Rob White has noted the challenges of identifying perpetrators for systematic environmental harms,[231] while others have highlighted the specific challenges of proving intent in cases where Nature may have been targeted for other purposes, such as economic gain or strategic advantage.[232]

Yet it is also important to acknowledge that not all protectees' interests are equally protected, and that this also has implications for the recognition of Nature. International criminal law 'rests on and confirms existing power imbalances,'[233] through the conduct it deems to be atrocities, as explored above, and then through selective processes of enforcement. In practice, courts recognise and respond to a relatively narrow category of victimisations, even when jurisdiction and resources allow them to carry out investigations and prosecutions. As Randle De Falco argues, and building on our discussions in Chapter 2, 'authoritative assessments' of which crimes are deserving of international criminal intervention have been 'overwhelmingly made by elite technocrats (lawyers, judges, investigators etc.) clustered in the Global North.'[234]

Thus, it is primarily the atrocities that 'offend the sensibilities of key consistencies clustered in the Global North' that will be 'deemed worth of recognition as international crimes.'[235] At the same time, and as noted in the previous chapter, the crimes for which the Global North might hold the most responsibility are overlooked. Drawing on Nils Christie's concept of the 'ideal victim,' Joris van Wijk has argued that for victims to obtain recognition, they need to have been harmed through 'well-timed' atrocities that

230 Cusato, "Beyond Symbolism."

231 Rob White, *Climate Change from a Criminological Perspective* (Springer, 2012).

232 Aurelie Lopez, "Criminal Liability for Environmental Damage Occurring in Times of Non-International Armed Conflict: Rights and Remedies," *Fordham Environmental Law Review* 18(2) (2007): 231–271; Tara Smith, "Creating a Framework for the Prosecution of Environmental Crimes in International Criminal Law," *The Ashgate Research Companion to International Criminal Law*, eds. William Schabas et al. (Routledge, 2013).

233 Posner, *Global Legalism*, 39.

234 Randle DeFalco, *Invisible Atrocities: The Aesthetic Biases of International Criminal Justice* (CUP, 2022), 8. See also Mikkel Christensen, "The Creation of an Ad Hoc Elite and the Value of International Criminal Law Expertise on a Global Market," *The Oxford Handbook of International Criminal Law*, eds. Kevin Heller et al. (OUP, 2020).

235 DeFalco, *Invisible Atrocities*, 21.

attract international (by which he primarily means Western) attention,[236] and they must be able to claim or 'sell' their own victim status.[237] These 'geopolitical distortions' mean that issues of more pressing concerns to the Global South – which might be intimately connected to issues around natural resource protection, use, and control – are less likely to be taken seriously as atrocities,[238] and communities who might be willing and able to advocate for Nature are silenced.[239]

The focus on certain types of rights violation is accompanied by the assumption that international crimes manifest as 'spectacles'[240] whose 'criminality is intuitively recognizable.'[241] As Aurelie Lopez argues, visceral atrocities against human beings 'will almost certainly have a greater impact on public opinion.'[242] The idea that international crimes involve 'a relatively large number of victims (e.g. a fairly significant number of deaths or casualties) or severe injury on non-combatant populations (e.g. massive destruction of private property)'[243] can obscure atrocities perpetrated through methods that are slow, attritive, and/or complex, and which involve social, economic, and cultural rights violations and – crucially – the targeting or deterioration of the natural world.[244] The non-recognition of these methods limits the protection and remedies available to the most vulnerable and marginalised communities around the world.[245]

This section has outlined the interests protected by international criminal law and the processes of selectivity that have shaped the field. The international criminal legal framework might be understood as a pyramid, with the range of atrocities perpetrated in our world at the bottom and those that are likely to be prosecuted at the top. In the following subsection, we briefly turn

236 Joris van Wijk, "Who is the 'Little Old Lady' of International Crimes? Nils Christie's Concept of the Ideal Victim Reinterpreted," *International Review of Victimology* 19(2) (2013): 159–179. See also Christine Schwöbel-Patel, "The 'Ideal' Victim of International Criminal Law," *European Journal of International Law* 29(3) (2018): 722.

237 Christine Schwöbel-Patel, *Marketing Global Justice* (CUP, 2021).

238 Alston, "Criminalizing Human Rights."

239 Filofteia Repez and Mirela Atanasiu, "The Environment – A 'Silent Victim' of Armed Conflicts," *Acta Universitatis Danubius: Relationes Internationales* 12(2) (2019): 123–133.

240 Christin Schwöbel-Patel, "Spectacle in International Criminal Law: The Fundraising Image of Victimhood," *London Review of International Law* 4(2) (2016): 247–274.

241 DeFalco, *Invisible Atrocities*, 30.

242 Lopez, "Criminal Liability."

243 David Scheffer, "Genocide and Atrocity Crimes," *Genocide Studies and Prevention* 1(3) (2006): 229–250.

244 Eliana Cusato, *The Ecology of War and Peace: Marginalising Slow and Structural Violence in International Law* (CUP, 2021), 232. See also Richard Clements, "Near, Far, Wherever You Are: Distance and Proximity in International Criminal Law," *European Journal of International Law* 32(1) (2021): 327–350.

245 Kiyani, "Politics of Criminal Theory."

to the legal concept of 'victim' to highlight the additional legal rules that narrow the pyramid of those who have suffered harm to those considered 'legally relevant' in international criminal law.[246]

3.4.2 Defining Victimhood in International Criminal Law

Over the last two and a half decades, 'victims' have become a central figure in domestic and international criminal discourse.[247] This rise in visibility has been accompanied by enhanced rights for victims in many jurisdictions.[248] In the international criminal context, a range of procedural and substantive rights have been granted in several courts and tribunals (such as the ICC, the Extraordinary Chambers in the Courts of Cambodia, the Special Tribunal for Lebanon, the Kosovo Specialist Chambers, and the Colombian Jurisdicción Especial para la Paz).[249] These developments can be linked to the merging of human rights and anti-impunity agendas. As the divisions between human rights and criminal law have become blurred, moves to bestow safeguards on victims of crime like those granted to victims of state abuses have emerged across domestic,[250] regional, and international contexts.[251] As a result, 'victimhood' is increasingly a legal rather than a descriptive category, with associated rights that can, in some instances, be asserted in courts.[252]

246 Sara Kendall and Sarah Nouwen, "Representational Practices at the International Criminal Court: The Gap between Juridified and Abstract Victimhood," *Law & Contemporary Problems* 76(3-4) (2013): 235–262.

247 Alessandra Cuppini, "The 'Ideal Victim': A Cage for Victims' Narratives at the International Criminal Court," *Leiden Journal of International Law* 37(2) (2024): 484–505; McEvoy and McConnachie, "Victims and Transitional Justice"; Schwöbel-Patel, "The 'Ideal Victim'"; Van Wijk, "Little Old Lady."

248 Rachel Killean, *Victims, Atrocity and International Criminal Justice* (Routledge, 2018), 16–39.

249 E.g. Mahmoud Cherif Bassiouni, "Victims' Rights and Participation in ICC Proceedings and in Emerging Customary International Law," *Contemporary Issues Facing the International Criminal Court*, ed. Richard Steinberg (Brill Nijhoff, 2020); Maria Elander, *Figuring Victims in International Criminal Justice: The Case of the Khmer Rouge Tribunal* (Routledge, 2018); Kinga Tibori-Szabó and Megan Hirst, *Victim Participation in International Criminal Justice: Practitioners Guide* (Springer, 2017); Christine Van den Wyngaert, "Victims before International Criminal Courts: Some Views and Concerns of an ICC Trial Judge," *Case Western Reserve Journal of International Law* 44(1–2) (2011): 475–496.

250 Jonathan Doak, *Victims' Rights, Human Rights and Criminal Justice: Reconceiving the Role of Third Parties* (Hart Publishing, 2008), 17.

251 E.g. ECtHR, *Bazorkina v. Russia*, App. No. 69481/01, 27 June 2006; ECtHR, *Jordan v. United Kingdom*, App. No. 24746/94, 4 May 2001; IACtHR, *Moiwana Community v. Suriname*, Preliminary Objections, Merits, Reparations and Costs, 15 June 2005.

252 Tyrone Kirchengast, "The Expressive Function of #VictimsLaw: Developing a Substantive and Enforceable Framework of Rights and Remedies in Response to Local Need and the Emerging Forms of Victimization," *Journal of Victimology and Victim Justice* 4(2) (2021): 103–118.

As with legal personhood, the category 'victim of crime' is socially and legally constructed.[253] Victims of crime, as with victims of human rights abuses, are generally understood as constituting humans or human-constructed entities.[254] In domestic contexts, it is frequently asserted that a victim is a 'person' that has been harmed by a crime.[255] These confines have been acknowledged and critiqued by various bodies of scholarship. Animal rights activists and scholars have advocated for animals' recognition as victims of crime,[256] arguing that recognition would enable 'the proper enforcement of current laws and the adequate representation and protection of animals.'[257] Scholars from green victimology,[258] earth jurisprudence,[259] eco-justice,[260] and environmental restorative justice[261] backgrounds have also considered the victimhood of 'natural objects.' Some have linked victim recognition to Rights of Nature movements,[262] discussed further in the next chapter. Others have explored the concept of equal redress for other-than-human species more broadly. Examples include Peter Singer's argument that the suffering of any being should be 'counted equally with the like suffering – in so far as rough comparisons can be made – of any other being'[263] and David Schlosberg's argument that ecological systems can experience injustice and conflicts requiring a response.[264]

253 Marian Duggan, *Revisiting the 'Ideal Victim': Developments in Critical Victimology* (Policy Press, 2018).
254 White, "Green Victimology"; Hall, "Environmental Harm and Environmental Victims."
255 Luis Chiesa, "Of Persons and the Criminal Law: (Second Tier) Personhood as a Prerequisite for Victimhood," *Pace Law Review* 28(4) (2008): 759–782.
256 Lacey Levitt, David Rosengard, and Jessica Rubin, *Animals as Crime Victims* (Elgar, 2024).
257 Andrew Ireland Moore, "Defining Animals as Crime Victims," *Journal of Animal Law* 1(1) (2005): 108. For a critique of this advocacy, see Justin Marceau, "Animal Rights and the Victimhood Trap," *Arizona Law Review* 63(3) (2021): 731–788.
258 Matthew Hall, *Victims of Environmental Harm: Rights, Recognition and Redress Under National and International Law* (Routledge, 2013).
259 Cormac Cullinan, *Wild Law: A Manifesto for Earth Justice* (Siber Ink and Green Books, 2003).
260 Rob White, "Environmental Victimology and Ecological Justice," *Crime, Victims and Policy: International Contexts, Local Experiences*, eds. Stuart Ross and Dean Wilson (Palgrave Macmillan, 2015).
261 Brian Preston, "The Use of Restorative Justice for Environmental Crime," *Criminal Law Journal* 35(3) (2011): 136–145.
262 David Boyd, *The Rights of Nature: A Legal Revolution that Could Save the World* (ECW Press, 2017).
263 Peter Singer, "All Animals are Equal," *Moral Reasoning*, ed. David. R. Morrow (OUP, 2018), 472. See also Heiner Bielefeldt, "Moving Beyond Anthropocentrism? Human Rights and the Charge of Speciesism," *Human Rights Quarterly* 43(3) (2021): 515–537.
264 David Schlosberg, "Justice, Ecological Integrity, and Climate Change," *Ethical Adaptation to Climate Change*, eds. Allen Thompson and Jeremy Bendik-Keymer (MIT Press, 2012).

In international criminal law, legal definitions of victimhood reflect the anthropocentric assumptions of the field as well as these broader understandings of victimhood. For example, the ICC's Rules of Procedure and Evidence (RPEs) define a victim as including a) natural persons who have suffered harm as a result of the commission of any crime within the jurisdiction of the Court; and b) organisations or institutions that have sustained direct harm to any of their property which is dedicated to religion, education, art, or science or charitable purposes, and to their historic monuments, hospitals, and other places and objects for humanitarian purposes.[265] The notion of 'personhood,' while not expressly defined in the ICC's legal documents, is exclusively tied to the human.[266] The Rome Statute's preamble, for example, refers to 'children, women and men' as victims, while the ICC's early jurisprudence makes clear that 'the ordinary meaning of the term "natural person" ... is ... in English, "a human being".'[267] The concept of 'legal person' has been understood in relatively broad terms, including:

> inter alia, nongovernmental, charitable and non-profit organisations, statutory bodies including government departments, public schools, hospitals, private educational institutes (primary and secondary schools or training colleges), companies, telecommunication firms, institutions that benefit members of the community (such as cooperative and building societies, or bodies that deal with micro finance), and other partnerships.[268]

However, the notion of 'personhood,' while not expressly defined in the ICC's legal documents, remains exclusively human-centric.[269]

Elsewhere, the Extraordinary Chambers in the Courts of Cambodia similarly defined a victim as a person or legal entity who suffered physical, psychological, or material harm as a direct consequence of the crimes under

265 ICC, Rules of Procedure and Evidence, Official Records of the Assembly of States Parties to the Rome Statute of the International Criminal Court, First session, New York, 3–10 September 2002, Rule 85: Definition of Victims.

266 Matthew Gillett, "Victim Participation and Reparations for Environmental Harm at the International Criminal Court," *Prosecuting Environmental Harm before the International Criminal Court*, ed. Matthew Gillett (CUP, 2022).

267 ICC, Decision on the Application for Participation in the Proceedings VPRS 1, VPRS 2, VPRS 3, VPRS 4, VPRS 5 and VPRS 6 (Public Redacted Version), Situation in the Democratic Republic of the Congo (ICC-01/04-101-tEN-Corr), Pre-Trial Chamber I, 16 January 2006, para 80.

268 ICC, Order for Reparations, *The Prosecutor v. Thomas Lubanga Dyilo*, (ICC-01/04-01/06-3129-AnxA) Appeals Chamber, 3 March 2015, para. 8.

269 Rachel Killean and Elizabeth Newton, "From Ecocide to Ecocentrism: Conceptualising Environmental Victimhood at the International Criminal Court," *International Review of Victimology* (2024), online access, https://doi.org/10.1177/026975802412694.

the Court's jurisdiction.'[270] At the Kosovo Specialist Chambers, a victim is 'a natural person who has suffered physical, material, or mental harm as a direct result of a crime alleged in an indictment confirmed by the Pre Trial Judge.'[271] Likewise, at the Special Tribunal for Lebanon, a victim was deemed to be 'a natural person who has suffered physical, material or mental harm as a direct result of an attack within the Tribunal's jurisdiction.'[272]

As Marina Lostal demonstrates through her analysis of the ICC's procedural framework, these definitions of victimhood are not framed in a way that creates space for expansion to the other-than-human.[273] As such, and mirroring the case in many domestic jurisdictions, environmental harms are considered 'victimless' in the absence of quantifiable damage to another rights-holding entity.[274] This has practical as well as symbolic implications. As noted above, several courts now enable victims to participate in their proceedings. Granting victims participatory rights can impact which crimes are recognised, enabling victims and their advocates to draw attention to harms that the investigators and prosecutors may have overlooked.[275] Moreover, increasingly, courts can make awards of reparations to victims harmed by the crimes prosecuted under their jurisdictions.[276] The anthropocentrism of 'victimhood' means that should harms against Nature be prosecuted using one of the existing core crimes, reparations would be limited to natural persons and specific organisations. As one of us has explored elsewhere, there are arguably avenues available that would enable reparations to have environmentally positive impacts while addressing the human suffering that results from atrocity crimes.[277] Yet the preclusion of other-than-human victimhood means that those positive impacts are entirely dependent on the

270 Victims Participation, ECCC Website, n.d., https://www.eccc.gov.kh/en/victims-support/participation#:~:text=Who%20does%20the%20ECCC%20consider,the%20jurisdiction%20of%20the%20ECCC.

271 Kosovo Specialist Chambers, Rules of Procedure and Evidence, adopted on 17 March 2017, revised on 29 May 2017, entered into force on 5 July 2017, KSC-BD-03/Rev2/2020/1, Rule 2.

272 Special Tribunal for Lebanon, Rules of Procedure and Evidence, adopted on 20 March 2009, STL-BD-2009-01-Rev.10, Rule 2.

273 Marina Lostal, "De-objectifying Animals: Could they Qualify as Victims before the International Criminal Court?" *Journal of International Criminal Justice* 19(3) (2021): 583–610.

274 Hamilton, *Environmental Crime and Restorative Justice.*

275 Rachel Killean and Luke Moffett, "Victim Legal Representation before the ICC and ECCC," *Journal of International Criminal Justice* 15(4) (2017): 713–740.

276 Christoph Sperfeldt, *Practices of Reparations in International Criminal Justice* (CUP, 2022).

277 Rachel Killean, "From Ecocide to Eco-sensitivity: 'Greening' Reparations at the International Criminal Court," *International Journal of Human Rights* 25(2) (2020): 323–347.

identification of a human victim, reasserting the anthropocentrism of the legal framework and arguably precluding a more holistic assessment of the harms caused by international crimes.[278]

3.5 Conclusion

This chapter has unpacked the concept of 'anthropocentric legalism' as it applies to transitional justice. It has done so by analysing the legal regimes that have played a central role in shaping transitional justice practice and discourse over the past 80 years, focusing in particular on human rights and international criminal law. We have demonstrated that both human rights and international criminal law have some capacity to recognise harms against Nature, and that there is extensive scholarship as well as some limited practice that seeks to expand this capacity. However, we have emphasised that power-knowledge dynamics have shaped the underlying framings of personhood, harm, and victimhood in both fields, and that these have in turn created blind spots in this regard. As we have explored, anthropocentrism is ingrained through the distinction between legal persons and objects, the prioritisation of certain (civil and political) human rights violations over others, the emphasis on particular understandings of atrocities as spectacular acts of violence against people and property, and the restriction of victimhood as a legal category to natural and legal persons. As a result, the natural world is reduced to a material resource or background context rather than a harmed entity deserving of redress. Taken together, these parameters of law reinforce prevailing 'human-centred visions of justice,'[279] depicting the natural world as something that surrounds us but remains separate from our social worlds.[280] Given the continued 'dominance of legalism' within mainstream transitional justice discourse and practice, these parameters arguably inhibit a more holistic, ecocentric, understanding of atrocity's impacts.

The following chapter builds on the themes explored here. We continue to examine the construction of victimhood and harm but turn our attention to the rise of 'eco-centric' legal movements around the world. As we will explore, these movements share a willingness to move (to varying extents) beyond the anthropocentric limitations contained within this chapter. Mirroring our focus above, we consider campaigns that seek to expand

278 Killean and Newton, "From Ecocide to Ecocentrism."

279 Michael Lynch et al., *Green Criminology and Green Theories of Justice* (Palgrave MacMillan, 2019), 129.

280 Daan van Uhm, "Atrocity Crimes and Ecocide: Interrelations between Armed Conflict, Violence and Harm to the Environment," *The Oxford Handbook on Atrocity Crimes*, eds. Barbora Holá et al. (OUP, 2022).

criminal law's protections to Nature, movements that seek to grant enhanced rights to natural entities, and legal developments that characterise Nature as a victim deserving of redress. We explore the possibilities that these initiatives might offer transitional justice. However, noting Audre Lorde's famous adage that the masters' tools will never dismantle the master's house, we retain some scepticism as to law's power to address law's own limitations.[281]

281 Audre Lorde, *The Master's Tools will Never Dismantle the Master's House* (Penguin Classics, 2018).

4

THE 'ECOCENTRIC TURN' IN LAW AND VICTIMHOOD

4.1 Introduction

Chapter 3 demonstrated how anthropocentric legalism has shaped transitional justice practice, contributing to a situation where harm to Nature is generally of consequence only insofar as it interferes with a relatively narrow range of human concerns. We drew attention to the ways in which this anthropocentrism manifests, through the distinction drawn between 'persons' and 'objects' in the law; the prioritisation of certain (civil and political) human rights violations over others (social, cultural, economic and environmental); the framing of atrocity crimes as spectacular incidences of violence perpetrated against people and their property; and the construction of victimhood as a legal category limited to humans and human organisations. Taken together, we argued that these legal parameters reinforce 'human-centred visions' of harm and justice and create a false dichotomy between humans and the natural world.[1]

In this chapter, we consider the emergence of challenges to this anthropocentrism. To do so, we set out a growing body of 'ecocentric' practice and scholarship in transitional justice and beyond. By 'ecocentric,' we mean approaches that recognise that 'nonhuman species and entire ecosystems exist not merely as elements in an anthropocentric utilitarian calculus or as extensions of human moral characteristics, but as entities with moral

1 Daan P. van Uhm, "Atrocity Crimes and Ecocide: Interrelations between Armed Conflict, Violence and Harm to the Environment," *The Oxford Handbook on Atrocity Crimes*, eds. Barbora Holá et al. (OUP 2022).

DOI: 10.4324/9781003264446-4

value in their own right.'[2] While often grounded in intrinsic reasoning, that is, an understanding that other-than-human entities are intrinsically entitled to moral consideration and duties of care,[3] ecocentric movements can also encompass instrumentalist reasoning; that is, enhanced rights for Nature will protect natural entities for future human generations. We do not consider instrumentalist reasoning to preclude a movement's framing as 'ecocentric'; to require ecocentric approaches to exclude all consideration of human interest would be to reinforce false distinctions between humans and Nature. Rather, by 'ecocentric,' we mean approaches that recognise the inherent moral value of nature and understand humanity as part of Nature rather than separate from it.[4]

The concept of legal 'ecocentrism' can be traced to Indigenous thought and Latin American neoconstitutionalist principles.[5] However, Nature-oriented legal initiatives have emerged and evolved in jurisdictions and communities around the world, and the turn towards 'ecocentrism' can now be witnessed in multiple legal settings, encompassing 'the interpretation of multilateral environmental agreements, domestic and case law, shifts in development agendas, and the struggles of diverse communities.'[6] Thus, ecocentrism is not one singular 'ontological turn' but rather a 'web of turns' scattered across numerous jurisdictions and contexts.[7] In practice, an ecocentric approach has been described as requiring 'either one or a combination of conceptions of the rights of Nature (both as subject with rights or object worthy of protection) and duties to Nature (its intrinsic worth which therefore imposes a moral obligation and duty of care).'[8] Building on our discussion in Chapter 3, we might therefore understand ecocentric approaches as framing Nature as a *protectee*, a *rights-bearer*, and/or a *victim* (encompassing elements of both).

In this chapter, we examine three examples of ecocentric approaches, before considering the possibility of a nascent 'ecocentric' turn in law and

2 Sarah Krakoff, "Mountains Without Handrails – Wilderness Without Cellphones," *Harvard Environmental Law Review* 27 (2003): 462.

3 Helen Kopnina et al. "Anthropocentrism: More than Just a Misunderstood Problem," *Journal of Agricultural and Environmental Ethics* 31 (2018): 109–127.

4 Kopnina et al. "Anthropocentrism." Rob White, "Ecocentrism and Criminal Justice," *Theoretical Criminology* 22(3) (2018): 342–362.

5 Laura Ordóñez-Vargas et al., "An Econcentric Turn in the Transitional Restorative Justice Process in Colombia," *International Journal of Transitional Justice* 17(1) (2023): 110.

6 Kristina Lyons, "'Nature' and Territories as Victims: Decolonizing Colombia's Transitional Justice Process," *American Anthropologist* 125(1) (2023): 73.

7 Joshua C. Gellers, "An Inconvenient Reflection on Human Rights: Comments on Choi-Fitzpatrick's article, 'Disruption and Emergence,'" *Journal of Human Rights* 23(3) (2024): 314–319, discussing: Austin Choi-Fitzpatrick, "Disruption and Emergence: How to Think about Human Rights Futures," *Journal of Human Rights* 23(1) (2023): 105–123.

8 White, "Ecocentrism."

transitional justice. The chapter proceeds as follows. In Part 2, we analyse the campaign to criminalise ecocide as an atrocity crime in both international and national law. This campaign is an example of attempts to frame Nature as an entity whose interests are protected by criminal law (a protectee). In Part 3, we track the evolution of Rights of Nature movements around the world, highlighting some of the ways in which Nature has been conceptualised as a rights-bearing entity. In Part 4, we turn to a specific transitional justice context, taking a closer look at the recognition of territories as victims of the armed conflict in Colombia. Understanding law as a constructive force,[9] we explore how these developments are creating new legal subjectivities, expanding notions of protectees, rights-bearers, and victims to encompass the other-than-human.

Having outlined these various developments, in Part 5 we analyse the possible benefits and limitations of a turn towards 'ecocentric legalism.' In particular, we argue that these ecocentric initiatives, while in their early stages, offer precedents that might inform more expansive understandings of 'victimhood' in transitional justice. We consider whether such a move might enhance the field's ability to respond to harms against Nature, arguing that the recognition of other-than-human victimhood could facilitate the platforming of a wider range of perspectives regarding the nature of victimhood and harm. Moreover, we argue that recognition could potentially lead to more holistic forms of justice and repair. However, we acknowledge the challenges of this approach, including those around representation, the possibility of new victim hierarchies and conflicts arising, and the limitations of addressing the problems of law through more law. Nonetheless, we conclude in Part 6 by arguing that an expansion of victimhood offers a way to think differently, and more inclusively, about what justice entails.

4.2 Nature as a 'Protectee' of Atrocity Crimes

In this part, we focus on calls to criminalise 'ecocide' as an example of a campaign that centres criminal law as a means of offering greater protection to other-than-human natural entities. As we will illustrate, this campaign initially emerged from the recognition of the environmental costs of conflict and as such has ongoing possible implications for transitional justice.

The concept of 'ecocide' first emerged as a term to describe the environmental destruction wrought during the Vietnam War, in particular the deforestation and related harms caused by the use of the herbicide Agent

9 See Michel Foucault, *Discipline and Punish* (Penguin Books, 1977) discussed in Chapter 3.

Orange.[10] As such, early attempts to define ecocide tended to frame it as a crime perpetrated during conflict.[11] This was reflected in international discussions about the possibility of introducing a new crime. In the 1980s, the UN Sub-Commission on Prevention of Discrimination and Protection of Minorities debated adding 'ecocide' to genocide's definition, ultimately rejecting this idea due to ecocide's perceived links with armed conflict.[12] The following decade, the International Law Commission (ILC) considered adding an environmental war crime and an environmental crime against humanity to their Draft Code of Offences Against the Peace and Security of Mankind.[13] However, as explored in Chapter 3, by the time international crimes were codified in the Rome Statute of the permanent International Criminal Court (ICC) in 1998, only the environmental war crime (Article 8(2)(b)(iv)) remained.[14] Nonetheless, the ILC's work on the Draft Code may have influenced early attempts to criminalise ecocide at a domestic level.[15] For example, criminal codes introduced in Vietnam and in several former Union of Soviet Socialist Republics (USSR) states in the 1990s and early 2000s include ecocide on their list of 'crimes against peace.'[16]

For the most part, twenty-first-century campaigns to criminalise ecocide internationally and/or domestically have moved away from a sole focus on conflict to crimes perpetrated in peace. A popular definition has been that of the Stop Ecocide Foundation's Independent Expert Panel, which foregoes any reference to war or peace, instead describing ecocide as 'unlawful or wanton acts committed with knowledge that there is a substantial likelihood of severe and either widespread or long-term damage to the environment being caused by those acts.'[17] However, scholarship has continued to interrogate

10 Richard A. Falk, "Environmental Warfare and Ecocide – Facts, Appraisal, and Proposals," *Security Dialogue* 4(1) (1973): 80–96.

11 Eliana Cusato, "From Ecocide to Voluntary Remediation Projects: Legal Responses to 'Environmental Warfare' in Vietnam and the Spectre of Colonialism," *Melbourne Journal of International Law* 19(2) (2018): 494–520; Falk, "Environmental Warfare."

12 UNESCOR, Revised and Updated Report on the Question of the Prevention and Punishment of the Crime of Genocide, Human Rights Sub-Commission on the Prevention of Discrimination and Protection of Minorities, 38th Sess., UN Doc. E/CN.4/Sub.2/1985/6.

13 International Law Commission, "Report of the International Law Commission on the work of its forty-third session (29 April–19 July 1991) (A/46/10)," *Yearbook of the International Law Commission* 2(2)(1991).

14 Anja Gauger et al., *Ecocide is the Missing 5th Crime Against Peace* (Human Rights Consortium, School of Advanced Study, University of London, 2012).

15 Gauger et al., *Ecocide is the Missing 5th Crime.*

16 Rachel Killean and Damien Short, *Scoping a Domestic Legal Framework for Ecocide in Scotland,* (Environmental Rights Centre for Scotland, 2024) https://www.ercs.scot/wp/wp-content/uploads/2024/04/Scoping-a-Domestic-Legal-Framework-for-Ecocide-in-Scotland_April24_online.pdf

17 Independent Expert Panel for the Legal Definition of Ecocide, *Commentary and Core Text*, Stop Ecocide, June 2021, www.stopecocide.earth/legal-definition.

the relationship between ecocide and atrocity. A particular contribution has been the theorisation of the 'genocide–ecocide nexus,'[18] an analytical tool used to describe the ways that environmental destruction and genocidal processes can facilitate, reinforce, and intertwine with one another. The genocide–ecocide nexus has been informed by Indigenous scholars, activists, and leaders, who have spoken of the central importance of Nature to their identities and drawn attention to the ways in which extraction harms their people.[19] Indeed, the concept arguably only seems relatively 'new' in academia due to the historic exclusion of Indigenous ontologies from academic scholarship.[20] The genocide–ecocide nexus has been used to describe the harms experienced by Indigenous communities in settler colonial states,[21] as well as harms perpetrated in South American[22] and African states.[23] Some have pointed to the nexus to argue for more ecocentric understandings of genocide, arguing that for Indigenous peoples, 'ecocide is an act of genocide because it literally eliminates, disfigures, and maims the other-than human members' of their communities.[24] Others have drawn on their analysis to advocate for ecocide's criminalisation, arguing that a new crime is needed to explicitly condemn this form of violence.[25]

A new international crime is yet to materialise, and changes to the ICC's Rome Statute require a two-thirds majority vote by its Assembly of

18 Michael J. Lynch et al., "Green Criminology and State–Corporate Crime: The Ecocide-Genocide Nexus with Examples from Nigeria," *Journal of Genocide Research* 23(2) (2021): 236–257; Damien Short and Martin Crook, eds. *The Genocide–Ecocide Nexus* (Routledge, 2022).

19 David R. Goyes et al., "Genocide and Ecocide in Four Colombian Indigenous Comunities: The Erosion of a Way of Life and Memory," *British Journal of Criminology*, 61(4)(2021): 965–984; Leane Makey et al., "(Un)Heard Voices of Ecosystem Degradation: Stories from the Nexus of Settler-Colonialism and Slow Violence," *Sustainability* 14(22)(2022): 14672.

20 Kelsey John, "Animal Colonialism: Illustrating Intersections between Animal Studies and Settler Colonial Studies through Diné Horsemanship," *Humanalia: A Journal of Human/Animal Interface Studies* 10(2) (2019): 44.

21 Jobb Dixon Arnold, "Bare Nature and the Genocide–Ecocide Nexus – The Conditions of General Threat and the Hope of Cultural Adaptation: The Case of Canada's Tar Sands," *Space and Culture* 21(1) (2018): 18–32; Donald A. Grinde and Bruce E. Johansen, "Ecocide of Native America: Environmental Destruction of Indian Lands and Peoples" (Clear Light Publishers, 1995); Jennifer Huseman and Damien Short, "'A Slow Industrial Genocide': Tar Sands and the Indigenous People of Northern Alberta," *International Journal of Human Rights* 16(1) (2012): 216–237.

22 Crook and Short, *Genocide-Ecocide*.

23 Lynch et al., "Green Criminology"; Kenneth Omeje, *High stakes and Stakeholders: Oil Conflict and Security in Nigeria* (Routledge, 2006).

24 Lauren J. Eichler, "Ecocide is Genocide: Decolonizing the Definition of Genocide," *Genocide Studies and Prevention: An International Journal* 14(2) (2020), 104–121.

25 Polly Higgins et al., "Protecting the Planet: A Proposal for a Law of Ecocide," *Crime, Law and Social Change* 59, Special issue (2023): 251–266.

State Parties,[26] making amendments a significant political challenge.[27] Yet, developments are afoot. At an international level, 2024 saw Vanuatu, Fiji, and Samoa submit a formal proposal to add the crime of ecocide to the Rome Statute.[28] At the same time, instances of domestic criminalisation are increasing, with more attention being paid to the importance of domestic accountability.[29] Moreover, the 2022 Russian invasion of Ukraine renewed interest in ecocide's role in a transitional justice context. Ukraine has investigated several alleged acts of ecocide since Russia's annexation of territory and subsequent invasion,[30] including the emission of chemicals in occupied land,[31] the decision of Russian-backed armed groups to flood an industrial nuclear explosion site,[32] attacks on the Zaporizhia nuclear power plant in Enerhodar in 2022,[33] and the destruction of the Kakhovka Dam in 2023.[34] In 2023, Maksym Popov, special advisor for environmental crimes to the Ukrainian Prosecutor General, identified additional potential ecocides[35] and expressed hopes that domestic prosecutions would be accompanied by investigations by the ICC.[36] Although there is no equivalent domestic legislation applicable to Israel/Palestine, it is notable that the language of ecocide has

26 UN General Assembly, *Rome Statute of the International Criminal Court* (last amended 2010), ISBN No. 92-9227-227-6, 17 July 1998, Article 121.
27 Shirleen Chin, "Lessons Learned from the Adoption of the Crime of Aggression: Ecocide to Charter its Own Path," *An International Crime of Ecocide: New Perspectives*, The Promise Institute for Human Rights, 2023, https://ecocidelaw.com/symposium/
28 Fiona Harvey, "Pacific Islands Submit Court Proposal for Recognition of Ecocide as a Crime" The Guardian, 10 September 2024, https://www.theguardian.com/law/article/2024/sep/09/pacific-islands-ecocide-crime-icc-proposal
29 Killean and Short, *Scoping*.
30 Russia has also investigated acts of ecocide allegedly perpetrated by Ukraine in occupied Crimea, but as these have dubious legal legitimacy considering Russia's illegal annexation, they are not included in our analysis.
31 Borys Babin and Oleksii Plotnikov, "Prosecution of Ecocide as a Weapon in Armed Conflict: Reflections on Crimea," *ICD Brief 29*, (October 2022); Lulia Mendel, "4,000 Children Flee Pollution Disaster on Ukraine-Crimea Border," *New York Times*, 14 September 2018, https://www.nytimes.com/2018/09/14/world/europe/crimea-ukraine-pollution.html.
32 Illia Ponomarenko, "Ecological Disaster Feared in Donbas as Russian-led Forces Inundate Infamous 'Nuclear Pit'," *Kyiv Post*, 13 April 2018, https://archive.kyivpost.com/ukraine-politics/ecological-disaster-feared-donbas-russian-led-forces-inundate-infamous-nuclear-pit.html. This investigation has reportedly since been downgraded to a less strict environmental offence (violation of environmental safety rules: Babin and Plotnikov, "Prosecution of Ecocide").
33 "Prosecutor General: Investigation into Ecocide in Connection with Attack of Russian troops on Zaporizhia NPP launched," *InterFax*, 4 March 2022, https://interfax.com.ua/news/general/807113.html
34 Yulia Kesaieva, "Ukraine Launches 'Ecocide' and War Crimes Probe into Nova Kakhovka Dam Incident," *CNN*, 7 June 2023, https://edition.cnn.com/europe/live-news/russia-ukraine-war-news-06-07 23/h_36848cd5abb76e0ddd522cd78f4f5f43 1/12
35 Kesaieva, "Ukraine Launches 'Ecocide'."
36 Kesaieva, "Ukraine Launches 'Ecocide'."

also been used to describe the environmental impact of settler colonialism in Palestine,[37] as well as the more recent destruction perpetrated by Israel in Gaza following the 7 October 2023 Hamas attacks.[38] Outside conflict contexts, France has taken its first steps towards prosecuting its own domestic criminal law of ecocide, focusing on an extreme incidence of land pollution.[39] It may be that we see more use of domestic ecocide provisions in future; since 2024, European Union states have been required to introduce crimes 'comparable to ecocide.'[40] However, considering the high gravity threshold of most definitions and the challenges surrounding proving causation, it is likely that prosecutions will remain relatively rare.

Advocates for a new crime of ecocide tend to frame its benefits in ecocentric terms, highlighting the recognition of Nature as a protectee of criminal law. For example, Philippe Sands, one of the Stop Ecocide Panel's co-chairs, identified the Panel's goal as creating a crime that would 'make the protection of the environment an end in itself.'[41] In academic scholarship, Ammar Bustami and Marie-Christine Hecken have described the criminalisation of ecocide as signalling a potential 'shift away from international criminal law's focus on humanitarian protection' through the introduction of 'genuine environmental protection.'[42] As Merle Kooijman observes, these arguments

37 Dina Abu Jaber, "Settler Colonialism and Ecocide: Case Study of Al-Khader, Palestine," *Settler Colonial Studies* 9(1) (2019): 135–154; Shourideh C. Molavi and Eyal Weizman, *Environmental Warfare in Gaza: Colonial Violence and New Landscapes of Resistance* (Pluto Press, 2024).

38 Kaamil Ahmed et al., "Ecocide in Gaza: Does Scale of Environmental Destruction Amount to a War Crime?" *The Guardian*, 29 March 2024, https://www.theguardian.com/environment/2024/mar/29/gaza-israel-palestinian-war-ecocide-environmental-destruction-pollution-rome-statute-war-crimes-aoe; Manal Shqair et al., "How Arab Eco-Normalisation of Israel Covers Up Its Crimes," *Al Jazeera*, 12 December 2023, https://www.aljazeera.com/opinions/2023/12/12/how-arab-eco-normalisation-of-israel-covers-up-its-crimes

39 Guilluame Lamy, "Ecocide à Grézieu-la-Varenne: l'ancien maire, candidat àl'élection du bâtonnat du barreau Lyon," *Lyon Capitale*, 13 November 2022, https://www.lyoncapitale.fr/actualite/ecocide-a-grezieu-la-varenne-l-ancien-maire-candidat-a-l-election-du-batonnat-du-barreau-lyon

40 European Parliament Legislative Resolution of 27 February 2024 on the Proposal for a Directive of the European Parliament and of the Council on the Protection of the Environment Through Criminal Law and Replacing Directive 2008/99/EC (COM (2021)0851 – C9-0466/2021 – 2021/0422(COD)).

41 Mia Stewart, "'The Revolution Does not Happen Overnight': Philippe Sands on Ecocide and its Links to Nuremberg," Al Jazeera, 29 June 2021, https://liberties.aljazeera.com/en/the-revolution-does-not-happen-overnight-aj-speaks-to-phillipe-sands-on-ecocide-and-a-life-in-environmental-lawyering/

42 Ammar Bustami and Marie-Christine Hecken, "Perspectives for a New International Crime against the Environment: International Criminal Responsibility for Environmental Degradation under the Rome Statute," *Goettingen Journal of International Law* 11(1) (2021): 145–190.

suggest that 'great importance is being attached to ecocide as an ecocentric core crime to redeem the anthropocentric tendencies in ICL.'[43]

Proponents have further argued that ecocide's criminalisation could assist in 'transform[ing] our understanding of nature from property to an equal partner with humans' by embedding nature's status as a *subject* in our legal institutions.[44] For example, Mark Gray, the former head of the Environmental Law Unit for the Australian Department of Foreign Affairs and Trade, has argued that 'the natural world's beauty, complexity and fragility suggest that it and its components in their own right have interests worthy of protection.'[45] He suggests that as the concept of ecocide gains recognition, 'acknowledgment of non-human rights, such as that of other species to exist, will broaden standing.'[46]

British barrister Polly Higgins also envisioned a framing of victimhood that extended beyond natural and legal persons. In 2011, she organised a Mock Trial to test the workability of her own draft ecocide law, incorporating a post-trial restorative justice conference in which other-than-human casualties – birds and the Earth itself – were recognised and represented as victims. Commenting on the process, solicitor and mediator Liz Rivers asserted that the experiment was proof of concept, demonstrating that 'it is possible to give voice to diverse and other-than-human elements of the system … in a meaningful way.'[47] In fact, real-life examples of environmental restorative justice practices are already emerging, with natural entities benefiting from reparative measures even in the absence of legal recognition of other-than-human victimhood.[48] It is notable that these examples arise in settler colonial contexts, where the emergence of restorative justice practices has been facilitated by non-Western legal norms,[49] such as 'Indigenous

43 Merle Kooijman, "From Anthropos to Oikos in International Criminal Law: A Critical-Theoretical Exploration of Ecocide as an 'Ecocentric'Amendment to the Rome Statute," *Netherlands Yearbook of International Law 2021: A Greener International Law – International Legal Responses to the Global Environmental Crisis*, eds. Daniëlla Dam-de Jong and Fabian Amtenbrink (T.M.C. Asser Press, 2023): 120.

44 Femke Wijdekop, "Against Ecocide: Legal Protection for Earth," *Great Transition Initiative*, August 2016, https://www.greattransition.org/images/Against-Ecocide.pdf.

45 Mark Allan Gray, "The International Crime of Ecocide," *California Western International Law Journal* 26(2) (1996): 215–272.

46 Gray, "The International Crime of Ecocide," 270.

47 Liz Rivers, "Shareholder Return: A Nuremberg Defence?" *Environmental Law & Management* 24(1) (2012): 17–19.

48 E.g. Auckland District Court, *Auckland City Council v. 12 Carlton Gore Road Ltd and Mary-Anne Catherine McKay Lowe*, McElrea DCJ, 11 April 2005; Auckland District Court, *Rodney District Council v. Sam Wong and Josh Topou*, JP Doogue DCJ, 28 February 2005.

49 Gema Varona, "Why an Atmosphere of Transhumanism Undermines Green Restorative Justice Concepts and Tenets," *International Journal of Restorative Justice* 4(1) (2021): 53.

and Aboriginal traditions of conflict resolution,'[50] enabling more varied 'cultural, emotional and spiritual values to be expressed.'[51] We return to environmental restorative justice in Part 5.

From these examples, it seems apparent that proponents of ecocide are linking Nature as a protectee with other framings, such as Nature as a rights-bearer and Nature as a victim and beneficiary of reparative measures. Parts 3 and 4 explore each of these in turn.

4.3 Nature as a Rights-Bearer

A growing transnational network of Rights of Nature movements has gained momentum over the last 20 years.[52] The growth of these movements can be attributed to a range of drivers. For one, the idea that humans and Nature exist in reciprocal relationships of obligation resonates with long-standing Indigenous ontologies and governance structures.[53] Another is the growth of theoretical approaches such as 'eco-feminism,'[54] 'deep ecology,'[55] 'earth jurisprudence,'[56] and 'wild law'[57] in Western legal theory, which share a belief in humans' dependency on and inextricable connection to Nature, as well the conviction that law should reflect this reality.[58] Both intrinsic and instrumental drivers are visible here: the law should reflect the reality of

50 Femke Wijdekop, "Restorative Justice Responses to Environmental Harm," *Amsterdam*: An IUCN Report (2019): 79–80, http://files.harmonywithnatureun.org/uploads/upload864.pdf.

51 Femke Wijdekop and Anneke van Hoek, "Green Criminology and Restorative Justice: Natural Allies?" *Environmental Justice Restoring the Future*, eds. Emanuela Biffi and Brunilda Pali (European Forum for Restorative Justice, 2019), 22.

52 Elizabeth Newton and Rachel Killean, "Global Rights of Nature Movements," *The Palgrave Handbook of Environmental Policy and Law*, eds. Robert C. Brears and Jade Lindley (Palgrave Macmillan, 2024); Alex Putzer et al., "Putting the Rights of Nature on the Map. A Quantitative Analysis of Rights of Nature Initiatives Across the World," *Journal of Maps* 18(1) (2022): 89–96.

53 Sequoia L Butler, "'I Am the River, the River Is Me': How Environmental Personhood Can Protect Tibal Food Systems," *Wisconsin International Law Journal* 38(1) (2020): 79–107; Erin O'Donnell et al., "Stop Burying the Lede: The Essential Role of Indigenous Law(s) in Creating Rights of Nature," *Transnational Environmental Law* 9(3) (2020): 403–427.

54 Discussed in Chapter 2. See also Verônica Maria Bezerra Guimarães, "Ecofeminism, Rights of Nature and Climate Justice: Relational Webs and Planetary Restoration," *Simbiótica. Revista Eletrônica*, 10(3) (2023): 15–30.

55 George Sessions, "The Deep Ecology Movement: A Review," *Environmental Review* 11(2) (1987): 105–125.

56 Judith E. Koons, "What is Earth Jurisprudence? Key Principles to Transform Law for the Health of the Planet," *Penn State Environmental Law Review* 18 (2009): 47–68.

57 Peter Burdon, "Wild Law: The Philosophy of Earth Jurisprudence," *Alternative Law Journal* 35(2) (2010): 62–65.

58 A leading Latin American thinker in this space was Godofredo Stutzin, who argued in favour of rights of nature in the context of environmental advocacy in Chile. See Godofredo

Nature's moral standing (intrinsic),[59] and doing so will address limitations in existing environmental law (instrumental).[60] In practice, Rights of Nature movements encompass a range of initiatives at community, national, and international levels,[61] and although not limited to these contexts, have been able to thrive the most when nurtured by Indigenous activism.[62]

Over time, the movements have branched into two 'rather distinct forms' of scholarship and practice:[63] the Nature's Rights model and the Legal Personhood model.[64] The former is premised on Nature's right to exist and flourish, leading to the granting of specific rights. An example of this approach is Ecuador, where Nature, or *Pacha Mama*, 'has the right to integral respect for its existence and for the maintenance and regeneration of its life cycles, structure, functions and evolutionary processes.'[65] The latter grants legal personhood to specific natural entities, presenting a profound challenge to the dominant framings of personhood discussed throughout Chapter 3.[66] Such initiatives draw from arguments that 'the inherent interests of natural objects ought to be protected through legal actions by the objects themselves.'[67] In several jurisdictions, particular natural entities have been recognised as legal persons endowed with associated capacities and rights.[68]

Perhaps the most well-known example of the Legal Personhood model is in Aotearoa, New Zealand, where the *Te Urewera Act 2014* extends legal personality to the forest, lakes, and rivers that make up the Te Urewera

Stutzin, "Un Imperativo Ecológico: Reconocer los Derechos de la Naturaleza," *Ambiente y Desarrollo* 1(1) (1984): 97–114.

59 Stutzin, "Un Imperativo Ecológico."

60 Christopher D. Stone, "Should Trees Have Standing? Towards Legal Rights for Natural Objects," *Southern California Law Review* 45 (1972): 450–501.

61 Oliver A. Houck, "Noah's Second Voyage," *Tulane Environmental Law Journal* 31(1) (2017): 1–50.

62 Anne Haluska, "Restorative Justice and the Rights of Nature: Using Indigenous Legal Traditions to Influence Cultural Change and Promote Environmental Protection," *Mitchell Hamline Law Review* 49(1) (2023): 92–125.

63 O'Donnell et al., "Stop Burying."

64 Craig M. Kauffman and Pamela L. Martin, *The Politics of Rights of Nature: Strategies for Building a More Sustainable Future* (MIT Press, 2021).

65 Constitution of Ecuador, Republic of Ecuador, entered into force 20 October 2008, Article 7.

66 Erin L. O'Donnell and Julia Talbot-Jones, "Creating Legal Rights for Rivers: Lessons from Australia, New Zealand, and India," *Ecology and Society* 23(1) (2018): 7.

67 Rob White, "Green Victimology and Non-Human Victims," *International Review of Victimology* 24(2) (2018): 241.

68 See Cristy Clark et al., "Can You Hear the Rivers Sing? Personhood, Ontology, and the Nitty-Gritty of Governance," *Ecology Law Quarterly* 45(4) (2019): 803.

area (formerly a national park) and appoints trustees to protect the area.[69] Similarly, the *Te Awa Tupua (Whanganui River Claims Settlement) Act 2017* confers full legal personality on the Whanganui River system, with all the rights, powers, duties, and liabilities of a legal person. The river is recognised as 'an indivisible and living whole,' incorporating 'all its physical and metaphysical elements.'[70]

Notably for our purposes, this is also an example of how Rights of Nature can be linked to the goals and approaches of transitional justice. The extension of legal personhood to natural entities is part of efforts to respond to Māori claims to restitution for breaches by the Crown of the Treaty of Waitangi, by which New Zealand was annexed to the British Crown in 1840.[71] The 2014 Act states its shared intention as being to contribute to resolving the grief of the Tūhoe iwi (tribe or nation),[72] while the 2017 Act also contains the government's acknowledgement of and apology to the Whanganui iwi.[73] The Acts are undoubtedly political compromises, using legal pluralism to draw from Crown and Māori law to create new collaborative legal frameworks.[74]

Although not explicitly framed as transitional justice by the New Zealand Crown, these initiatives can be understood as part of attempts to address legacies of colonial harms and pursue national reconciliation.[75] Importantly, the initiatives tie together redress for historic wrongs and safeguarding natural entities and ecosystems in future.[76] While they have been critiqued

69 Christopher Rodgers, "A New Approach to Protecting Ecosystems: The Te Awa Tupua (Whanganui River Claims Settlement) Act 2017," *Environmental Law Review* 19(4) (2017): 266–279.

70 O'Donnell and Talbot-Jones, "Creating Legal Rights," 7; Rodgers, "A New Approach."

71 Toni Collins and Shea Esterling, "Fluid Personality: Indigenous Rights and the Te Awa Tupua (Whanganui River Claims Settlement) Act 2017 in Aotearoa New Zealand," *Melbourne Journal of International Law* 20 (2019): 197–220.

72 Te Urewera Act 2014, Public Act 2014 No 51, Section 3.

73 Te Awa Tupua (Whanganui River Claims Settlement) Act 2017, Public Act 2017 No 7, Section 70.

74 Miriama Cribb et al., "Beyond Legal Personhood for the Whanganui River: Collaboration and Pluralism in Implementing the Te Awa Tupua Act," *International Journal of Human Rights* (2024): 1–24.

75 Richard Boast, "The Waitangi Tribunal and Transitional Justice," *Human Rights Research Journal* 4.

(2006): 1–13; Jacinta Ruru, "Can Recognition of Māori Law Achieve Greater National Unity?" *The Big Questions. What Is New Zealand's Future?* (Penguin, 2018); Augustine S.J Park, "Settler Colonialism, Decolonization and Radicalizing Transitional Justice," *International Journal of Transitional Justice* 14(2) (2020): 260–279.

76 Andrew Geddis and Jacinta Ruru, "Places as Persons: Creating a New Framework for Māori–Crown Relations" *The Frontiers of Public Law*, ed. Jason Varuhas (Hart Publishing, 2019).

for not going far enough to recognise Indigenous claims,[77] they have also been praised for promoting 'human well-being through a more ecologically sustainable approach.'[78] As such, they offer one interesting, if imperfect, example of how Rights of Nature can be encompassed in, and advance, transitional justice endeavours.

Colombia provides a further example of expanding legal personhood in a transitional context. In 2016, the Constitutional Court recognised the Atrato River as a rights holder with 'rights that imply [the river's] protection, conservation, maintenance and ... restoration.'[79] This case has been noted for its important recognition of the connections between the protection of natural entities and the cultural, spiritual, and physical well-being of the communities that rely upon those entities.[80] This connection has been acknowledged by the Court through the framework of 'biocultural rights.'[81] Since then, Colombian judges have recognised rivers, national parks, wetlands, and the Colombian Amazon rainforest as rights-holders, and have acknowledged the 'biocultural' relationship between communities and natural entities.[82]

These judgments sit outside Colombia's formal transitional justice framework (discussed below). However, some of the decisions draw clear links between present harms and the legacy of armed conflict.[83] In the Atrato River case, the Constitutional Court noted how illegal mining in the river basin was 'generating worrying socio-environmental conflicts that materialize in an indiscriminate struggle for the control of territories and natural

77 Brad Coombes, "Nature's Rights as Indigenous rights? Mis/recognition through Personhood for Te Urewera," *Space, Population Society* 1(2) (2020) Although see Cribb et al., "Beyond Legal Personhood," for an analysis as to how subsequent practice has evolved in ways that recognise Indigenous law.

78 Craig M. Kauffman, "Managing People for the Benefit of the Land: Practising Earth Jurisprudence in Te Urewera, New Zealand," *ISLE: Interdisciplinary Studies in Literature and Environment* 27(3) (2020): 578–595.

79 Isabella Ariza-Buitrago and Luisa Gómez-Betancur, "Nature in Focus: The Invisibility and Re-Emergence of Rivers, Land and Animals in Colombia's Transitional Justice System," *International Journal of Transitional Justice* 17(1) (2023): 86, citing Colombian Constitutional Court, Judgement T-622/16, 10 November 2016 (the 'Atrato River case').

80 Elizabeth Macpherson et al., "Constitutional Law, Ecosystems and Indigenous Peoples in Colombia: Biocultural Rights and Legal Subjects," *Transnational Environmental Law* 9(3) (2020): 521–540.

81 Macpherson et al., "Constitutional Law, Ecosystems and Indigenous Peoples in Colombia." See also Craig M. Kauffman and Pamela L. Martin, "How Courts Are Developing River Rights Jurisprudence: Comparing Guardianship in New Zealand, Colombia, and India," *Vermont Journal of Environmental Law* 20(3) (2019): 260–289.

82 Ariza-Buitrago and Gómez-Betancur, "Nature", 86; Ximena Sierra Camargo, "The Ecocentric Turn of Environmental Justice in Colombia," *King's Law Journal* 30(2) (2019): 224–233.

83 Ariza Buitrago and Gómez Betancur, "Nature," 86.

resources,'[84] and causing harm to the natural environment as well as the cultural heritage of the Colombian people. The recognition of the river as a rights holder, represented by a Guardians' Council comprised of the local population, was seen as a way to protect the ecosystem from further harm.[85] Drawing closer links between Rights of Nature and transitional justice in Colombia has been flagged as a 'promising path to fill in the gaps of transitional justice mechanisms,'[86] as well as a way of 'decolonising' the transitional justice process by incorporating greater recognition of Indigenous perspectives.[87]

In terms of real-life benefits of Rights of Nature, it seems results have been mixed. For example, commenting four years after the Atrato River decision, Phillip Wesche observed that implementation of its public policy order faced substantial barriers due to weak governance and the continued reliance on environmentally harmful extractive practices.[88] However, Wesche also observed that the communities in the Atrato region had gained a stronger voice through the Guardians' Council, and that the River's recognition as a legal subject had 'resulted in some important advances with respect to the formulation of environmental policies.'[89] In Ecuador, subsequent judicial decisions have continued to flesh out the contours of *Pacha Mama's* rights, guided by the Andean Indigenous concept of *sumak kawsay* (*Buen Vivir* or 'good life', discussed in Chapter 6), meaning to live in harmony with Nature.[90] Important developments have included the repeated linking of Rights of Nature with those of Indigenous communities, and practical examples of environmental protections such as the annulment of mining concessions.[91]

These examples suggest that Rights of Nature, whether through the Nature's Rights or Legal Personhood model, offers some promise as a way of recognising harm perpetrated against Nature (including the human communities who rely on protected ecosystems), and of pursuing more environmentally sustainable futures. As such, it is a concept of potential value to transitional justice. However, the Colombian example demonstrates the limits of Rights of Nature as a means of bringing about meaningful change

84 Ariza-Buitrago and Gómez-Betancur, "Nature," 86, citing Atrato River case at 9.35.
85 Ariza-Buitrago and Gómez-Betancur, "Nature," 86.
86 Ariza-Buitrago and Gómez-Betancur, "Nature," 86.
87 Lyons, "Nature."
88 Philipp Wesche, "Rights of Nature in Practice: A Case Study on the Impacts of the Colombian Atrato River Decision," *Journal of Environmental Law* 33(3) (2021): 531–555.
89 Wesche, "Rights of Nature in Practice," 540.
90 Craig M. Kauffman and Pamela Martin, "How Ecuador's Courts are Giving Form and Force to Rights of Nature Norms," *Transnational Environmental Law* 12(2) (2023): 366–395.
91 Kauffman and Martin, "How Ecuador's Courts are Giving Form."

in the absence of effective governance. We further explore the challenges of justice in the absence of structural change in Chapter 5.

4.4 Nature as a Victim

In this section, we return to Colombia to consider the first (and to date only) explicit legal recognition of Nature as a victim of armed conflict. Following a 2016 peace agreement made between the national government and the Revolutionary Armed Forces of Colombia – People's Army (FARC-EP), Colombia established a range of transitional justice measures to address the harmful legacies of its almost six decades of conflict, including judicial and non-judicial mechanisms.[92] These included the *Jurisdicción Especial para la Paz* (JEP), a court mandated with administering justice in response to conflict-related crimes committed between 1 January 1990 and 1 December 2016. This institution encompasses both retributive and restorative justice concepts.[93] On the one hand, it is mandated to judge and punish large-scale patterns of criminality and rights violations.[94] On the other hand, it seeks 'truth through consciousness, reconciliation, healing, and harmonization between victims and accused that allows for the strengthening of the community fabric, as well as the harmonization of the territory.'[95] The latter becomes particularly interesting when considering the notion of other-than-human victimhood.

Colombia has adopted a novel approach to who and what is considered a victim of its conflict.[96] The 2011 Victims' Law for Indigenous peoples (Decree-Law 4633), which sets out victims' rights to truth, justice, reparation, and non-repetition, acknowledges territory as a living entity that 'suffers harm when violated or desecrated by the internal armed conflict.'[97] Providing 'an important starting point in the consideration of the long-lasting effects of war,'[98] this recognition of territories as victims has been

92 Ordóñez-Vargas et al., "Econcentric," 113.

93 Jermey Julian Sarkin and Ines Pereira Lopes, "Reaching for Both Justice and Peace in Colombia: Understanding the Special Jurisdiction for Peace's Mixed Approach (Using Both Retributive and Restorative Justice) to Deal with International Crimes," *Contemporary Justice Review* 26(2) (2023): 123–144.

94 Lyons, "Nature."

95 General Regulation 2018, Article 44, cited in Belkis Izquierdo and Lieselotte Viaene, "Decolonizing Transitional Justice from Indigenous Territories," *Peace in Progress* 34 (June 2018): 5.

96 Alexandra Huneeus and Pablo Rueda Saiz, "Territory as a Victim of Armed Conflict," *International Journal of Transitional Justice* 15(1) (2021): 210–229.

97 Colombian Congress, Decree-Law 4633, Comprehensive Reparation for Indigenous People, December 2011, Article 45.

98 Daniel Ruiz-Serna, "Transitional Justice beyond the Human: Indigenous Cosmopolitics and the Realm of Law in Colombia," *Cultural Politics* 19(1) (2023): 58.

enhanced by five resolutions passed by the JEP since 2019. These resolutions recognise the Katsa Su, the Cxhab Wala Kile, and the Esperera Euja (territories of the Awá, Nasa, and Eperara Siapidara Indigenous people) and the territories of the Black communities of Tumaco, Ricaurte and Barbacoas, and the Cauca River as victims of the conflict.[99]

This recognition followed campaigns and demands from Indigenous, Afro-descendent, and *campesino* organisations and communities – including significant interventions by Indigenous women[100] – who argued that their territories should be recognised as living beings and the subject of rights.[101] It also exists alongside the Rights of Nature initiatives discussed above.[102] The JEP Judge Belkis Izquierdo Torres[103] has acknowledged the importance of Rights of Nature initiatives 'in terms of their extension of legal personhood to what were only recently understood to be objects, resources, or property.' She has expressed hope that they might 'buttress her chamber's attempts to broaden public perception and juridical concepts of victimization.'[104] As such, the work of the JEP should be situated in this broader 'ecocentric' legal turn in Colombia.

The recognition of *territories* as victims is somewhat different from recognising 'Nature' as a rights-holder.[105] Reflecting the worldviews of the impacted communities, 'territories' are understood as encompassing human beings, natural entities such as rivers, the relationships between humans and between humans and nature, and *Pacha Mama* as her own 'living being.'[106] In this sense, they are broader than a natural entity such as a mountain, river, or forest, which would not necessarily encompass the spiritual or cultural elements of territory.[107] The centrality of human relationality to 'territory'

99 Huneeus and Rueda Sáiz, "Territory"; Ordóñez-Vargas et al., "Econcentric."

100 On the frequent overlooking of women's advocacy, see Lejandrina Pastor and Angela Santamaria, "Experiences of Spiritual Advocacy for Land and Territorial Itineraries for the Defense of Wiwa Women's Rights in Postconflict Colombia," *International Journal of Transitional Justice* 15(1) (2021): 86–107; Angela Santamaría et al., "Decolonial Sketches and Intercultural Approaches to Truth: Corporeal Experiences and Testimonies of Indigenous Women in Colombia," *International Journal of Transitional Justice* 14(1) (2020): 56–79.

101 See e.g., JEP, Auto SRVBIT 079/19, Case 002, 12 November 2019. See also Lyons, "Nature"; Ruiz-Serna, "Transitional."

102 See the Atrato River case.

103 An Indigenous judge in the JEP's Chamber for the Recognition of Truth, Responsibility and the Determination of Facts and Conduct and former Indigenous Auxiliary Judge of the High Council of the Judiciary in Colombia.

104 Lyons, "Nature."

105 Lyons, "Nature."

106 Huneeus and Rueda Sáiz, "Territory," 221; Ariza-Buitrago and Gómez-Betancus, "Nature."

107 Lyons, "Nature."

is reflected, for example, in the Indigenous and Decolonial feminist concept of the *Cuerpo-Territorio* (body-territory), used to describe the deep connection between women's bodily autonomy and territorial integrity.[108] As Daniel Ruiz-Serna notes: 'territory is not something that is complete in and of itself, nor is it separate from or prior to the values, practices, and relations that render places and lives meaningful.'[109] Notably, the territories are also considered agentive: 'legal subjects with rights to justice, truth and reparation, and the right to participate in each stage of the legal process.'[110]

These territories are now subjects of Colombia's 2016 peace treaty regime.[111] There are currently three 'territorial cases' before the JEP, meaning the judges will be tasked with exploring what retributive and restorative justice looks like in the context of other-than-human victims. The JEP's resolutions have been praised for 'breaking new ground'[112] in their legal recognition of the fact that conflicts victimise ecosystems, other-than-human entities, and the spiritual relationships that can exist between them.[113] They can also at least in part be understood as part of a broader ecocentric shift in Colombian jurisprudence, characterised by a willingness to recognise natural entities as rights holders.[114]

4.5 Towards Other-than-Human Victimhood?

While at varying stages of development and implementation, the 'ecocentric' legal initiatives we have outlined here 'converge in attempting to provide a legal basis for enhanced protection of the environment in its own right.'[115] In particular, they expand understandings of environmental protection, disrupt ideas that only humans and manmade entities can hold rights or deserve justice, and offer potential pathways to environmental redress. As such, they offer a challenge to the anthropocentrism of the legal frameworks that have traditionally dominated the transitional justice field. Attending to

108 See e.g. Diana Garcés, "When the Forest Does Not Sing Anymore. Cuerpoterritorio Approach of Amazonian Indigenous Women to the Concepts of Conflict and Violence," *Blanquerna School of Communication and International Relations* 51 (2021): 69–83.

109 Ruiz-Serna, "Transitional," 60.

110 Lyons, "Nature"; Huneeus and Rueda Sáiz, "Territory," 210.

111 Daniel Ruiz Serna, "Territory as Victim. Political Ontology and the Laws for Victims of Indigenous and Afrodescendant Communities in Colombia," *Revista Colombian Journal of Anthropology* 53(2) (2017): 85–113.

112 Alexandra Huneeus, "Territory as a Victim of Colombia's War," *Blog of the European Journal of International Law: Talk!* May 7, 2020, www.ejiltalk.org/territory-as-a-victim-of-colombias-war/#:~:text=In%20two%20recent%20resolutions%2C%20Colombia's,Colombia's%2050%2Dyear%20civil%20war

113 Lyons, "Nature."

114 Camargo Ximena, "The Ecocentric Turn."

115 White, "Ecocentrism," 244.

these initiatives, we argue, may offer ideas that might better equip transitional justice to recognise and respond to harms against the natural world.

A particularly noteworthy point of connection between the initiatives outlined above is their understanding that Nature can experience harm and should have some entitlement to redress in such circumstances. Drawing on these initiatives, in this section we argue that the legal expansion of victimhood to include other-than-human natural entities has the potential to beneficially inform transitional justice theory and practice by platforming a broader range of perspectives on what justice might entail, and by offering more holistic forms of recognition and repair. The appropriate approach to transitional justice will depend on the specificities of the context (including the nature of the harm, the communities involved, the political situation, and the applicable legal culture). For that reason, we keep our observations relatively general, rather that advocating for a specific legal framework or mechanism. We are also aware that there are limits to what law can achieve and are cautious of implying that recognition of victimhood is any guarantee of justice – the expansive literature critiquing victims' rights and access to justice in transitional justice contexts demonstrates that this is not the case.[116] We therefore also highlight some potential difficulties of other-than-human victim recognition and 'ecocentric legalism,' in particular the challenges of representation and the risk of new victim hierarchies and conflicts.

4.5.1 Ecocentric Recognition and Decolonising Justice

Our first argument is that the expansion of victimhood could have expressive value, expanding (or recovering) our understanding of violence as something which threatens entire social and ecological systems.[117] Proponents of ecocentric approaches to law and justice have cited this expressive potential. For example, Darryl Robinson has argued that recognising Nature as a protectee of international criminal law could play an important 'social expressive function … reframing massive environmental wrongdoing … as one of

116 See e.g., Mijke De Waardt and Sanne Weber, "Beyond Victims' Mere Presence: An Cmpirical Analysis of Victim Participation in Transitional Justice in Colombia," *Journal of Human Rights Practice* 11(1) (2019): 209–228; Rachel Killean, "Constructing Victimhood at the Khmer Rouge Tribunal: Visibility, Selectivity and Participation," *International Review of Victimology* 24(3) (2018): 273–296; Kieran McEvoy and Kirsten McConnachie, "Victims and Transitional Justice: Voice, Agency and Blame," *Social & Legal Studies* 22(4) (2013): 489–513; Simon Robins, "Failing Victims: The Limits of Transitional Justice in Addressing the Needs of Victims of Violations," *Human Rights & International Legal Discourse* 11 (2017): 41–58.

117 Ordóñez-Vargas et al., "Econcentric," 110; Huneeus and Rueda Sáiz, "Territory."

the gravest crimes.'[118] In their discussion on multispecies justice, Danielle Celermajer and Anne O'Brien argue that expanding transitional justice to encompass the other-than-human can have 'educational dimensions aimed at informing communities about wrongs that have been explicitly concealed.'[119] As we have explored, law can both reflect and shape societal values,[120] and the inclusion of other-than-human victimhood may open the door to greater recognition of the moral value of natural entities.[121] Furthermore, an ecocentric approach arguably enables greater awareness not only of harms against Nature, but also of associated cultural and spiritual losses experienced by human beings and, importantly, of the harm done to relationships as well as individual entities.[122]

The inclusion of other-than-human victims could also be an important mark of respect to the experiences, beliefs, and laws of victimised human communities. As Part 4 illustrated, Indigenous advocacy, philosophies, and laws have played a central role in the recognition of territories as victims in Colombia and the development of Rights of Nature movements around the world. While ecocide does not share the same foundational connections to Indigenous law, the genocide–ecocide nexus has been used as a framework for understanding harms experienced by Indigenous peoples,[123] linked to attempts to 'decolonise' the law on atrocity crimes,[124] and used as an advocacy tool by Indigenous activists.[125] Indeed, 'ecocentrism' can be

118 Darryl Robinson, "Ecocide – Puzzles and Possibilities," *Journal of International Criminal Justice* 20(2) (2022): 313–347.

119 Danielle Celermajer et al., "Justice through a Multispecies Lens," *Contemporary Political Theory* 19 (2020): 475–512.

120 Holly Doremus, "The Rhetoric and Reality of Nature Protection: Toward a New Discourse," *Washington and Lee Law Review* 57(1) (2000): 11–74.

121 Gary Steiner and Marc Lucht, "Law and Nature: Human, Non-human, and Ecosystem Rights," In *Speciesism in Biology and Culture*, eds. Brian Swartz and Brent D. Mishler (Springer, 2022).

122 Lyons, "Nature."

123 Martin Crook et al., "Ecocide, Genocide, Capitalism and Colonialism: Consequences for Indigenous Peoples and Glocal Ecosystems Environments," *Theoretical Criminology* 22(3) (2018): 298–317; Michael J. Lynch, "Green Criminology and Native Peoples: The Treadmill of Production and the Killing of Indigenous Environmental Activists," *Theoretical Criminology* 22(3) (2018): 318–341.

124 Eichler, "Ecocide"; Tim Lindgren, "Ecocide, Genocide and the Disregard of Alternative Life-Systems," *International Journal of Human Rights* 22(4)(2018): 525–549.

125 See e.g. Katie Surma, "Indigenous Leaders and Human Rights Groups in Brazil Want Bolsonaro Prosecuted for Crimes Against Humanity," *Inside Climate News*, June 24, 2021, https://insideclimatenews.org/news/24062021/bolsonaro-amazon-brazil-deforestaiton-climate-change-indigenous-rights-ecocide/; Libby Brooks, "Indigenous Women Speak out at Cop26 Rally: 'Femicide is Linked to Ecocide'" *The Guardian*, 11 November 2021, https://www.theguardian.com/environment/2021/nov/10/indigenous-women-speak-out-at-cop26-rally-femicide-is-linked-to-ecocide.

understood as having roots in, and being informed by, decolonial thought.[126] If approached with appropriate care, avoiding extractive practices or simplistic, romantic notions of Indigenous justice mechanisms,[127] it is possible to understand a more expansive recognition of victimhood as offering one response to increasing calls for a 'decolonisation' of transitional justice.[128]

Bringing other-than-human entities under the 'empire of law' can raise its own concerns. As Andrew Woolford and Wanda Hounslaw note, doing so brings the risk that Nature 'will become more subject to the power' of law than 'protected by it.'[129] Carol Smart has made similar arguments in the context of feminist strategy: law's claim to truth and unity continues to have the 'power to disqualify alternative discourse,'[130] and law can neutralise alternative approaches to justice even as it purports to absorb them. For example, Indigenous scholars have raised concerns that the incorporation of restorative justice principles into settler legal systems can be ultimately disempowering to Indigenous communities.[131] This concern forms part of broader debates as to whether and how Indigenous peoples should engage with settler law at all.[132] Similar concerns arise in transitional justice contexts, where, as Daniel Ruiz-Serna has argued, there is a risk that states will reduce Indigenous perspectives to social or cultural constructions rather than 'reality.'[133] Transitional justice's mechanisms have been critiqued for being institutionalised, technical, and physically distanced from the communities they purportedly serve.[134] A failure to take community perspectives seriously can result in a 'deep disjunction' between communities and

126 Ordóñez-Vargas et al., "Econcentric."

127 Indigenous feminist scholars, for example, have urged caution regarding Indigenous rituals that might reinforce harmful or oppressive cultures, see e.g., Joyace Green, ed., *Making Space for Indigenous Feminism* (Fernwood Publishing, 2017).

128 Jennifer Balint et al., "Rethinking Transitional Justice, Redressing Indigenous Harm: A New Conceptual Approach," *International Journal of Transitional Justice* 8(2), (2014) 194–216; Hugo Van der Merwe and M. Brinton Lykes, "Racism and Transitional Justice," *International Journal of Transitional Justice* 14(3) (2021): 415–422; Park, "Settler Colonialism."

129 Andrew Woolford and Wanda Hounslow, "Symbiotic Victimisation and Destruction: Law and Human/Other-than-Human Relationality in Genocide," in *Genocide and Victimology*, ed. Yarin Eski (Routledge, 2020).

130 Carol Smart, *Feminism and the Power of Law (*Taylor and Francis, 1989), 5.

131 Juan Marcellus Tauri, "Restorative Justice as a Colonial Project in the Disempowerment of Indigenous Peoples," in *Routledge International Handbook of Restorative Justice*, ed. Theo Gavrielides (Routledge 2018).

132 See e.g. Asch Michael, ed. *Resurgence and Reconciliation: Indigenous–Settler Relations and Earth Teachings* (University of Toronto Press, 2018).

133 Ruiz-Serna, "Transitional," 71.

134 Rosemary Nagy, "Transitional Justice as Global Project: Critical Reflections," *Third World Quarterly* 29(2) (2008): 275–289.

justice processes[135] and responses to harm 'which are at times detrimentally abstracted from lived realities.'[136]

Too narrow a focus on 'ecocentric' legal solutions also risks simply replicating the challenges of marginalisation currently encountered by human victims. There is a wide-ranging literature critiquing whether the growth of victims' rights has delivered on its promise of justice for victims, or whether legal responses to harm continue to reinforce what Nils Christie termed the 'theft of the conflict' from those most directly impacted by it.[137] The continued faith in legal processes, written law, and the presence of legal professionals to determine punishment and redress is – as we have explored – born of the dominance of Western legalism.[138] For a more expansive notion of victimhood to offer real decolonial potential, it may require an accompanying radical rethinking of what 'justice' beyond the human really means.[139] As Alexandra Huneeus and Pablo Rueda Sáiz caution, decolonisation should not be limited to recognition, but should involve substantive work towards repairing 'broken relations not only between humans, but also between humans and non-humans.'[140]

Centring the voices of impacted communities and making space for diverse knowledges and understandings of the natural world would be crucial in this regard. Considering the critiques we have explored throughout this book so far, it is clear to us that neither one-size-fits-all approaches nor those solely shaped from the top down are ethically defensible.[141] To that end, a legal pluralism approach to transitional justice would ideally move beyond dialogue or consultation, recognising Indigenous laws and/or other local legal cultures as legitimate legal sources capable of informing transitional justice practice.[142] Such an approach arguably offers pathways towards new legal institutional arrangements that challenge anthropocentrism and Western Nature/culture dualism.[143]

135 Kora Andrieu, "Confronting the Dictatorial Past in Tunisia," *Human Rights Quarterly* 38(2) (2016): 261–293.
136 Nagy, "Transitional," 276.
137 Nils Christie, "Conflicts as Property," *The British Journal of Criminology* 17(1) (1977): 1–15.
138 Dana Zartner, "The Culture of Law: Understanding the Influence of Legal Tradition on Transitional Justice in Post-Conflict Societies," *Indiana International & Comparative Law Review* 22(2) (2012): 297–316.
139 Celermajer et al., "Justice."
140 Huneeus and Rueda Sáiz, "Territory"; Ruiz-Serna, "Transitional."
141 See also Kirsten Anker, *Declarations of Interdependence: A Legal Pluralist Approach to Indigenous Rights* (Routledge, 2014).
142 See Ordóñez-Vargas et al., "Econcentric"; Zartner, "Culture."
143 Elizabeth Macpherson and Felipe Clavijo Ospina, "The Pluralism of River Rights in Aotearoa, New Zealand and Colombia," *Journal of Water Law* 25(6) (2018): 283–293; Macpherson et al., "Constitutional"; O'Donnell et al., "Stop Burying," 403.

Going further, recognition of ecocentric victimhood invites considerations of the perspectives of the other-than-human members of victimised communities. As Danielle Celermajer and others have explored, introducing the other-than-human 'onto the scene of justice' immediately raises questions around the meaning of justice, and around communication and representation.[144] Given the primacy of human language as the 'medium for claims-making ... the possibility of beings other than humans representing themselves seems precluded.'[145] In the absence of radical new forms of interspecies translation, there are risks of misinterpreting these interests through the process of assimilating them via human forms of understanding.[146]

The question therefore arises: who should be given the role of articulating the harms and needs of the other-than-human victim?[147] Indigenous peoples are often at the forefront of advocating for Nature and are sometimes assumed to be 'uniquely positioned' to act as spokespersons for other-than-human victims.[148] The examples highlighted above suggest that foregrounding Indigenous understandings of Nature, harm, and justice[149] may facilitate 'a field of interlocution and transaction ... in which different communities can describe the effects that go beyond human beings.'[150] However, while we have emphasised the connections between the two, not all conflicts that lead to harms against Nature involve Indigenous peoples.[151] Moreover, it is important that Indigenous peoples are not expected to act as 'convenience representatives'[152] for other-than-human victims. As evidenced by the growth of Rights of Nature movements across multiple jurisdictions, membership in an Indigenous group is not a prerequisite for recognising other-than-human victimhood;[153] the possibility of experiencing harm as a result of harms against Nature transcends specific social groupings or ethnic affiliations.[154] Careful and collaborative engagement with relevant groups would be required to avoid the adoption of simplistic, orientalising narratives about

144 Celermajer et al., "Justice."
145 Celermajer et al., "Justice."
146 Astrida Neimanis, "No Representation without Colonisation? (Or, Nature Represents Itself)," *Somatechnics*, 5(2) (2015): 135–153.
147 Gómez-Betancur, "Rights of Nature," 77; Izquierdo and Viaene, "Decolonizing."
148 Wijdekop, "Restorative Justice," 45.
149 Mark McMillan and Sophie Rigney, "Race, Reconciliation and Justice in Australia," *Ethnic and Racial Studies* 41(4) (2018): 759–777.
150 Ruiz Serna, "Territory," 103.
151 Although it is also the case that Indigenous peoples' harms during conflict are overlooked. See e.g. Prabindra Shakya, "Indigenous Peoples: Expanding the Realm of Justice," *Peace Insight*, 26 March 2014, https://www.peaceinsight.org/en/articles/indigenous-peoples-expanding-realm-justice/?location=&theme=human-rights.
152 Mark Hamilton, *Environmental Crime and Restorative Justice* (Palgrave, 2021), 217.
153 Haluska, "Restorative Justice," 96.
154 Ruiz-Serna, "Transitional," 73.

the connection between Indigenous groups and Nature.[155] Other 'friends of a natural object'[156] could be found in environmental organisations, human rights organisations, community groups, scientists, forest-dwellers, local landowners, and/or local governmental bodies, if appropriate.[157]

None of this is straightforward. Scientists might represent harm in very different ways from landowners, for example, and there may be significant multiplicity of perspectives, both in relation to how other-than-human victims should be represented and in terms of how the harm should be understood. Individuals within groups may also have different and potentially conflicting interpretations of the harms experienced; for example, some may perceive environmental destruction's impacts as spiritual, while others may perceive the harm solely in terms of plants and animals in the physical world.[158] As noted above, the concept of 'territory' may mean very different things from 'Nature,' and yet both terms might be used to refer to the same area or ecosystem. Representing this nuance, and translating it into meaningful forms of truth, justice, and repair, is likely to be a key challenge for any transitional justice process that seeks to address complex environmental and cultural harms.[159] However, as we argue in the following subsection, there are potential material benefits of engaging with this challenge.

4.5.2 Facilitating Holistic Repair

Our second argument is that the inclusion of other-than-human victims might facilitate or inform more holistic forms of justice in the aftermath of mass violence. Expanding notions of victimhood would not only provide recognition and representation to a greater range of subjects but also expand notions of victims' rights to other-than-humans, such as the right to access justice through accountability mechanisms, the right to information about what happened, and the right to remedies.[160] Granting other-than-human entities (or, more accurately, their human guardians or representatives) access to accountability and information could be important, enabling those guardians or representatives to pursue more holistic official narratives about the harm perpetrated by mass violence. However, it is not straightforward to transpose human concepts such as 'truth' and 'accountability' onto

155 White, "Ecocentrism"; Macpherson et al., "Constitutional," 521.
156 Stone, "Should Trees," 464.
157 Haluska, "Restorative Justice," 123.
158 Lyons, "Nature."
159 Lyons, "Nature."
160 UN General Assembly, *Basic Principles and Guidelines on the Right to a Remedy and Reparation for Victims of Gross Violations of International Human Rights Law and Serious Violations of International Humanitarian Law*, UNGA Res 60/147.

the concept of justice for other-than-human beings.[161] While we argue that the lack of human reflexivity and interiority does not preclude other-than-human entities from moral consideration, it is clear that certain aspects of justice, such as access to information, are to some extent premised on the assumption that there is a victim who can consciously experience injustice and desire truth.

In other cases, the expansion of justice appears somewhat more intuitive, such as the right to remedy.[162] Sentient and non-sentient life alike can flourish, and the interruption of the capacity to flourish can be understood as an injustice requiring reparation.[163] Taken together, the recognition and representation discussed above could enable advocacy for reparative measures in which the human is no longer 'the exclusive subject of reparation.'[164] Reparation for the destruction of Nature is far from a new concept,[165] and established jurisprudence and practice can be found in international, human rights, and specialist environmental courts and tribunals.[166] However, it is somewhat more rare in the context of criminal trials, and transitional justice's focus on judicial mechanisms could pose some barriers to the pursuit of environmental repair. Investigating and gathering evidence regarding the destruction of Nature would require complex forms of scientific and technical expertise,[167] and the slow and uncertain effects of human action may cause considerable complexities around determining causal links in a system based on individual criminal liability.[168] Furthermore, a focus on individual

161 Gema Varona, "Restorative Pathways after Mass Environmental Victimisation: Walking in the Landscapes of Past Ecocides," *Oñati Socio-Legal Series* 10(3) (2020): 664–685.

162 See e.g. Luke Moffett, *Reparations and War: Finding Balance in Repairing the Past* (OUP, 2022); Christoph Sperfeldt, *Practices of Reparations in International Criminal Justice* (CUP, 2022).

163 Katy Fulfer, "The Capabilities Approach to Justice and the Flourishing of Nonsentient Life," *Ethics and the Environment* 18(1) (2013): 19–42.

164 Ruiz Serna, "Territory," 104.

165 A. Dwight Baldwin et al., eds., *Beyond Preservation: Restoring and Inventing Landscapes* (University of Minnesota Press, 1994).

166 Rachel Killean, "Imagining Future Reparations for Environmental Destruction," *Futures of International Criminal Justice*, eds. Emma Palmer et al. (Routledge, 2022); Lingjie Kong and Yuqing Zhao, "Remedying the Environmental Impacts of War: Challenges and Perspectives for Full Reparation," *International Review of the Red Cross* 105 (924) (2023) 1441–1462.

167 Nabil Ahmed, "Proof of Ecocide: Towards a Forensic Practice for the Proposed International Crime Against the Environment," *Archaeological and Environmental Forensic Science* 1(2) (2017): 139–146; Gillett Matthew, *Prosecuting Environmental Harm before the International Criminal Court* (Leiden University 2018).

168 Eliana Cusato, *The Ecology of War and Peace* (CUP, 2021), 123–127; Pauline Martini et al., "Mass Deforestation as a Crime against Humanity?" *International & Comparative Law Quarterly* 72(3) (2023): 1013–1046.

criminal liability could obscure forms of 'systemic responsibility'[169] that might be particularly salient to harms against Nature, and – depending on the mechanism's approach to liability – limit the resources available for funding reparative projects. This reflects broad critiques that have been made of 'corrective justice,' that is, reparations that respond to specific harms while failing to account for deeper underlying inequalities.[170] We return to this theme in Chapter 5.

It is also the case that some of the forms of reparation are more suitable than others in the aftermath of Nature's destruction.[171] In transitional justice, reparations can encompass forms of restitution, compensation, rehabilitation, and guarantee of non-recurrence.[172] Environmental restitution or rehabilitation[173] may be impossible. The injury may have 'tipped an element of the environment into a new system state, like cumulative impacts of pollution on a river or the atmosphere.'[174] Some have even referred to the notion of 'authentic' environmental restoration as a human 'fantasy' due to the complexity around determining a 'natural' base line to which an ecosystem could be restored.[175] Environmental restoration is highly technical and may require scientific research and experimentation as scientific knowledge of all the variables involved in maintaining healthy ecosystems continues to evolve. Considering the potential scale of atrocity-related environmental destruction, restoration may also be expensive, posing challenges in resource-depleted contexts. These challenges must be understood in the context of mass violence, where reparations are already faced with the paradox of repairing the irreparable, and often have a symbolic quality.[176]

169 Zinaida Miller, "Effects of Invisibility: In Search of the 'Economic' in Transitional Justice," *International Journal of Transitional Justice* 2(3)(2008): 275.

170 Simeon Gready, "The Case for Transformative Reparations: In Pursuit of Structural Socio-Economic Reform in Post-Conflict Societies," *Journal of Intervention and Statebuilding* 16(2) (2022): 182–201.

171 Rachel Killean, "From Ecocide to Eco-sensitivity: 'Greening' Reparations at the International Criminal Court," *International Journal of Human Rights* 25(2) (2021): 323–347.

172 Killean, "From Ecocide to Eco-sensitivity."

173 Although rehabilitation and restitution can mean different things in transitional justice, they are interchangeable in the literature on environmental repair and so are taken to mean the same thing here. See e.g. Mike Mentis, "Environmental Rehabilitation of Damaged Land," *Forest Ecosystems* 7(19)(2020): 7–19.

174 Hamilton, *Environmental*, 162.

175 Celermajer,et al., "Justice."

176 Rachel Killean and Luke Moffett, "What's in a Name? 'Reparations' at the Extraordinary Chambers in the Courts of Cambodia," *Melbourne Journal of International Law* 21(1) (2020): 115.

Compensation also has limitations from an other-than-human justice perspective. Examples of compensation for environmental harms can certainly be found. These include the practice of the Environmental Panel of the UN Compensation Commission,[177] the International Court of Justice,[178] and, most notably, the Inter-American Court of Human Rights (ICtHR),[179] where Indigenous communities have sought compensation for the loss of culturally significant land and natural resources. In this context, the IACtHR has previously ordered compensation for material damage caused by 'despoiled subsistence resources' and 'destruction' of forests, as well as the immaterial damage caused to a people's spiritual connection with their territory.[180] While undeniably a valued aspect of repair to those communities, a focus on compensation alone risks offering little to the other-than-human victims of the harm, unless steps are taken to place compensatory payments into environmental trusts or appropriate organisations.[181]

Yet, other approaches to reparations are more encouraging, particularly those that move beyond the challenges of corrective justice and consider future transformation. Guarantees of non-repetition, for example, are designed to prevent the reoccurrence of crimes by addressing the structural causes of violations. Such measures might be usefully adapted to other-than-human victims, including in the absence of criminal convictions.[182] More commonly found in the context of human rights violations and state-led reparations than in criminal contexts, guarantees of non-recurrence can encompass training for law enforcement, promoting mechanisms for conflict resolution, and reforming laws that enabled the violations to take place.[183] Such measures offer the potential to entrench greater respect for Nature and

177 UN Compensation Commission, Governing Council, Report and Recommendations made by the Panel of Commissioners concerning the fifth instalment of 'F4' claims (S/AC.26/2005/10), 4 April 2005, para 80.

178 Diane Desierto, "Environmental Damages, Environmental Reparations, and the Right to a Healthy Environment: The ICJ Compensation Judgment in *Costa Rica v Nicaragua* and the IACtHR Advisory Opinion on Marine Protection for the Greater Caribbean," *Blog of the European Journal of International Law: Talk!* 14 February 2018, https://www.ejiltalk.org/environmental-damages-environmental-reparations-and-the-right-to-a-healthy-environment-the-icj-compensation-judgment-in-costa-rica-v-nicaragua-and-the-iacthr-advisory-opinion-on-marine-protection/.

179 Thomas M. Antkowiak, "A Dark Side of Virtue: The Inter-American Court and Reparations for Indigenous Peoples," *Duke Journal of Comparative and International Law* 25(1) (2014): 1–80.

180 Inter-American Court of Human Rights, *Case of the Saramaka People v. Suriname*, Preliminary Objections, Merits, Reparations, Costs, Series C, No. 172, 28 November 2007.

181 There is precedent for this in domestic case law; see e.g. Hamilton, *Environmental*.

182 Nita Shala, *Guarantees of Non-Repetition in International Human Rights Law and Transitional Justice: Building Peace after Conflict* (Routledge, 2024).

183 UN Basic Principles.

to reduce future harms. Danielle Celemajer and Anne O'Brien have used the example of soil to explore such potentials, arguing that changes to agriculture policies might present one such forward-looking initiative.[184] We return to the possibilities of pursuing structural change through transitional justice in the following chapter.

Practice concerning reparations for natural entities in a transitional justice context is likely to evolve as the Colombian territories' cases progress.[185] While neither the JEP resolutions nor the 2016 Peace Accord prescribe specific modes of repair for other-than-human victims, the concept of the territory as victim is likely to influence the JEP tribunal's approach to determining appropriate reparative measures.[186] This was already envisioned to some extent in the Colombian Peace Agreement's chapter on victims' rights,[187] which established that certain ex-combatants, as part of their contributions to 'restorative sanctions,'[188] may participate in programs to clear regions of anti-personnel mines or explosive remnants, to substitute illicit crops, and to repair environmental damage through reforestation.[189]

Colombia is arguably the first example of environmental restorative justice in a transitional justice context. Environmental restorative justice can be understood as an approach that incorporates 1) an orientation towards healing, inclusive of nature; 2) participation of those with power to take responsibility and those who have suffered harm, inclusive of other-than-humans; 3) the use of storytelling and dialogue; 4) the identification of harm, victims, and those responsible; and 5) accountability in the pursuit of relational justice. It can occur in conjunction with other forms of adjudication, but it need not do so.

The JEP promotes practices which resonate with these restorative justice concepts, such as seeking 'truth through consciousness, reconciliation, healing, and harmonization between victims and accused that allows for the strengthening of the community fabric, as well as the harmonization of the territory.'[190] Spiritual healing is identified as 'part of the integral reparation of the territory' in the 2011 Victims Law,[191] and the Investigation and

184 Celermajer et al., "Justice."
185 Ariza-Buitrago and Gómez-Betancur, "Nature," 87.
186 Ariza-Buitrago and Gómez-Betancur, "Nature," 79.
187 Final Agreement to End the Armed Conflict and Build a Stable and Lasting Peace, Colomombia-FARC-EP, 24 November 2016, Chapter V, Comprehensive System for Truth, Justice, Reparations and Non-Recurrence.
188 Ordóñez-Vargas et al., "Econcentric," 116.
189 Luisa Gómez-Betancur, "The Rights of Nature in the Colombian Amazon: Examining Challenges and Opportunities in a Transitional Justice Setting," *UCLA Journal of International Law and Foreign Affairs* 25(1) (2020): 41–84.
190 General Regulation 2018, Article 44.
191 Decree-Law 4633 of 2011, Article 8.

Prosecution Unit of the JEP has also indicated that it is seeking environmental reparation mechanisms and guarantees of non-recurrence in the context of its investigations in the south of the country.[192] As Ruiz-Serna explores, there are possibilities for symbiotic reparations here. For example, reforestation is on the one hand an important measure to re-establish biodiversity, but on the other could be a necessary step in re-establishing communities' relationships with spiritual beings that may have been lost during the conflict.[193] As this example demonstrates, the recognition of other-than-human victims could draw attention to the relationship between restoring natural environments and repairing the harm experienced by human individuals and communities.[194] Turning towards environmental restorative justice may therefore offer valuable prospects, moving away from the idea of restitution towards the repair of relationships[195] and relational healing.[196] We explore the benefits of the environmentally restorative justice approach for navigating potential conflicts between victimised groups in the follow subsection.

4.5.3 New Hierarchies of Victimhood

One significant potential challenge regarding the introduction of other-than-human victimhood centres around the concept of 'victim hierarchies.' Challenges of victim hierarchy and contestation are not new to transitional justice;[197] hierarchisation can be multilayered and reflect distinctions of class, ideology, gender, and the nature of the harm suffered. This process can leave some victims 'outside the reach' of transitional justice or lead to conflict between different 'categories' of victim.[198] The introduction of other-than-human victims could bring additional tensions in this regard.[199] Environmental harm can be 'victim-full,'[200] a reality exacerbated

192 Gómez-Betancur, "Rights of Nature," 79.
193 Ruiz-Serna, "Transitional," 66.
194 Merryl Lawry-White, "Victims of Environmental Harm During Conflict: The Potential for 'Justice'," *Environmental Protection and Transitions from Conflict to Peace*, eds. Carsten Stahn et al. (OUP, 2017).
195 Wendy Lambourne, "Power Struggles and the Politics of Knowledge Production in the Burundian Transitional Justice Process," *Knowledge for Peace: Transitional Justice and the Politics of Knowledge in Theory and Practice*, eds. Briony Jones and Ulrike Lühe (Cheltenham: Edward Elgar Publishing Ltd., 2021), 114.
196 Miranda Forsyth et al., "A Future Agenda for Environmental Restorative Justice?" *International Journal of Restorative Justice* 4(1) (2021): 17–40.
197 Kevin Hearty, "Victims of Human Rights Abuses in Transitional Justice: Hierarchies, Perpetrators and the Struggle for Peace," *International Journal of Human Rights*, 22(7) (2018): 888–909; Tshepo Madlingozi, "On Transitional Justice Entrepreneurs and the Production of Victims," *Journal of Human Rights Practice* 2(2) (2010): 208–228.
198 Hearty, "Victims."
199 White, "Green Victimology."
200 Wijdekop, "Restorative Justice," 31.

by the severe and widespread nature of atrocity-related violence. Examples of tensions between victim groups are already evident in Colombia. The connections made between territories and specific ethnic groups has been critiqued for excluding others who have also experienced harm as a result of crimes perpetrated against the territory.[201] This has led to some *campesino* groups calling for territories to be understood in more intercultural terms.[202]

There is also scope for tensions between the needs of other-than-human victims and humans/groups. These tensions have been noted in the Rights of Nature discourse, where scholars have observed that the proliferation of rights is not always a path to a widening sense of community.[203] Indigenous scholar Virginia Marshall has argued that such an approach can sever or disrupt Indigenous governance of territory, overlooking the importance of pre-existing relationships of obligation and care.[204] Furthermore, while expanding rights to Nature can be a way of creating a more level playing field,[205] it can lead to a growing number of individualised rights that risk coming into conflict with one another.[206] As Erin O'Donnell argues in the context of river rights, this can isolate humanity from Nature: 'rather than a community, we become merely individual rights holders, in conflict with each other as much as the world around us.'[207] For example, the restoration of access to land for traditional hunting practices may be culturally significant for community but clash with conservationist perspectives,[208] while eco-tourism projects might restore livelihoods but risk significant environmental damage.[209] Examples can also be found outside transitional justice contexts: one of the first outcomes of a case granting rights to Bangladesh

201 Ruiz-Serna, "Transitional," 72–73.

202 Ordóñez-Vargas et al., "Econcentric," 115–116.

203 Erin O'Donnell et al., "Rights and Relationality: Competing Discourses in Water Regulation," *Water Alternatives* 17(2) (2024): 207–238.

204 Virginia Marshall, "Removing the Veil from the 'Rights of Nature': The Dichotomy between First Nations Customary Rights and Environmental Legal Personhood," *Australian Feminist Law Journal*, 45(2) (2019): 233–248.

205 Stone, "Should Trees."

206 See e.g. Michelle Maloney and Peter Burdon, eds., *Wild Law – In Practice* (Routledge, 2014).

207 Erin O'Donnell, "Repairing our Relationship with Rivers: Water Law and Legal Personhood," *Research Agenda for Water Law*, eds. Vanessa Casado Pérez and Rhett Larson (Elgar, 2023), 113–114. See also Usha Natarajan, "Human Rights in a Time of Ecological Change," *Locating Nature: Making and Unmaking International Law*, eds. Usha Natarajan and Julia Dehm (CUP, 2022), 217.

208 Hamilton, Environmental, 217; White, "Ecocentrism."

209 Ordóñez-Vargas et al., "Econcentric," 117.

in 2019 was the forcible removal of slum dwellers in accordance with the court's directives to protect the interests of the river.[210]

These tensions display the limits of legal solutions to legal challenges and emphasise the need to more radically re-imagine justice practices as well as outcomes. Adopting adversarial approaches to these tensions, whereby other-than-human victims and communities are understood as rights bearers in conflict, would risk returning transitional justice to its dualistic foundations, whereby humankind and Nature are seen as separate and opposing forces.[211] Worse, pursuing an 'essentialist ecocentric approach' that divorces other-than-human victims from local communities could risk problematic conservationism at the expense of communities' needs.[212] To avoid such an approach, Colombian researchers Laura Ordóñez-Vargas, Peralta Gonzalez, and Enrique Prieto-Rios advocate a hybrid or biocentric approach in which 'the human and the non-human are part of a common environment (without hierarchies).'[213] Rather than considering competing rights and liabilities, a greater emphasis on relationality and the 'shared vulnerabilities'[214] of humans and other-than-humans in the aftermath of mass violence might better facilitate the navigation of justice conflicts.[215]

Environmental restorative justice could prove valuable in this regard, as restorative justice envisions and enables multiple perspectives to be heard. Rather than shying away from conflict, proponents of restorative justice suggest that constructively engaging in disagreements can create opportunities for developing deeper understandings of what justice might entail.[216] This could prove particularly important in conflicts involving Indigenous communities, given the 'deep and fundamental disconnects' that can arise between Indigenous and non-Indigenous worldviews.[217] Embracing constructive disagreement through appropriate restorative justice practices might create safe spaces to discuss the past and the future, playing an important role in promoting reconciliation.[218] In the context of harms against nature, creating this safe space may even enable difficult conversations about how to bal-

210 Rina Chandran, "Fears of Evictions as Bangladesh Gives Rivers Legal Rights," *Reuters Asia*, 5 July 2019, https://www.reuters.com/article/us-bangladesh-landrights-rivers/fears-of-evictions-as-bangladesh-gives-rivers-legal-rights-idUSKCN1TZ1ZR.
211 Gómez-Betancur, "Rights of Nature," 76.
212 Gómez-Betancur, "Rights of Nature," 76.
213 Ordóñez-Vargas et al., "Ecocentric," 111.
214 Val Plumwood, *Environmental Culture: The Ecological Crisis of Reason* (Routledge 2002).
215 Celermajer et al., "Justice."
216 Kerry Clamp, *Restorative Justice in Transitional Settings* (Routledge, 2016), 3.
217 Brunilda Pali and Ivo Aersten, "Inhabiting a Vulnerable and Wounded Earth: Restoring Response-ability," *International Journal of Restorative Justice* 4(1) (2021): 5.
218 Pali and Aersten, "Inhabiting a Vulnerable and Wounded Earth."

ance economic recovery, the rights of individuals and communities, and the Rights of Nature in a post-conflict context.[219]

4.6 Conclusion

This chapter has explored how the rise of 'ecocentric legalism,' both in transitional justice contexts and beyond, challenges some of the underlying assumptions and framings of victimhood contained within the field of transitional justice. Focusing on initiatives that seek to reframe Nature as a protectee, rights-bearer, and victim, including the campaign to criminalise ecocide, Rights of Nature movements, and the recognition of territories as victims in Colombia, we have demonstrated a growing willingness to understand harm and justice as concepts that extend beyond the human.

The implications of expanding victims' rights to other-than-human victims are interesting. The expansion of rights-holders (e.g., to include women, people of colour, or children) has had a profound impact on regulatory regimes, while the recognition of previously marginalised groups and the growth of 'victims' rights' have opened new ways of thinking about dealing with the past. In such contexts, who (or what) is recognised as a subject of rights becomes both practically and normatively important.

We do not wish to seem naïve about the ability of transitional justice to meaningfully address other-than-human victims' rights claims. Victim-centric rhetoric has rarely been matched in practice, and a turn to 'ecocentric law' retains the trappings of legalism. Lawyers can be accused of assuming every problem has a legal solution, including those created by law, and is important to avoid simply reinforcing the legal fetishism we discussed in Chapter 3.[220] However, what we have hoped to achieve is a demonstration of how the expansion of victimhood might offer a way to think differently about what justice entails. For example, a more inclusive framing of victimhood might offer one tool for 'decolonising' transitional justice through its respectful engagement with and recognition of Indigenous laws. As we unpacked in Chapter 2, it is an ongoing act of epistemic violence to continue denying the validity of worldviews that are more holistic in their understanding of which entities deserve protection and respect.[221] It is therefore a moral obligation to unpack and move beyond these ontological binaries. Moreover, while the delivery of reparations is no small task in the aftermath of atrocity, enabling the interests of Nature to be heard could also lead to the design of more symbiotic forms of repair.

219 Varona, "Restorative," 668.
220 Natarajan, "Human Rights," 222.
221 Gellers, "Inconvenient Reflection."

We acknowledge that the introduction of a new category of victimhood would bring its own challenges, including risks of new hierarchies and victim conflict. Yet conflict, if well handled, can be a constructive force. It can provide space to engage with the messiness of recovering from periods of mass violence. Drawing on environmental restorative justice, both as a way of thinking beyond criminal frameworks and as a platform for navigating multiple perspectives, we have argued that the expansion of victimhood could further a more holistic recognition of conflict's harmful impacts on humans, other-than-humans, and the relationships between them.

One critique that emerged in our discussion was the limitations of 'corrective justice' – an approach to justice that seek to address acute harms while leaving underlying relationships and dynamics intact. Law and the expansion of rights alone cannot address structural inequalities and other root causes of violence.[222] A sole focus on the rights of victims can even distract from these structural violations[223] by emphasising what is owed *to* those harmed rather than what might be owed *by* those who ultimately benefit(ed) from the harm.[224] We continue this theme in the following chapter, which turns to the structures that underlie and influence transitional justice, and their implications for the field's engagement with harm to Nature.

222 Peter D. Burdon, "On the Limits of Political Emancipation and Legal Rights," *International Journal for the Semiotics of Law* 34 (2019): 319.

223 Rachel Killean and Luke Moffett, "What's in a Name? Reparations at the Extraordinary Chambers in the Courts of Cambodia," *Melbourne Journal of International Law* 21(1) (2020): 1–29.

224 Natarajan, "Human Rights," 215.

5

STRUCTURAL HARM AND SLOW VIOLENCE

5.1 Introduction

Throughout this book, we have argued that various power hierarchies have narrowed the scope of transitional justice scholarship and practice in ways that have historically precluded the recognition of harms against Nature. In Chapter 2, we explored how the intellectual foundations and development of the field have been shaped by power-knowledge dynamics, leading to the dominance of anthropocentric assumptions throughout the field. We demonstrated some of the ways that powerful actors can draw parameters around the type of situations that are deemed to require transitional justice intervention. In Chapter 3, we took this analysis further, focusing on the dominance of particular legal frameworks and the ways in which those frameworks further narrowed the field. We noted how transitional justice tends to focus on direct and/or interpersonal violence towards and between individual human beings and their property. While Chapter 4 was dedicated to exploring how an ecocentric conceptualisation of victimhood might challenge this anthropocentrism, we concluded the chapter on a cautionary note, observing that a sole focus on the definition and rights of victims might risk obscuring more structural harms. This chapter picks up this thread, turning to the ways in which structural harm and 'slow violence'[1] are often excluded by transitional justice's 'implied temporal parameters,'[2] and interrogating

1 Rob Nixon, *Slow Violence and the Environmentalism of the Poor* (Harvard University Press, 2011).
2 Cynthia M. Horne, "Transitional Justice and Temporal Parameters," *International Journal of Transitional Justice* 14(3) (2020): 544.

DOI: 10.4324/9781003264446-5

the implications of these exclusions for grappling with harms against Nature. Scholarly engagement with time and temporality in transitional justice has evolved from a rather narrow focus on 'institutional mandates or temporal jurisdiction' to one which engages more deeply with temporality as a 'fundamental frame for justice.'[3] We have found that there are aspects of this literature which are relevant for the field's ability to respond to harms against Nature. These are introduced here and further unpacked throughout the chapter.

First, the framing of certain justice initiatives as 'transitional' self-evidently assumes 'temporal parameters.'[4] Transitional justice is often considered a 'bounded process,'[5] or, as Rosemary Nagy describes, 'a fixed interregnum period with a distinct end.'[6] As such, transitional justice mechanisms tend to impose a constructed sense of a 'before' and 'after' in which the 'before' is understood as a specific, delineated, period of violence from which a society will undertake a fixed period of transition.[7] Decisions relating to the temporal scope of transitional justice interventions can influence which harms are investigated (for instance prioritising torture over longer patterns of displacement), decisions as to when individuals 'become responsible for their choices,' and the overall scope and depth of investigations into past violence.[8] These choices are political, there is no 'neutrality in the treatment of time' in transitional justice.[9] As we explore below, these decisions often come at the expense of excluding complex, long-lasting, or 'slow' manifestations of violence that may pre- and/or post-date the period of atrocity demarcated by a transitional justice process.[10]

Relatedly, and as articulated by Jennifer Balint, Julie Evans and Nesam McMillan:

3 Zinaida Miller, "Transitional Justice Temporalities," *The Oxford Handbook of Transitional Justice,* eds. Jens Meierhenrich et al. (OUP, 2023).

4 Horne, "Transitional," 544.

5 Sarah Maddison and Laura J. Shepherd, "Peacebuilding and the Postcolonial Politics of Transitional Justice," *Peacebuilding* 2(3) (2014): 253.

6 Rosemary Nagy, "Transitional Justice as Global Project: Critical Reflections," *Third World Quarterly* 29(2) (2008): 280. See also Miller, "Transitional."

7 E.g., Paige Arthur, "How Transitions Reshaped Human Rights," *Human Rights Quarterly* 31(2) (2009): 321–367; Jennifer Balint et al., "Rethinking Transitional Justice, Redressing Indigenous Harm: A New Conceptual Approach," *International Journal of Transitional Justice* 8(2) (2014): 194–216; Horne, "Transitional"; Maddison and Shepherd, "Peacebuilding"; Miller, "Transitional"; Dustin N. Sharp, "Introduction: Addressing Economic Violence in Times of Transition," *Justice and Economic Violence in Transition,* ed. Dustin N. Sharp (Springer, 2014).

8 Miller, "Transitional."

9 Miller, "Transitional."

10 Miller, "Transitional."

> Transitional justice is premised on ... a certain understanding of the past, the present and the future as discrete and sequential. As such, transitional justice assumes a linear notion of time as progress, in which the past and the future are seen as separable and successive, instead of intertwined and co-implicated.[11]

Transitional justice has a 'progress narrative'[12] of transition 'from one *time* to another,' and particularly from a time of 'crisis' and 'horror' to a time of 'peace' and 'hope.'[13] It therefore involves 'a before-and-after narrative of change.'[14] This idea of a rupture followed by linear progress suggests the past has 'ended' and that circumstances can be improved upon moving forward.[15] As Jon Elster notes, transitional justice is for some about 'how societies close their open accounts.'[16] This creates a transitional justice which not only overlooks some past harms, but also allows for unrecognised or unaddressed harms to continue. This has implications, for example, for the use of and access to natural resources. In what follows, we will engage with Zinaida Miller's argument that a focus 'on continuity rather than rupture' might allow 'the longer legacies of deeper violence,' including forms of violence perpetrated against the natural world, to 'become more apparent.'[17]

Building on these themes, this chapter explores how the temporal focus of transitional justice measures obscures contexts where harms have been perpetrated across generations[18] and prevents 'deep engagement with structural injustices and the types of interventions needed to address them.'[19] As we will demonstrate, these temporal parameters operate alongside the

11 Balint et al., "Rethinking," 200. See also Bronwyn Leebaw, "The Irreconcilable Goals of Transitional Justice," *Human Rights Quarterly* 30(1) (2008): 95–118; Miller, "Transitional."

12 Miller, "Transitional."

13 Miller, "Transitional." See also Marcus Zunino, *Justice Framed* (CUP, 2019).

14 Kimberley Theidon, "Editorial Note," *International Journal of Transitional Justice* 3(3) (2009): 295. See also Zunino, *Justice.*

15 For a related critique of international law as preoccupied with 'crisis' to the exclusion of structural problems, see Hilary Charlesworth, "International Law: A Discipline of Crisis," *The Modern Law Review* 65(3) (2002): 377.

16 Jon Elster, *Closing the Books: Transitional Justice in Historical Perspective* (CUP, 2004), ix.

17 Miller, "Transitional."

18 Jennifer Matsunaga, "Two Faces of Transitional Justice: Theorizing the Incommensurability of Transitional Justice and Decolonization in Canada," *Decolonization: Indigeneity, Education and Society* 5(1) (2016): 24–44. See also Daniela Jara et al., "Tracing Mapuche Exclusion from Post-Dictatorial Truth Commissions in Chile: Official and Grassroots Initiatives," *International Journal of Transitional Justice* 12(3) (2018): 479–498.

19 Balint et al. "Rethinking," 198. See also Miller, "Transitional."

exclusions we have noted in previous chapters: certain periods of time in particular sites are selected for intervention and, within these, 'specific acts of violence' are prioritised.[20]

We argue that these temporal boundaries have significant implications for recognising and understanding harms against Nature. Periods of armed conflict, genocide, or authoritarianism may highlight, exacerbate, intensify or give new form to the destruction of Nature. However, periods of acute violence and human suffering can also be situated against much longer-term forms of environmental harm and natural resource exploitation. Indeed, human-perpetrated harm towards Nature is the norm rather than the exception,[21] and forms the motivation, method, and collateral damage of many atrocity crimes. Against this backdrop, transitional justice processes offer at best a temporary interruption, at worst their own stage in the continuum of harm against Nature (see Chapter 6). Therefore, we argue that the field of transitional justice cannot adequately engage with, or respond to, atrocity-related harm against Nature without challenging its temporal boundaries.

This chapter proceeds as follows. In Part 2, we examine two forms of harm that have been overlooked as a result of transitional justice's temporal boundaries: structural and slow violence. We consider the implications of this oversight for the field's ability to recognise and respond to harm against Nature. In Part 3, we draw on multidisciplinary scholarship to consider how the temporal boundaries of transitional justice might be challenged. We consider how transitional justice might be 'reconceived,' examining the utility of the crimes of the powerful scholarship and transformative justice approaches for identifying the structural harms that are often overlooked in transitional justice. In Part 4, we then consider the potential of environmental justice and Nancy Fraser's tripartite justice model as approaches which challenge the inequalities that pre- and post-date mainstream transitional justice efforts. In Part 5, we conclude by drawing together the scholarship explored in Part 4 to suggest some ways in which transitional justice could be adapted to better capture harm against Nature. We are cautious of overstating the possibilities, so the conclusion also highlights some of the limitations of the field that may hinder such efforts.

20 Simeon Gready, "The Case for Transformative Reparations: In Pursuit of Structural Socio-Economic Reform in Post-Conflict Societies," *Journal of Intervention and Statebuilding* 16(2) (2022): 184.

21 E.g., Gustavo Rojas-Páez, "Resisting Colonial State Crime: The Experience of the Peace Community of San José de Apartadó," *Oñati Socio-Legal Series* 14(1) (2024): 119–144.

5.2 Structural Harm, Slow Violence, and Harms Against Nature

5.2.1 Structural Harm, Slow Violence, and Transitional Justice

Coined by Johan Galtung, the term 'structural violence' is used to refer to forms of violence that are 'built into the structure,' that manifest as 'unequal power and consequently as unequal life chances' and are directly related to who has 'the power to decide over the distribution of resources.'[22] Offered as a counterpart to the notion of 'personal' or 'direct' violence,[23] it can be understood as comprising 'silent'[24] forms of violence such as social marginalisation, political exclusion, and economic exploitation.[25] These forms of violence are intertwined and mutually reinforcing, and shape everyday patterns of behaviour by differently impacting the lives of groups and individuals.[26] Structural violence can feature significant violations of social, economic and cultural rights[27] – rights which are often 'ignored or sidelined' in transitional justice.[28] In her book *The Ecology of War and Peace*, Eliana Cusato adapts Galtung's theory of structural violence to interrogate the linkages between Nature and war. As she notes, a focus on structural violence offers a rejection of the notion that violence occurs only when there is a visible perpetrator to whom responsibility can be afforded, a lens for exposing root causes of wars and insecurity, and an invitation to move from a focus on negative peace (i.e. the absence of personal violence) to positive peace (the absence of structural violence).[29] The usefulness of structural violence as a lens for interrogating harms against Nature during conflict is returned to below.

The exclusion, or marginalisation, of structural violence from transitional justice's purview is a key critique of the field. For example, René

22 Johan Galtung, "Violence, Peace and Peace Research," *Journal of Peace Research* 6(3) (1969): 171.

23 Galtung, "Violence, Peace," 167.

24 Johan Galtung and Tord Höivik, "Structural and Direct Violence: A Note on Operationalization," *Journal of Peace Research* 8(1) (1971): 73.

25 Daire McGill, "Different Violence, Different Justice? Taking Structural Violence Seriously in Post-conflict and Transitional Justice Processes," *State Crime Journal* 6(1) (2017): 79–101.

26 Paul Farmer, "On Suffering and Structural Violence: A View from Below," *Daedalus* 125(1) (1996): 261–283; Gready, "The Case."

27 Amanda Cahill-Ripley, "Foregrounding Socio-Economic Rights in Transitional Justice: Realising Justice for Violations of Economic and Social Rights," *Netherlands Quarterly of Human Rights* 32(2) (2014): 183–213.

28 Gready, "The Case," 184. See also Jennifer Balint et al., "'Post-conflict' Reconstruction, The Crimes of the Powerful and Transitional Justice," *State Crime* 6(1) (2017): 4–12; Sean Molloy, "Conceptualising the Transformative Justice Potential of Peace Processes," *The International Journal of Human Rights* 27(2) (2023) 307–334.

29 Eliana Cusato, *The Ecology of War and Peace* (CUP, 2020), 24.

Urueña and María Angélica Prada-Uribe contend that 'transitional justice risks weakening its objective if it fails to address the fundamental causes of conflict, such as inequality, land and resource redistribution, and socioeconomic violence.'[30] This type of critique has been advanced by proponents of transformative justice,[31] who argue that dealing with the past requires changes to pre-conflict structures in ways that make society more inclusive and equal in future.[32] There have been some developments in this regard within the field of transitional justice. For instance, Dustin Sharp has drawn attention to a number of truth commissions (Chad, Ghana, Kenya, Liberia, Sierra Leone, East Timor, and the Solomon Islands) that – he argues – 'represent an important step' in foregrounding economic and social rights violations, exploitation of natural resources and other economic crimes including corruption and fraud.[33] However, to the extent that structural violence is acknowledged in transitional justice, it is more often framed as the backdrop to more serious violations of civil and political rights rather than as a series of rights violations in itself.[34] As we will examine below, the general tendency of the field to overlook structural harm impacts upon its recognition of harm against Nature.

The notion of 'slow violence' can also be traced to Galtung, in his consideration of violence as 'indirect' or 'latent.'[35] The concept was isolated and given shape by Rob Nixon, and it shares some similarities with Galtung's theory of structural violence; both are offered as concepts that can be used for 'widening the field of what constitutes justice.'[36] We can understand slow violence as 'violence that occurs gradually and out of sight, a violence of delayed destruction that is dispersed across time and space, an attritional

30 René Urueña and María Angélica Prada-Uribe, "Transitional Justice and Economic Policy," *Annual Review of Law and Social Science* 14(1) (2018): 398.

31 See e.g. Rosemary Nagy, "Transformative Justice in a Settler Colonial Transition: Implementing the UN Declaration on the Rights of Indigenous Peoples in Canada," *The International Journal of Human Rights* 26(2) (2022): 195; Matthew Evans, "Structural Violence, Socioeconomic Rights, and Transformative Justice," *Journal of Human Rights* 15(1) (2016): 1–20; Paul Gready and Simon Robins, *From Transitional to Transformative Justice* (CUP, 2019). Rojas-Páez, "Resisting."

32 Molloy, "Conceptualising."

33 Dustin N. Sharp, "Economic Violence in the Practice of African Truth Commissions and Beyond," *Justice and Economic Violence in Transition*, ed. Dustin N. Sharp (Springer, 2014), 80.

34 Cahill-Ripley, "Foregrounding." See also Nagy, "Transitional," 287 for structural violence as 'largely in the background' in cases where it does feature.

35 Galtung, "Violence," discussed in Shannon O'Lear, "Geographies of Slow Violence: An Introduction," *A Research Agenda for Geographies of Slow Violence*, ed. Shannon O'Lear (Elgar, 2021).

36 Cusato, *Ecology*, 23.

violence that is typically not viewed as violence at all.'[37] Slow violence can result from inaction and subtle, incremental processes, such as 'slowly unfolding environmental catastrophes,'[38] and so it can be difficult to identify and address. Its legacy can also be long-term and intergenerational; Rachel Pain and Caitlin Cahill suggest that 'we might imagine slow violence creeping, or even bleeding through spaces, through families, through soils and land ... embedded and entrenched in place, lingering, extending the time-frame of targeted harm.'[39]

It is easy to see how the fixed and narrow temporal boundaries of transitional justice can exclude slow violence. As Nixon notes, slow violence can disrupt lives and cause harm due to the 'unequal attention given to spectacular and unspectacular time.'[40] The exclusion of slow violence means that more gradual and longer-term forms of environmental degradation can be overlooked, as can the related harms experienced by human populations.[41] However, as a concept, it 'provokes us to expand our imaginations of what constitutes harm' and 'insists we take seriously forms of violence that have, over time, become unmoored from their original causes.'[42] Indeed, the spectacular and unspectacular are often intertwined, as Nixon demonstrates using the example of the Gulf War. Aperiod of acute violent conflict, the Gulf War also caused long-term harm against Nature and people due to the United States' use of depleted uranium weapons.[43] As Cusato notes, Nixon's work therefore invites us to 'think critically about how the temporal dispersion of slow violence affects the way institutions and the law respond' to forms of acute violence.[44]

It is evident from the above that there are 'inextricable links' between structural and slow violence.[45] Although not all slow violence can necessarily be described as structural,[46] both concepts seek to expand conceptualisations of violence, engage with underlying structural inequalities, shed light

37 Nixon, *Slow*, 2.

38 Nixon, *Slow*, 2. See also Rachel Pain and Caitlin Cahill, "Critical Political Geographies of Slow Violence and Resistance," *Environment & Planning C: Politics and Space* 40(2) (2022): 357–372.

39 Pain and Cahill, "Critical," 362

40 Nixon, *Slow*, 6, cited in Cusato, *Ecology*, 19.

41 Leane Makey et al., "(Un)Heard Voices of Ecosystem Degradation: Stories from the Nexus of Settler-Colonialism and Slow Violence," *Sustainability* 14(22) (2022): 14672.

42 Thom Davies, "Slow Violence and Toxic Geographies: 'Out of Sight' to Whom?" *Environment & Planning C: Politics and Space* 40(2) (2022): 410. See also Chloe Ahmann, "'It's Exhausting to Create an Event Out of Nothing': Slow Violence and the Manipulation of Time." *Cultural Anthropology* 33(1) (2018): 142–171.

43 Cusato, *Ecology*, 20.

44 Cusato, *Ecology*, 20.

45 Davies, "Slow," 413.

46 Nixon, *Slow*.

on violence that is difficult to recognise as such, and deal with harm where questions of responsibility and accountability are especially challenging to answer.[47] Due to this overlap, we examine structural harm and slow violence together, considering the particular impacts of these forms of violence on Nature.

5.2.2 Slow and Structural Violence Against Nature

The exclusion of structural harm and slow violence has implications for the transitional justice field's engagement with harm to Nature. It can limit understandings of the root causes of conflict and periods of atrocity, exclude many (human and other-than-human) victims of harm from the remit of transitional justice mechanisms, and blinker the field to the culpability or complicity of some actors who bear responsibility for harm against Nature. Furthermore, by not engaging with slow violence or structural harm, transitional justice processes may facilitate the continuation of these types of harm beyond the point of the perceived 'transition.' We consider each of these points in turn, before exploring South Africa as an example that demonstrates each of these limitations.

As Dustin Sharp emphasises, 'conflicts do not begin in a vacuum, isolated from deeper socioeconomic and historical forces.'[48] Competition over natural resources is often an overlooked root cause of conflict. While recognition of the connections between natural resources and conflict has certainly grown within the literature, transitional justice scholarship and practice continues to frequently overlook the structural dimensions of resource distribution which may have 'paved the way' to periods of violence.[49] Rather, structural and slow violence is reduced to providing the 'context' in which the 'real' violence occurs, with only the latter requiring remedy.[50] Transitional justice's exclusion of structural harm can thereby lead to an incomplete or decontextualised understanding of more acute periods of mass violence.[51]

One example of a decontextualised approach to violence is the use of the term 'resource curse' to explain 'the adverse effects of a country's

47 Davies, "Slow"; Nixon, *Slow*.

48 Sharp, "Economic," 79.

49 Cusato, *Ecology*, 651.

50 Cusato, *Ecology*, 663, citing Sarah Nouwen, "As You Set Out for Ithaka: Practical, Epistemological, Ethical and Existential Questions about Socio-Legal Empirical Research in Conflict," *Leiden Journal of International Law* 27(1) (2014): 227–260.

51 Mark Drumbl, *Accountability for Property Crimes and Environmental War Crimes: Prosecution, Litigation, and Development*, International Center for Transitional Justice, 2009, https://www.ictj.org/sites/default/files/ICTJ-Development-PropertyCrimes-FullPaper-2009-English.pdf.

natural resource wealth on its economic, social or political well-being.'[52] This framing implies mismanagement and corruption on the part of the state, but can obscure the 'historical and structural dimensions of inequality and poverty in the Global South, as well as the role of external actors, notably former colonial powers and transnational corporations, in producing such evils.'[53] As Michael Beevers describes, resource extraction 'can create unequal patterns of development, and yield instability and conflict.'[54] For example, in Liberia, Beevers suggests that 'every conflict ... has deep roots in competition over land and resources and much of the social conflict is due to state control over natural resources, which for most of Liberia's history has been predatory and exploitative.'[55] Decontextualised approaches which focus on the eruption of conflict but not its more complex origins can lead to incomplete forms of justice, leaving untouched the deeper inequalities that facilitate unfair and unsustainable natural resource exploitation.

A focus on a specific time period inevitably means some victims' harms falls outside of the temporal boundaries of transitional justice. Slow violence, for example, can involve 'scientifically convoluted cataclysms in which casualties are postponed, often for generations.'[56] We noted the Gulf War example above; there are many others. Arguably one of the most notorious examples is President Richard Nixon and Henry Kissinger's use of Agent Orange during the Vietnam War. This led to the deaths of hundreds of thousands of people after the war had 'officially' ended through the buildup of dioxins through biomagnification in plants and animals. Those affected included people who were not born at the time of the chemical's use.[57] Rob Nixon cites an Institute of Medicine committee that has connected 17 medical conditions – including ischemic heart disease and

52 Michael L. Ross, "What Have We Learned About the Resource Curse?" *Annual Review of Political Science* 18(1) (2015): 239–256.

53 Cusato, *Ecology*, 656, citing Michael Watts, "Oil, Development, and the Politics of the Bottom Billion," *Macalester International* 24 (2009): Article 11; Lee Wengraf, "The Pillage Continues: Debunking the Resource Curse," *Review of African Political Economy*, January 24, 2017, https://roape.net/2017/01/24/pillage-continues-debunking-resource-curse/.

54 Michael Beevers, "Forest Governance and Post-conflict Peace in Liberia: Emerging Contestation and Opportunities for Change?" *The Extractive Industries and Society* 3(2) (2016): 322.

55 Beevers, "Forest," 325.

56 Nixon, *Slow*, 3.

57 Nixon, *Slow*. See also Matthias Baumann and Tobias Kuemmerle, "The Impacts of Warfare and Armed Conflict on Land Systems," *Journal of Land Use Science* 11(6) (2016): 672–688; Giacomo Certini et al., "The Impact of Warfare on the Soil Environment," *Earth-Science Review* 127 (2013): 1–15.

Parkinson's disease – to Agent Orange.[58] Looking beyond the human, the use of Agent Orange led to the widespread loss of mangroves vital to the Delta region's coastal ecology, and the deaths of thousands of animals, including from rare species such as the Irrawaddy dolphin, the Saurus crane, the wild Asian Elephant, different species of deer, the Giant Ibis, and the White Shouldered Ibis.[59] These other-than-human harms remain largely overlooked in scholarship and in the legal responses to the conflict over half a century later.[60]

Overlooking structural and slow violence also creates a culture of impunity with regards to the perpetrators of harms against Nature. As Clara Sandoval, Leonardo Filippini, and Roberto Vidal emphasise, 'addressing the causes and consequences of conflict and repression requires considering the role of all actors that caused or contributed to the commission of mass atrocities.'[61] This would include economic actors involved in the perpetration of violence[62] and 'the broader population of beneficiaries,' an extension of liability that can prove challenging to transitional justice mechanisms which are often the product of compromises between powerful actors.[63] Transitional justice mechanisms have been particularly critiqued for precluding corporate liability,[64] with scholars advocating for criminal liability to be extended to corporations as well as other forms of accountability.[65] While Leigh A. Payne, Gabriel Pereira, and Laura Bernal-Bermúdez have argued that 'transitional justice has, in fact, taken on corporate complicity' (for instance, the Nuremberg Trials included the complicity of businessmen

58 Nixon, *Slow*.

59 Nathalie de Pompignan, "Ecocide," *Mass Violence & Résistance – Research Network*, November 3, 2007, https://www.sciencespo.fr/mass-violence-war-massacre-resistance/en/document/ecocide.html.

60 See Kiem N. Truong and Khuong V. Dinh, "Agent Orange: Haft-Century Effects on the Vietnamese Wildlife Have Been Ignored," *Environmental Science and Technology* 55(22) (2021):15007–15009; Eliana Cusato, 'From Ecocide to Voluntary Remediation Projects: Legal Responses to "Environmental Warfare" in Vietnam and the Spectre of Colonialism," *Melbourne Journal of International Law* 19(2) (2018): 494–520.

61 Clara Sandoval et al., "Linking Transitional Justice and Corporate Accountability," *Corporate Accountability in the Context of Transitional Justice*, ed. Sabine Michalowski (Routledge, 2014).

62 Leigh A. Payne et al., "The Business of Transitional Justice," *The Oxford Handbook of Transitional Justice*, eds. Jens Meierhenrich et al. (OUP, 2023); Eduardo Saad-Diniz, "The Idea of Corporate Justice: Paths to Corporate Criminology in Brazil," *Criminal Justice Review* 46(4) (2021): 435–449.

63 John Torpey, *Politics and the Past: On Repairing Historical Injustices* (Rowman and Littlefield, 2003), 7–8. See Chapter 6.

64 Gready, "The Case."

65 Sabine Michalowski, ed., *Corporate Accountability in the Context of Transitional Justice* (Routledge, 2013).

and bankers,[66] and approximately half of all truth commissions that have published a final report have referred to the role of economic actors),[67] they assert that 'corporate accountability ... remains highly limited, largely invisible, and innovative in the rare situations in which it occurs.'[68] Notably, where such findings have emerged, this has generally been a result of mobilisation by civil society or victim testimony.[69] Certainly, engagement with corporate accountability has not developed into an institutionalised or formalised element of transitional justice.[70] This can result in those with responsibility for past harm remaining in positions of power. For example, in Brazil, many corporations and economic, industry, and business sectors who financially and institutionally supported the military dictatorship 'are still protagonists in the public sphere,'[71] and there has been little accountability for those who have financially benefited from land grabs across the country.[72]

To consider Nature specifically, overlooking corporate responsibility means overlooking the 'plurality of actors, such as transnational corporations, local and global elites [and] international financial institutions' who benefit from unsustainable resource exploitation and extraction.[73] In their assessment of over 100 cases in which corporations were accused of involvement in atrocity crimes, Wim Huisman and Daniel Sidoli found that 'most clearly overrepresented are the extractive industries.'[74] Yet, a focus on actors perceived to be more 'proximate' to the harm can distract from the 'culpability of those who benefited from the system'[75] and who have caused lasting harm to the natural world.[76] For instance (and reflecting 'resource curse' logic), the Sierra Leonean Truth Commission framed the conflict as something brought about by internal contradictions and the bad governance of

66 Jonathan Kolieb, "Through the Looking-Glass: Nuremberg's Confusing Legacy on Corporate Accountability under International Law," *American University International Law Review* 32(2) (2015): 570–602.

67 See also Cusato, *Ecology*.

68 Payne et al., "The Business."

69 Payne et al., "The Business."

70 Payne et al., "The Business." See also Sandoval et al., "Linking."

71 Saad-Diniz, "The Idea," 437.

72 Fabricio Teló et al., "Land and Transitional Justice in Brazil," *International Journal of Transitional Justice* 15(1) (2021): 190–209.

73 Cusato, *Ecology*, 657, citing Cyril Obi, "Oil as the 'Curse' of Conflict in Africa: Peering Through the Smoke and Mirrors," *Review of African Political Economy* 37(126): 483.

74 Wim Huisman and Daniel Sidoli, "Corporations, Human Rights and the Environmental Degradation–Corruption Nexus," *Asia Pacific Journal of Environmental Law* 22(1) (2019): 80.

75 Vasuki Nesiah, "Theories of Transitional Justice: Cashing in the Blue Chips," *The Oxford Handbook of the Theory of International Law*, eds. Anne Orford and Florian Hoffmann with Martin Clark (OUP, 2016), 795.

76 Steve Tombs and David Whyte, "The Shifting Imaginaries of Corporate Crime," *Journal of White Collar and Corporate Crime* 1(1) (2020): 16–23.

the domestic elites. While transnational networks associated with diamond trading are mentioned in the Truth Commission's report, blame was placed on 'the local government and its weak governance system'.[77] Similarly, although the Liberian Truth Commission acknowledged that foreign corporations had benefited from the conflict and related absence of rule of law in Liberia, the Commission primarily blamed the Charles Taylor regime for the conflict and its economic crimes.[78] This failure to account for corporate liability continues to attract substantial discussion in the literature.[79] We return to the issue of corporate criminality below.

Finally, failure to address structural violence may allow harm to continue after the transitional period.[80] This can be particularly damaging to marginalised populations, who may be returned to 'pre-conflict situations of poverty, discrimination, and exclusion.'[81] As Clara Sandoval sets out, significant inequalities remain in a number of post-transitional justice sites, including East Timor, Guatemala, Sierra Leone, and South Africa.[82] This also has implications for harms against Nature. Returning to the example of Liberia, the framing of conflict by international actors as rooted in illegal extraction and trade in natural resources by rebel groups overlooked the structural reality – that the 'predatory and exploitative' nature of state control of natural resources lay at the heart of conflict in the region. This resulted in the imposition of reforms that reconstructed state-led extractive

77 Cusato, *Ecology*, 658.

78 Cusato, *Ecology*, 660.

79 See e.g. Evelyne Owiye Asaala, "The Politics of Transitional Justice and Corporate Accountability for Atrocities: Options under International Law," *International Journal of Transitional Justice* 16(3) (2022): 467–477 for a review of three monographs on the topic: Irene Pietropaoli, *Business, Human Rights and Transitional Justice* (Routledge, 2020); Joanna Kyriakakis, *Corporations, Accountability and International Criminal Law: Industry and Atrocity* (Elgar, 2021); and Leigh A. Payne et al., *Transitional Justice and Corporate Accountability from Below* (CUP, 2020) The challenges of holding corporations accountable in so-called 'ordinary' domestic and international contexts are also well documented, see e.g. Ronald Burns, "Corporate Crimes and the Problems of Enforcement," *The Routledge International Handbook of Crimes of the Powerful*, ed. Gregg Barak (Routledge, 2015); Lisa Lähteenmäki and Anne Alvesalo-Kuush, "The Imaginary Social Order of Corporate Criminal Liability," *Revisiting Crimes of the Powerful: Marxism, Crime and Deviance,* eds. Steven Bittle et al. (Routledge, 2018); Michael Levi and Nicholas Lord, "White-Collar and Corporate Crime," *The Oxford Handbook of Criminology*, eds. Alison Liebling et al., 6th Edition (OUP, 2017); Dawn L. Rothe and David Kauzlarich, *Crimes of the Powerful: White-Collar Crime and Beyond*, 2nd Edition (Routledge, 2022).

80 Balint et al., 'Post-conflict," 6.

81 Gready, "The Case," 184. See also Makey et al., "(Un)heard."

82 Clara Sandoval, "Transitional Justice and Social Change," *Sur: International Journal on Human Rights* 11(20) (2014): 180–189.

approaches of the past and allowed corruption and unsustainable natural resource exploitation to continue.[83]

To weave the threads of this part together, we turn to the example of South Africa. This is a site where the structural violence of apartheid was not fully explored in its formal transition mechanism. This has allowed significant structural inequalities to continue. Although it is now well-established that the physical violence of apartheid took place on a continuum of structural harm and repression,[84] this backdrop was not comprehensively addressed by the Truth and Reconciliation Commission. Amanda Cahill-Ripley has highlighted that the Commission framed violations of economic and social rights as contextual information needed in order to understand 'narrowly defined gross human rights violations.'[85] Race was not fully dealt with, the 'brutality of the apartheid system *in toto*' was 'evaded,'[86] and decades later, high levels of inequality and poverty remain.[87] Although 'neo-colonial business interests' helped to sustain apartheid violence,[88] this aspect of the conflict has also been a gap in the country's transitional justice efforts.

Overlooking the structural nature of apartheid-era violence has negatively impacted Nature. Phia Steyn reports that 'the environmental impact of apartheid lingered on long after' the election of a democratic government in 1994.'[89] A 1999 government report on the state of the environment indicated a high extinction rate of plant and animals, high levels of air and water pollution and soil erosion, the generation of too much waste to be safely disposed of, and the disposal of untreated hazardous waste.[90] While, as Steyn notes, weak environmental governance at a domestic level and isolation from international developments in environmental issues are an important part of this picture, so too was 'the profoundly detrimental environmental impact' of apartheid on 'the human and natural environments of

83 Beevers, "Forest," 325.
84 Richard Peacock, "Institutional and Structural Victimisation: Apartheid South Africa," *Towards a Victimology of State Crime*, eds. Dawn Rothe and David Kauzlarich (Routledge, 2014).
85 Cahill-Ripley, "Foregrounding," 191. See also Sharp, "Introduction."
86 Miller, "Transitional."
87 Evans, "Structural"; Sharp, "Introduction."
88 Susan Forde et al., "Peacebuilding, Structural Violence and Spatial Reparations in Post-Colonial South Africa," *Journal of Intervention and Statebuilding* 15(3) (2021): 327–346.
89 Phia Steyn, "The Lingering Environmental Impact of Repressive Governance: The Environmental Legacy of the Apartheid Era for the New South Africa," *Globalizations* 2(3) (2005): 392. See also Patrick Bond, "Sub-Imperial Ecosystem Management in South Africa: Continental Implications of South African Environmental Injustice," *The Routledge Handbook of Environmental Justice*, ed. Ryan Holifield et al. (Routledge, 2018).
90 Steyn, "Lingering."

all people of colour in South Africa.'[91] For example, the Bantu Authorities Act of 1951 legalised the forced resettlement of Black South Africans to the poorest rural lands.[92] Overpopulation in these areas caused widespread soil erosion and – when combined with poverty and a lack of electricity – overexploitation of forests for wood fuel.[93] Although the Truth and Reconciliation Commission referred to the forced removals, Valerie Stull, Michael M. Bell, and Mpumelelo Ncwadi argue that this 'environmental apartheid' continues today, with some Black communities forced to cultivate poor land.[94] The mining industry provides a second example. During apartheid, a lack of effective regulation of the industry facilitated 'enormous environmental destruction.'[95] Since 1994, as a result of the continuation of corrupt relationships between mining companies and government and continued poverty creating a pool of labour (in addition to the establishment of an economic agenda which prioritised industrial expansion over the environment – see Chapter 6), the environmental harms of mining have continued – albeit 'to a lesser degree.'[96] In this case, overlooking the structural roots of apartheid resulted in the provision of an incomplete picture by the Commission, impunity for corporate actors, and the continuation of serious harm against Nature into the present.

To summarise the arguments put forward in this part: we agree with the now fairly substantial scholarship which argues that the temporal boundaries of transitional justice have limited the field's engagement with structural harm, slow violence, and the historical causes of armed conflict.[97] Following Rosemary Nagy, Eliana Cusato, and others, we find that the artificial time frames of transitional justice and the associated 'zones of impunity'[98] produce restricted accounts of violence and only partial remedy. We further argue that this blind spot has particular implications for the recognition of harm against Nature, which are often rooted in structural inequalities and manifest as slow violence, that is, 'attritional catastrophes that overspill clear boundaries in time and space.'[99] We note that these forms of violence can be difficult to recognise, raise challenges regarding the attribution of

91 Steyn, "Lingering," 394.
92 Valerie Stull et al., "Environmental Apartheid: Eco-Health and Rural Marginalisation in South Africa," *Journal of Rural Studies* 47 (2016): 369–390.
93 Steyn, "Lingering"; Stull, Bell, and Newadi, "Environmental."
94 Stull, Bell, and Newadi, "Environmental."
95 Leonard Llewellyn, "Mining Corporations, Democratic Meddling, and Environmental Justice in South Africa," *Social Sciences* 7(12) (2018): 259.
96 Llewellyn, "Mining Corporations, Democratic Meddling," 272.
97 Belkis Izquierdo and Lieselotte Viaene, "Decolonizing Transitional Justice from Indigenous Territories," *Peace in Process* 34 (2018): 11–19.
98 Nagy, "Transitional," 287.
99 Nixon, *Slow*, 7. See also Cusato, *Ecology*.

responsibility, and both pre-date and outlive the temporal boundaries of transitional justice. In the next section, we consider approaches to justice that might offer useful tools for tackling these challenges.

5.3 Engaging with Structural Injustice

Scholars have long argued in favour of a broader lens when considering violations that require transitional justice intervention. There have been calls for a more 'holistic interpretation' of transitional justice,[100] a 'thicker' approach that looks beyond legalistic measures,[101] and 'a more nuanced, contextualized, and balanced approach to a wider range of justice issues.'[102] Some critiques explicitly interrogate the temporality of transitional justice and its failure to address structural violence. For example, in 2007, Louise Arbour argued that the field 'must reach to – but also beyond – the crimes and abuses committed during the conflict that led to the transition, and it must address the human rights violations that pre-dated the conflict and caused or contributed to it.'[103] In 2018, Hakeem Yusuf argued that a 'paradigm shift' is needed in transitional justice, so that both 'theory and practice ... engender discussion of the dynamics of continuities of structural injustice.'[104] Simeon Gready asserted in 2022 that the 'pursuit of a deeper justice' requires transitional justice 'to consider its temporal mandate.'[105] Sarah Maddison and Laura Shepherd have suggested that 'keeping open' the 'temporal window on the past may broaden the application of transitional justice measures by demanding more from the concept of "transition" itself.'[106] The continuation of these calls reflects the lack of meaningful change in this area, despite the proliferation of the forms transitional justice can take and the circumstances to which it applies.

In this section, we examine how transitional justice might engage with 'the dynamics of continuities of structural injustice'[107] that can often incorporate or cause harm against Nature. We identify two lenses that may shed

100 Alex Boraine, "Transitional Justice: A Holistic Interpretation," *Journal of International Affairs* 60(1) (2006): 17.

101 Kieran McEvoy and Lorna McGregor, eds., *Transitional Justice from Below: Grassroots Activism and the Struggle for Change* (Hart 2008).

102 Sharp, "Introduction," 4.

103 Louise Arbour, "Economic and Social Justice for Societies in Transition," *New York University Journal of International Law and Politics* 40(1) (2007): 3. See also Stahn, "Confronting."

104 Hakeem O. Yusuf, "Colonialism and the Dilemmas of Transitional Justice in Nigeria," *International Journal of Transitional Justice* 12(2) (2018): 276.

105 Gready, "The Case," 191.

106 Maddison and Shepherd, "Peacebuilding," 269.

107 Yusuf, "Colonialism," 276.

light on these dynamics and subsequently two approaches that could contribute to reshaping transitional justice in a way that captures structural harm. First, the crimes of the powerful and transformative justice scholarships are examined for their potential to help identify the structures that provide the backdrop to transitional justice. Second, we consider the potential of environmental justice and Nancy Fraser's tripartite model of redistribution, recognition, and representation as means of usefully informing a more holistic and 'greener' transitional justice project.

5.3.1 Crimes of the Powerful

'Crimes of the powerful' is a body of scholarship primarily developed in the field of criminology, which interrogates state crime, corporate crime, state–corporate crime, and the global context in which harms occur. In this section, we focus on the utility of the concepts of corporate and state–corporate crime for expanding the gaze of transitional justice.[108] Corporate crime involves those '*crimes and harms committed in the name of or on behalf of the organisation and/or major stakeholders for gain of the organisation*, with recognition of self gain as a component though not necessary.'[109] State–corporate crime involves interactions between two or more organisations, 'at least one of which is private and one public.'[110] It can include acts of violence, corrupt practices, and conduct that might fall outside traditional ideas of crime.[111] Criminology and transitional justice have a closely intertwined relationship.[112] Given that transitional justice is often a response to state crime, state violence, or state terror, there is an inevitable and persistent relationship between state crime and transitional justice – though we agree with Huma Saeed that state crime as a concept is often dealt with in a 'rather broad and vague' way by transitional justice scholars.[113] However there has been less crossover between transitional justice and the scholarship

108 We turn to the global context in Chapter 6.

109 Dawn Rothe and David Kauzlarich, *Crimes of the Powerful: White-Collar Crime and Beyond* (Routledge, 2022), 78.

110 Ronald Kramer at the 1990 Annual Meeting of the Society for the Study of Social Problems, cited in Ronald C. Kramer et al., "The Origins and Development of the Concept and Theory of State–Corporate Crime," *Crime and Delinquency* 48(2) (2002): 263–282.

111 Balint, Laslett, and McDonald, 'Post-conflict," 6.

112 See Kieran McEvoy et al., "Criminology and Transitional Justice," *The Oxford Handbook of Criminology*, eds. Alison Liebling et al. (OUP, 2017); Huma Saeed, *Transitional Justice and Socio-Economic Harm: Land Grabbing in Afghanistan* (Routledge, 2022), Chapter 7.

113 Saeed, *Transitional*, 172.

on corporate and state–corporate crime.[114] We suggest that thinking about these categories might open transitional justice up to closer engagement with structural harm, particularly in the context of harm against Nature.

To first think about the contribution of the concepts of corporate and state–corporate crime to transitional justice at a general level, as introduced above, transitional justice in its current form often overlooks corporate responsibility for harm and corporate and other beneficiaries of harmful practices. The actions of powerful economic actors can be overlooked either 'inadvertently or by design' in a context where there are many competing demands[115] and the focus is on political violence.[116] We agree with Leigh A. Payne, Gabriel Pereira, and Laura Bernal-Bermúdez that 'businesses complicit in authoritarian regimes could, and should, be held accountable,'[117] and propose that applying a 'crimes of the powerful' framework may help to capture a broader spectrum of accountability, including corporate and state–corporate crime.

There has been some recognition of this form of criminality in transitional justice, as evidenced by the expanding literature on corporate liability. This has the potential to extend the field's boundaries. As Eduardo Saad-Diniz argues, furthering engagement with corporate accountability and complicity could facilitate 'broader debates about the historical *continuum* and different forms and aspects of harming and victimizing by means of business contributions.'[118] The rise of the movement to criminalise ecocide (discussed in Chapter 4) has further invigorated this debate, leading to calls for domestic and international tribunals such as the International Criminal Court to expand their liability frameworks to incorporate legal persons – although such a move would encounter the same non-retroactive application challenges as any new crime.[119] However, what Dawn Rothe and Raymond Kauzlarich emphasise is that corporations 'exist and operate within a system that facilitates criminogenic behaviour, mostly driven by a

114 Some exceptions to this include Michalowski, *Corporate*; Rojas-Páez, "Resisting"; Saad-Diniz, "The Idea"; Saeed, *Transitional.*

115 Balint et al., 'Post-conflict," 4.

116 Richard Falk, "Predicaments of Transformative Justice in a Neoliberal and State-Centric World Order," *From Transitional to Transformative Justice*, eds. Paul Gready and Simon Robins (CUP, 2019), 59.

117 Payne, Pereira, and Bernal-Bermúdez, "The Business."

118 Saad-Diniz, "The Idea," 435.

119 See e.g. Marco Colacurci, "The Draft Convention Ecocide and the Role for Corporate Remediation. Some Insights from the International Monsanto Tribunal and a Recent Research Proposal," *International Criminal Law Review* 21(1) (2021): 154–180; Donna Minha, "The Possibility of Prosecuting Corporations for Climate Crimes Before the International Criminal Court: All Roads Lead to the Rome Statute?" *Michigan Journal of International Law* 41(3) (2020): 491–539.

capitalist logic.'[120] While examining corporate crime can shed light on these dynamics, it arguably does not go deep enough. Clara Sandoval, Leonardo Filippini, and Roberto Vidal have highlighted this challenge in the current transitional justice landscape, emphasising 'the close interaction between states and other important international actors, such as multinational corporations' and the challenge that transitional justice faces in 'catching up with a changing world' that is arguably no longer one of state dominance.[121] To this end, applying the concept of state–corporate crime could broaden the gaze of transitional justice so that it better captures 'the changed realities of a globalized world' where economic interests and corporations have become much more powerful in the context of capitalism – potentially more powerful than states themselves.[122] Adopting a state–corporate lens therefore requires transitional justice actors to both 'take seriously the crimes of political, social and economic elites,'[123] and to turn away from spectacular acts of atrocity towards analysing underlying power relations.[124]

These state–corporate relationships have particular implications for Nature. Harms against Nature are often the responsibility (directly or indirectly) of a 'plurality of actors,' including international financial institutions (IFIs) and multinational corporations.[125] While engaging with corporate crime can contribute to capturing accountability for harm against Nature,[126] to comprehensively understand and establish responsibility for harm against Nature often requires a state–corporate lens.[127] The state–cor-

120 Rothe and Kauzlarich, *Crimes*, 78

121 Sandoval et al., "Linking."

122 Michalowski, *Corporate*, 247. By 'capitalism,' we mean the economic model that prioritises free markets, competition, privatisation and economic deregulation (see Chapter Six).

123 Lieselot C. J. Bisschop et al., "Getting Into Deep Water: Coastal Land Loss and State–Corporate Crime in the Louisiana Bayou," *British Journal of Criminology* 58 (2018): 887.

124 Ignasi Bernat and David Whyte, "State–Corporate Crime and the Process of Capital Accumulation: Mapping a Global Regime of Permission from Galicia to Morecambe Bay," *Critical Criminology* 25(1) (2017): 71–86. See also Bisschop, Strobi, and Viollaz, "Getting."

125 Cusato, *Ecology*, 657.

126 Huisman and Sidoli, "Corporations"; David O. Friedrichs, *Trusted Criminals: White Collar Crime in Contemporary Society*, 4th Edition (Wadsworth Cengage Learning, 2010).

127 See e.g. Busisiwe Kamolane-Kgadima and Thandeka Kathi, "The Mpumalanga Highveld Air Pollution Crisis: A South African Reparations Framework for Environmental State–Corporate Harm," *International Journal for Crime, Justice and social Democracy* 13(1) (2024): 1–13; Damián Zaitch and Laura Gutiérrez Gómez, "Mining as State–Corporate Crime: The Case of AngloGold Ashanti in Colombia," *The Routledge International Handbook of Crimes of the Powerful*, ed. Gregg Barak (Routledge, 2015). The state–corporate relationship is also examined in the literature on Allan Schnaiberg's concept of the

porate crime scholarship facilitates exploration of the 'deeper, structural relation' between corporations and the state,[128] and the exposure of their role in the consolidation and reproduction of structural harms.[129] For instance, emphasising state–corporate criminality can draw attention to the land concessions that facilitate harmful practices of resource extraction. Examples include Liberia, where timber corporations funded Charles Taylor's regime; and the Democratic Republic of Congo, where AngloGold Ashanti paid the Nationalist and Integrationist Front paramilitary group for mining access.[130] A state–corporate crime lens also draws attention to the role of arms dealers, a group of people and organisations that are rarely acknowledged within transitional justice. Their role is intertwined with harms to Nature in various ways: for example, corporations have been known to supply arms in exchange for access to natural resources.[131]

Other examples of state–corporate crime have more overt connections to the destruction of Nature. One of the earliest applications of the state–corporate crime concept – David Kauzlarich and Ron Kramer's analysis of the environmental damage caused by nuclear weapons production – involved conflict-related harm to nature. They found that nuclear weapons production in the United States resulted in the production of hazardous and radioactive waste and contamination of land. Although the production activity was carried out by private firms, they were working under contract with the US Department of Energy and Atomic Energy Commission.[132] While this

'Treadmill of Production' (see e.g. Michael J. Lynch et al., "The Treadmill of Production and the Treadmill of Law: Propositions for Analyzing Law, Ecological Disorganization and Crime," *Capitalism Nature Socialism* 31(1)(2020): 107–122; Michael Lynch et al., "Green Criminology and State–Corporate Crime: The Ecocide–Genocide Nexus with Examples from Nigeria," *Journal of Genocide Research* 23(2) (2021): 236–257; Paul B. Stretesky et al., *The Treadmill of Crime: Political Economy and Green Criminology* (Routledge, 2014).

128 David Whyte, "Regimes of Permission and State–Corporate Crime," *State Crime Journal* 3(2) (2014): 238.

129 Payne et al., "The Business."

130 Huisman and Sidoli, "Corporations."

131 Huisman and Sidoli, "Corporations."

132 David Kauzlarich and Ronald Kramer, "State–Corporate Crime in the US Nuclear Weapons Production Complex," *Journal of Human Justice*, 5(1) (1993): 4–28, cited in Rothe and Kauzlarich, *Crimes*. The United States is not unique in this. The International Campaign to Abolish Nuclear Weapons has reported that states including the United Kingdom, France, and Russia have also been responsible for significant environmental damage linked to the production or testing of nuclear weapons (International Campaign to Abolish Nuclear Weapons, *Nuclear Weapons, the Environment, and the Climate Crisis*, https://assets.nationbuilder.com/ican/pages/3178/attachments/original/1677630121/Climate_Crisis_Policy_Paper-2.pdf?1677630121).

example is a relatively clear case of 'state-initiated state corporate crime,'[133] the relationships that contribute to state–corporate crime are not always clear cut or easily identifiable due to the symbiotic nature of state–corporate relationships.[134] As Steve Tombs articulates, 'what appear at first sight to be discrete events brought into view by the lens of state–corporate crime are in fact better understood as processes.'[135]

State–corporate crime poses challenges for transitional justice processes in practice; for one, investigatory mechanisms may struggle to 'interrogate instances of suffering that have no obvious author.'[136] Dealing with state–corporate criminality raises the challenge of untangling webs of responsibility, particularly when corporations operate through multiple subsidiaries and states through multiple branches and partnerships.[137] As David Whyte has noted in the context of ecocide, corporations are remarkably good at evading responsibility and surviving critiques of their environmental practices.[138] As such, it may remain difficult for transitional justice measures to deliver on some of its purported goals. For example, individualised accountability may be very difficult to establish, further highlighting the limitations of the legalistic approach interrogated in Chapter 3.

Forms of transitional justice that are removed from an emphasis on criminal accountability may be better equipped in this regard. For example, one might imagine lustration processes that target political actors who are demonstrated to have granted concessions or enabled extractivism in exchange for arms or other benefits.[139] In relation to corporations, lustration might apply to the board of directors of a company responsible for violations or even extend to the dismantling of entire corporations and/or their subsidiaries. As Naomi Roht-Arriaza argues, 'techniques like asset declarations,' 'screening of personnel for previous participation in human rights violations,' and acceding to anticorruption frameworks offer ways to curb the worst crimes of the powerful.[140] Clara Sandoval, Leonardo Filippini, and Roberto Vidal have argued that such institutional reforms are 'the most

133 Dawn Rothe and David Kauzlarich, *Crimes of the Powerful: An Introduction* (Routledge, 2016).
134 Steve Tombs, "State–Corporate Symbiosis in the Production of Crime and Harm," *State Crime Journal* 1(2) (2012): 170–195. See also Rothe and Kauzlarich, *Crimes*.
135 Tombs, "State–Corporate," 177.
136 Davies, "Slow," 413.
137 David Whyte, *Ecocide: Kill the Corporation Before it Kills Us* (Manchester University Press, 2020).
138 Whyte, *Ecocide*.
139 On the positive impact of lustration on corruption, see Peter Rožič and Yuliy A. Nisnevich, "Lustration Matters: A Radical Approach to the Problem of Corruption," *Studies in Comparative International Development* 51 (2016) 257–285.
140 Roht-Arriaza, "Natural," 148–149.

needed measure to stop business from feeling that they have immunity that protect them. Yet, it is the area of transitional justice where the least is done in practice.'[141] In part, this may be because it requires long-term efforts, and, as Roht-Arriaza emphasises, will involve 'difficult, highly political struggle.' However, if successful, they offer a means of 'at least containing the toxic mixture of corrupt elites, rent-seeking officials, and organized crime that has used state power for its own benefit, and to the detriment of its environment and people.'[142]

More victim-centred mechanisms, such as collective reparations, also offer potential here. Even in the absence of criminal accountability, one might imagine the possible benefits of requiring corporate actors to return resources or make non-judicial reparations to communities, potentially greatly expanding the economic resources available to fund reparative projects.[143] Guarantees of non-recurrence – the most forward-looking of the reparation modalities – might involve increased regulation around the relationship between private and public actors to prevent future corruption and unsustainable and/or unjust resource extractivism.[144] As Irene Pietropaolo has argued, the potential for guarantees of non-recurrence to combat corporate harm has remained relatively underexplored, and yet it offers real potential as a way of exercising future control over corporate behaviour.[145] However, it is also the case that powerful actors are able to assert influence over the scope of transitional justice mechanisms, additionally highlighting the limitations of state-led, top-down approaches. This theme is explored further in the following subsection.

5.3.2 Transformative Justice

Transformative justice theories emerged 'as a critique of the liberal peace, the "top-down", elite nature of transitional justice.'[146] As captured by Rosemary Nagy, 'there is no consensus within the literature on whether transformative

141 Sandoval et al., "Linking," 24.

142 Roht-Arriaza, "Natural," 149.

143 Rachel Killean, "Ecocide in the International Criminal Court: The Prosecutor v Mr X (Reparations Order)," *UK Earth Judgments Project*, eds. Helen Dancer et al. (Hart, 2024).

144 Naomi Roht-Arriaza, "Natural Resources, Transitional States and Grand Corruption," *Research Handbook on International Law and Environmental Peacebuilding*, eds. Daniëlla Dam-de Jong and Britta Sjöstedt (Elgar, 2023).

145 Pietropaoli, *Business*.

146 Nagy, "Transformative": 195. See also Cahill-Ripley, "Foregrounding"; Evans, "Structural"; Matthew Mullan, "Reassessing the Focus of Transitional Justice: The Need to Move Structural and Cultural Violence to the Centre," *Cambridge Review of International Affairs* 28(3) (2015): 462–479; Gready and Robins, *From*.

justice is meant to replace, radically revise, or complement transitional justice.'[147] For instance, some have proposed that transitional justice be adapted to incorporate transformative elements, or that it has the potential to be transformative.[148] Others have articulated a transformative justice that is 'broader than and separate to' transitional justice.[149] While cognisant of these differing approaches, we find that these are largely definitional questions that do not need resolved for our purposes. Rather, in this subsection, we examine some proposed benefits of transformative approaches that seek to challenge transitional justice's temporal boundaries in order to better respond to structural harms. We also consider some of the critiques or proposed limitations of transformative justice.

For Dáire McGill, 'transformative justice is the framework required for transitional justice's redemption.'[150] Advocates of transformative approaches believe that addressing the underlying structural violence, and the social, economic, and cultural rights violations that accompany periods of mass violence, is crucial to achieving and sustaining peace. They push for a more holistic grappling with the past, one that exposes these 'deeper, structural systems that produce inequalities and forms of discrimination.'[151] Transformative approaches therefore seek to foreground the broader socioeconomic, political, and ecological contexts of mass violence[152] and propose a shift away from the 'short-term nature of dominant transitional justice practice' to more long-term processes of change.[153] For Simeon Gready and Simon Robins, transformative justice entails a shift in focus from legalism and the imposition of top-down, external legal frameworks or institutional models to bottom-up understandings of harm, communities, and their everyday concerns and needs.[154] Ideologically, proponents of a transformative approach seek 'a much more ambitious approach to transitional justice'[155] involving 'radical new ways of framing and responding to violence that is

147 Nagy, "Transformative," 194.

148 E.g. Balint et al., "Rethinking"; Pablo De Greiff, "The Future of the Past: Reflections on the Present State and Prospects of Transitional Justice," *International Journal of Transitional Justice* 14(2) (2020): 251–259; Wendy Lambourne, "Transitional Justice and Peacebuilding after Mass Violence," *International Journal of Transitional Justice* 3(1) (2009): 28–48.

149 Evans, "Structural"; see also Gready and Robins, *From.*

150 McGill, "Different," 96.

151 Molloy, "Conceptualising," 312. See also Matthew Evans, "Structural"; Nagy, "Transformative."

152 Lambourne, "Transitional." See also Molloy, "Conceptualising"; Evans, "Structural."

153 Sonya Klinsky and Jasmina Brankovic, *The Global Climate Regime and Transitional Justice* (Routledge, 2019), 157. See also Nagy, "Transformative."

154 Gready and Robins, *From.* See also Matthew Evans, "Structural."

155 Falk, "Predicaments," 60.

both relational and structural, holistic, sustainable and locally owned.'[156] In sum, a transformative approach centres structural injustices or inequalities; challenges the dominance of legalistic, top-down, or state-led approaches to transitional justice; and creates space for the agency of marginalised populations.

Applying these priorities to the identification of harm against Nature demonstrates the potential of a transformative justice perspective. First, it could broaden the scope of harms to include structural inequalities that are rooted in, and/or contribute to, the environmental destruction that can motivate or sustain conflict. To consider the example of the conflict in the Niger Delta, where decades of oil extraction have destroyed ecosystems,[157] a transformative approach might centre consideration of the colonial dynamics that have continued to generate conflict and are the source of the ongoing and severe environmental destruction.[158] Second, as examined in Chapter 3, the dominance of legalistic approaches has restricted transitional justice's capacity to recognise or respond to harms against Nature by asserting and maintaining the difference and separation of the natural world from that of humankind, and we would echo the transformative call to challenge these types of approaches. Third, creating space for grassroots agency is key to 'greening' transitional justice. For instance, in Chapter 4, we explored the potential of ecocentric developments; these are often initiated, promoted, and driven by activists rather than top-down institutions. The example of Colombia detailed in that chapter demonstrates the potential for grassroots-led movements to contribute to the development of 'official' or state-led transitional justice mechanisms that answer real need on the ground. A further example will be explored below, which is the potential of environmental justice , a movement which centres affected communities themselves in the identification and articulation of the harms they are experiencing.

Transformative justice approaches have also been criticised, and some of these criticisms are relevant to our analysis. It has been suggested that while the transformative scholarship clearly demonstrates the limitations of transitional justice, less well demonstrated is how transformative justice might be implemented in practice.[159] As observed above, addressing structural violence requires engagement with how political power is held, both locally

156 Nagy, "Transformative," 192. See also Falk, "Predicaments."

157 Lynch, Fegadel, and Long, "Green." See also Kenneth Omeje, *High Stakes and Stakeholders: Oil Conflict and Security in Nigeria* (Routledge, 2006); Ken Saro-Wiwa, *Genocide in Nigeria: The Ogoni Tragedy* (Saros, 1992).

158 Lynch et al., "Green"; Yusuf, "Colonialism."

159 Padraig McAuliffe, *Transformative Transitional Justice and the Malleability of Post-Conflict States* (Elgar, 2017).

and globally, and dismantling unequal power dynamics and systems of discrimination that may be built into the fabric of institutions of the state.[160] Some practical suggestions as to how this is to be achieved have been put forward, such as inclusive participation of victim populations in efforts to build a more fair and equal society,[161] and the employment of 'longer term and less individualized' economic models.[162] However, it is difficult to envisage how transitional justice might lead to a 'greener' and more just future without accompanying fundamental change in how states, businesses, and other elites operate. The dominance of neoliberalism in particular makes it very challenging to sustain claims for transformative outcomes.[163] Relatedly, due to the focus in the scholarship on 'empowering victims,' transformative justice 'has yet to address issues of complicity, benefit, indifference or hostility amongst those who feel they are being required to "give up" power and privilege or grant "special treatment" to minorities.'[164] In short, and paraphrasing Matthew Evans' analysis of land inequalities in South Africa, tensions can emerge between 'protecting the rights' of those who have, while 'realizing the rights' of those who have not.[165] The sharp end of this challenge relates to those who hold politically influential positions. As Rosemary Nagy has also noted, it may be difficult to motivate support for transformative change from those who benefit from, or are comfortable with, the status quo.[166]

Sean Molloy has highlighted transformative justice's 'diagnostic and prescriptive potential.'[167] While transformative justice approaches may remain somewhat aspirational, we agree with Matthew Evans that 'the concept of transformative justice is useful as an analytical tool.'[168] Transitional justice cannot adequately respond to harm against Nature and its implications for people's long-term well-being without taking into account socioeconomic and structural issues, and the transformative justice scholarship provides us with a way of, and rationale for, identifying and thinking through these manifestations of harm. In the next part, we turn to two further justice approaches that we argue may be useful for 'transforming' transitional justice into a more environmentally conscious field.

160 Molloy, "Conceptualising," 312–313.
161 Molloy, "Conceptualising," 312–313.
162 Evans, "Structural," 7.
163 Falk, "Predicaments," 71.
164 Nagy, "Transformative," 198.
165 Evans, "Structural," 10.
166 Nagy, "Transformative," 195; See also McAuliffe, *Transformative*; Sharp, "Introduction."
167 Molloy, "Conceptualising," 325.
168 Evans, "Structural," 9.

5.4 Transforming Justice

5.4.1 Environmental Justice

Transformative justice advocates have at times acknowledged the specific environmental harms that comprise structural violence (such as the spoiling of land by corrupt officials, the violation of the right to water, food, etc.). Yet, it has not generally been a dominant focus of this scholarship. However, important contributions to thinking through structural harms and Nature exist outside the context of mass violence. Transformative justice ideas find resonance with 'environmental justice,' a body of scholarship and advocacy that works to expose the disproportionate impacts of environmental degradation and the unequal distribution of natural resources in a wide range of contexts.[169] This subsection explores the potential of environmental justice to inform and expand transitional justice to better capture the inequalities that can drive or result from harm against Nature.

Grounded in the experiences of Black communities in the United States, the term 'environmental justice' gained prevalence in the 1980s. Activists and scholars have drawn attention to the range of structural inequalities at a local, national, and international level that create 'the socioecological dynamics that imperil black [sic] life.'[170] Central to this is an emphasis on the 'need to honour and acknowledge' those most affected by environmental injustice, something that is 'especially important' when those affected 'are often rendered invisible and ignored.'[171] Given the relative invisibility of structural harm and slow violence in transitional justice, such a perspective is a valuable one, and one that resonates with the victim-centric approach we have adopted throughout this book.

In response to environmental injustices, and recognising the challenges associated with pushing people in positions of power to make (or at least not

169 Robert Bullard, ed., *The Quest for Environmental Justice: Human Rights and the Politics of Pollution* (Sierra Club Books, 2005); Ryan Holifield et al., "Introduction: The Worlds of Environmental Justice," *The Routledge Handbook of Environmental Justice*, eds. Ryan Holifield et al. (Routledge, 2018); Thomas Sikor and Peter Newell, "Globalizing Environmental Justice?" *Geoforum* 54 (2014): 151–157; Gordon Walker, "Beyond Distribution and Proximity: Exploring the Multiple Spatialities of Environmental Justice," *Antipode* 41(4) (2009): 614–636.

170 Michael Warren Murphy et al., "Black Ecology and Critical Environmental Justice," *Environmental Justice* 14(6) (2021): 393–397. See also Tatiana Height et al., "Call for Environmental Justice Amplification Among Ecology Scholars and Practitioners: A Black Ecology Perspective," *The Bulletin of the Ecological Society of America* 104(1) (2022): e02039; Holifield et al., "Introduction"; Esme G. Murdock, "A History of Environmental Justice: Foundations, Narratives, and Perspectives," *Environmental Justice*, ed. Brendan Coolsaet (Routledge, 2020).

171 Murdock, "A History," 9.

hinder) change, David Pellow and others have advocated for 'transformative (rather than primarily reformist) approaches to realize environmental justice."'[172] Pellow has argued that greater attention should be paid to 'the expendability of human and nonhuman populations that face socioenvironmental threats.'[173] From this perspective, environmental justice requires the interrogation and confrontation of the structural contexts in which harm to Nature occurs,[174] and measures which pursue fundamental social change.[175] More recently, Pellow and others have advocated for what they term a 'critical environmental justice.'[176] Such an approach has four pillars, which we will briefly examine in turn.

5.4.1.1. Intersectionality

The first is 'intersectionality.' First conceptualised by Kimberlé Crenshaw to examine the impact of the intersection of race and gender in discrimination law,[177] 'intersectionality' usefully demonstrates how 'the multiple and intermeshed oppressions experienced by marginalized communities and environments around the world *kill*.'[178] While environmental justice has traditionally emphasised race and class as determining factors in exposure to environmental risks and inequalities, critical environmental justice calls attention to the roles of 'colonialism, racism, cisheteropatriarchy, classism, nativism, ableism, ageism, speciesism, imperialism, and so on' as intersecting determinants of environmental injustice.[179] Building on above critiques regarding transitional justice's overlooking of the historic contexts in which violence becomes possible, critical environmental justice theorists highlight

172 David Pellow, "Toward a Critical Environmental Justice Studies," *Du Bois Review* 13(2) (2016): 224. See also Leah Temper, "Blocking Pipelines, Unsettling Environmental Justice: From Rights of Nature to Responsibility to Territory," *Local Environmental* 24(2) (2019): 94–112.

173 Murphy et al., "Black," 394.

174 Michael J. Lynch et al., *Green Criminology and Green Theories of Justice: An Introduction to a Political Economic View of Eco-Justice* (Palgrave Macmillan, 2019).

175 Rob White, "The Conceptual Contours of Green Criminology," *Emerging Issues in Green Criminology: Exploring Power, Justice and Harm*, eds. Reece Walters et al. (Palgrave MacMillan, 2013), 27.

176 David N. Pellow, *What is Critical Environmental Justice?* (Polity Press, 2018).

177 Kimberlé Crenshaw, "Demarginalizing the Intersection of Race and Sex: Black Feminist Critique of Antidiscrimination Doctrine, Feminist Theory and Antiracist Politics," *University of Chicago Legal Forum* 1989(1): 139–167; Kimberlé Crenshaw, "Mapping the Margins: Intersectionality, Identity Politics and Violence against Women of Color," *Stanford Law Review* 43(6) (1991): 1241–1299.

178 Giovanna Di Chiro, "Mobilizing 'Intersectionality' in Environmental Justice Research and Action in a Time of Crisis," in *Environmental Justice*, ed. Brendan Coolsaet (Routledge, 2020).

179 Murphy et al., "Black," 395.

how 'chattel slavery not only formed the bedrock of racial domination, but along with Indigenous dispossession and elimination, constituted a racial-colonial and ecological order imbued with violence.'[180] This theorisation resonates with the concept of *Cuerpo-Territorio* ('body territory'), a concept that captures the intertwined nature of the harm caused by domination of (Indigenous women's) bodies and territory at a cultural and spiritual level as well as a physical level.[181] Intersectionality invites a more expansive understanding of harm, facilitating more nuanced understandings of who might have a claim to justice, and for what.

While transitional justice literature has primarily used intersectionality to deepen our understanding of gendered harms,[182] drawing on critical environmental justice invites an intersectionality that moves beyond transitional justice's traditional focus on physical and property-oriented harm. A critical environmental approach, we argue, would consider the intersections between human and other-than-human harm, as well as how those harms are differentially experienced by those who hold marginalised identities. Reflecting critical environmental justice's emphasis on thinking beyond the state (discussed below), engaging with intersections of oppression also provides opportunities for collaboration and mobilisation across organisations and borders, inviting recognition of shared experiences and resistance to overly narrow framings of justice.[183]

5.4.1.2. Multi-scalarity

The second pillar is 'multi-scalarity.' Critical environmental justice research seeks to uncover 'the complex spatial and temporal causes, consequences, and possible resolutions of environmental justice struggles.'[184] Such an approach acknowledges the 'deep ecological entanglements of (earthly) existence.'[185] Furthermore, consideration of scale can help us to see how 'environmen-

180 Murphy et al., "Black," 395.

181 Marcela Tovar-Restrepo and Clara Irazábal, "Indigenous Women and Violence in Colombia: Agency, Autonomy, and Territoriality," *Latin American Perspectives* 41(1) (2014): 39–58; Elizabeth L. Sweet and Sara Ortiz Escalante, "Engaging Territorio Cuerpo-Tierra through Body and Community Mapping: A Methodology for Making Communities Safer," *Gender, Place & Culture* 24 (2017): 1–13.

182 For early calls, see Eilish Rooney and Fionnuala Ni Aolaín, 'Underenforcement and Intersectionality: Gendered Aspects of Transition for Women,' *International Journal of Transitional Justice* 1(3) (2007): 338–354; and for a more recent assessment, see Ruth Amir, "Transitional Justice and Intersectionality in Post-Conflict Societies," in *Human Rights and International Humanitarian Law*, eds. Andreas Zimmermann and Norman Weiß (Elgar, 2022).

183 Di Chiro, "Mobilizing," 321.

184 Pellow, "What," 22.

185 Murphy et al., "Black," 396.

tal injustices are facilitated by decision-makers' who may seek to distance themselves from the impacts of their actions on both humans and Nature.[186] Returning to our examination of transitional justice's tendency to overlook the complicity or direct responsibility of corporations or others responsible for harm against Nature, we can see how taking a multi-scalar view could help to broaden the scope of accountability. Even in the absence of legal liability for powerful actors, adopting a multi-scalar approach might invite more holistic approaches to truth telling and memorialisation, for example by resisting the 'resource curse' narratives discussed above and reckoning with the broader causes of injustice.

5.4.1.3 Horizontality

'Horizontality' challenges the traditional approach of environmental justice activists of looking to the state and the legal system to deliver justice and regulate industry. Critical environmental justice challenges this reliance on state structures, drawing attention to the entrenched modes of power that are only reinforced by state apparatus. Instead of looking to the state, critical environmental justice activists called for a deepened 'direct democracy.'[187] Horizontality involves 'enhanced participation in environmental decision-making.'[188] Such an approach draws from an awareness in Black and anticolonial radical activism that justice cannot be found in modifications of the existing state. As Esme Murdock contends,

> environmental justice is, importantly, a movement, which means that it starts and lives with the people: in the communities that are experiencing the harms ... environmental justice ... is primarily a grassroots and people-driven movement ... an important principle of environmental justice that emerges from activist communities is the maxim: 'We speak for ourselves.'[189]

This activist-led movement resonates with the literature on transitional justice 'from below'[190] and our own arguments throughout the book: that for transitional justice to recognise and meaningfully respond to harm against

186 David N. Pellow, "Critical Environmental Justice Studies," *Environmental Justice*, ed. Brendan Coolsaet (Routledge, 2020), 294.

187 Pellow, *What*, 24.

188 Tamara Stegerm et al., "Environmental Justice in Central and Eastern Europe: Mobilization, Stagnation and Detraction," *The Routledge Handbook of Environmental Justice*, eds. Ryan Holifield et al. (Routledge, 2018): 649.

189 Murdock, "A History," 9.

190 McEvoy and McGregor, "From Below."

Nature requires the empowerment and platforming of those directly affected by these harms. Bringing together transitional justice 'from below' and critical environmental justice perspectives might necessitate asking different kinds of questions and being open to hearing about communities' perspectives beyond the narrow scope of usually accepted 'harms.'

5.4.1.4 Indispensability

Indispensability is the idea that 'the dominated, human or otherwise' should no longer be viewed as 'expendable but rather as indispensable to our collective futures.'[191] As Pellow argues, 'socially, politically, philosophically, and ecologically, what this means is that we are all linked in webs of interdependence, so that what happens to one group affects, in some way, all others.'[192] Michael Murphy, George Weddington, and AJ Rio-Glick note that 'black [sic] studies have consistently sought to challenge modes of thought and action that are deeply invested in the captivity of (black) life and that (re) produce alienation from our human and more-than-human relatives, and even the earth itself.'[193] We argue that any attempt to meaningfully 'green' transitional justice requires greater foregrounding of 'relational ontologies' that emphasise the relationships between all natural organisms. Centring the critical environmental justice principle of indispensability in the design and implementation of transitional justice and combining it with the notions of other-than-human justice and restoration, as explored in Chapter 4, present ways that relationality could be made meaningful in the field. [194]

In sum, as Esme Murdock articulates, 'environmental justice ... expands the space of possibility for examining the intersectional sites of humans and environments while also multiplying the number of those whom we consider when we talk about environmental degradation.'[195] As such, we argue that critical environmental justice in particular offers a lens which can be used to 'expand the space of possibility' for what transitional justice incorporates in ways that better acknowledge the interconnections between structural

191 Murphy et al., "Black," 397.
192 Pellow, *What*, 27.
193 Murphy et al., "Black."
194 Andrea Doucet, "Shorelines, Seashells, and Seeds: Feminist Epistemologies, Ecological Thinking, and Relational Ontologies," *The Palgrave Handbook of Relational Sociology*, ed. François Dépelteau (Palgrave Macmillan, 2018).
See also Lorraine Code, *What Can She Know? Feminist Theory and the Construction of Knowledge* (Cornell University Press, 1991).
195 Murdock, "A History," 13. Murdock does however critique environmental justice's focus on environmental racism and oversimplification of the challenges faced by diverse communities and populations.

injustice, the destruction of Nature, periods of mass violence, and human suffering.

5.4.2 Trivalent Justice

In this final subsection, we consider the influential work of Nancy Fraser. Both transformative justice and environmental justice advocates have been influenced by aspects of Fraser's trivalent justice theorisation.[196] This encompasses redistribution (to promote equal access to resources), recognition (through the designation of social and cultural standing or status), and representation (participation and increased marginalised voices in positions of power).[197] Fraser argues that an integrated approach to justice is necessary in order to address the injustices that encompass both economic and cultural harms, that is, we need to address inequity and the 'why' of the inequity.[198] For Fraser, this tripartite approach is particularly effective for addressing transnational concerns, as the representation strand can challenge 'misframing' of global inequalities as national problems.[199] While Fraser's focus is on gender inequality, a justice framework aimed at transnational issues has utility for challenging harm against Nature.

As Fraser cautions, responses to injustice may encompass affirmative remedies which reduce inequalities without challenging underlying social relations. Instead, transformative remedies should be pursued which correct 'inequitable outcomes by restructuring the underlying generative framework.'[200] Fraser's approach speaks to critiques of transitional jus-

196 See e.g., Brendan Coolsaet and Pierre-Yves Néron, "Recognition and Environmental Justice," *Environmental Justice*, ed. Brendan Coolsaet (Routledge, 2020); Andrea Durbach and Louise Chappell, "Leaving Behind the Age of Impunity: Victims of Gender Violence and the Promise of Reparations," *International Feminist Journal of Politics* 16(4) (2014): 543–562; Daniela Lai, *Socioeconomic Justice: International Intervention and Transition in Post-War Bosnia and Herzegovina* (CUP, 2020); David Schlosberg, *Defining Environmental Justice: Theories, Movements and Nature* (OUP, 2009); Sarah Williams and Emma Palmer, "Transformative Reparations for Women and Girls at the Extraordinary Chambers in the Courts of Cambodia," *International Journal of Transitional Justice* 10(2) (2016): 311–331; Özge Yaka, "Rethinking Justice: Struggles for Environmental Commons and the Notion of Socio-Ecological Justice," *Antipode* 51(1) (2019): 353–372.

197 See, for example, Nancy Fraser, *Scales of Justice: Reimagining Political Space in a Globalizing World* (Columbia University Press, 2009); Nancy Fraser, "From Redistribution to Recognition? Dilemmas of Justice in a 'Post-Socialist' Age," *New Left Review* 1(212) (1995): 82.

198 Fraser, "From Redistribution"; David Schlosberg, "Reconceiving Environmental Justice: Global Movements and Political Theories," *Environmental Politics* 13(3) (2004): 517–540.

199 Fraser, *Scales*.

200 Fraser, "From Redistribution."

tice as leaving issues of distribution untouched,[201] while also aligning with environmental justice advocates who have argued that 'justice' calls for much more than 'just distribution.'[202] Approaches to justice which encompass issues of redistribution, recognition and representation have clear links to transformative justice ways of thinking about mass atrocity. We have found that this framework, and the work of environmental activists in pursuing transformation, offers an insight into what environmentally transformative justice might necessitate in the aftermath of mass violence. In the remainder of this subsection, we will examine each of the three strands and their potential relevance for transitional justice.

5.4.2.1 Redistribution

For Nancy Fraser, redistribution 'might involve redistributing income, reorganizing the division of labour, subjecting investment to democratic decision-making, or transforming other basic economic structures.'[203] 'Redistributive justice' as a term has not been widely used in transitional justice scholarship,[204] which has tended to focus more on notions of restitution.[205] To the extent that the scholarship has engaged with notions of redistribution, it has understood transitional justice and redistribution as differing spheres of justice.[206] This can be linked to both transitional justice's history, which grounds it in liberal ideas of individual rights, and its related emphasis on backward-looking justice for 'victims' (narrowly defined), rather than forward-looking measures for broader social groups.[207]

Similarly, few transitional justice mechanisms have featured redistributive measures. These have been mixed in their results. For example, in her discussion on the Sierra Leone Truth Commission, Eliana Cusato notes that the Commission considered colonial legacies. However, 'under the

201 See e.g. Hannah Franzki and Maria Carolina Olarte, "Understanding the Political Economy of Transitional Justice: A Critical Theory Perspective," *Transitional Justice Theories*, eds. Susanne Buckley-Zistel et al. (Routledge, 2013).

202 Schlosberg, *Defining.*

203 Fraser, "From Redistribution," 75.

204 Katie Boyle, "Reconceptualising Socio-Economic Rights in the Transitional Justice Discipline," *Law, Social Justice & Global Development* 2 (2016): 2–10.

205 Boyle, "Reconceptualising Socio-Economic Rights." Khanyisela Moyo, "Mimicry, Transitional Justice and the Land Question in Racially Divided Former Settler Colonies," *International Journal of Transitional Justice* 9 (2015): 70–89.

206 Felix E. Torres, "On Deserving Victims and the Undeserving Poor: Exploring the Scope of Distributive Justice in Transitional Justice Theory and Practice," *Human Rights Quarterly* 45(2) (2023): 306–334.

207 Torres, "On Deserving Victims and the Undeserving Poor."

title of "Community Empowerment", few recommendations were aimed at redistributing wealth from diamond experts for the benefits of communities in mining areas,' and Cusato describes the recommendation that a 'higher percentage of export tax on diamonds be made available to communities through the "Community Development Programme"' as the 'only (timid) effort to redress inequality as a factor leading to violent conflict'.[208] She further notes that such measures were only of 'symbolic' value, rather than bringing about meaningful redistribution. Elsewhere, in Zimbabwe, Mugabe's land redistribution efforts have been 'driven ... by violence, corruption and favoritism,' resulting in a system that has been 'grossly unfair to the majority African population.'[209] In South Africa, redistribution efforts sought 'a compromise between protecting the economy and redressing the legacy of unjust land dispossessions.'[210] Redistribution has been slow, and has often involved transfer of land to 'a few farmers with money' rather than more impoverished rural populations.[211]

These examples demonstrate that not only is redistribution relatively rare in transitional justice, it can also be limited and even harmful if not done in good faith. As Ismael Muvingi cautions, 'the challenges of redistribution are many and serious ... [and] a huge undertaking.'[212] He emphasises that individual reparations are insufficient, and that what is required is an overhaul of 'systemic arrangements of inequality.'[213] Khanyisela Moyo emphasises a particular challenge in post-colonial contexts, where 'on the face of it,' one might think that transitional justice should avoid using 'the binaries of black and white.' However, 'these binaries cannot be ignored in any meaningful rendition of land injustices' as there is a need to 'correct bifurcated colonial/apartheid racialized land redistribution patterns that favoured white commercial farms and marginalized black communal areas.'[214] We can see here echoes of Fraser's 'redistribution-recognition dilemma,' where recognition requires the affirmation of difference, while redistribution requires the collapsing of difference.[215] Following Fraser, we suggest that involving previously marginalised groups in decision-making processes (*representation*) and applying all three dimensions of justice 'in

208 Cusato, *Ecology*, 659.

209 Moyo, "Mimicry"; Ismael Muvingi, "Sitting on Powder Kegs: Socioeconomic Rights in Transitional Societies," *International Journal of Transitional Justice* 3 (2009): 181–182; Tafadzwa Pasipanodya, "A Deeper Justice: Economic and Social Justice as Transitional Justice in Nepal," *The International Journal of Transitional Justice* 2 (2008): 378–397.

210 Moyo, "Mimicry," 81.

211 Moyo, "Mimicry," 82. See also Evans, "Structural."

212 Muvingi, "Sitting," 180.

213 Muvingi, "Sitting," 180.

214 Moyo, "Mimicry," 72.

215 Fraser, "From Redistribution," 74.

a balanced way' could facilitate the development of the most 'just' solution to these types of tension.[216]

While the examples above demonstrate the challenges, we argue that redistribution need not be seen as a separate arena of justice. Indeed, it is entirely possible to contemplate reparations for material deprivations and unequal socioeconomic power relations.[217] Doing so may offer promising pathways towards responding to harms against Nature. René Urueña and María Angélica Prada-Uribe suggest (using the terminology of redistributive and distributive justice interchangeably) that this would involve transitional justice mechanisms 'looking further back' to the root causes of conflict.[218] We can see the potential here for expanding the temporal gaze of transitional justice. In addition, Moyo suggests a shift away from viewing land issues through a property or contract lens to take into account issues of 'unjust enrichment' and the experiences of all previously marginalised groups.[219] Such an argument finds resonance with theories we have outlined above, including the recognition of a broader range of accountability, the indispensability of marginalised groups, and adopting a more relational approach to harm. In the context of transitional justice responses to harms against Nature, aspects of redistributive justice could be encompassed by guarantees of non-recurrence, lustration mechanisms, and forms of collective rehabilitative reparations for harmed groups. It could include, for example, systemic changes to the management of energy production and natural resources,[220] the re-establishing of Indigenous or community land practices and custodianship,[221] and enabling communities to re-access land-based livelihoods that may have been lost.[222] It may also encompass more equitable ways of distributing environmental 'bads' as well as

216 Fraser, *Scales.*

217 Torres, "Deserving."

218 Urueña and Prada-Uribe, "Transitional," 402.

219 Moyo, "Mimicry," 72. Relatedly, Mark McMillan and Sophie Rigney have written of the importance of Indigenous people 'naming the harm they have survived' in "Race, Reconciliation, and Justice in Australia: from Denial to Acknowledgment," *Ethnic and Racial Studies* 41(4) (2017): 771.

220 Avi Brisman and Nigel South, "Resource Wealth, Power, Crime and Conflict," *Emerging Issues in Green Criminology: Exploring Power, Justice and Harm*, eds. Reece Walters et al. (Palgrave MacMillan, 2013), 67; Cameron Holley et al., *The New Environmental Governance* (Routledge, 2012).

221 For the particular challenges of applying transitional justice to settler colonial contexts, see Park, "Settler"; Margaret Mutu, "Behind the Smoke and Mirrors of the Treaty of Waitangi Claims Settlement Process in New Zealand: No Prospect for Justice and Reconciliation for Māori without Constitutional Transformation," *Journal of Global Ethics* 14(2) (2018): 208–221.

222 Schlosberg, "Reconceiving," 524.

goods,[223] resonating with the environmental justice principles outlined above and requiring recognition of intersectional forms of marginalisation. This approach in turn resonates with the second aspect of Fraser's framework: recognition.

5.4.2.2. Recognition

'Recognition' calls for engagement with the role of identity and status in shaping access to and control over natural resources.[224] Fraser outlines a range of possible manifestations of 'recognition.' As she argues, this could involve challenging 'patterns of cultural value or status hierarchies,'[225] 'upwardly revaluing disrespected identities ... recognizing and positively valorizing cultural diversity,' or even 'the wholesale transformation of societal patterns of representation, interpretation and communication.'[226] This finds resonance with the critical environmental justice literature, which emphasises the need to adopt intersectional understandings of environmental harm and justice claims.

Given that 'the recognition paradigm identifies failure in societal institutions to acknowledge or respect *difference* as a source of systematic wrongdoing,'[227] we can see how this aligns with and might help to counter transitional justice's overlooking of structural inequalities. For some environmental justice scholars, recognition is a 'significant and distinct paradigm for understanding environmental injustice.'[228] In any effort to 'green' transitional justice, recognition would require acknowledgement of the full range of environmental harms experienced. Going further, it might extend to recognition of cultural connections and claims to environments, the historic territorial sovereignty of targeted groups, or, indeed, the rights and standing of Nature itself, as protected by guardians or representatives.[229] Cultural recognition is in many ways central to environmental justice, particularly when Indigenous peoples have been denied sovereignty or excluded from their ancestral lands, and where damage to the environment is also expe-

223 Schlosberg, "Reconceiving," 523.
224 Women and children are some of the most vulnerable to environmental risk and face additional barriers to meaningful voice and participation. See, for example, Karen J. Warren, *Ecofeminist Philosophy: A Western Perspective on What It Is and Why It Matters* (Rowman and Littlefield, 2000); Vandana Shiva, *Staying Alive: Women, Ecology and Development* (Southend Press, 2010).
225 Fraser, *Scales*, 105.
226 Fraser, "From Redistribution," 73.
227 Kyle Whyte, "The Recognition Paradigm of Environmental Injustice," *The Routledge Handbook of Environmental Justice*, eds. Ryan Holifield et al. (Routledge, 2018), 117.
228 Whyte, "The Recognition Paradigm," 113.
229 Temper, "Blocking," 97–98. See Chapter Four.

rienced as an attack on family and community. As Kyle Whyte discusses, this is a potentially very substantial undertaking as 'genuine recognition is deeply ecological ... certain forms or expressions of differences ... require a particular range of ecological processes and access to large territories of land and water ecosystems.'[230] Embracing recognition may help to facilitate a form of environmentally transformative justice that could facilitate a shift beyond the maintenance of unequal and harmful 'human social and economic organization'[231] towards more egalitarian principles.[232] As Fraser notes in her own discussions around recognition, 'it is unjust that some individuals and groups are denied the status of full partners in social interaction simply as a consequence of institutionalized patterns of cultural value in whose construction they have not equally participated and which disparage their distinctive characteristics or the distinctive characteristics assigned to them.'[233] What recognition therefore entails is 'that everyone has an equal right to pursue social esteem under fair conditions of equal opportunity.'[234]

In a transitional justice context, a body of work exists on transitional justice as 'recognition,' originating with Frank Haldemann's 2008 article.[235] Haldemann's conceptualisation focuses on 'human suffering' (as transitional justice traditionally does), and for him, recognition is 'individual-centered.'[236] As we have argued throughout this book, to respond to harms against Nature, transitional justice must broaden its gaze beyond the human and move away from the individualism inherent to the field. Setting the anthropocentrism of Haldemann's work to the side, the tenets of this approach could be beneficial for 'greening' transitional justice. For Haldemann, recognition 'requires the just redistribution of resources and rights' and this 'must reach beyond distributive systems of goods in the society to investigate the full dimension of injustice and the sense of victimization it arouses.'[237] Haldemann 'endorses a rather broad notion of victimhood' including direct and secondary victims, incorporating those 'affected by structural violence and systemic injustice.'[238] Such a 'recognition' approach to transitional

230 Whyte, "The Recognition Paradigm," 120.
231 Lynch et al., *Green Criminology*, 10.
232 Rob White, *Environmental Harm: An Eco-Justice Perspective* (Bristol University Press, 2013), 20.
233 Nancy Fraser, "Social Justice in the Age of Identity Politics: Redistribution, Recognition, Participation," Discussion Paper, 1998, https://nbn-resolving.org/urn:nbn:de:0168-ssoar-126247.
234 Fraser, "Social Justice in the Age of Identity Politics."
235 Frank Haldemann, "Another Kind of Justice: Transitional Justice as Recognition," *Cornell International Law Journal* 41(3) (2008): 675–738.
236 Haldemann, "Another Kind of Justice," 678.
237 Haldemann, "Another Kind of Justice," 679.
238 Haldemann, "Another Kind of Justice," 679.

justice could potentially allow for the extension of rights or victimhood to Nature. Haldemann also advocates for recognising the 'collective nature of "macro" instances of evil' and the 'inherently societal, macro-level, and systemic dimension' of 'extraordinary evil.'[239] While we do not find the idea of 'evil' a particularly useful one, looking at 'macro' harms resonates with a crimes of the powerful approach and could facilitate more comprehensive engagement with harms against Nature in transitional contexts.

To consider an example of the application of 'recognition' in transitional justice in practice, Camilo Tamayo Gomez's work indicates potential for centring, or at least mainstreaming, notions of recognition in transitional justice. Gomez suggests that there is a 'mutual' relationship between recognition and transitional justice 'from below,' with 'from below' efforts determining 'the content and nature of recognition' and 'recognition' being a prerequisite for justice, truth, reparation, and the other major functions of transitional justice.[240] As Fraser originally articulated, 'redistributive remedies generally presuppose an underlying conception of recognition' and 'recognition remedies sometimes presuppose an underlying conception of redistribution.'[241] Gomez's work provides practical examples of 'recognition' work, demonstrating the importance of recording, documenting, or describing harm as a way of 'constructing a social narrative of recognition' and displaying these accounts in a public place.[242]

Visible displays of the harms caused to Nature may provide one way to recognise this type of harm. As authors, we have both been struck by the images of conflict-related harm against Nature we have seen in recent years from Ukraine, Palestine, Syria, and other contexts of armed conflict, mass atrocity, or genocide. One particularly striking example is of Mahfodah Shtayyeh, a Palestinian farmer pictured in 2005 hugging an olive tree after it was attacked by Israeli settlers.[243] Such images demonstrate the interconnected and multilayered harm experienced as a result of attacks on Nature, encompassing human anguish just as much as environmental destruction. While Shtayyeh has spoken to the media about the image, there are ethical

239 Haldemann, "Another Kind of Justice," 679.

240 Camilo Tamayo Gomez, "Recognition as Transitional Justice 'From Below': Analysing Victims' Grassroots Activism in Postconflict Colombia," *International Journal of Transitional Justice* 16 (2022): 319.

241 Fraser, "From Redistribution," 73.

242 Gomez, "Recognition," 323.

243 Al Jazeera English, "The Tree Hugger: Settler Attacks on Palestinian Farmers and their Olive Trees" (YouTube: https://www.youtube.com/watch?v=fslr2bZs864&t=50s). This photograph is on the cover of Joseph Pugliese's *Biopolitics of the More-Than-Human: Forensic Ecologies of Violence* (Duke University Press, 2020).

considerations in using images of victims of violence,[244] and there has been criticism of the use of victim imagery in the 'marketisation' of transitional justice.[245] However, we suggest that increasing the visibility of harm against Nature – if done sensitively and with consent – could be a useful first step in moving environmental harm onto the transitional justice agenda. Gomez has suggested that 'by scrutinizing victims' initiatives as expressions of recognition, the idea of transitional justice "from below" can be revigorated.'[246] For example, *Asociación Kuyanakuy*, a group of displaced Peruvian women, created an *arpillera* (an appliquéd textile) for presentation at the Peruvian Truth Commission in 2002. This *arpillera*, entitled *Ayer–Hoy* (Yesterday–Today) depicted the women's previous lives in villages in the Andes alongside their present displaced lives in an urban area of Lima. What is most striking about the *arpillera* is the contrast between the Nature depicted in village life (including mountains, waterways, trees and other flora, animals) and the brown and barren cityscape. This *arpillera* powerfully visualises how these women have been separated from Nature.[247] A further example can be found in Gema Varona's analysis of the *Prestige* case as ecocide. *Prestige* was an oil tanker that sank, resulting in the spillage of over 77,000 tonnes of oil and pollution of some 2,000 kilometres of coastline. A range of official and unofficial memorials have been created along the affected coast to 'remind us of a wounded landscape.'[248] Both these examples could be considered examples of 'recognition' – pressing upon the audience (be that a formal transitional justice body or the public) the value of Nature and the interrelated experiences of harm. From this perspective, transitional justice already has many of the tools needed, and they can be adapted to draw attention to harm against Nature.

5.4.2.3. Representation

Finally, we turn to representation, which involves ensuring 'equal political voice' for marginalised communities within 'already constituted political

244 See e.g. Judith Butler, "Torture and the Ethics of Photography," *Environment and Planning D: Society and Space*, 25 (2007): 951–966; Eamonn Carrabine, "Just Images: Aesthetics, Ethics and Visual Criminology," *The British Journal of Criminology* 52(3) (2012): 463–489; Aoife Duffy, "Bearing Witness to Atrocity Crimes: Photography and International Law," *Human Rights Quarterly* 40(4) (2018): 776–814.

245 See e.g. Christine Schwobel-Patel, "The 'Ideal' Victim of International Criminal Law," *The European Journal of International Law* 29(3) (2018): 703–724.

246 Gomez, "Recognition," 330.

247 Asociación Kuyanakuy, *Ayer–Hoy/Yesterday–Today*, viewable at https://cain.ulster.ac.uk/conflicttextiles/search-quilts2/fulltextiles1/?id=198.

248 Gema Varona, "Restorative Pathways After Mass Environmental Victimization: Walking in the Landscapes of Past Ecocides," *Oñati Socio-Legal Series* 10(3) (2020): 673.

communities.'[249] Fraser added this third dimension in a 'major revision' of her original framework,[250] and as such representation is not necessarily always discussed alongside the other two strands. However, while Fraser's 'representation' strand is not explicitly engaged with to the same extent as her work on recognition, the concept of 'participation' in the environmental justice scholarship captures a similar approach to justice.[251] This would involve 'policy-making procedures that encourage active community participation, institutionalize public participation, recognize community knowledge, and utilize cross-cultural formats and exchanges to enable the participation of as much diversity as exists in a community.'[252] As such, this concept finds resonance with the emphasis on 'horizontality' explored in the critical environmental justice scholarship.

Fraser developed the concept of 'parity of participation' in an effort to square the circle of how to facilitate both redistribution and recognition against the backdrop of 'complex relations between interest and identity, economy and culture, class and status in contemporary globalizing capitalist society.'[253] Parity of participation 'requires social arrangements that permit all (adult) members of society to interact with one another as peers.'[254] While some environmental justice scholars have used Fraser's notion of 'recognition' to explore participation, her shift to 'representation' better encapsulates questions around who is 'entitled to participate' in a political space, and how.[255] In the environmental justice context, David Schlosberg's work connects the notion of recognition to participation, suggesting a 'direct link between a lack of respect and recognition and a decline in a person's membership and participation in the greater community, including the political and institutional order.'[256] In this way, Schlosberg contends that recognition 'brings the political parity necessary for participation'[257] and that this could be extended to Nature to allow for recognition of Nature across political, cultural, and social institutions. Taking this further, Schlosberg proposes that ecological and environmental

249 Fraser, *Scales*, 114.
250 Fraser, *Scales*, 145.
251 For instance, for David Schlosberg, it is 'improved participatory mechanisms' that can address issues with distribution or recognition, in a similar vein to Fraser's use of representation; and for Brendan Coolsaet and Pierre-Yves Néron, it is Fraser's theory of 'parity of participation' that 'combines' demands for recognition and redistribution (Schlosberg, *Defining* and Coolsaet and Néron, "Recognition," 56).
252 Schlosberg, "Reconceiving," 522.
253 Fraser, "Social Justice."
254 Fraser, "Social Justice," 5. See also Nancy Fraser, *Fortunes*.
255 Fraser, in interview with Kate Nash and Vikki Bell, *Scales*, 147.
256 Schlosberg "Reconceiving," 519.
257 Schlosberg, *Defining*.

justice requires recognition and representation of 'views from the margins, the remote, and the natural world ... either directly or through proxies.'[258] Such an approach finds resonance with our arguments regarding the possibilities of expanding representation to Nature.

5.5 Conclusion

We have argued in this chapter that the temporal boundaries of transitional justice preclude much structural and slow violence from the field's purview. As such, these temporal choices impact upon the visibility of phases or forms of harm, and the ways in which these harms are responded to. We have argued for a broadening of these temporal parameters, to capture harm against Nature that may pre-date the period of conflict or authoritarianism that the transitional justice process has been designed to address. Such a broadening would not be without challenges, given that harm against Nature is often deeply embedded in structural inequalities and, in many contexts, rooted in historic and continuing colonial violence. However, we argue that transitional justice must be more ambitious in scope if it is to engage effectively with environmental harm. To this end, our conclusions to this chapter can be framed in two ways: the first is that this chapter has demonstrated the continued importance of themes we have examined throughout this book, and the second is that transitional justice already has at least some of the tools required for pursuing the change needed.

To first turn to themes, this chapter has demonstrated that the power hierarchies that have narrowed the scope of transitional justice through the dominance of legalism (see Chapter 3) have further narrowed the field's scope by artificially isolating specific periods of time for investigation. Such decisions are not neutral and might exclude much harm, including serious environmental harm, which continues to manifest once the period of mass violence has come to an end. A second theme is the extent of exclusion of harm as a result of transitional justice's focus on extreme or 'spectacular' acts of violence – an additional result of the dominance of legalism. These limitations demonstrate the need to (as transformative justice and environmental justice advocates contend) challenge state-led, top-down approaches to addressing injustice and critically reflect on who is designing and implementing transitional justice efforts (see Chapter 2).

In this regard, this chapter has further demonstrated the importance of creating space for victimised communities to identify transitional justice

258 Schlosberg, *Defining*, 187. See also White, "Recognition."

priorities, rather than having agendas imposed from above. Along with transformative justice scholars and environmental justice advocates, we emphasise the need to centre those impacted by harm and for whom conflict-related harms against Nature may manifest in subtle, everyday ways that have long contributed to structural inequality. The importance of listening to those with direct experiences of harm comes up again and again in the literature, whether through theories of transitional justice 'from below,' intersectionality, horizontality, or recognition and representation. While there is clearly still much work to be done in this regard, examples discussed above already demonstrate the benefits of taking this seriously. Where corporate accountability has been engaged with in transitional justice, this has often been as a result of efforts by the local population,[259] and the recognition of territory as a victim in Colombia was the result of decades of activism by affected communities (see Chapter 4). These examples demonstrate the value of platforming the lived experiences of those affected by harm in the design of transitional justice measures. In the context of harms against Nature, this engagement also needs to expand past transitional justice's temporal boundaries. The impacts of harm against Nature can stretch across multiple generations, and identifying them will require continued engagement with communities for whom these harms are lived reality.[260]

In part, our engagement with diverse conceptualisations of justice is an attempt to push forward transitional justice scholarship. We believe that doing so can assist in the intellectual maturation of the field. Alternative frameworks can shine a light on cultural, social, and historical complexities that are often overlooked in traditional models. Integrating multidisciplinary perspectives fosters critical reflection, challenges normative assumptions, and promotes innovative solutions. However, this chapter has also shown that transitional justice already has tools that could be adapted to redress some of the structural and slow forms of violence outlined above. To this end, we echo Cynthia Horne's advice 'to constantly reevaluate what we think we know about measures'[261] and suggest that critical analysis of existing mechanisms might shed light on ways in which they might be adapted to better respond to harm against Nature. To summarise some of the arguments we have made above: guarantees of non-recurrence and lustration offer ways to address the structural inequalities that enabled both the unequal access to, and unsustainable exploitation of, the natural world. Collective reparations (whether judicial or non-judicial) might recognise Indigenous connection to land, restore community custodianship, and offer

259 Payne et al., "The Business."
260 Makey et al., "(Un)heard," 4 of 27.
261 Horne, "Transitional," 564.

forms of rehabilitation that address interconnected human and other-than-human harm. Expanding liability frameworks to corporations and recognising the role of corruption in facilitating mass violence[262] provide potential routes to meaningful accountability for the crimes of the powerful. Truth commissions offer ways to recognise context and highlight how structural and slow violence caused and/or facilitated periods of mass violence. More ambitiously, perhaps, encompassing mechanisms that facilitate redistributive justice offers long-term measures that both address structural violence and prevent its return.

The shift toward a broader, more inclusive, and ecologically aware transitional justice faces significant challenges. As this chapter has highlighted, it is not straightforward to push traditional justice frameworks beyond their fixed temporal boundaries. Confronting entrenched power dynamics and holding state–corporate actors accountable is complex, as these entities frequently resist change. Transformative justice demands dismantling unequal structures, but this faces opposition from powerful elites and requires extensive political will and resources. Practical implementation remains underdeveloped, with redistributive and participatory measures difficult to enact in deeply divided societies. The dominance of neoliberal ideologies further complicates efforts to prioritise structural and environmental justice, while intersectional harms involving race, gender, class, and ecology add layers of complexity. Ensuring the inclusion of marginalised voices within traditionally top-down frameworks is another challenge. This potentially adds further emphasis to the need for grassroots activism from those impacted by harm against Nature to challenge existing power relations and work to place the environment on the transitional justice agenda. Despite these barriers, the chapter emphasises the need for interdisciplinary collaboration, grassroots participation, and systemic rethinking to address these challenges and achieve more equitable and sustainable justice. We continue our examination of the influence of the powerful in Chapter 6.

262 Roht Arriaza, "Natural."

6

NEO(LIBERALISM), CAPITALISM, AND THE FUTURE HARMS OF TRANSITION

6.1 Introduction

In this chapter, we interrogate the relationships between liberalism, neoliberalism, and transitional justice. In doing so, we highlight the potential impact of these interconnected relationships on Nature. To briefly introduce these concepts (discussed further below): liberalism is an ideology that emerged in the seventeenth century and focuses on the pursuit and protection of individual freedom and reduced state interference in people's lives.[1] Neoliberalism came to prominence in the United States and the United Kingdom in the 1970s and has since become a dominant ideology globally, prioritising privatisation, deregulation, and market growth.[2] Both are associated with capitalism and have driven a significant and often damaging shift in human–Nature relationships, defining 'the right way to live, not only with other humans, but *also with the more than human world*.'[3]

1 See e.g. Norberto Bobbio, *Liberalism and Democracy* (Verso, 1999); Samuel Freeman, *Liberalism and Distributive Justice*; John Gray, *Liberalism* (Open University Press, 1995); Paul-Jacques Lehman, *Liberalism and Capitalism Today* (Wiley, 2021); John Rawls, *The Law of Peoples* (Harvard University Press, 1999); Jeremy Waldron, *Liberal Rights: Collected Papers 1981–1991* (CUP, 1993).

2 See e.g. Kean Birch and Vlad Mykhnenko, "Introduction: A World Turned Right Way Up," in *The Rise and Fall of Neoliberalism*, eds. Kean Birch and Vlad Mykhnenko (Bloomsbury Publishing, 2010); David Harvey, *A Brief History of Neoliberalism* (OUP, 2007); Jason Hickel, "Neoliberalism and the End of Democracy," in *The Handbook of Neoliberalism*, eds. Simon Springer et al., (Routledge, 2016); Stephanie Mudge, "The State of the Art: What is Neo-liberalism?" *Socio-Economic Review* 6(4) (2008): 703–731.

3 Rosemary-Claire Collard et al., "Re-regulating Socioecologies Under Neoliberalism," in *The Handbook of Neoliberalism*, eds. Simon Springer et al. (Routledge, 2016), 469, emphasis ours.

DOI: 10.4324/9781003264446-6

Throughout this chapter, we continue the book's focus on the more top-down, formal institutions of transitional justice (e.g. trials, truth commissions, administrative reparations programmes, etc.). This focus is for two reasons. First, these elite-led mechanisms remain the dominant format of transitional justice despite the diversification of the field, and second, it is in these formal mechanisms that the relationship with (neo)liberalism most clearly manifests. As Marcus Zunino articulated in 2019, the field of transitional justice has a 'liberal imprint,' resulting in a 'sympathy for capitalism.'[4] This sympathy, and its effects, are still largely overlooked in transitional justice. Where they are mentioned, this is generally as a passing critique and rarely engaged with in depth.[5] This chapter seeks to address this gap. We contend that an analysis of the field's ability to engage with harm against Nature is incomplete without interrogating the ideologies in which the field is embedded.

Transitional justice has both backward- and forward-looking dimensions. Our focus in this chapter is on the latter – what transitional justice involves transitioning *to*. We take a question raised by Richard Falk as the chapter's starting point: when a state is going through a period of transitional justice, 'what kind of justice is capable of being realised, given the mix of pressures and constraints in each national setting?'[6] In response, we interrogate the influence of liberalism and particularly neoliberalism on the field of transitional justice, arguing that external and international pressures, combined with the needs of societies in transition, provide a fertile ground for the spread of neoliberalism – an ideology associated with widespread and often severe harm against Nature.

This analysis builds on earlier chapters, examining how the previously interrogated limitations and critiques of transitional justice may influence what accompanies, or follows, transition. To wit: in Chapter 2, we highlighted the dominance of the Global North in both scholarship and practice. In this chapter, we take this further, demonstrating how this has shaped transitional justice into a neoliberalising project. Chapter 3 interrogated how legalism and particular frameworks of international law shape transitional justice. In this chapter, we explore how international law is in turn shaped by global power dynamics – within which capitalism, liberalism, and neoliberalism are dominant ideologies. In Chapter 5, we examined the overlooking of structural harm in transitional justice; here we discuss how, as

4 Zunino, *Justice*, 47; 53.

5 There are occasional exceptions, such as the work of John Bowsher and Marcus Zunino, both cited in this chapter.

6 Richard Falk, "Predicaments of Transformative Justice in a Neoliberal and State-Centric World Order," in *From Transitional to Transformative Justice*, eds. Paul Gready and Simon Robins (CUP, 2019), 59.

a result, transitional justice neglects the continued influence of pre-existing harmful structures and fails to consider the potential for other structures or ideologies to influence societies experiencing transition.

The chapter proceeds as follows. In Part 2, we introduce liberalism and neoliberalism in more depth and explain their relationship to capitalism. We examine how these ideologies have facilitated grave harms to Nature. In Part 3, we explore the relationship between liberalism, neoliberalism, and transitional justice. As the links between transitional justice and neoliberalism have received less attention in the literature and form a central part of our argument, we dedicate Part 3.2 to making our case that transitional justice is often accompanied by, or is a prelude to, a shift towards neoliberalism. We argue that there has been insufficient interrogation of the ideological underpinnings of the field of transitional justice and a more rigorous examination of the influence of neoliberalism is necessary. In Part 4, we argue that transitional justice assumes a transition to neoliberal capitalism when this is neither inherent nor inevitable. We then explore potential alternative models that challenge and undermine the global dominance of capitalism, particularly in its neoliberal form. Building on our earlier arguments for the need to engage with decolonial and feminist epistemologies (Chapter 2) and the 'ecocentric turn' in law (Chapter 4), these alternative approaches are situated in Indigenous knowledges that we suggest can provide the radical reimagining of human–Nature relationships required to counteract the naturalisation of capitalism.

We conclude in Part 5 by acknowledging the limits on what transitional justice can achieve, recognising that some of what we discuss concerns the pursuit of justice in broader terms than those applicable to a period of 'transition'. Yet, we also note that transitional justice mechanisms accompany moments of rupture, setting in motion longer-term changes and interventions.[7] We therefore argue that it is worth considering some ways in which transitional justice scholars and practitioners could actively challenge the dominance of neoliberal ideology in transitional justice. In doing so, there is the potential to shift towards a transitional justice that better enables the protection of Nature in the aftermath of transition and works towards rebalancing relations between humankind and Nature, from a dynamic of dominance to one of reciprocity.

7 Felix E. Torres, "On Deserving Victims and the Undeserving Poor: Exploring the Scope of Distributive Justice in Transitional Justice Theory and Practice," *Human Rights Quarterly* 45(2) (2023): 306–334.

6.2 Liberalism, Neoliberalism, and Harm to Nature

6.2.1 Introducing Liberalism and Neoliberalism

Liberalism can be understood as a political ideology, an intellectual tradition, and a social and political doctrine. Dating from the seventeenth century, liberalism became the dominant ideology in the Western world[8] and has since remained a contested area in theory and practice.[9] Liberalism has 'no single, unchanging nature or essence';[10] a range of definitions 'have enjoyed more or less wide currency.'[11] While we do not have the need, nor the space, to provide an in-depth analysis here of the vast scholarship relating to liberalism,[12] it is worth summarising three key components of liberalism which underpin our subsequent discussions regarding neoliberalism.

First is the centrality of individual freedom.[13] Norberto Bobbio argues that 'without individualism, there can be no liberalism.'[14] Liberalism's emphasis on responsibilised individuals finds its origins in particular strands of Christian thought, and the 'deep interpellation' between Christianity, liberalism, and individualism has led to this characteristic being described as almost 'unassailable.'[15] The implication of this enhanced individualism is that collective identity and/or agency is simultaneously reduced.[16] Second, and relatedly, is the reduction of the role of the state – its powers limited by the need to allow for individual freedom, rights, and agency and its functions reduced to those involving the maintenance of public order, or the provision of other services in a 'non-coercive fashion.'[17] Third is what John Gray describes as 'meliorism' – the 'corrigibility and improvability of all social institutions and political agreements.'[18] In liberal thought, conflict or opposition between individuals and groups is 'fruitful' as a driver of progress, and

8 Freeman, *Liberalism*; Onur Ulas Ince, *Colonial Capitalism and the Dilemmas of Liberalism* (OUP, 2018).
9 Freeman, *Liberalism*; Gray, *Liberalism*, xi.
10 Gray, *Liberalism*, xi.
11 Bobbio *Liberalism*, 92.
12 See e.g. Bobbio, *Liberalism*; Freeman, *Liberalism*; Gray, *Liberalism*; John Rawls, *A Theory of Justice* (OUP, 1973); Waldron, *Liberal*.
13 Bobbio, *Liberalism*; Freeman, *Liberalism*; Lehman, *Liberalism*; Rawls, *The Law*; Waldron, *Liberal*.
14 Bobbio, *Liberalism*, 9.
15 Kathleen Lynch and Manolis Kalaitzake, "Affective and Calculative Solidarity: The Impact of Individualism and Neoliberal Capitalism." *European Journal of Social Theory* 23(2) (2020): 238–257.
16 Bobbio, *Liberalism*, 43
17 Bobbio, *Liberalism*, 73; Lehman, *Liberalism*; Rawls, *The Law*.
18 Gray, *Liberalism*, xii.

progress is perceived as something to which individuals and society should aspire.[19]

Despite its roots in liberalism, neoliberalism differs in its separation of the market from, and elevation above, political intervention.[20] While the origins of neoliberal thought can be traced to the 1930s, it was not until the 1970s that the implementation of neoliberal policies really took hold.[21] Post–World War II, a phase of what has been described as 'embedded liberalism' brought with it a prioritisation of social welfare, higher taxes on the rich, and improved conditions for workers.[22] While such policies were unpopular with the wealthy elites of the United States and the United Kingdom, voters were unwilling to support any shift towards neoliberal economic models that would bring with it a reduction in both workers' rights and welfare provision. The first 'experiments in neoliberalism' were therefore 'imposed by force' in the 1970s in the Global South, in Argentina, Brazil, Chile, and Uruguay.[23] Over time, rhetoric and lobbying in favour of neoliberalism gained traction in the Global North.[24] By the 1980s, voters were more ready to accept the neoliberal economic reforms advocated by Ronald Reagan in the United States and Margaret Thatcher in the United Kingdom in response to economic downturns.[25] Political liberalism is argued to have provided 'a means' for this shift, with its prioritisation of individualism and reduced role for the state facilitating market logics.[26]

Under neoliberalism, the state's role is reduced in order to 'maximise' competition and free trade.[27] This means a reduction in state welfare provision and pushback against labour rights to ensure the pursuit of capitalist accumulation, unimpeded by any need to support workers.[28] 'An oft-invoked

19 Bobbio, *Liberalism*, 22.

20 Wendy Brown, "Neoliberalism and the End of Liberal Democracy," in *Edgework: Critical Essays on Knowledge and Politics*, ed. Wendy Brown (Princeton University Press, 2005), 37–59; Pierre Dardot and Christian Laval, "Neoliberalism and the Alternative of the Common," *The Routledge Companion to Theatre of the Oppressed*, eds. Kelly Howe et al. (Routledge, 2019); Mudge, "The State."

21 Birch and Mykhnenko, "Introduction"; Mudge, "The State."

22 Harvey, *A Brief*; Hickel, "Neoliberalism."

23 Harvey, *A Brief*; Hickel, "Neoliberalism."

24 Harvey, *A Brief*; Hickel, "Neoliberalism."

25 Birch and Mykhnenko, "Introduction"; Hickel, "Neoliberalism"; Mudge, "The State"; Thomas Perreault and Patricia Martin, "Geographies of Neoliberalism in Latin America," *Environment and Planning A* 37(2) (2005): 191–201.

26 Bobbio, *Liberalism*, 81.

27 Brown, "Neoliberalism."

28 Harvey, *A Brief*.

but ill-defined concept,'[29] it is difficult to simply define neoliberalism.[30] A relatively consistent view in the scholarship is that 'neoliberalism' does not refer to one particular phenomenon, but rather can be used to describe a discourse,[31] a worldview,[32] or a set of policies or processes.[33] For current purposes, we can understand neoliberalism through 'five core principles': privatisation, trade liberalisation, monetarism, deregulation, and marketisation.[34] From a neoliberal perspective, individual entrepreneurial freedom within a structure of 'private property rights, free markets, and free trade' is key to the improvement of human well-being.[35]

From this brief introduction alone, we can see echoes in neoliberalism of some of the limitations of transitional justice explored previously, including the focus on individualism and property (Chapter 3) and the influence of neocolonialism (Chapter 2). We will expand on the neoliberalism–transitional justice relationship further in Part 3. First, we look to the connections between liberalism, neoliberalism, and capitalism and explore what this means for Nature. We argue that any effort to 'green' transitional justice must consider the insidious effects of capitalism on Nature to prevent future environmental harm from arising out of efforts to redress past injustices.

6.2.2 Capitalism and Harm Against Nature

Economic liberalism and neoliberalism are both manifestations of capitalism, an economic model that involves privatisation, competition, free markets, and economic deregulation.[36] Matthew Eagleton Pierce suggests that

29 Mudge, "The State," 703. See also Josh Bowsher, "'Omnus et Singulatim': Establishing the Relationship Between Transitional Justice and Neoliberalism," *Law Critique* 29(1) (2018): 83–106; Noel Castree, "Neoliberalism and the Biophysical Environment: A Synthesis and Evaluation of the Research," *Environment and Society* 1(1) (2010): 5–45.

30 Perreault and Martin, "Geographies," 191. See also Kim England and Kevin Ward, "Theorizing Neoliberalization," in *The Handbook of Neoliberalism*, eds. Simon Springer et al. (Routledge, 2016); Simon Springer et al., "An Introduction to Neoliberalism," in *The Handbook of Neoliberalism*, eds. Simon Springer et al., (Routledge, 2016).

31 Castree, "Neoliberalism"; Mudge, "The State"; Perreault and Martin, "Geographies."

32 Castree, "Neoliberalism."

33 Castree, "Neoliberalism"; Mudge, "The State"; Perreault and Martin, "Geographies."

34 Birch and Mykhnenko, "Introduction," 5. See also Brown, "Neoliberalism"; Collard, Dempsey, and Rowe, "Re-regulating"; Mudge, "The State."

35 Harvey, *A Brief*, 2.

36 Bowsher "'Omnus'"; Brown, "Neoliberalism"; Nancy Fraser, *Fortunes of Feminism From State-Managed Capitalism to Neoliberal Crisis* (Verso, 2020); Freeman, *Liberalism*; Matthew Hinley, "Geographies of Environmental Governance: The Nexus of Nature and Neoliberalism," *Geography Compass* 2(2) (2008), 433–451; Hélène Mayrand, "From Classical Liberalism to Neoliberalism: Explaining the Contradictions in the International Environmental Law Project," in *Locating Nature: Making and Unmaking International*

capitalism is the 'master concept' or 'larger object of analysis' behind both liberalism and neoliberalism.[37] While the expansion of capitalism was a function and goal of colonialism,[38] liberalism is argued to have been key to its spread due to the centrality of individual freedom introduced above. The liberal prioritisation of 'the *homo economicus*,' that is, the belief that 'each individual seeks to maximize their own well-being,' provided a fertile ground for the growth of capitalism.[39] Further expansion in both scope and influence came with neoliberalism, an ideology less hindered by the social, political, and regulatory 'constraints' that existed under economic liberalism.[40] Thus, neoliberalism as a variant of capitalism became internationalised, globalised,[41] 'amorphous and extra-territorial.'[42] As an economic system, capitalism is premised on

> (1) free enterprise and the competitive market; (2) the pursuit of profit and its private appropriation; (3) wage labour and the production of commodities; (4) property rights; (5) the financial infrastructure of money and investment that makes possible credit and debt; (6) a highly variable degree of state regulation; and (7) a propensity for growth as the productive reinvestment of profit.[43]

However, capitalism is more than an economic system; it also permeates our social and political systems.[44] Given that the contemporary global economy is dominated by capitalism, any attempt to understand environmental harm must take its influence into account.[45]

Law, eds. Usha Natarajan and Julia Dehm (CUP, 2022); Mudge, "The State"; Perreault and Martin, "Geographies."

37 Matthew Eagleton-Pierce, "Historicizing the Neoliberal Spirit of Capitalism," in *The Handbook of Neoliberalism*, eds. Simon Springer et al. (Routledge, 2016), 19.

38 Ince, *Colonial*; Ntina Tzouvala, *Capitalism as Civilization* (CUP, 2020), drawing on Marx's *Capital*.

39 Lehmann, *Liberalism*.

40 Harvey, *A Brief*, 11.

41 Freeman, *Liberalism*, 1.

42 Gerard Delanty and Neal Harris, *Capitalism and its Critics* (Routledge, 2023), 156.

43 Delanty and Harris, *Capitalism*, 3.

44 Freeman, *Liberalism*, 19.

45 Michael J. Lynch et al., *Green Criminology and Green Theories of Justice: An Introduction to a Political Economic View of Eco-Justice* (Palgrave, 2019), 7. See also Michael J. Lynch et al., "Green Criminology and Native Peoples: The Treadmill of Production and the Killing of Indigenous Environmental Activists," *Theoretical Criminology* 22(3) (2018): 318–341.

There is an 'identifiable nexus between capitalism as a system, and environmental degradation.'[46] Karl Marx described capitalism as having created an 'irreparable rift' in the 'metabolic interaction' between humans and the earth.[47] This involved 'the forcible expropriation of the people from the soil' and the reduction of 'land, like man' to 'the level of a venal object.'[48] The individual pursuit of labour and capital that intensified under liberalism required individuals to 'dominate' Nature to meet the ever-increasing needs of 'progress' in a civilising society.[49] Noel Castree contends that Nature itself has since been 'neoliberalised': privatised, propertised, and marketised in a context of state deregulation and re-regulation to facilitate the market.[50] In the remainder of this part, we examine five characteristics of neoliberal capitalism that have severe negative repercussions for Nature: increased extractivism, capitalisation, deregulation, decollectivisation, and the impact of neoliberalism beyond the economic sphere.

While *extractivism* is not new, being 'central to colonization,'[51] neoliberalism has expanded the extractivist project. Extractive industries are now 'central to global trade dynamics in a form reminiscent of classical imperialism.'[52] Such practices are deeply intertwined with both periods of mass violence and the structural harms and inequalities that underpin them. John Bellamy Foster and Brett Clark have used the term 'ecological imperialism' to describe (building on Marx):

> the pillage of the resources of some countries by others and the transformation of whole ecosystems upon which states and nations depend; massive movements of population and labour that are interconnected with

46 Rob White, "Climate Change, Ecocide and the Crimes of the Powerful," in *The Routledge International Handbook of Crimes of the Powerful*, ed. Gregg Barak (Routledge, 2015), 214. See also Alexander Dunlap, "The Politics of Ecocide, Genocide and Megaprojects: Interrogating Natural Resource Extraction, Identify and the Normalization of Erasure," *Journal of Genocide Research* 23(2) (2021): 212–235.

47 Karl Marx, *Capital: A Critique of Political Economy, Volume III*, ed. Friedrich Engels (International Publishers, 1894), 588. See also John Bellamy Foster and Brett Clark, "Ecological Imperialism: The Curse of Capitalism," in *The New Imperial Challenge*, eds. Leo Panitch and Colin Leys (Socialist Register, 2004); John Bellamy Foster, "Marx's Theory of Metabolic Rift: Classical Foundations for Environmental Sociology," *American Journal of Sociology* 105(2) (1999): 366–405.

48 Foster and Clark, "Ecological," 188.

49 Gray, *Liberalism*.

50 Castree, "Neoliberalism."

51 Sonja Killoran-McKibbin and Anna Zalik, "Rethinking the Extractive/Productive Binary Under Neoliberalism," in *The Handbook of Neoliberalism*, eds. Simon Springer et al. (Routledge, 2016), 538; Tzouvala, *Capitalism*.

52 Killoran-McKibbin and Zalik, "Rethinking," 539.

> the extraction and transfer of resources; the exploitation of ecological vulnerabilities of societies to promote imperialist control; the dumping of ecological wastes in ways that widen the chasm between centre and periphery; and overall, the creation of a global 'metabolic rift' that characterizes the relation of capitalism to the environment, and at the same time limits capitalist development.[53]

Rosa Luxembourg was arguably the first Marxist to develop a 'comprehensive theory of imperialism,'[54] recognising that the continued existence of capitalism requires imperialism.[55] Luxembourg highlighted that 'capitalism arises and develops historically amidst a non-capitalist society,' arguing that the European capitalist state's position – surrounded by non-capitalist countries – provides 'the setting for the accumulation of capital' as these countries provide 'a market for its surplus value ... a source of supply for its means of production and ... a reservoir of labour power for its wage system.'[56] Christine Schwobel-Patel has captured the continuation of this dynamic at a global level, arguing that states continue to facilitate the conversion of natural resources and land into 'commercial assets' for exploitation by foreign investors.[57] As summarised by Nigel South in the specific context of environmental harm, 'today's pursuit of empire is the corporate variety.'[58]

Under capitalism 'everything' – including Nature – is 'transformed' into capital,[59] what Pierre Dardot and Christian Laval refer to as '*capitalization*' [sic].[60] Natural entities become commodities or resources to be exploited rather than other life forms with which humans share the world. Within

53 Foster and Clark, "Ecological," 187.

54 George Lee, "Rosa Luxembourg and the Impact of Imperialism," *The Economic Journal* 81(324) (1971): 847–848. See also Andreas Bieler et al., "The Enduring Relevance of Rosa Luxemburg's *The Accumulation of Capital*," *Journal of International Relations and Development*, 19 (2016): 420–447; Paul M. Sweezy, "The Accumulation of Capital," *Science and Society* 31(4) (1967): 474–485; Kishen Pattnayak, "Visions of Development: the Inevitable Need for Alternatives," *Futures: The Journal of Policy, Planning and Futures Studies*, 36(6) (2004): 671–678.

55 Rosa Luxembourg, *The Accumulation of Capital* (reprinted by Routledge, 2003).

56 Luxembourg, *The Accumulation*, 348–349. See also analysis in Lee, "Rosa."

57 Christine Schwobel-Patel, "Real (E)State: Valuing a Nation under Imperial Rentier Capitalism," in *Constitutions of Value: Law, Governance, and Political Ecology*, eds. Isabel Feichtner and Geoff Gordon (Routledge, 2023).

58 Nigel South, "The 'Corporate Colonisation of Nature': Bio-prospecting, Bio-piracy and the Development of Green Criminology," *Transnational Environmental Crime*, ed. Rob White (Routledge, 2016), 352.

59 Bowsher, "'Omnus,'" 88.

60 Dardot and Laval, "Neoliberalism," 204. See also Mayrand, "From."

both the liberal and neoliberal projects, natural entities become 'less valuable ... available to be sacrificed, developed for the supposed "common good".'[61]

To facilitate this capitalisation, states have engaged in deregulation.[62] The role of the state is debated in the literature, with some keen to add nuance to the notion of deregulation. Rosemary Collard, Jessica Dempsey, and James Rowe avoid using the term – arguing that regulation has been repositioned or reconfigured, rather than removed.[63] For Noel Castree, neoliberalism involves increased governance, rather than less.[64] Similarly, Ian Bruff contends that the neoliberal agenda 'has been less interested in giving free rein to markets than in engineering and managing the markets that it wishes to see.'[65] Nonetheless, what connects these perspectives is the observance of a shift in the role of the state – away from regulation and towards the facilitation of optimal market conditions by promoting privatisation and investment.[66] To this end, and of relevance to our discussion, is one of neoliberalism's 'most sacred principles': 'a laissez-faire approach to environmental regulation in order to facilitate economic development.'[67]

Beyond these more tangible manifestations of policy and strategy is a shift in mindset or worldview that comes with decollectivisation and the centring of the individual. Under liberalism, the individual became 'the basis and irreducible unit of society.'[68] This philosophy has continued, with individual freedom, responsibility, and choice each argued to be another of neoliberalism's 'most sacred principles.'[69] 'Decollectivisation' is 'a prerequisite for the implementation of a "market society"'[70] as this relies on a philosophy of 'personal responsibility,'[71] and 'the superiority of individualised,

61 Collard, Dempsey and Rowe, "Re-regulating," 469
62 On the imposition of deregulation on the Global South and related human rights violations, see Maria Laura Böhm, *The Crime of Maldevelopment* (Routledge, 2018).
63 Collard, Dempsey, and Rowe, "Re-regulating."
64 Castree, "Neoliberalism."
65 Ian Bruff, "Neoliberalism and Authoritarianism," in *The Handbook of Neoliberalism*, eds. Simon Springer et al. (Routledge, 2016), 107. See also Steven Bittle et al., *Revisiting Crimes of the Powerful: Marxism, Crime and Deviance* (Routledge, 2021), xxxiii–xlviii.
66 Mayrand, "From"; Perreault and Martin, "Geographies"; David Whyte, "Regimes of Permission and State–Corporate Crime," *State Crime Journal* 3(2) (2014): 237–246.
67 Collard, Dempsey, and Rowe, "Re-regulating"; See also Castree, "Neoliberalism."
68 Stephanie Vielle, "Transitional Justice: A Colonizing Field?" *Amsterdam Law Forum* 4(3) (2012): 60. See also Makau Mutua, "A Critique of Rights in Transitional Justice: The African Experience," in *Rethinking Transitions: Equality and Social Justice in Societies Emerging from Conflict*, eds. Gaby Oré Aguilar and Gómez Isa (Intersentia, 2020); Mudge, "The State"; Judith N. Shklar, "The Liberalism of Fear," in *Liberalism and the Moral Life*, ed. Nancy L. Rosenbaum (Harvard University Press, 1989).
69 Collard, Dempsey, and Rowe, "Re-regulating," 469. See also Shklar, "The Liberalism."
70 Bowsher, "'Omnus,'" 101.
71 Fraser, *Fortunes*, 295.

market-based competition.'[72] Humans become '*homo economicus* ... cast in terms of market rationality.'[73] For *homo economicus*, the world – 'including social relations with the natural environment' – is understood via an 'economic rationality' of production, accumulation, and exploitation.[74]

Within liberalism in both its classical and neo forms, the relationship between Nature and humans becomes one of the individual pursuit of economic self-interest through the exploitation of Nature as a resource.[75] While this is relevant for capitalisation, it also speaks to a way of being in the world that runs counter to protecting, or experiencing a sense of relationality with, Nature. This brings us back to the logic of domination discussed in Chapter 2. For instance, Nancy Fraser has captured how 'market mediated processes of subordination are the very life-blood of neoliberal capitalism.'[76] More specifically, Sabrina Fernandes argues that 'a key aspect of capitalist modernity is its treatment of humans as separate from nature, as its tamers or overlords.'[77] From this perspective, Nature is reduced to 'a body of resources, free to be utilised as raw materials for the upkeep of basic necessities and the production of commodities.'[78] This becomes a self-reinforcing relationship, as the increased appropriation and commodification of Nature further detaches humans from the natural world, ultimately perpetuating Marx's 'irreparable rift between humans and nature.'[79] In short, the role of the individual under the neoliberal project is fundamentally at odds with the relationality that is needed if we are to build and maintain mutually supporting relationships with Nature.

The fifth and final strand we consider is the extension of *neoliberalism's influence beyond the economic sphere* to become an all-encompassing and transformative force. As Pierre Dardot and Christian Laval articulate, neoliberalism

72 Mudge, "The State," 705. See also Harvey, *A Brief*.
73 Brown, "Neoliberalism," 40.
74 Mayrand, "From," 55.
75 Collard, Dempsey, and Rowe, "Re-regulating."
76 Fraser, *Fortunes*, 305.
77 Sabrina Fernandes, "Right-Wing Authoritarianism Against Nature: The Latin American Context," *Global Authoritarianism Perspectives and Contestations from the South* (International Research Group on Authoritarianism and Counter-Strategies, 2022), 59.
78 Fernandes, "Right-Wing," 58.
79 Fernandes, "Right-Wing," 62. See also José Castro-Sotomayor and Paola Minoia, "Cultivating Post-development: Pluriversal Transitions and Radical Spaces of Engagement," in *Challenging Global Development: Towards Decoloniality and Justice*, eds. Henning Melber et al. (Palgrave, 2014). The extractive industries also involve the exploitation of human labour, leading to some questioning the strict human/non-human nature binary (see Killoran-McKibbin and Zalik, "Rethinking").

> relies on … the accumulation of legal, judicial, regulatory, and institutional constraints that aim to guarantee the inviolability of the very foundations of the system … neoliberalism is thus a method for expanding the reach of capitalism beyond the economic sphere by diffusing throughout society a system of norms for action.[80]

Neoliberalism's spread is captured by Wendy Brown, who argues that 'neoliberal rationality …involves extending and disseminating market values to all institutions and social action, even as the market itself remains a distinctive player.'[81] As we will examine below, the ubiquitous influence of neoliberalism in the context of transitional justice is particularly evident in the intertwined relationship between post-conflict development and neoliberalism. Michael Beevers draws our attention to how neoliberal economic policies link development efforts to both resource extraction and the funding of infrastructure projects, reinforcing the connections between 'economic development' and 'extractivism.'[82] The results are too often violent, as 'development's insistent prescription of new interventions by outsiders to release the riches lying dormant in the ground risks planting the seeds for a chaotic future, in an already bloodied soil.'[83]

Before concluding this section, it is worthwhile highlighting how the above characteristics of neoliberal capitalism can manifest in 'post-transition' contexts. To take the example of Colombia: while the conflict itself had serious environmental impacts,[84] the end of the conflict brought with it increased resource extraction, as the Revolutionary Armed Forces of Colombia (FARC) lost control of large tracts of forest. A range of actors filled the void, including guerilla groups, large landowners, drug cartels, and criminal gangs.[85] The end of FARC's so-called 'gunpoint conservation'[86]

80 Dardot and Laval, "Neoliberalism," 205.

81 Brown, "Neoliberalism," 39–40.

82 Michael D. Beevers, "Forest Governance and Post-Conflict Peace in Liberia: Emerging Contestation and Opportunities for Change?" *The Extractive Industries and Society* 3(2) (2016): 322.

83 Mark Evenhuis, "Developmental Faith, Sacrifice and the Betrayal of Transitional Justice A Bouganvillean Case Study," *State Crime Journal* 6(1) (2017): 126.

84 Jerónimo Ríos et al., "Environment and Armed Conflict in Colombia: Terrorist Attacks Against Water Resources and Oil Infrastructure in Norte de Santander (2010–2020)," *Small Wars & Insurgencies* 34(8) (2023): 1429–1457; Chad Smith et al., "The War on Drugs in Colombia: The Environment, the Treadmill of Destruction and Risk-Transfer Militarism," *Journal of World-Systems Research* 20(2) (2014): 185–206.

85 Eoghan Darbyshire, *Deforestation in Conflict Areas in 2020*, Conflict Environment and Observatory, *https://ceobs.org/assessment-of-recent-forest-loss-in-conflict-areas/*; Paulo J. Murillo-Sandoval et al., "The End of Gunpoint Conservation: Forest Disturbance after the Colombian Peace Agreement," *Environmental Research Letters* 15(3) (2020): 034033.

86 Murillo-Sandoval et al., "The End."

has brought an estimated 70% of deforestation, resulting from land grabbing and the subsequent use of this land for the creation of pasture and coca farms and exploitation via logging and mining.'[87] We can also see the effects of deregulation in post-conflict contexts. For instance, in post-conflict Guatemala, the international development community viewed the construction of a gold and silver mine by *Montana Exploradora de Guatemala*[88] in the San Marcos region as 'an opportunity for post-conflict economic development.'[89] However, mining activity has been challenged by the community for various reasons, including environmental pollution and violation of regulations relating to the need for free, prior, and informed consent of Indigenous communities prior to granting the mining license.[90] .

To sum up, neoliberal capitalism manifests in ways that involve a transformation of human–Nature relations. Under a neoliberal capitalist system, 'the entire planet is given to those who are most capable of exploiting it';[91] thus, environmental destruction is an inherent feature of neoliberalism. This 'Treadmill of Production'[92] has resulted in increased resource extraction and unsustainable environmental exploitation, with environmental law and regulation adapted or minimised to prioritise the needs of economic actors rather than the preservation of balanced ecosystems.[93] Having established the role of capitalism in causing significant environmental harm, in the next section we turn to examining the relationship between liberalism, neoliberalism, and transitional justice. This will facilitate an exploration of the

87 Darbyshire, "Deforestation."

88 As a subsidiary of the Canadian company Goldcorp, this example also demonstrates the continued relevance of Rosa Luxembourg's argument that imperialism is necessary to capitalism.

89 Volker Boege and Daniel M. Franks, "Reopening and Developing Mines in Post-Conflict Settings: The Challenge of Company-Community Relations," in *High-Value Natural Resources and Post-Conflict Peacebuilding*, eds. Päivi Lujala and Siri Aas Rustad (Routledge, 2011), 103.

90 Boege and Franks, "Reopening and Developing Mines in Post-Conflict Settings."

91 Vincenzo Ruggiero and Nigel South, "Toxic State–Corporate Crimes, Neo-liberalism and Green Criminology: The Hazards and Legacies of the Oil, Chemical and Mineral Industries," *International Journal for Crime, Justice and Social Democracy* 2(2) (2013): 13. See also Brown, "Neoliberalism"; Collard, Dempsey, and Rowe, "Re-regulating"; Hinley, "Geographies."

92 Michael J. Lynch et al., "The Treadmill of Production and the Treadmill of Law: Propositions for Analyzing Law, Ecological Disorganization and Crime," *Capitalism Nature Socialism* 31(1) (2020): 107–122; Michael J. Lynch et al., "Green Criminology and State–Corporate Crime: The Ecocide–Genocide Nexus with Examples from Nigeria," *Journal of Genocide Research* 23(2) (2021): 236–256.

93 See e.g. Ruchi Anand, "Free-market Economics, Multinational Corporations and Environmental Justice in a Globalized World," in *The Routledge Handbook of Environmental Justice*, ed. Ryan Holifield et al. (Routledge, 2017); Lynch et al., "The Treadmill."

ways in which these ideologies may influence transitional justice's processes, outcomes, and aftermath.

6.3 Neoliberal Transitional Justice

While the relationship between transitional justice and liberalism is relatively widely acknowledged and has been touched upon in previous chapters,[94] the connections between transitional justice and neoliberalism remain generally overlooked in both scholarship and practice.[95] We therefore dedicate some space below to establishing these links. However, we first provide some context by briefly summarising the more well-established relationship between liberalism and transitional justice. This is bi-directional – with the field having been strongly influenced and shaped by liberalism,[96] and having a liberalising effect on those states in which it operates.[97] These are considered in turn.

6.3.1 Liberalism and Transitional Justice

Transitional justice has been described as 'steeped in Western liberalism.'[98] As we have explored in previous chapters, this influence can be traced to the

94 See e.g. Kris Brown and Fionnuala Ní Aoláin, "Through the Looking Glass: Transitional Justice Futures Through the Lens of Nationalism, Feminism and Transformative Change," *International Journal of Transitional Justice* 9(1) (2015): 127–149; Rosemary Nagy, "Transitional Justice as Global Project: Critical Reflections," *Third World Quarterly* 29(2) (2008): 275; Chandra Lekha Sriram, "Justice as Peace? Liberal Peacebuilding and Strategies of Transitional Justice," *Global Society* 21(4) (2007): 579–591; Falk, "Predicaments"; Zunino, *Justice*.

95 Bowsher "'Omnus,'" 90.

96 See e.g. Kora Andrieu, "Civilizing Peacebuilding: Transitional Justice, Civil Society and the Liberal Paradigm," *Security Dialogue* 41(5)(2010): 537 558; Kora Andrieu, "Political Liberalism After Mass Violence: John Rawls and a 'Theory' of Transitional Justice," in *Transitional Justice Theories*, eds. Susanne Buckley-Zistel et al. (Routledge, 2014); Hannah Franzki and Maria Carolina Olarte, "Understanding the Political Economy of Transitional Justice: A Critical Theory Perspective," in *Transitional Justice Theories*, eds. Susanne Buckley-Zistel et al. (Routledge, 2013); Nagy, "Transitional"; Ruti G. Teitel, *Transitional Justice* (OUP, 2000); Zunino, *Justice*.

97 See e.g. Tshepo Madlingozi, "On Transitional Justice Entrepreneurs and the Production of Victims," *Journal of Human Rights Practice* 2(2) (2010): 208–228; Vielle, "Transitional."

98 Nagy, "Transitional," 275. See also e.g. Andrieu, "Civilizing"; Andrieu, "Political"; Sirkku K. Hellsten, "Transitional Justice as a Philosophical and Practical Challenge: Critical Notes on Colleen Murphy's New Theory of the 'Conceptual Foundations of Transitional Justice,'" in *Reconciliation, Transitional and Indigenous Justice*, eds. Krushil Watene and Eric Palmer (Routledge, 2020); Patricia Lundy and Mark McGovern, "Whose Justice? Rethinking Transitional Justice From the Bottom Up," *Journal of Law and Society* 35(2) (2008): 265–292; Nagy, "Transitional"; Teitel, *Transitional*; Zunino, *Justice*.

field's origins in a presumed 'liberal consensus ... after the end of the Cold War.'[99] As a result of these origins, it is often assumed that 'the aim of the "transition" is the establishment of a liberal regime, both politically and economically.'[100] In her germinal work, Ruti Teitel proposed that 'the term *transition* has come to mean change in a liberalizing direction.'[101] While it has since been argued that transitional justice can also encompass other political goals, depending on domestic political contexts,[102] it remains the case that 'paradigmatic transitions' are associated with liberalisation.[103]

This relationship lies at the heart of arguments that transitional justice is a neocolonial project seeking to 'repair' countries transitioning from conflict and authoritarianism (often located in the Global South) in the image of the Global North – or at least in the Global North's self-image. As Tshepo Madlingozi contends, transitional justice can be viewed 'as a global project aimed at reconstructing Third World states in Western liberal democratic terms.'[104] Transitional justice therefore has been framed as having a liberalising tendency that shapes not only the mechanisms and processes of transition, but also the type of society that is envisioned after the transitional phase has come to an end.

The 'liberal imprint'[105] of transitional justice has been described in the literature as encompassing various components, many of which we have touched upon in previous chapters. These include an emphasis on political violence, civil and political rights violations, and states' negative obligations rather than structural harms, social, economic, and cultural rights and states' positive obligations (see Chapters 3 and 5); a centring of individuals rather than collective or relational understandings of victimhood (see Chapter 4); and the dominance of legalism and the rule of law (see Chapters

99 Franzki and Olarte, "Understanding," 202.

100 Andrieu, "Civilizing," 544. See also Franzki and Olarte, "Understanding"; Nagy, "Transitional"; Zinaida Miller, "Effects of Invisibility: In Search of the 'Economic' in Transitional Justice," *The International Journal of Transitional Justice* 2(3) (2008): 266–291; Makau W. Matua, "A Problem of Utopia: Human Rights and Transitional Justice," in *The Oxford Handbook of Transitional Justice*, edS. Jens Meierhenrich et al. (OUP, 2023).

101 Teitel, *Transitional Justice*, 5. See also Andrieu, "Civilizing."

102 See e.g. Bosmat Yefet, "Egypt after the 2011 Uprising: The Implications of Transitional Justice in a Non-Liberal Transition," *The Journal of North African Studies* 29(2) (2024): 332–358.

103 Augustine SJ Park, "Transitional Justice and Decolonization," in *The Routledge International Handbook on Decolonizing Justice*, eds. Chris Cuneen et al. (Routledge, 2023), 402. See also Hellsten, "Critical Notes."

104 Madlingozi, "Entrepreneurs," 212. See also Lundy and McGovern, "Whose Justice?" Nagy, "Transitional."

105 Zunino, *Justice*, 47.

3 and 4).[106] These liberal features of transitional justice are accompanied by 'the assumption that transitioning to liberal democracy is an unalloyed good.'[107] From such a perspective, transitional justice brings with it political liberalisation, which in turn brings economic liberation.[108] This – the theory goes – provides the foundation for good governance, and this then leads to lasting peace.[109] However, such assumptions are at a minimum highly contestable. Furthermore, we argue that transitional justice has also been shaped, perhaps even more so, by the parallel rise of neoliberalism as a dominant global ideology. It is to this that we now turn.

6.3.2 The Influences of Neoliberalism

As with liberalism, we argue that the relationship between transitional justice and neoliberalism is bidirectional, with transitional justice both 'a product and ... an agent of neoliberal globalisation.'[110] We primarily focus on transitional justice as an agent of neoliberalisation, as it is this characteristic of transitional justice that links it to potential future harm against Nature. While cognisant that 'tracing the processes through which places, economies, and societies become neoliberalised remains ... complicated,'[111] in this section we endeavour to unpack the connections between transitional justice and neoliberalism, and how the elements and mechanisms of a transition may motivate a turn towards neoliberal policies.

Scholars have occasionally questioned the strength of neoliberalism's influence on the field.[112] Geoff Dancy and Eric Wiebelhaus-Brahm suggest that while the expansion of transitional justice has undoubtedly occurred simultaneously with the spread of neoliberalism, 'the relationship ... may be more tenuous than it appears.'[113] Similarly, Padraig McAuliffe has urged

106 See e.g. Vielle, "Transitional"; Zunino, *Justice*. For discussion of the relationship between liberalism and the rule of law, see e.g. Gray, *Liberalism*; Rawls, *The Law*.

107 Josh Bowsher, "The South African TRC as Neoliberal Reconciliation: Victim Subjectivities and the Synchronization of Affects," *Social & Legal Studies* 29(1) (2020): 44. See also Nagy, "Transitional."

108 Andrieu, "Civilizing," 54.

109 Miller, "Effects of Invisibility," 272; Ismael Muvingi, "Donor-Driven Transitional Justice and Peacebuilding," *Journal of Peacebuilding and Development* 11(1) (2016): 11.

110 Pierre Hazan, *Judging War, Judging History: Behind Truth and Reconciliation* (Stanford University Press, 2010), 151.

111 Perreault and Martin, "Geographies," 193.

112 Padraig McAuliffe, "Rhetoric and Realpolitik: Interrogating the Relationship Between Transitional Justice and Socio-Economic Justice," *Finnish Yearbook of International Law* 23 (2013): 239–307.

113 Geoff Dancy and Eric Wiebelhaus-Brahm, "Bridge to Human Development or Vehicle of Inequality? Transitional Justice and Economic Structures," *The International Journal of Transitional Justice* 9(1) (2015): 51–69.

caution in too closely linking neoliberal economic approaches to transitional justice. McAuliffe emphasises that capitalism is not the aim of transitional justice and argues that claims that transitional justice processes usher in a new age of neoliberal economics 'wildly overstate' the field's 'relevance and impact.'[114] While heeding these calls to be cautious, we argue that there are at least two influences on the field which evidence a relationship between transitional justice and neoliberalism: (i) transitional justice's legalism and associated individualism; and (ii) the relationship between transitional justice and economic development. Drawing on these two influences, we argue that (iii) dominant approaches to transitional justice can be understood as agents of neoliberalisation.

6.3.2.1 Transitional Justice and Individualism

Dominant conceptualisations of transitional justice share certain assumptions with neoliberalism, most notably a commitment to individualism. These assumptions are entrenched through the dominance of legalism explored in Chapter 3. This legalism, and the associated technical discourse, can give transitional justice a somewhat 'apolitical façade,'[115] with law framed as a neutral rather than political force. Yet, this façade can hide both local, context-specific dynamics[116] and the ideologies that underpin purportedly 'universal' legal norms. As outlined in Chapter 3, transitional justice has been particularly shaped by international human rights law and international criminal law. These bodies of law are deeply 'entangled' with the emergence of neoliberal globalisation and demonstrate the influence of individualism on the field.[117]

Human rights – as formalised through the post–World War II international human rights framework – have been described as 'inextricably – inherently – bound up' with both Western political democracy and free market norms.[118] This is particularly true of the narrower framing of human rights that emerged across the Global North in the 1970s, a framing that prioritised civil and political rights while undermining 'broader claims to social distribution and self-determination emanating from the Global South.'[119] Transitional

114 McAuliffe, "Rhetoric," 301.

115 Zunino, *Justice*, 43.

116 Zunino, *Justice*, 43. See also Line Engbo Gissel, "The Standardisation of Transitional Justice," *European Journal of International Relations* 28(3) (2022): 859–894.

117 Bowsher "TRC," 43.

118 Matua, "A Problem of Utopia."

119 Michelle Burgis-Kasthala and Barrie Sander, "Contemporary International Criminal Law After Critique: Towards Decolonial and Abolitionist (Dis-)Engagement in an Era of Anti-Impunity," *Journal of International Criminal Justice* 22(1) (2024): 127–150.

justice's evolution corresponds with this shift towards a narrower formulation of human rights[120] and the parallel emphasis on markets and reduced state intervention that emerged during this period. As such, transitional justice has been critiqued for sidelining those socioeconomic rights violations that might require more redistributive outcomes.[121] This critique, and its links to neoliberalism, have been repeated in the context of several transitional justice initiatives. For example, Vasuki Nesiah has argued that the Truth Commissions established in Chile and South Africa both 'defined their remit in ways that were compatible with neoliberal policies,'[122] involving individual hearings and individualised experiences of harm, to the exclusion of those harms that were socioeconomic, structural, collective, and relational.[123] Makau W. Matua has similarly contended that truth commissions 'seek to institute and reproduce a model of state that does not address the shortcomings of either the human rights project, market-driven economies, or the liberal state'[124] – the implication being that by overlooking the influence of neoliberalism, these mechanisms enable this ideology to shape society in the aftermath of the transition. More broadly, Paige Arthur has explained that the very notion of 'transition' was popular amongst pro–free market elites across Latin America because it enabled short-term legalistic measures to transition from authoritarianism, while avoiding the necessity of more redistributive justice.[125]

Transitional justice has also been critiqued for prioritising individual rights claims over collective framings of both harm and justice. Focusing on the transition in Tunisia, Saerom Han has explored how the focus on violent crimes against individuals, 'replicated the hierarchy of rights entrenched in the global neoliberal regime.'[126] Han argues that this focus on individualism may have undermined collective or relational ways of thinking while allowing individuals to follow their own interests, make their own choices, and essentially be active, autonomous agents of capitalism.[127] Eliana Cusato has similarly highlighted how placing the 'liberal individual' at the centre

120 Ismael Muvingi, "Sitting on Powder Kegs: Socioeconomic Rights in Transitional Societies," *The International Journal of Transitional Justice* 3(2) (2009): 163–182.
121 Saerom Han, "Transitional Justice for Whom? Contention Over Human Rights and Justice in Tunisia," *Social Movement Studies* 21(6) (2022): 823.
122 Vasuki Nesiah, "Transitional Justice and Development: Governance at the End of History," *The Oxford Handbook of International Law and Development*, edS. Ruth Buchanan et al. (OUP, 2023): 661–662.
123 Nesiah, "Transitional Justice and Development."
124 Matua, "A Problem of Utopia."
125 Paige Arthur, "How 'Transitions' Reshaped Human Rights: A Conceptual History of Transitional Justice," *Human Rights Quarterly* 31(2) (2009): 337.
126 Han, "Transitional Justice for Whom?" 823.
127 Jessica Whyte, *The Morals of the Market: Human Rights and the Rise of Neoliberalism* (Verso, 2019).

of rights discourses 'may come at the expense of collective demands for more radical changes over the way wealth is managed and distributed at the domestic and global level.'[128] In the context of reparations, Henry Theriault has argued that even instances of collective repair are often premised on harm experienced by individuals, reducing group harm and repair to 'individual benefits' and even 'individual self-interest.'[129] Taken together, these examples demonstrate a recognition that transitional justice prioritises individuals, alongside a concern that this focus overlooks serious harms while laying the groundwork for potential future inequalities.[130]

International criminal law also shares a history, and underpinning assumptions, with neoliberalism. The flurry of activity in the 1990s, during which several international criminal institutions were created, coincided with the expansion of neoliberalism and an associated emphasis on criminal responses to social harms.[131] As neoliberalism spread, emphasis was placed on a 'punitive state,' with criminal law playing 'an important role in economic restructuring and rule of law projects.'[132] An individualised, punitive approach to justice was seen to offer a way to further individual capitalist interests by protecting property rights[133] while overlooking the potentially harmful role of international financial institutions (IFIs) and transnational economic activity.[134] As such, the increased focus on individual criminal responsibility for atrocity crimes has been described as mirroring 'the individualist ideologies of neoliberalism.'[135] For example, Michelle Burgis-Kasthala and Barrie Sander contend that the increased use of international criminal law to prosecute individuals for large-scale political violence 'entails

128 Eliana Cusato, "International Law, the Paradox of Plenty and the Making of Resource-Driven Conflict," *Leiden Journal of International Law* 33(3) (2020): 660, citing Antony Anghie, "Whose Utopia? Human Rights, Development and the Third World," *Qui Parle* 22(1) (2013): 63.

129 Henry C. Theriault, "Reparations for Genocide: Group Harm and the Limits of Liberal Individualism," *International Criminal Law Review* 14, Special Issue: Armenian Genocide Reparations (2014): 456.

130 Bowsher "'Omnus,'" 103.

131 See e.g. Karen Engle, "Anti-Impunity and the Turn to Criminal Law in Human Rights," *Cornell Law Review* 100(5) (2015): 1069–1128.

132 Engle, "Anti-Impunity and the Turn," 1076.

133 Engle, "Anti-Impunity and the Turn." See also B.S. Chimni, "Third World Approaches to International Law: A Manifesto," *International Commmunity Law Review* 8(1) (2006): 3–28.

134 Tor Krever, "International Criminal Law: An Ideology Critique," *Leiden Journal of International Law* 26(3) (2013): 701–723.

135 Sophie Rigney, "Building an Abolition Movement for International Criminal Law?" *Journal of International Criminal Justice* 22(1) (2024): 211–233, p. 214. See also Zunino, *Justice*.

a concern for the accountability of individuals' and a focus on specific incidents rather than harmful structures.[136] As explored in the previous chapter, such an approach can also overlook the important historical context that created the conditions for mass violence, such as histories of colonialism or inequality.

Relatedly, both international human rights and international criminal law are strongly influenced by the perspectives of political, legal, and other professional actors from the Global North.[137] Indeed, in Chapter 2 we explored the argument that transitional justice can be critiqued as a neocolonial project, in which ideas and approaches from the Global North are imposed onto transitional societies.[138] These structures shape a 'global economy of knowledge' in which neoliberalism and individualism have a major presence[139] and through which states are 'transformed ... networked and externally regulated in accordance with global priorities and standards.'[140] This is not to suggest that all Global North transitional justice actors are involved in a deliberate attempt to further the goals of neoliberalism, nor that such values are absent across the Global South. However, individualism and individualisation are particularly pervasive values in Global North cultures, being embedded through a long history of political and religious tradition[141] and then further entrenched through neoliberal attempts to resist calls for social redistribution and self-determination from the Global South.[142] As Berit Bliesemann de Guevara and Roland Kostić tell us, academics, experts, and other professionals are 'bound by broader dominant structures of their times.'[143] Thus, the centring of international legal regimes arguably creates within both the practice and practitioners of transitional justice a fertile territory for the (potentially tacit and/or unintentional) spread of dominant neoliberal ideologies.

In the following section, we shift from law to economics, examining the relationship between transitional justice and development as an intersection

136 Burgis-Kasthala and Sander, "Contemporary."
137 Matua, "A Problem of Utopia"; Mikkel Jarle Christensen, "The Professional Market of International Criminal Justice: Divisions of Labour and Patterns of Elite Reproduction," *Journal of International Criminal Justice* 19(4) (2021): 783–802.
138 Berit Bliesemann de Guevara and Roland Kostić, "Knowledge Production In/About Conflict and Intervention: Finding 'Facts', Telling 'Truth,'" *Journal of Intervention and Statebuilding* 11(1) (2017): 4.
139 Raewyn Connell and Nour Dados, "Where in the World Does Neoliberalism Come From: The Market Agenda in Southern Perspective," *Theory and Society* 43(2) (2014), 117–138.
140 Gissel, "Standardisation," 876.
141 Lynch and Kalaitzake, "Affective."
142 Burgis-Kasthala and Sander, "Contemporary."
143 de Guevara and Kostić, "Knowledge," 4.

where the influence and appeal of neoliberalism in post-atrocity contexts is particularly strong.

6.3.2.2 Transitional Justice and Economic Development

Armed conflict, authoritarianism, and mass violence leave legacies of poverty, damaged or destroyed infrastructure, and depleted resources.[144] There are environmental challenges also, such as the need to manage stresses on natural resources, address environmental damage, establish or re-establish environmental governance structures, and find sustainable ways to rebuild.[145] However, it is economic growth that is often seen as the prerequisite for recovery.[146] As a result, transitional 'settings frequently usher in powerful discourses of economic development or reconstruction,' often involving the promotion of foreign investment or involvement of IFIs.[147] Increased resource exploitation is also a common feature of peacebuilding in the aftermath of mass violence and/or armed conflict. As Michael Beevers describes, 'the view among many international peacebuilders is that natural resources can foster economic revival, create employment, address poverty and provide a source of public revenue.'[148] In practice, Beevers notes that this view has led to significant environmental costs.[149] Taking these links between economic recovery and future environmental harm as our starting point, in this section we examine the place of economic development in transitional contexts, the appeal of neoliberal economic models and prioritisation of foreign investment, and the role of external actors – particularly IFIs – in shaping transitional justice.

144 See e.g. Vesna Bojicić-Dzelilović, "World Bank, NGOs and the Private Sector in Post-War Reconstruction," *International Peacekeeping* 9(2) (2002): 81–98; Rama Mani, "Editorial: Dilemmas of Expanding Transitional Justice, or Forging the Nexus between Transitional Justice and Development," *The International Journal of Transitional Justice* 2(3) (2008): 253–265; Daniel Bertrand Monk and Jacob Mundy, *The Post-Conflict Environment: Investigation and Critique* (University of Michigan Press, 2014); Paul Williams and Milena Sterio, *Research Handbook on Post-conflict State Building* (Elgar, 2020).

145 Ken Conca and Jennifer Wallace, "Environment and Peacebuilding in War-torn Societies: Lessons from UN Environment Programme's Experience with Postconflict Assessment," *Global Governance* 15(4) (2009): 485.

146 Kepa Artaraz et al., "Introduction: Vivir Bien/Buen Vivir and Post-Neoliberal Development Paths in Latin America – Scope, Strategies, and the Realities of Implementation," *Latin American Perspectives* 48(3) (2021): 4.

147 Jennifer Balint et al., "'Post-conflict' Reconstruction, The Crimes of the Powerful and Transitional Justice," *State Crime* 6(1) (2017): 6.

148 Beevers, "Forest," 321.

149 Beevers, "Forest," 322.

Sirrku Hellsten argues that there is a 'conceptual closeness' in 'Western academic and political thinking' between economic development and transitional justice.[150] The two have, as Vasuki Nesiah has described, 'parallel and intersecting lives' in policy and law.[151] As Nesiah further argues, transitional justice can be seen as laying the groundwork for subsequent development, and both domains place importance on good governance.[152] An example of this relationship can be found in transitional justice's close and long-standing connection to the rule of law. Transitional justice is generally assumed to strengthen the rule of law, and the use of trials has long been argued to have provided a major foothold for the re-establishment of the rule of law in the aftermath of atrocities.[153] While definitions vary, the preservation of liberty has been argued by many scholars to be a (or *the*) key function of the rule of law.[154] On the face of it, this is a separate concern from development. However, the rule of law also provides the basis for governance, which in turn shapes economic activity.[155] The rule of law therefore plays a role in the entrenchment of economic norms[156] and is 'an integral aspect of advanced capitalist societies.'[157] Furthermore, promotion of the rule of law is key to the mandates of institutions such as the World Bank and the UN General Assembly, which describe the rule of law as both a pathway to and product of economic development.[158] The result, as Hannah Franzki and Maria Carolina Olarte suggest, is that 'transitional justice's "innocent" championing of the liberal rule-of law thereby provides legitimacy for a general rule-of-law promotion which models states according to the needs of the market.'[159] Indeed, John Bowsher contends that, in practice, 'most, if not all, of the transitions that transitional justice has attended have been defined by neoliberal imperatives of marketisation and the production of states as arbiters of market competition.'[160]

150 Hellsten, "Critical Notes," 39. For more on the transitional justice–development relationship please see Andrieu, "Civilizing"; Balint et al. "Post-Conflict"; Nesiah, "Transitional"; Wendy Lambourne, "Transitional Justice and Peacebuilding After Mass Violence," *International Journal of Transitional Justice* 3(1)(2008): 28–48.

151 Nesiah, "Transitional," 655.

152 Nesiah, "Transitional," 655.

153 Matua, "A Problem of Utopia"; Zunino, *Justice*, 52.

154 Brian Z. Tamanaha, "Functions of the Rule of Law," in *Cambridge Companion to the Rule of Law*, eds. Jens Meierhenrich and Martin Loughlin (CUP, 2021).

155 Matua, "A Problem of Utopia"; Tamanaha, "Functions."

156 Matua, "A Problem of Utopia"; Tamanaha, "Functions."

157 Tamanaha, "Functions," 232.

158 Shane Chalmers and Sundhya Pahuja, "Economic Development and the Rule of Law," in *Cambridge Companion to the Rule of Law*, eds. Jens Meierhenrich and Martin Loughlin (CUP, 2021).

159 Franzki and Olarte, "Understanding," 216.

160 Bowsher "'Omnus,'" 94–95; Sriram, "Justice."

One implication of the 'conceptual closeness' between transitional justice and economic development is that the 'transitional justice–development nexus' is embedded within broader processes of neoliberal transformation.[161] In the next few paragraphs, we take a closer look at three aspects of the 'transitional justice–development nexus' that enable neoliberal agendas: the perceived need for economic growth, the role of foreign direct investment, and the influence of external actors.

Previous practice in transitional contexts suggests that a need for economic growth can cause a shift towards capitalist economic models. As Marcos Zunino highlights, transitions in Argentina, post-communist Eastern Europe, and Southern Europe were all followed by the continuation of, or reform to, a capitalist economic model.[162] Internally, such a shift may have been appealing due to the need to rebuild, and further motivated by external influences or pressures. For example, the turn to neoliberalism by the African National Congress (ANC) in South Africa is argued to have been in part a response to the severe socioeconomic legacies of the apartheid regime[163] and the perceived need for rapid economic growth. In Peru, the end of internal conflict was followed by Fujimori introducing a range of neoliberal economic reforms, including deregulation of financial markets, erosion of workers' rights, and increased privatisation.[164] As Rama Mani describes, the 'overriding priority' for those involved in economic development efforts 'is rapid economic growth and integration into global markets.'[165]

To this end, foreign direct investment is 'widely recognised as one of the most important engines of economic development.'[166] In its turn, foreign direct investment is often focused on resource extraction.[167] For governments in transitional societies, incentivising investment is often a priority, and transitional justice is one tool that can be used to further this goal. From the perspective of potential investors, Marco Polizzi and Jeffrey King have argued that by implementing a transitional justice process, a state is

161 Daniela Lai, "Transitional Justice and its Discontents: Socioeconomic Justice in Bosnia and Herzegovina and the Limits of International Intervention," *Journal of Intervention and Statebuilding* 10(3) (2016): 361–381.

162 Zunino, *Justice*.

163 Paul Williams and Ian Taylor, "Neoliberalism and the Political Economy of the 'New' South Africa," *New Political Economy* 5(1) (2000): 21–40.

164 Anthony Bebbington, *Governing Extractive Industries: Politics, Histories, Ideas* (OUP, 2018); Maritza Felices Luna, "The Pacification of Peru and the Production of a Neoliberal Populist Order," *State Crime* 6(1) (2017): 156–174.

165 Mani, "Editorial," 254.

166 Benjamin J. Appel and Cyanne E. Loyle, "The Economic Benefits of Justice: Post-Conflict Justice and Foreign Direct Investment," *Journal of Peace Research* 49(5) (2012): 685.

167 Michael A. Long et al., "Foreign Direct Investment, Ecological Withdrawals, and Natural-Resource-Dependent Economies," *Society & Natural Resources* 30(1) (2017): 1261–1276.

demonstrating that it is 'open for business.'[168] Accompanying economic reforms such as structural adjustment programmes, increased privatisation, deregulation of the market, and new trade agreements are similarly understood as indicating a willingness to ultimately integrate the country into the global economy.[169] Indeed, economic liberalisation programmes have been implemented alongside transitional justice in a number of contexts, including El Salvador, Guatemala, and Liberia.[170] Such moves can have serious negative implications for Nature. For example, in Northern Ireland, Juneseo Hwang describes how 'the environment ... has been sacrificed to feed a pro-growth agenda' by the government in the post Good Friday/Belfast Agreement period, through the prioritisation of motivating international investment (for example by reducing corporation tax) over environmental regulation.[171] This has resulted in 'large-scale environmental crime' that has continued into the present.[172]

Linked to the perceived need for development is the role of external actors. Ismael Muvingi tells us that transitional justice has 'from its inception ... been characterised by a heavy presence' of external actors, including 'donors for transitional justice initiatives.'[173] As examined in Chapter 2, the professionals and experts involved in transitional justice are key to the development and spread of particular approaches, priorities, and mechanisms. Often intermediaries between the international and national level, experts translate 'purported universal ordering principles into concrete institutions and practices.'[174] While external expertise is often necessary as states emerging from conflict often lack capacity nationally, it is generally accompanied by the agendas of, and conditions set by, the state or organisation providing assistance.[175] These agendas have been argued to amount to 'an amalgam of

168 Marc Polizzi and Jeffrey King, "Aid for Justice? Analysing the Impact of Foreign Aid on Recipient Transitional Justice Implementation," *The International Journal of Human Rights* 26(4) (2022): 627.

169 Birte Vogel, "Everyday Economic Experiences and Peace Processes," in *Contemporary Peacemaking: Peace Processes, Peacebuilding and Conflict*, eds. Roger MacGinty and Anthony Wanis-St John (Palgrave, 2022).

170 Zunino, *Justice*.

171 Juneseo Hwang, "The Political Economy of the Mubuoy Dump in Northern Ireland: A Green Criminology Perspective," *International Journal for Crime, Justice and Social Democracy*, advanced online 2024.

172 Hwang, "The Political Economy of the Mubuoy Dump in Northern Ireland."

173 Muvingi, "Donor-Driven."

174 Maj Grasten and Ntina Tzouvala, "The Political Economy of International Transitional Administration: Regulating Food and Farming in Kosovo and Iraq," *Contemporary Politics* 24(5) (2018): 588–606.

175 Amanda Cahill-Ripley, "Challenging Neoliberalism: Making Economic and Social Rights Matter in the Peacebuilding Agenda," in *Economic and Social Rights in a Neoliberal World* ed Gillian McNaughton and Diane F. Frey (CUP, 2018).

human rights, liberal democracy, the rule of law and market economics.'[176] The international community's role is 'increasingly prevalent' in '*funding* and potentially *dictating* the implementation of [transitional justice].'[177] This involvement again speaks to the connection between transitional justice and development. While Marc Polizzi and Jeffrey King found that foreign aid is used to fund transitional justice mechanisms, particularly prosecutions, the 'official purpose' behind this support is the 'promotion of economic development.'[178]

The role of IFIs like the World Bank and the International Monetary Fund (IMF) has been highlighted by several scholars. The 'assumptions and agendas' of these institutions have been argued to shape transitional justice and the economy in recipient countries.[179] The World Bank's involvement in conflict and post-conflict situations has been described as 'extensive,'[180] involving poverty reduction plans agreed in conjunction with the IMF and relatively consistent 'adherence to its main "orthodox" economic policy principles.'[181] In Peru, for example, Fujimori's economic reforms were encouraged and financially supported by the World Bank and other institutions,[182] and led to Peru being readmitted to the international financial community. Peru's relative exclusion from this community under the left-wing Garcia government had been a response to, and contributing factor in, an economic crisis.[183]

This is relevant to our discussion because IFIs can be critiqued for being 'imbued' with an 'ideology of neoliberal economic modernization,'[184] and as a result, their involvement can lead to, for instance, increased privatisation.[185] For example, both transitional periods in Tunisia since independence

176 Muvingi, "Donor-Driven," 12.

177 Polizzi and King, "Aid for Justice?" 612.

178 Polizzi and King, "Aid for Justice?"

179 Muvingi, "Donor-Driven," 14. For the role of IFIs in contributing to or exacerbating conflict, please see Antony Anghie and B. S. Chimni, "Third World Approaches to International Law and Individual Responsibility in Internal Conflicts," *Chinese Journal of International Law* 2(1) (2003): 77–103. More broadly, see Sundhya Pahuja, *Decolonizing International Law: Development, Economic Growth and the Politics of Universality* (CUP, 2011).

180 Pieter van Houten, "The World Bank's (Post-)conflict Agenda: The Challenge of Integrating Development and Security," *Cambridge Review of International Affairs* 20(4) (2007): 645. See also Vesna Bojicić-Dzelilović, "World Bank."

181 van Houten, "The World Bank," 651.

182 Bebbington, *Governing*.

183 Luna, "Pacification."

184 Lundy and McGovern, "Whose Justice?" 276.

185 Jeffrey Atteberry, "Turning the Widening Gyre: History, Corporate Accountability and Transitional Justice in the Postcolony," *Chicago Journal of International Law* 19(2) (2019): 333–374. See also M Rodwan Abouharb and David L. Cingranelli, "The Human

(the first from the Bourguiba regime, and the second from Ben Ali) have been followed by agreements with the IMF, which have contributed to deregulation and liberalisation, including increased public–private partnerships and international ownership of land.[186] In South Africa, it has been suggested that the influence of the World Bank was a factor in the neoliberalisation that followed the ANC's coming to power.[187] In Bosnia, following the signing of the Dayton Peace Accords, the international community – in particular the World Bank, the IMF, the United States, and the European Union – sought 'to reconstruct the Bosnian economy along neoliberal lines,' introducing an economic reform package focused on privatisation, liberalisation, and the transition to a market economy.[188] It is relevant to note that these pushes towards neoliberalisation often fail to deliver real-world improvements for the societies involved and can in fact lead to greater inequalities,[189] arguably increasing the chances of future violence.

6.3.2.3 Transitional Justice as a Neoliberalising Project

This part has sought to articulate the relationship that exists between dominant approaches to transitional justice practice and policy, neoliberalism, and capitalism. As we have explored, neoliberalism has become a global norm,[190] and its expansion has coincided with the spread of transitional justice.[191] Neoliberal globalisation therefore 'provides the inescapable background' to transitional justice.[192] We do not wish to overstate the relationship between transitional justice and neoliberalism. Transitional justice mechanisms are not the same as economic reform, nor can they unilaterally cause a shift towards neoliberal policy. However, the sections above demonstrate some of the ways that transitional justice can indirectly become 'an agent of neoliberal globalisation'[193] and 'a further step in the development of *homo economicus*.'[194] Makau Mutua argues that 'by failing to interrogate and

---

Rights Effects of World Bank Structural Adjustment, 1981–2000," *International Studies Quarterly* 50(2) (2006): 233.

186 Jihen Chandoul, *Tunisia and IMF: Transitional Injustice*, Policy Brief prepared for Arab NGO Network for Development, September 2017.

187 Sagie Narsiah, "Neoliberalism and Privatisation in South Africa," *GeoJournal* 57(1/2) (2002): 3–13; Williams and Taylor, "Neoliberalism."

188 Timothy Donais, *The Political Economy of Peacebuilding in Post-Dayton Bosnia* (Routledge, 2005), 13.

189 Valentin Lang, "The Economics of the Democratic Deficit: The Effect of IMF Programs on Inequality," *The Review of International Organisations* 16 (2020): 599–623.

190 See e.g. Dardot and Laval, "Neoliberalism"; Falk, "Predicaments"; Hinley, "Geographies."

191 Dancy and Wiebelhaus-Brahm, "Bridge," 69.

192 McAuliffe, "Rhetoric," 299.

193 Hazan, *Judging War*, 151.

194 Bowsher, "'Omnus,'" 103.

wrestle with economic and political philosophies and systems, the human rights movement [for Mutua, transitional justice is part of this movement] indirectly sanctions capitalism and free markets.'[195] We similarly argue that the failure to examine transitional justice's underpinning ideologies can result in the field legitimising neoliberalism as the 'economic counterpart' of liberal democracy – the rarely questioned purported end goal of transitional justice.[196] While there is an emerging literature that highlights these risks, it is often the case that transitional justice's neoliberal underpinnings remain uninterrogated.[197] This relationship, we believe, means that transitional justice measures can fail to account for harms against Nature, and play a role in creating the circumstances in which further harms against Nature become possible. The risks associated with these blind spots are not insignificant; inequalities and unsustainable natural resource exploitation can sow the seeds of future conflict and violence. Given the scale of the ecological crises in which we find ourselves and given that the field does have 'forward-looking aspects,'[198] we suggest that transitional justice scholars and practitioners have a responsibility to at least attempt to ensure that transition does not contribute to future ecological destruction. By more closely interrogating the relationship between transitional justice, neoliberalism, and harm against Nature, the field will arguably be in a better position to design approaches that can protect Nature. Moreover, transitional justice's alignment with capitalism is, we argue, neither inherent nor unchangeable. This brings us to Part 4, where we challenge the idea that capitalism is an inevitable outcome of transition by considering alternative models that might lay the groundwork for more protective or relational approaches to Nature.

6.4 Alternative Pathways

Building on one of the book's key threads – the need to engage with diverse knowledges – here we propose alternative models to neoliberalism that we argue could inspire or shape economic approaches that are less harmful towards Nature than those that currently accompany periods of transition. Of course, there are limitations on transitional justice as a vehicle for radical change. As Khanyisela Moyo argues, 'transitional justice's foundational concepts … were invented by patriarchal societies and colonial masters and are sometimes appropriated for neocolonial ends.'[199] The very existence of

195 Mutua, "A Critique," 37. See also Zunino, *Justice.*
196 Franzki and Olarte, "Understanding," 202. See also Bowsher, "'Omnus.'"
197 Zunino, *Justice.*
198 Andrieu, "Civilizing," 538.
199 Khanyisela Moyo, "Mimicry, Transitional Justice and the Land Question in Racially Divided Former Settler Colonies," *International Journal of Transitional Justice* 9 (2015): 71.

transitional justice in any context will be the result of compromise, including with powerful actors with strong incentives to place parameters around what the field can achieve. Furthermore, transitional justice is embedded in liberalism, which generally involves 'progressive and moderate change relying on liberal law and institutions,' restricting the potential for 'emancipatory change.'[200] A further aspect of this is the continued dominance of scholars, practitioners, and expertise from the Global North. If the same categories of people, with the same educational and cultural backgrounds, are doing the same type of work, this limits the potential for new, different approaches from the existing transitional justice 'toolkit.'[201] While we agree with Rosemary Nagy that 'radical new ways of framing and responding to violence' are required,[202] we acknowledge that the capacity for transitional justice in its current form to embrace transformative or radical change is limited.

At the same time, we are living in a climate crisis that is simply 'not manageable' within existing dominant worldviews.[203] Indeed, the harms of neoliberalism have motivated the emergence of 'innovative ideas … from communities and subjects that have historically been economically, politically, and culturally marginalized' and that are often rooted in 'Indigenous epistemologies.'[204] Scholars have looked to the theory and practice of 'pluriversal knowledge and agency to cultivate post-development futures,'[205] exploring 'visions of the world' that embrace 'diverse and multiple knowledges, realities and perspectives.'[206] As indicated previously, some Indigenous cosmovisions centre Nature in ways that dominant Western approaches do

200 Zunino, *Justice*, 232.

201 Rosemary Nagy, "Transformative Justice in a Settler Colonial Transition: Implementing the UN Declaration on the Rights of Indigenous Peoples in Canada," *The International Journal of Human Rights* 26(2) (2022): 199.

202 Nagy, "Transformative Justice in a Settler Colonial Transition," 192. See also Falk, "Predicaments."

203 Ashish Kothari et al., "Introduction: Finding Pluriversal Paths," in *Pluriverse: A Post-Development Dictionary*, eds. Ashish Kothari et al. (Tulika Books, 2019).

204 Artaraz et al., "Introduction," 4. See also Miriam Lang, "Buen Vivir as a Territorial Practice. Building a More Just and Sustainable Life Through Interculturality," *Sustainability Science* 17 (2022): 1287–1299.

205 Castro-Sotomayor and Minoia, "Cultivating." See also Ashish Kothari, "In Search of Alternatives to Development: Learning from Grounded Initiatives," in *Challenging Global Development: Towards Decoloniality*, eds. Henning Melber et al. (Springer, 2024). Kothari et al. define 'pluriverse' (drawing on the Zapatista conceptualisation) as 'a world where many worlds fit' (Kothari et al., "Introduction," xxviii).

206 María Fernanda Ordóñez et al., "The Materialization of the *Buen Vivir* and the Rights of Nature: Rhetoric and Realities of *Guayaquil Ecológico* Urban Regeneration Project," *City, Territory and Architecture* 9(1) (2022): 3.

not.[207] In a pluriversal world, 'people re-learn what it means to be a humble part of "nature," leaving behind narrow anthropocentric notions of progress based on economic growth.'[208] Building on the growing literature that engages with pluriversal perspectives, the next sections examine three value systems that may provide pathways that the field of transitional justice could take towards an alternative vision of the future: *Buen vivir*, *Ubuntu*, and *Swaraj*.

6.4.1 Buen Vivir

Buen vivir provides an alternative to modern modes of development based in capitalism and neoliberalism.[209] Translating directly as the 'good life'[210] (though it differs in nature from Western conceptualisations of 'the good life'),[211] '*Buen vivir*' is the Spanish expression of a non-colonial concept, known for example in Quecha as *sumak kawsay*, or *suma qumaña* in Aymara.[212] While first utilised in the context of the constitutions of Latin American countries, including Bolivia, Ecuador, and later Nicaragua and Venezuela, the international community (including NGOs, academics and activists) has since begun to consider the potential of *Buen vivir*.[213] As the concept emerges from diverse Indigenous epistemologies, has multiple conceptualisations, and manifests differently across a range of policies,

207 See Chapter 2. See also Dorine E. van Norren, "The Sustainable Development Goals Viewed Through Gross National Happiness, Ubuntu, and Buen Vivir," *International Environmental Agreements* 20 (2020): 431–458.

208 Kothari et al., "Introduction," xviii.

209 Artaraz et al., "Introduction"; Mónica Chuji et al., "Buen Vivir" in *Pluriverse: A Post-Development Dictionary*, eds. Ashish Kothari et al. (Tulika Books, 2019); Lang, "Buen Vivir"; Roger Merino, "An Alternative to 'Alternative Development'?: *Buen Vivir* and Human Development in Andean Countries," *Oxford Development Studies* 44(3) (2016): 271–286. For critique of this idea, see e.g. Pablo Alonso González and Alfredo Macías Vázquez, "An Ontological Turn in the Debate on *Buen Vivir – Sumak Kawsay* in Ecuador: Ideology, Knowledge and the Common," *Latin American and Caribbean Ethnic Studies* 10(3) (2015): 315–334; Rafael Domínguez et al., "*Buen Vivir*: Praise, Instrumentalization, and Reproductive Pathways of Good Living in Ecuador," *Latin American and Caribbean Ethnic Studies* 12(2) (2017): 133–154.

210 Artaraz et al., "Introduction."

211 Chuji et al., "Buen Vivir," 111–114.

212 Maria Chiara Fatigato, *Buen Vivir: An Opportunity to Re-thnk the Development and Sustainability Model* (Departimento Di Scienze Sociali Ed Economiche Working Papers Series: 2023).

213 Artaraz et al., "Introduction"; Chuji et al., "Buen Vivir"; Domínguez et al., "Buen Vivir"; Merino, "Alternative"; Salvatore Monni and Massimo Pallottino, "A New Agenda for International Development Cooperation: Lessons Learnt From the *Buen Vivir* Experience," *Development*, 58(1) (2015): 49–57.

development plans, and constitutions, it is challenging to provide a specific definition.[214] However, a number of key characteristics can be identified.

First, and of particular relevance for our purposes, is the presence of a view of Nature that involves a 'symbiotic relationship' between 'humans and Mother Earth.'[215] *Buen vivir* emphasises 'the principles of reciprocity, complementarity and relationality in human interactions and in relation to the cycles of nature.'[216] Thus, it challenges the 'logic of domination' that prioritises humankind over Nature. Second is the importance of community, including 'mutual aid,' 'collective work,' and 'reciprocity.'[217] This is 'diametrically opposed to the individuality of Western societies'[218] and the dominance of individualism for neoliberalism, as explored above. Third is 'an economy based on solidarity and community life,' and fourth is 'respect for ancestral knowledge.'[219] In contrast to capitalism, *Buen vivir* 'is not part of an expansive or accumulative logic of progress, and infinite growth, but rather seeks plenitude in balance and sufficiency.'[220]

Buen vivir is not without its challenges. Indigenous communities and states can clash over what the concept means, and some critics have highlighted instances where *Buen vivir* has been exploited by state institutions to support government-led, neoliberal, extractivist agendas.[221] Nonetheless, the concept has proven 'pretty successful' in challenging consumptionist lifestyles.[222] For instance, *Buen vivir* has provided 'the basis for concrete alternatives to development,' including temporary prohibitions on drilling in the Amazon.[223] Furthermore, the concept is a valuable tool for resistance, utilised for instance by Indigenous and non-Indigenous activists in Ecuador, Peru, and Bolivia.[224] Importantly, it breaks with modern Western

214 Artaraz et al., "Introduction"; Chuji et al., "Buen Vivir"; Monni and Pallottino, "A New Agenda."

215 Artaraz et al., "Introduction," 7. See also Chuji et al., "Buen Vivir"; Lang, "Buen Vivir"; Merino, "Alternative."

216 Merino, "Alternative," 272–273. See also Monni and Pallottino, "A New Agenda."

217 Artaraz et al., "Introduction," 8. See also Fatigato, *Buen Vivir*; Monni and Pallottino, "A New Agenda."

218 Artaraz et al., "Introduction."

219 Artaraz et al., "Introduction," 8.

220 Lang, "Buen Vivir," 1287.

221 González and Vázquez, "Ontological Turn"; Artaraz et al., "Introduction"; Merino, "Alternative."

222 Domínguez et al., "*Buen Vivir*," 134. See Merino, "Alternative," for a critique. Merino argues that *Buen vivir* can be understood as a 'reconstruction of traditional principles re-invented by contemporary indigenous and non-indigenous social movements' (p. 273).

223 Chuji et al., "Buen Vivir," 113.

224 Chuji et al., "Buen Vivir."

assumptions about society–nature dualism and Eurocentric univeralism;'[225] such a breakage is necessary if transitional justice is to better recognise and respond to harm against Nature.

In terms of what this might look like for transitional justice, *Buen vivir* principles could be written into transitional justice mechanisms to provide a remit for the consideration of Nature alongside humankind (for example, *Pacha Mama's* rights in Ecuador were guided by *Buen vivir*).[226] Specific transitional justice measures could be established to address harm against Nature (thus challenging the logic of domination), for example as we have seen in Colombia. Furthermore, transitional justice mechanisms could make forward-looking provision for future land use and resource extraction, whether framed as guarantees of non-recurrence or as broader policy recommendations. For example, Sri Lanka's *Commission of Inquiry on Lessons Learnt and Reconciliation* recommended that land-use plans 'ensure protection of environment and bio-diversity; sustainable economic development ... with a view to improving the quality of life of the present and future generations.'[227] The incorporation of *Buen vivir* into the constitutions of several Latin American countries, as noted above, demonstrates its potential as a step towards institutional reform and the provision of some form of bulwark against the environmental deregulation that can be welcomed in the aftermath of conflict to facilitate economic growth. More broadly, a *Buen vivir* approach to transitional justice would be one which emphasises the pursuit of harmony (both between humans and between humans and the natural world),[228] meaning a shift away from retributive justice towards restorative, reparative, and rehabilitative measures.

6.4.2 Ubuntu

Next we move to the concept of *Ubuntu*, which is a 'value system' or philosophy across many countries on the African continent that 'stresses the

225 Merino, "Alternative," 280.

226 Sarah Kerremans and Tine Destrooper, "Exploring the Nexus between Transitional Justice and Ecoterritorial Conflict Resolution: Time for an Ecoterritorial Turn in Transformative Transitional Justice?" *The International Journal of Transitional Justice* 17(1) (2023): 54–70.

227 Government of Sri Lanka, *The Report of the Commission of Inquiry on Lessons Learnt and Reconciliation.* Available https://reliefweb.int/report/sri-lanka/report-commission-inquiry-lessons-learnt-and-reconciliation, para 9.151.

228 Thaddeus Metz, "The Role of Economic Goods in National Reconciliation: Evaluating South Africa and Colombia," in *Transitional Justice, Distributive Justice and Transformative Constitutionalism*, eds. David Bilchitz and Raisa Cachalia with Magdalena Inés Correa Henao and Nathalia Bautista Pizarro (OUP, 2023).

value of compassion, human relations and life as mutual aid.'[229] *Ubuntu* means 'I am, because we are.'[230] In a similar vein to *Buen vivir*, community is prioritised over individualism, and this includes connections between ancestors, future generations, and nature.[231] *Ubuntu* is 'rooted in notions of communitarianism, reconciliation, relationality, and interdependence.'[232] It has previously been linked to transitional justice efforts in South Africa, in particular its Truth and Reconciliation Commission.[233] While *Ubuntu* can influence various spheres of life, including for instance justice and the economy, we are particularly interested in what the concept means for relationships with Nature.

Ubuntu 'concerns the unfolding of the human being in relation to other human beings and the more-than-human world of non-human nature.'[234] According to Dorine van Norren, *Ubuntu* creates a 'form of guardianship of nature,' and failure to protect Nature is considered 'a violation of *Ubuntu*.'[235] Mathew Bukhi Mabele, Judith E. Krauss, and Wilhelm Kiwango conceptualise Ubuntu as 'an ethic of care predicated on the practices of mutuality and sharing between humans and nonhumans.'[236] The anthropocentrism of transitional justice is one of the major barriers to the field's engagement with harm against Nature; however, 'in the *Ubuntu* ethic, there is no conception of anthropocentrism, as humans and nonhumans are moral counterparts.'[237] A second facet of interest is the extension of connectedness and care to future generations;[238] transitional justice's forward-looking aspects matter – not only to avoid harm to Nature, but also for the potential impact upon future generations. The notions of 'guardianship'[239] and 'care'[240] are of relevance for the 'ecocentric' turn in victimhood, with advocates for a crime

229 Dorine E. van Norren, "African Ubuntu and Sustainable Development Goals: Seeking Human Mutual Relations and Service in Development," *Third World Quarterly* 43(12) (2022): 2793. See also Mathew Bukhi Mabele et al., "Going Back to the Roots: *Ubuntu* and Just Conservation in South Africa," *Conservation and Society* 20(2) (2022): 92–102.

230 van Norren, "African Ubuntu"; J. Marc Foggin, "We Still Need the Wisdom of *Ubuntu* for Successful Nature Conservation," *Ambio* 50(3) (2021): 723–725.

231 van Norren, "African Ubuntu"; Foggin, "We Still Need"; Lesley Le Grange, "Ubuntu" in *Pluriverse: A Post-Development Dictionary*, eds. Ashish Kothari et al. (Tulika Books, 2019).

232 Mabele et al., "Going Back," 93. See also van Norren, "African Ubuntu"; Le Grange, "Ubuntu."

233 Desmond Tutu, *No Future Without Forgiveness* (Doubleday, 1999).

234 Le Grange, "Ubuntu," 323.

235 van Norren, "African Ubuntu," 2793.

236 Mabele et al., "Going Back," 96.

237 Mabele et al., "Going Back," 96.

238 Mabele et al., "Going Back," 96; van Norren, "African Ubuntu."

239 van Norren, "African Ubuntu," 2793.

240 Mabele et al., "Going Back," 96.

of ecocide proposing the recognition of Nature as a 'protectee' of criminal law and rights of nature approaches involving guardianship of natural entities by humans.[241] As argued in Chapter 4, recognising the victimhood of other-than-human beings can help to expand understandings of victimhood and harm in transitional justice. We suggest that embedding understandings of victimhood into transitional justice mechanisms that make provision for some form of protection or guardianship over Nature may help to offer the future-facing protection that Nature needs in the face of the onset of neoliberalism that often accompanies post-conflict development.

As with *Buen vivir*, implementing *Ubuntu* in practice has proved challenging,[242] and there is a risk of co-option 'by supranational organizations, governments and the corporate world to suit their own agendas.'[243] Again, as with *Buen vivir*, the concept of *Ubuntu* exists across multiple communities and cultures, and has been somewhat 'generalised.'[244] However, we agree with Dorine van Norren that it remains 'a worthwhile concept to consider when designing new economic, developmental and legal concepts.'[245] In a transitional justice context, the idea that the failure to protect Nature constitutes a violation of *Ubuntu* could promote a stretching of transitional justice to ensure that its measures capture harm against Nature. This could include, for instance, the broadening of remits of truth commissions to allow for testimony relating to longer-term, structural harms that often incorporate impacts on Nature; or the memorialisation of violence perpetrated against the natural world as a reminder of the duty to protect it. There is already a literature that explores its possibility as a framework for pursuing 'environmentally just' reparations and restorative justice, with Busisiwe Kamolane-Kgadima and Thandeka Kathi arguing that severe pollution should be addressed through mechanisms which recognise the interdependence of humans and Nature and that focus on future-oriented, participatory processes.[246] Thus, as with *Buen vivir*, *Ubuntu* lays the groundwork for forward-looking environmental protections. Advocating for the need to value *Ubuntu*, J. Marc Foggin proposes that 'in order to maintain healthy

241 See also Hercules Wessels, "Nature's Rights and Developing Remedies: Enabling Substantive and Restorative Relief in Civil Litigation," in *The Palgrave Handbook of Environmental Restorative Justice*, eds. Brunilda Pali et al. (Palgrave, 2022).
242 van Norren, "African Ubuntu," 2806.
243 Le Grange, "Ubuntu," 326.
244 Mabele et al., "Going Back"; van Norren, "African Ubuntu."
245 van Norren, "African Ubuntu," 2806.
246 Busisiwe Kamolane-Kgadima and Thandeka Kathi, "The Mpumalanga Highveld Air Pollution Crisis: A South African Reparations Framework for Environmental State–Corporate Harm" *International Journal for Crime, Justice and Social* Democracy 13(1) (2024): 8–9.

ecosystems,' there is a need to 'promote co-existence' and 'build on the long-standing knowledge and institutions of local peoples and communities such as indigenous peoples, in tandem with science.'[247] As we will revisit below, a thread that runs through all of these alternative approaches is the need to engage with diverse and potentially previously overlooked knowledges.

6.4.3 Ecological Swaraj

Moving to the Asian continent, we turn now to Mohandas Karamchand Gandhi's concept of *Swaraj*. While Gandhi did not refer to Nature in his writings, his work has been interpreted as applicable to thinking about ecological and environmental concerns – particularly more recently, in light of the global environmental crisis.[248] Gandhi used the term to mean both 'self-control and self-realisation' of the nation (i.e. India's independence from British colonialism) and the individual.[249] Indeed, *Swaraj* is derived from *swarajya*, the Sanskrit word meaning 'self-control' or 'self-mastery.'[250] It is this application to the individual that is argued to be of relevance for thinking about Nature, as this involved self-control, restraint, rejecting consumerism, and cautious use of natural resources.[251] Gandhi is argued to have 'fully understood the primordiality of man–nature relationship' and 'premised that every community was inextricably bound up with a specific natural environment ... Gandhi viewed a community's culture as its "soul" or "spirit" and its natural habitat as its "body": the two formed an indissoluble unity.'[252]

Swaraj differs from *Buen vivir* and *Ubuntu* in its focus on individuals rather than human–Nature relationality. As such, it speaks to a different aspect of transitional justice than the mechanisms themselves, placing responsibility on individuals to protect and respect Nature. We propose two dimensions of this, one being top-down and the other bottom-up. In relation to the former, 'Ecological *Swaraj*' (sometimes referred to as Radical Ecological Democracy) has a 'strong democratic and egalitarian impulse' with an emphasis on social well-being, direct political democracy and the

247 Foggin, "We Still Need," 724.
248 Ambarish Mukherji, "Gandhi's Views on Environment: The Search for an Alternative," *Bulletin of the Ramakirshna Mission Institute of Culture* (July 2022), 22–27. See also Sumanas Koulagi, *Development as Swaraj: Towards a Sustainable and Equitable Future* (Routledge, 2022).
249 Mukherji, "Gandhi's Views on Environment."
250 Koulagi, *Development*, 5.
251 Mukherji, "Gandhi's Views"; Koulagi, *Development.*
252 Mukherji, "Gandhi's Views," 26.

plurality of knowledge, and the localisation of the means of production.[253] Running counter to the priorities and nature of capitalist economy as discussed above, *Swaraj* involves restraining overconsumption, the need for direct interactions between consumers and producers (so that consumers can 'comprehend all the social and environmental impacts of production'), and 'conscious' disposal of goods.[254] Institutional reforms and guarantees of non-recurrence in the aftermath of mass violence, if informed by such principles, would align with arguments we have made regarding the need for inclusion, as well as encouraging forms of development far removed from neoliberal principles.

In relation to the latter, bottom-up dimension, *Swaraj* might inspire agency from communities themselves to ensure that Nature is taken into account in the context of transitional justice, in a similar vein to the critical environmental justice approaches examined in Chapter 5. This is not about denying victims of harm the right to claim redress from the state when appropriate. Rather, it is about adopting approaches that 'deprive the state of the power to define the issues and their solutions' and empower communities to name the issues they face and develop appropriate responses.[255] It is a bottom-up approach which encourages communities to think and act 'beyond the state.'[256] Given that it is often the state that is promoting (or at least facilitating) extractive projects,[257] if communities mobilise to challenge this in the aftermath of conflict or transition, this could motivate alternative approaches that better protect Nature. As examined in Chapter 4, the developments in Colombia in terms of greening transitional justice were the product of years of mobilisation and activism.

Guarantees of non-recurrence might also be relevant here. For instance, *Swaraj* and the notion of individual responsibility towards Nature could be incorporated into education, and space could be given for civil society to mobilise and articulate demands. Such an approach also resonates with community-oriented environmental peacebuilding efforts, whereby communities engage in activism to ensure their consultation and consent on projects that affect their territories, interests, cultures, and livelihoods.[258] *Swaraj* therefore might inspire an activist and political bottom-up movement that

253 Ashish Kothari et al., "Buen Vivir, Degrowth and Ecological Swaraj: Alternatives to Sustainable Development and the Green Economy," *Development* 57(3–4) (2014): 362–375.

254 Koulagi, *Development*, 33.

255 Augustine SJ Park, "Settler Colonialism, Decolonization and Radicalizing Transitional Justice," *International Journal of Transitional Justice* 14(2) (2020): 260–279.

256 Pellow, *Towards a Critical*, 229.

257 Temper, *Blocking Pipelines*, 105.

258 Ken Conca, "Environmental Peacebuilding: Yesterday, Today and Tomorrow," *The Journal of Social Encounters* 8(1) (2024): Article 3.

can potentially challenge the rise of neoliberalism in transitional contexts. Such an activist approach may be essential if transitional justice processes are to begin taking harms against Nature into account.

6.4.4 Pushing the Boundaries

To conclude this section, we acknowledge the concerns raised by Roger Merino (in relation to *Buen vivir*) that there is risk of reductionism and appropriation in seeking to transpose or adapt these Indigenous worldviews into a Western mindset,[259] and we agree that fulsome understanding of 'Indigenous thinking' is required 'before any attempt at conceptual assimilation.'[260] The decolonial and feminist approaches to knowledge production detailed in Chapter 2 arguably provide a workable basis for this. Drawing from the scholarship on *Buen vivir*, we contend that engaging with Indigenous worldviews can – if handled sensitively and in a spirit of genuine co-production – provide 'inspiration,'[261] 'disrupt' dominant modes of thinking, and challenge 'the present boundaries of our political imagination.'[262]

Indeed, these Indigenous approaches have already inspired the development of 'Western' alternatives to capitalism. For instance, 'Doughnut Economics' is an economic model based on systems-thinking, in which societies and economies are 'complex and interdependent systems that need to thrive after growth.' The type of economy envisioned by such an approach is distributive and regenerative.[263] As discussed above and articulated by Marama Davidson of the Green Party of Aotearoa New Zealand, 'the principle of Doughnut Economics is nothing new to Indigenous peoples and Indigenous economies.' Indeed, the Māori leadership has reframed the Doughnut Economic model as the Te Reo Māori model, with the ecological ceiling at the centre.[264] A second alternative is Mutual Aid, which involves 'collective coordination to meet each other's needs, usually from an

259 Merino, "Alternative," 282.
260 Merino, "Alternative," 280.
261 Monni and Pallottino, "A New Agenda," 55.
262 Merino, "Alternative," 283.
263 Elisa Aracil and Ibrahim Sancak, *Essential Concepts of Sustainable Finance: An A–Z Guide* (Routledge, 2024), 61. See also Rachel A. Turner and Jane Wills, "Downscaling Doughnut Economics for Sustainability Governance," *Current Opinion in Environmental Sustainability Governance* 56 (2022): 1–10.
264 Tim Hollo, "Uncomfortable with Power: Strategies, Policies and Approaches of the Green Part of Aotearoa NZ in Government," *Green Agenda Journal* No. 1 (2022). Available https://greenagenda.org.au/2022/04/uncomfortable-with-power/; Native Land Information System, "Data Sovereignty," https://nativeland.info/about/data-sovereignty/.

awareness that the systems we have in place are not going to meet them.'[265] It is focused on meeting needs, mobilisation and solidarity, and participatory problem-solving.[266] Mutual aid is not a Western concept; its 'central tenets ... have always been a tradition of many Black, Indigenous, queer, and disabled communities.'[267] For instance, the notion of 'life as mutual aid' is central to the *Ubuntu* philosophy discussed above,[268] and also of relevance for *Buen vivir* – as noted above. While these approaches are rooted in Indigenous worldviews, they provide some indication of how alternative cosmovisions might be incorporated into new economic models.

Over the past 20 years, 'an immense variety of radical alternatives to ... [the] dominant regime and to its roots in capitalist, patriarchal, racist, statist and anthropocentric forces' has emerged.[269] We have considered just a sample of these here. We contend that fulsome and collaborative engagement with alternative models can inspire and shape the development of economic models that are much less harmful to Nature than neoliberalism. Transformative change is needed, and that will likely require a radical approach that extends far beyond what transitional justice can achieve. However, the approaches we have outlined here revisit several arguments made throughout this book with regards to how transitional justice might be 'greened.' First is the need to rethink the human–Nature relationship and move away from the capitalisation of Nature, which is in turn a symptom of the 'logic of domination' (see Chapter 2). The 'ecocentric turn' in law (see Chapter 4) has already provided possibilities for expanding understandings of victimhood to incorporate the other-than-human. Second, consideration of these Indigenous worldviews demonstrates the value of the co-construction of knowledge and of engaging with knowledge produced outside of the Global North. Third is the importance of connectedness and relationality. The concept of relationality is key to recognising the victimhood of Nature and also counters the individualism that accompanies and supports neoliberalism.

265 Dean Spade, *Mutual Aid: Building Solidarity During This Crisis (and the Next)* (Verso, 2020), 7.
266 Spade, *Mutual Aid*, 10–13.
267 Rachel G. McKane et al., "Mutual Aid as a Praxis for Critical Environmental Justice: Lessons from W.E.B. Du Bois, Critical Theoretical Perspectives, and Mobilising Collective Care in Disasters," *Antipode* 56(2) (2023): 587.
268 C. Ewuoso and S. Hall, "Core Aspects of *Ubuntu*: A Systematic Review," *South African Journal of Bioethics and Law* 12(2) (2019): 93–103; van Norren, "African Ubuntu."
269 Ashish Kothari et al., "Postscript: The Global Tapestry of Alternatives," in *Pluriverse: A Post-Development Dictionary*, edS. Ashish Kothari et al. (Tulika Books, 2019). See also Eija Ranta, "Alternative Development Approaches: Utopias, Co-Options, Transitions," in *The Routledge Handbook on the History of Development*, eds. Corinna R. Unger et al. (Routledge, 2022).

6.5 Conclusion

A key aim of this chapter was to highlight the need for transitional justice scholars and practitioners to be cognisant of the potential harm against Nature that can result during, or in the aftermath of, transition as a result of the relationship between transitional justice and neoliberalism. Echoing Makau W. Matua,[270] we contend that transitional justice is not a 'utopia' – rather it is a space where the dominance of the Global North and, as argued in this chapter, the influence of neoliberalism has created a field that may lay the groundwork for the continuation of, or the emergence of future, harm against Nature. Throughout, we have tried to remain cognisant of the limits of transitional justice as a means of bringing about radical societal change, while nonetheless arguing for the pursuit of a reimagined, less ecologically disastrous, future. By way of conclusion, therefore, we wish to offer some final reflections on what it might look like for transitional justice scholars and practitioners to actively challenge neoliberal capitalism and its associated ecological destruction. We articulate three guiding principles which – we argue – can contribute to such an effort: (i) comprehensive engagement with the forward-looking aspects of transitional justice; (ii) recognition of transitional justice's political nature; and (iii) adopting and building on the feminist and decolonial approaches introduced in Chapter 2.

First, we suggest that transitional justice scholars and practitioners must engage comprehensively and practically with the forward-facing aspects of transitional justice.[271] Transitional justice is argued to be teleological, with a clear aim of transition from a period were things were 'worse' to a future where things are 'better.'[272] For many, the field's 'forward-looking' dimension is looking forward to a future that is stable and peaceful, where state institutions are (re)established and functioning, justice is upheld, and the rule of law and liberal democracy shape society.[273] The influence of transitional justice's liberal roots is evident here. As noted above, meliorism is a key strand of liberalism, and this assumption of progress is evident in the 'progress narrative' embedded in transitional justice institutions.[274] Yet, as we hope to have demonstrated in this chapter, this progress narrative can

270 Matua, "A Problem of Utopia."

271 Andrieu, "Civilizing," 538.

272 Kimberley Theidon, "Editorial Note," *The International Journal of Transitional Justice* 3(3) (2009): 295–300; Zunino, *Justice*.

273 See e.g. Andrieu, "Civilizing"; Cynthia M. Horne, "Transitional Justice and Temporal Parameters," *International Journal of Transitional Justice* 14(3) (2020): 544–565; Zinaida Miller, "Embedded Ambivalence: Ungoverning Global Justice," *Transnational Legal Theory* 11(3) (2020): 353–381; Zinaida Miller, "Transitional Justice Temporalities," *The Oxford Handbook of Transitional Justice*, eds. Jens Meierhenrich et al. (OUP, 2023).

274 Miller, "Transitional Justice Temporalities."

mask substantial future harms, and the economic models that accompany transition should not be assumed to be 'good' because they are embedded in an assumed idea of progress. Rather, their real-world impacts must be interrogated and the tensions between short term 'progress' and the long-term deterioration of the natural world should be taken seriously.[275]

A pragmatic philosophical approach could be useful in this regard. Such an approach 'stresses the dynamic relationship between theory and practice' and prioritises the identification of issues by those affected, rather than an approach driven by disciplinary paradigms or priorities.[276] We are not suggesting that transitional justice seeks to encapsulate all future harm against Nature. However, we argue that the relatively unquestioned ideological dominance of neoliberalism in transitional justice has harmful environmental impacts that should be given more attention. Where there is sufficient suggestion of a connection between transitional justice and harm against Nature via the economic shifts that accompany or follow transition, we contend that transitional justice scholars and practitioners have a responsibility to recognise, seek to understand, and, to the extent possible, highlight, challenge, or prevent this harm.

Second, we contend that transitional justice must be recognised and presented as the political project that it is, and those who research or work in the field should critically reflect on their positionality and the political power of the project of which they are a part. We repeat here the words of Walter D. Mignolo: 'all thinking is located.'[277] In a similar vein, Donna Haraway's concept of 'situated knowledge' emphasises that the 'knower' has a specific and limited location from which they see.[278] We suggest that explicit acknowledgement of transitional justice's 'situatedness' is required – this could for instance include increased critical engagement with our locations as 'knowers' and the influence of the 'global economy of knowledge'[279] on what we know and how we know what we know. This has the potential to provide the basis for a field that more openly acknowledges the ideologies that underpin and are furthered by its work. If the field is to engage with the influence of capitalism – be that in its neoliberal form or otherwise – the perception that transitional justice is a benign or perhaps benevolent tech-

275 Jens Iverson, "Managing the Tensions between a Maximalist Approach to Environmental Protection and Anthropocentric Peacebuilding," in *Research Handbook on International Law and Environmental Peacebuilding*, eds. Daniëlla Dam-de Jong and Britta Sjöstedt (Elgar, 2023).

276 Shannon Sullivan, "Pragmatism," in *The Blackwell Guide to Feminist Philosophy*, eds. Linda Martín Alcoff and Eva Feder Kittay (Blackwell Publishing, 2007).

277 Walter D. Mignolo, "Epistemic Disobedience and the Decolonial Option: A Manifesto," *Transmodernity* 1(2) (2011): 52.

278 Donna Haraway, *Simians, Cyborgs and Women* (Free Association Books, 1991).

279 Connell and Dados, "Where."

nocratic exercise must be explicitly challenged. As Rosemary Nagy stated in 2008, 'transitional justice is a discourse and practice imbued with power.'[280] This remains the case.[281] Not only does a focus on technocratic transitional justice overlook the harms that can result from its own dominant ideologies, but it is also arguably an opportunity missed. As Jeffrey Atteberry suggests, 'transitional justice has the chance to promote, if pursued from a properly internationalist perspective, the development of a more acute consciousness within the international community concerning the neocolonialist forces at work within its own structures of governance.'[282] Interrogating the structures and ideologies that shape transitional justice will facilitate greater self-reflection in the field, as well as a more comprehensive, complex, and nuanced understanding of past and present-day harms that may go some way towards addressing the epistemic injustice that is currently a feature of dominant approaches to the field.

Third, and finally, we return to the feminist epistemology and decolonial scholarship that we introduced in Chapter 2. We argue that the points of connection identified across these bodies of literature provide the foundations for an approach to transitional justice that can challenge the dominance of capitalism in the field. First is recognition of the interconnected and structural nature of harm against Nature. As we have argued, harm against Nature is often rooted in colonialism and continued via an ecological imperialism that supports the perpetuation of capitalism. Until this is recognised, any effort by transitional justice to address harm against Nature will be partial. Second is a collaborative approach to knowledge production that engages with and values equally diverse knowledges. Engaging with different knowledges can bring transitional justice into conversation with worldviews that offer potential alternatives to capitalism and present understandings of relational (rather than exploitative) connections with Nature. Relatedly, the field's emphasis on individualism is fundamentally at odds with a sense of connection to others. Any movement towards a multispecies justice requires 'an acute sense of loyalty and connection to other human beings ... and the natural world.'[283]

Incentivising a fundamentally different approach to transitional justice, one that responds to legacies of past harm while remaining cognisant of the risk of causing future harm, may require collective mobilisation by citizens

280 Nagy, "Transitional," 286–287.

281 See e.g. Madlingozi, "Entrepreneurs," 212. See also Lundy and McGovern, "Whose Justice?"; Nagy, "Transitional"; Matua, "A Problem of Utopia."

282 Atteberry, "Widening Gyre," 357.

283 Kristian Laslett, "Marx Reloaded for the 21st Century: Capitalism, Agency and the Crimes of the Powerful," in *Revisiting Crimes of the Powerful: Marxism, Crime and Deviance*, eds. Steven Bittle et al. (Routledge, 2021), 130.

to pressure the state into changing course. This raises the question of who will do this work. While transitional justice is a space of significant victim activism – it is often only through the efforts of victims and survivors of armed conflict that states take any action to address legacies of harm – the dominance of individualised legal frameworks is potentially a barrier to more collective attempts to effect change. Given that there are multiple, overlapping, and potentially competing needs in the aftermath of conflict, consideration should be given to where calls for greening transitional justice might come from in practice.[284] Re-imagining economic futures is one potential site of such work, and a place where we can potentially engage meaningfully with Françoise Vergès' 'struggle for epistemic justice ... a struggle that demands equality between knowledges and contests the order of knowledge imposed by the West.'[285] Third is the need to break down binaries – specifically the physis/nomos binary that is exploited and exacerbated by capitalism. A key step in this direction was explored in Chapter 4; by moving away from anthropocentrism and recognising non-human beings and ecosystems as 'entities with moral value in their own right'[286] within transitional justice, the field will be in a stronger position to challenge the exploitation of Nature.

In sum, we argue that failing to acknowledge and interrogate the influence of neoliberalism on transitional justice creates a situation in which transition can be accompanied or proceeded by economic activity that is harmful against Nature. To counter this, there is a need to more rigorously interrogate the forward-facing dimensions of the field, to engage openly and critically with the political nature of the transitional justice project, and – building on feminist and decolonial scholarship – to recognise the interconnected and structural roots of environmental harm, embrace diverse knowledges, and pursue approaches that seek to rebalance human–Nature relations.

284 We are grateful to our colleague, Dr Chulani Kodikara, for drawing our attention to this challenge. See also Iverson, "Managing."

285 Françoise Vergès, *A Decolonial Feminism* (Pluto Press, 2021), 13.

286 Sarah Krakoff, "Mountains Without Handrails ... Wilderness Without Cellphones," *Harvard Environmental Law Review* 27(2) (2003): 462.

7

GREENING TRANSITIONAL JUSTICE

7.1 Introduction

Throughout this book, we have sought to highlight what we believe is a pressing need to transform transitional justice into an ecologically aware and inclusive process that recognises Nature as a legitimate subject of justice in the aftermath of mass violence. Our central argument is that dominant approaches to transitional justice, in their current form, are offering incomplete justice. By focusing exclusively on human-centered narratives, transitional justice often fails to recognise the complex web of harm connected not only to conflict, repression, and authoritarian violence but also to neoliberal recovery. 'Greening' transitional justice, as we envision it, requires reimagining the field's underpinning anthropocentric, legalistic, temporal, and neoliberal assumptions and integrating new perspectives, particularly those rooted in Indigenous, feminist, and decolonial thought. In proposing a more ecocentric transitional justice, we are arguing that the field must better recognise the interdependence of human and ecological well-being as essential to achieving peace in the aftermath of mass violence. In this brief conclusion, we revisit the book's key themes, analyse the challenges and implications of a green transitional justice framework, and explore examples that demonstrate how these ideas could usefully inform the field.

We want to acknowledge here that some (or perhaps a lot) of what we have argued for in this book may seem pointlessly utopian to some transitional justice scholars and practitioners. Calls for a more expansive transitional justice have consistently attracted such critiques. These tend to highlight the need for caution about what transitional justice can realistically achieve. This is sometimes with an eye on practical limitations, with

DOI: 10.4324/9781003264446-7

Clara Sandoval suggesting that 'it is better to see the field … in *realistic terms*.'[1] Similarly, Lars Waldorf has argued that transitional justice barely delivers on its 'original promises of truth, justice and reconciliation' and that it should retain short temporal parameters and its focus on a limited category of civil and political rights.[2] For Waldorf, considerations of social, economic, and cultural harms belong in the realm of democratic process and distributive justice. Others have called for modesty when exploring the transformative potential of transitions from mass violence, noting that 'no process or set of transitional justice processes can by itself fundamentally transform a community.'[3] For example, Rosemary Nagy reminds us that transitional justice is 'predominantly state-centred and state-driven,' meaning it can be 'difficult to motivate support for transformative change from those who benefit from or are comfortable with the status quo.'[4] Similarly, Dustin Sharp argues that 'the concepts and practices at the core of peace and justice work … are essentially contested' and 'any approach to transitional justice that truly broke with liberal principles more radically would be unlikely to garner support in many circles.'[5]

We are conscious of the need for humility within the field. We agree that spreading the concept of transitional justice too thin may negatively impact its legitimacy, with negative implications for victimised communities. However, we remain convinced that 'ignoring a significant portion of the drivers of conflict and resulting violations' carries substantial risks.[6] Furthermore, we believe in the importance of pushing 'beyond reform,'[7] by which we mean challenging the field to 'disinvest' in norms that no longer serve us, embrace a more diverse range of 'global imaginaries,' and reach for

1 Clara Sandoval, "Transitional Justice and Social Change," *SUR – International Journal on Human Rights* 11(20) (2014): 185.

2 Lars Waldorf, "Anticipating the Past: Transitional Justice and Socio-Economic Wrongs," *Social and Legal Studies* 21(2) (2012): 171.

3 Colleen Murphy, "On Principled Compromise: When Does A Process of Transitional Justice Qualify as Just?" *Proceedings of the Aristotelian Society* 120(1) (2020): 57. See also Padraig McAuliffe, *Transformative Transitional Justice and the Malleability of Post-Conflict States* (Elgar, 2017).

4 Rosemary Nagy, "Transformative Justice in a Settler Colonial Transition: Implementing the UN Declaration on the Rights of Indigenous Peoples in Canada," *International Journal of Human Rights* 26(2) (2022): 195.

5 Dustin N. Sharp, "Crisis, Faith, and Transformation in Transitional Justice," *Beyond Transitional Justice*, ed. Matthew Evans (Routledge, 2022), 31–32.

6 Dustin N. Sharp, "Introduction: Addressing Economic Violence in Times of Transition," *Justice and Economic Violence in Transition*, ed. Dustin N. Sharp (Springer, 2014), 19.

7 Vanessa de Oliveira Andreotti et al., "Mapping Interpretations of Decolonization in the Context of Higher Education," *Decolonization: Indigeneity, Education & Society* 4(1) (2015): 21–40.

an 'ecologically wise and socially just world, that is, a world where "many worlds fit."'[8] While transitional justice is a field associated with legacies of past harm, we are unable and unwilling to ignore the global context of climate disaster. For us, this renders necessary more ambitious, radical, and transformative thinking to ensure that our field of scholarship does not ignore or exacerbate harm against Nature.

7.2 Principles for a Greener Transitional Justice

Throughout the book, we have presented a series of potential approaches that we argue might contribute to a transitional justice that better recognises and responds to harm to Nature. Inspired by the approach of Eleni Dimou, we do not suggest that any of these provides a universal solution. Rather, we present them as *options* – 'one of the many paths' that could be taken.[9] While aware of the limitations of transitional justice and its underlying structures, in this final chapter, we respond to Clara Sandoval's prompt that transitional justice can provide 'a unique window of opportunity'[10] to effect change. In this spirit, we make the case for a series of guiding principles, which we argue might go some way towards challenging the structures that underlie and shape transitional justice, limiting its ability to recognise and respond to harm against Nature. These are the following:

1. A green transitional justice requires a decolonised justice.
2. A green transitional justice looks beyond the state.
3. Victimhood is not a uniquely human experience.
4. Transitional justice is better conceived of as a process than a mechanism.
5. Neoliberalism should not be accepted as the inevitable consequence of transition.
6. There is always value in pursuing a more holistic transitional justice project.

For each, we highlight some of the examples that we have found instructive while bringing this book together.

8 M. Brinton Lykes and Colleen Murphy, "Decolonising Transitional Justice: Soft, Radical, or Beyond Reform," *The International Journal of Transitional Justice* 17(3) (2023): 361–369.

9 Eleni Dimou, "Decolonizing Southern Criminology: What can the 'Decolonial Option' Tell Us About Challenging the Modern/Colonial Foundations of Criminology?" *Critical Criminology* 29(3) (2021): 433.

10 Sandoval, "Transitional," 184.

7.2.1 A Green Transitional Justice Requires a Decolonised Justice

A key theme throughout the book has been the importance of incorporating Indigenous, feminist, and decolonial epistemologies into transitional justice. Without wishing to oversimplify or romanticise Indigenous perspectives, we have drawn on numerous examples to demonstrate how engagement with such epistemologies can advance a more ecologically inclusive framework. Western legal frameworks, grounded in property rights and individualism, are often insufficient for addressing collective, relational forms of harm. This has implications for the field's recognition of Nature as well as for the justice available for certain human harms, such as those affecting Indigenous communities whose cultural and spiritual practices are deeply interconnected with their natural surroundings. As discussed in Chapter 2, the dominance of Global North (and particularly Eurocentric) perspectives in transitional justice's knowledge production has had profound implications in this regard, leading to the entrenching of individualistic, anthropocentric understandings of legal personhood; a relatively narrow formulation of victimhood; and the marginalising of Indigenous worldviews that see Nature as a co-equal actor in justice processes.

While we have been cautious of overemphasising the potential benefits of expanding rights frameworks, we have explored the Rights of Nature movements across Latin America and elsewhere, considering whether they might provide one potential model for integrating Indigenous perspectives into transitional justice. As explored throughout the book, Ecuador's Constitution, which grants legal rights to Nature, reflects Indigenous cosmovisions that recognise the intrinsic worth of rivers, mountains, and forests.[11] Similarly, in Colombia, the Atrato River was declared a legal person with rights to protection and restoration following advocacy from Indigenous communities.[12] In an explicitly transitional justice context, Colombia's JEP has extended notions of victimhood to encompass Indigenous and Black communities' territories.[13] These forms of legal recognition potentially allow Indigenous and other communities to defend their territories against ecological harm and offer one pathway towards a more inclusive form of justice that respects both human and ecological rights. Future research into how transitional justice might encompass Rights of Nature, and greater legal pluralism, could be beneficial in this regard.

11 Ecuador, Constitution of Ecuador, Republic of Ecuador, entered into force 20 October 2008.

12 Philipp Wesche, "Rights of Nature in Practice: A Case Study on the Impacts of the Colombian Atrato River Decision," *Journal of Environmental Law* 33(3) (2021): 531–555.

13 Sierra Camargo Ximena, "The Ecocentric Turn of Environmental Justice in Colombia." *King's Law Journal* 30(2) (2019): 224–233.

The literature has consistently highlighted the room for improvement regarding the field's engagement with decolonial and Indigenous perspectives. Transitional justice could far better account for the lived realities of Indigenous communities, whose experiences of harm extend beyond the immediate impacts of conflict. Expanding this model to include a more multispecies justice could allow transitional justice to recognise the compound impacts of environmental and cultural harm, acknowledging that for many Indigenous communities, destruction of the land is as harmful as physical violence against their people.

7.2.2 A Green Transitional Justice Looks Beyond the State

Another key theme throughout the book has been that effective green transitional justice may require a shift 'beyond the state,' using but also enhancing 'from below' methods that empower local communities, civil society, and marginalised groups to define and pursue justice on their own terms. State-led processes often fail to address the diverse needs of communities affected by conflict, especially when state institutions are weak or complicit or lack legitimacy. Furthermore, state-led processes can overlook the ecological dimensions of conflict and may be complicit in the same or subsequent environmental destruction. As examined in Chapter 2 and linked to the discussion above, power imbalances and dominant knowledge systems frequently shape state-led approaches, reinforcing Global North paradigms and leaving little room for alternative perspectives, particularly from marginalised or Indigenous communities. In contrast, 'from below' approaches enable community-driven truth-telling and reparations that may be more open to ecological harms. For example, community-led truth initiatives allow survivors to document their experiences of environmental degradation alongside human rights abuses, such as the destruction of forests, water sources, and biodiversity that frequently accompany armed conflicts. These processes empower communities to articulate their relationships to their natural surroundings and seek justice for harms that extend beyond anthropocentric frameworks.

Chapter 5 underscored the importance of integrating local ecological knowledge and traditional practices of environmental stewardship, particularly from Indigenous communities, which often emphasise relational accountability and care for Nature. Many Indigenous justice frameworks, for instance, include practices that honour the land and prioritise the long-term health of the community and its environment over punitive measures. By recognising the cultural and ecological value of forests, rivers, and other natural resources, 'from below' approaches may encourage justice models to go beyond state-imposed frameworks and acknowledge Nature as a legitimate victim of conflict.

Moreover, 'from below' approaches rely on the involvement of those directly impacted by harm, often working alongside civil society organisations or transnational networks. This speaks to the imperative, emphasised in feminist epistemology and decolonial scholarship, to centre those with lived experience in knowledge production and to work collaboratively in efforts to effect change, as examined in Chapter 2. There is potential for such collectives to advocate for both human and environmental accountability, as has been witnessed in Colombia, for example. Transnational networks can offer critical support for community-led environmental restoration projects, such as reforestation and soil rehabilitation, which might otherwise be deprioritised by state-led recovery efforts. By mobilising resources and support, these decentralised networks help marginalised communities address harms to Nature in ways that reinforce local priorities and cultural values. We suggest that (and speaking also to guiding principle 4) viewing transitional justice as a tool for activism rather than a series of mechanisms could be effective here. Reflecting Michael Ignatieff's approach to human rights, we suggest that transitional justice can be a tool for 'empowering' victims and provides a 'language' or 'shared vocabulary' from which our arguments can begin.[14] As explored in this book, transitional justice has many tools which – while imperfect – have potential in efforts to 'green' the field. Using the language of transitional justice to articulate claims, needs, and wants could be a valuable dimension in mobilisation and activism.

Furthermore, we argued in Chapter 6 for taking seriously the forward-looking aspects of transitional justice, having built a case for transitional justice as a neoliberalising project. We suggest that there is real potential here for grassroots work to make a meaningful intervention. We know from our own experience of living in Northern Ireland that victims and survivors of conflict, and the organisations that support them, must remain vigilant and informed with regards the detail, progress, and implementation of any proposed transitional justice mechanism. With this in mind, we propose that those working at the grassroots – be they victims of conflict or environmental activists – could monitor transitional justice processes to assess their potential environmental impacts and, where necessary, challenge and suggest alternatives to approaches that may introduce or exacerbate harms against Nature.

14 Michael Ignatieff, *Human Rights as Politics and Idolatry* (Princeton University Press, 2001), 8; 95. See also Lauren Dempster, "Northern Ireland: The Right to Life, Victim Mobilisation and the Legacy of Conflict," *International Conflict and Security Law: A Research Handbook*, eds. Sergey Sayapin et al. (TMC Asser Press/Springer, 2022).

7.2.3 Victimhood is Not a Uniquely Human Experience

One fundamental shift we have explored in this book is the need to broaden the concept of victimhood within transitional justice to include environmental damage as a direct form of harm, experienced by both human beings and other-than-human natural entities. Transitional justice mechanisms typically focus on justice and repair for human victims, largely overlooking environmental destruction except where it directly impacts human livelihoods, health, or property. However, we argue that ecological harm itself is a significant injustice that can have lasting impacts on ecosystems, biodiversity, and human societies alike.

In Chapter 3, we highlighted the limitations of anthropocentric legalism as a core issue restricting transitional justice's capacity to address environmental damage. Anthropocentric legalism, by focusing on individual human rights and property ownership, sets boundaries on what constitutes 'victimhood.' For instance, environmental destruction during conflicts is often classified in transitional justice frameworks as property damage rather than a standalone harm that warrants redress. We used the example of the Guatemalan civil war to illustrate this point, amongst others, noting that the 'scorched earth' tactics which destroyed Mayan lands and crops were framed as damage to people's property rather than as extensive harm to both Mayan cosmologies and the ecosystems themselves.

We argue that a more ecocentric approach would recognise that environmental damage is not just a backdrop to human suffering but a harm in its own right, meriting justice. Drawing from the emergence of more 'ecocentric' legal debates, in Chapter 4 we argued that examples are available of a shift towards this recognition. An emerging example of this shift is the campaign to criminalise 'ecocide' under international criminal law, which at the time of writing has been proposed as a formal amendment to the International Criminal Court's (ICC) Statute. While we are aware that international criminal prosecutions would be difficult (as evidenced by the ineffectiveness of the ICC's environmental war crime – see Chapter 3) and likely very rare in practice, we argue that recognising ecocide as a crime in transitional justice contexts could at a minimum prevent environmental harm from being dismissed as collateral damage and at most offer the prospects of reparation to ecosystems in post-atrocity rebuilding processes. As we explored in Chapter 4, existing reparation forms and mechanisms already offer prospects for adaptation to harms experienced by ecosystems.

Bringing other-than-human victimhood into the remit of transitional justice raises complex questions about how to represent Nature legally and might require significant legal adaptations. Unlike a human victim, an ecosystem does not have a singular 'voice' that we can hear and understand, and questions of who can advocate for them remain contentious. If Nature were to be recognised as a legal rights-holder in a transitional justice framework, who would represent ecosystems in these proceedings? One possible solution is that of guardianship, where representatives from local communities and/or environmental organisations act on behalf of Nature. Ecocentric legal frameworks such as those seen in Ecuador, Colombia, and New Zealand, where rivers and forests are granted legal standing and rights, offer pathways forward. In Colombia, the recognition of the Atrato River as a legal entity with rights to protection and restoration, particularly within Indigenous contexts, signals a shift towards more inclusive and ecologically respectful justice systems. In these cases, and in others, representatives are entrusted with the responsibility of advocating for the ecosystem's interests, ensuring that its intrinsic value is upheld in legal processes. Establishing such mechanisms within transitional justice might require new policies, training, and cooperation across legal, environmental, and Indigenous institutions. However, they demonstrate the potential for a green transitional justice that honours Nature as an integral part of justice rather than as a subsidiary issue.

7.2.4 Transitional Justice is a Process, not a Mechanism

As we explored in Chapter 5, traditional transitional justice mechanisms often focus on discrete periods of violence, bounded by a 'before' and 'after' narrative in which transitional justice is the mechanism that enables the shift from one to the other. However, harms against Nature frequently unfold over extended periods and are not limited to acute, visible acts of violence. One of our key critiques is therefore that the temporal limitations of transitional justice hinder the recognition of and engagement with harms against Nature, with the field's episodic focus excluding forms of 'slow violence'[15] – gradual, dispersed, and often invisible damage that accumulates over time. This concept, discussed in Chapter 5, usefully expands understandings of violence to include protracted ecological degradation, which may be directly linked to acts of mass violence but may also form part of the structural violence that often underpins more acute periods of conflict. In either case, such harms can be highly destructive to both human and ecological well-being.

As we highlighted, the Gulf War provides a stark example of slow violence, where the environmental consequences of military actions have outlasted the conflict itself. The United States' use of depleted uranium weapons caused radioactive contamination that persisted in the soil and water long after the war ended, affecting ecosystems and public health in Iraq through

15 Rob Nixon, *Slow Violence and the Environmentalism of the Poor* (CUP, 2013).

generations.[16] Traditional transitional justice frameworks, focusing solely on the immediate effects of warfare, would disregard these long-term environmental impacts as outside the scope of justice. However, as we argue in Chapter 5, including slow violence within transitional justice would allow for a more comprehensive engagement with environmental harm, acknowledging the prolonged suffering caused by ecological degradation. Such a shift would require recognition that transitional justice is perhaps best understood not a discrete series of mechanisms with a beginning and an end, but as a politically informed process that might need to evolve over time to respond to emerging harms. Such argumentation is common in the transformative justice literature, a body of scholarship that has consistently argued for greater recognition of social, economic, and cultural rights violations within the transitional justice field. Bringing transformative justice literature into conversation with environmental justice and Nancy Fraser's trivalent justice framework, we argue for transitional justice to move beyond narrow legal remedies and adopt a transformative framework that addresses environmental harm, structural violence, and long-term inequality. Such an integrated approach would emphasise the importance of restructuring societal relationships with both human and non-human entities to build lasting, inclusive peace.

Returning to a theme noted above, Indigenous epistemologies offer alternative ways of understanding time and justice that could help transitional justice better address structural and slow violence. Indigenous knowledge systems, as discussed in Chapter 2, often view time as cyclical rather than linear, recognising that past actions continue to impact the present and future. From this perspective, harm to Nature is seen not as a discrete event but as part of an ongoing process that affects generations. Adopting this approach within transitional justice would allow for longer-term accountability and reparations that address a fuller range of environmental harms, including their delayed and cumulative effects on both ecosystems and communities.

7.2.5 Neoliberalism Should Not Be Accepted as the Inevitable Consequence of Transition

A core challenge of greening transitional justice is the field's entrenchment within neoliberal ideology. As explored in Chapter 6, neoliberalism's emphasis on market expansion, privatisation, and economic growth often directly conflicts with environmental stewardship. Transitional justice mechanisms, particularly those implemented under international

16 See also Eliana Cusato, *The Ecology of War and Peace* (CUP, 2020).

guidance or funding, are frequently embedded in neoliberal paradigms that prioritise economic recovery over ecological sustainability. We argue that without greater critical reflexivity, transitional justice will continue to play a role in perpetuating conditions that facilitate further environmental harm.

Of course, all human endeavour has an environmental cost – we do not argue that there is a prospect of an untouched pristine environment, or that such a prospect is desirable. But as we have argued throughout Chapter 6, our current neoliberal model of capitalism is leading to the widespread destruction of the natural world. A pertinent example of how this dynamic can manifest in a transitional justice context is Liberia's post-conflict economic recovery, which relied heavily on resource extraction as a revenue stream.[17] After the Liberian civil war, the government granted numerous logging and mining concessions to multinational corporations to stimulate economic growth. While this influx of investment was seen as essential for rebuilding infrastructure and generating employment, it led to extensive deforestation, drastic biodiversity loss, and contamination of waterways, severely affecting local ecosystems and the livelihoods of Indigenous and rural communities who rely on these natural resources. By prioritising economic growth over environmental preservation, the post-conflict recovery strategy in Liberia highlighted the pitfalls of neoliberal recovery models that treat Nature as an expendable asset.

Integrating more forward-looking environmental concerns into transitional justice arguably requires a two-stage reflexive process: questioning the underlying economic structures that often drive environmental harm, and considering the role of transitional justice in 'normalising' a particular goal or end point. As Chapter 6 argues, environmental justice cannot be fully achieved within a framework that views the protection of Nature as secondary to economic growth. 'Greening' transitional justice is not suggested as the only or even the main vehicle for long-term environmental justice. However, what greening might involve is the contemplation of whether and how transitional justice processes might facilitate and encourage more sustainable development models. Again, there are limits to what is possible in this regard. Transitional justice is not the same as economic reform, and the influence of international financial institutions, foreign investment, and economic pressures, all serve to nudge transitioning states towards the global economic model.

17 Michael D. Beevers, "Forest Governance and Post-Conflict Peace in Liberia: Emerging Contestation and Opportunities for Change?" *The Extractive Industries and Society* 3(2) (2016): 320–328.

We have argued that there are nonetheless shifts in thinking that transitional justice scholars and practitioners might usefully employ. Some are linked to arguments above, such as greater recognition of structural and slow violence, and the design of mechanisms that address economic, social, and environmental rights violations. For example, truth commissions and reparative programmes could focus on reclaiming communal lands, protecting cultural practices related to resource use, and recognising collective rights over individual property rights. Others include learning from related disciplines. We argue that critical criminology, and the crimes of the powerful literature in particular, offer lenses that can help expose forms of systemic violence that can flourish in transitional contexts. Indigenous, feminist, and decolonial perspectives are again of value here, presenting justice frameworks that emphasise care, reciprocity, and interdependence rather than extraction. By integrating these principles, transitional justice could promote forms of recovery that respect and protect Nature as an essential component of a sustainable peace.

7.2.6 There is Value in Pursuing a More Holistic Transitional Justice Project

Expanding transitional justice to encompass harms against Nature is not without legal and practical challenges. Throughout this book, we have examined how current legal frameworks are ill-equipped to accommodate other-than-human victims, as they may lack mechanisms for assigning legal standing to ecosystems or species. Another challenge is balancing the immediate needs of transitioning societies with long-term ecological justice. Post-conflict societies often prioritise human-centered issues such as economic recovery, housing, and public health, and they may view environmental concerns as secondary or even obstructive. We argue that such an approach is understandable but dangerous, as ignoring environmental degradation in the pursuit of short-term recovery can exacerbate underlying social and ecological issues, ultimately undermining the sustainability of peace. A green transitional justice, therefore, would seek ways to balance the urgency of human recovery with a commitment to environmental restoration, recognising that healthy ecosystems are essential for the long-term resilience of both human and other-than-human communities.

7.3 Final Thoughts

In sum, this book calls for a reconceptualisation of transitional justice that embraces ecological inclusivity, recognising the interconnectedness of human and natural systems. By adopting an ecocentric framework, transitional justice could extend its mandate to address the enduring impacts of mass violence on the natural world, which are often as damaging, and sometimes longer-term, than the direct human atrocities they accompany. This shift necessitates a departure from anthropocentric legal norms, temporally bounded approaches, and neoliberal recovery models, paving the way for a transformative justice that honours Nature as an integral participant in peace and recovery.

At its most ambitious, a 'green' transitional justice is not merely about reforming legal structures or other mechanisms; it is also about fostering a deeper ethical commitment to ecological stewardship, relationality, and reciprocity. This inclusive vision recognises that justice for ecosystems, biodiversity, and human communities are interdependent, and that true peace cannot be achieved without addressing the environmental harm that underpins so many conflicts. The future of transitional justice, as envisioned here, is one that challenges power structures, redefines legal categories, and advocates for ecological restoration alongside human reparations. In doing so, transitional justice may evolve towards a field that not only addresses past injustices but also lays the foundation for a sustainable, equitable, and inclusive future – one in which human and ecological flourishing are understood as mutually reinforcing goals.

BIBLIOGRAPHY

Abbott, Pamela, Melissa Tyler and Claire Wallace. *An Introduction to Sociology: Feminist Perspectives.* Routledge, 2006.

Abouharb, M. Rodwan and David L. Cingranelli. "The Human Rights Effects of World Bank Structural Adjustment, 1981–2000." *International Studies Quarterly* 50(2) (2006): 233–262.

Acosta, Mónica, Angela Castañeda, Daniela García, Fallon Hernández, Dunen Muelas, Angela Santamaria. "The Colombian Transitional Process: Comparative Perspectives on Violence against Indigenous Women." *International Journal of Transitional Justice* 12(1) (2018): 108–125.

Adébísí, Folúké. *Decolonisation and Legal Knowledge: Reflections on Power and Possibility.* Bristol University Press, 2024.

Adler, Emanuel and Peter Haas. "Conclusion: Epistemic Communities, World Order, and the Creation of a Reflective Research Programme." *International Organization* 46(1) (1992): 367–390.

Ahmann, Chloe. "'It's Exhausting to Create an Event out of Nothing': Slow Violence and the Manipulation of Time." *Cultural Anthropology* 33(1) (2018): 142–171.

Ahmed, Kaamil, Damien Gayle and Aseel Mousa. "Ecocide in Gaza: Does Scale of Environmental Destruction Amount to a War Crime?" *The Guardian*, March 29, 2024. https://www.theguardian.com/environment/2024/mar/29/gaza-israel-palestinian-war-ecocide-environmental-destruction-pollution-rome-statute-war-crimes-aoe.

Ahmed, Nabil. "Proof of Ecocide: Towards a Forensic Practive for the Proposed International Crime against the Environment." *Archaeological and Environmental Forensic Science* 1(2) (2017): 139–146.

Ahren, Mattias. "Indigenous Peoples' Culture, Customs, and Traditions and Customary Law - The Saami People's Perspective." *Arizona Journal of International and Comparative Law* 21(1) (2004): 63–112.

Ake, Claude. *Social Science as Imperialism.* Ibadan University Press, 1982.

Akoleowo, Victoria Openif'Oluwa. "Critical Pedagogy, Scholar Activism and Epistemic Decolonisation." *South African Journal of Philosophy* 40(4) (2022): 436–451.

Alario, Margarita. "Environmental Policy Enactment under the Military: Some Generalities Between Brazil and Chile." *International Journal of Comparative Sociology* 34(3–4) (1993): 222–230.

Alcoff, Linda Martin and Eva Feder Kittay, eds. *The Blackwell Guide to Feminist Philosophy*. Blackwell Publishing, 2007.

Alcoff, Linda Martín and Eva Feder Kittay. "Defining Feminist Philosophy." In *The Blackwell Guide to Feminist Philosophy,* ed. Linda Martín Alcoff and Eva Feder Kittay. Blackwell Publishing, 2007.

Allman, Jean. "Kwame Nkrumah, African Studies, and the Politics of Knowledge Production in the Black Star of Africa." *The International Journal of African Historical Studies* 46(2) (2013): 181–203.

Alston, Philip. "Criminalizing Human Rights." *Journal of Human Rights Practice* 15(3) (2023): 660–677.

Ambos, Kai. "Punishment without a Sovereign? The Ius Puniendi Issue of International Criminal Law: A First Contribution towards a Consistent Theory of International Criminal Law." *Oxford Journal of Legal Studies* 33(2) (2013): 293–315.

Ambos, Kai. "The Legal Framework of Transitional Justice: A Systematic Study with a Special Focus on the Role of the ICC." In *Building a Future on Peace and Justice*, eds. Kai Lambos, Marieke Wierda and Judith Large. Springer, 2009.

Amir, Ruth. "Transitional Justice and Intersectionality in Post-Conflict Societies." In *Human Rights and International Humanitarian Law,* ed. Andreas Zimmermann and Norman Weiß. Elgar, 2022.

An-Na'im, Abdullahi Ahmed. "Editorial Note: From the Neocolonial 'Transitional' to Indigenous Formations of Justice." *International Journal of Transitional Justice* 7(2) (2013): 197–204.

Andreotti, Vanessa de Oliveira, Sharon Stein, Cash Ahenakey and Dallas Hunt. "Mapping Interpretations of Decolonization in the Context of Higher Education." *Decolonization: Indigeneity, Education &* Society 4(1) (2015): 21–40.

Anand, Ruchi. "Free-Market Economics, Multinational Corporations and Environmental Justice in a Globalized World." In *The Routledge Handbook of Environmental Justice*, eds. Ryan Holifield, Jayajit Chakraborty and Gordon Walker. Routledge, 2017.

Andrieu, Kora. "Civilizing Peacebuilding: Transitional Justice, Civil Society and the Liberal Paradigm." *Security Dialogue* 41(5) (2010): 537–558.

Andrieu, Kora. "Confronting the Dictatorial Past in Tunisia: Human Rights and the Politics of Victimhood in Transitional Justice Discourses." *Human Rights Quarterly* 38(2) (2016): 261–293.

Andrieu, Kora. "Political Liberalism after Mass Violence: John Rawls and a 'Theory' of Transitional Justice." In *Transitional Justice Theories,* eds. Susanne Buckley-Zistel, Teresa Koloma Beck, Christian Braun and Friederike Mieth. Routledge, 2014.

Anghie, Antony. "Whose Utopia? Human Rights, Development and the Third World." *Qui Parle* 22(1) (2013): 63–80.

Anghie, Antony and B. S. Chimni. "Third World Approaches to International Law and Individual Responsibility in Internal Conflicts." *Chinese Journal of International Law* 2(1) (2003): 77–103.

Anker, Kirsten. *Declarations of Interdependence: A Legal Pluralist Approach to Indigenous Rights*. Routledge, 2014.

Antkowiak, Thomas M. "A Dark Side of Virtue: The Inter-American Court and Reparations for Indigenous Peoples." *Duke Journal of Comparative and International Law* 25(1) (2014): 1–80.

Anton, Donald. "Adding a Green Focus: The Office of the Prosecutor of the International Criminal Court Highlights the "Environment" in Case Selection and Prioritisation." *Griffith Law School Research Paper* 17(3) (2016): 1–13.

Appel, Benjamin J. and Cyanne E. Loyle. "The Economic Benefits of Justice: Post-Conflict Justice and Foreign Direct Investment." *Journal of Peace Research* 49(5) (2012): 685–699.

Aracil, Elisa and Ibrahim Sancak. *Essential Concepts of Sustainable Finance: An A-Z Guide*. Routledge, 2024.

Arbour, Louise. "Economic and Social Justice for Societies in Transition" *New York University Journal of International Law and Politics* 40(1) (2007): 1–28.

Ariza-Buitrago, Isabella and Luisa Gómez-Betancur. "Nature in Focus: The Invisibility and Re-Emergence of Rivers, Land and Animals in Colombia's Transitional Justice System." *International Journal of Transitional Justice* 17(1) (2023): 71–88.

Armenian, Andre. "Selectivity in International Criminal Law: An Assessment of the 'Progress Narrative'." *International Criminal Law Review* 16(4) (2016): 642–672.

Arnold, Jobb Dixon. "Bare Nature and the Genocide–Ecocide Nexus—The Conditions of General Threat and the Hope of Cultural Adaptation: The Case of Canada's Tar Sands." *Space and Culture* 21(1) (2018): 18–32.

Arowosegbe, Jeremiah O. "Decolonising the Social Sciences in the Global South: Claude Ake and the Praxis of Knowledge Production in Africa." Working Paper 79/2008; Leiden, African Studies Centre, 2008.

Arriaza, Laura and Naomi Roht-Arriaza. "Social Reconstruction as a Local Process." *International Journal of Transitional Justice*, 2(2) (2008): 152–172.

Arstein-Kerslake, Anna, Erin O'Donnell, Rosemary Kayess and Joanne Watson. "Relational Personhood: A Conception of Legal Personhood with Insights from Disability Rights and Environmental Law." *Griffith Law Review* 30(3) (2021): 530–555.

Artaraz, Kepa, Melania Calestani, and Mei L Trueba. "Introduction: Vivir Bien/Buen Vivir and Post-Neoliberal Development Paths in Latin America: Scope, Strategies, and the Realities of Implementation." *Latin American Perspectives* 48(3) (2021): 4–16.

Arthur, Paige. "How 'Transitions' Reshaped Human Rights: A Conceptual History of Transitional Justice." *Human Rights Quarterly* 31(2) (2009): 321–367.

Atteberry, Jeffrey. "Turning the Widening Gyre: History, Corporate Accountability and Transitional Justice in the Postcolony." *Chicago Journal of International Law* 19(2) (2019): 333–374.

Babin, Borys and Oleksii Plotnikov. "Prosecution of Ecocide as a Weapon in Armed Conflict: Reflections on Crimea." *ICD Brief 29* (October 2022). https://www.internationalcrimesdatabase.org/upload/documents/20221024T110657-Prosecution%20for%20Ecocide%20as%20a%20weapon%20in%20armed%20conflict%20reflections%20on%20Crimea.pdf.

Baker, Catherine and Jelena Obradovic-Wochnik. "Mapping the Nexus of Transitional Justice and Peacebuilding." *Journal of Intervention and Statebuilding* 10(3) (2016): 281–301.

Balint, Jennifer and Julie Evans, "The Australian and New Zealand Critical Criminology Conference 2010 Proceedings: Transitional Justice and Settler States." (2011), http://hdl.handle.net/2123/7361.

Balint, Jennifer, Julie Evans and Nesam McMillan. "Rethinking Transitional Justice, Redressing Indigenous Harm: A New Conceptual Approach." *International Journal of Transitional Justice* 8(2) (2014): 194–216.

Balint, Jennifer, Kristian Laslett and Kate Macdonald. "'Post-conflict' Reconstruction, The Crimes of the Powerful and Transitional Justice." *State Crime* 6(1) (2017): 4–12.

Bano, Abida. "Hegemony and Decolonising Research Praxis: A Researcher's Journey in the Perepheries of Pakistan." In *Thinking with the South,* eds. Andrea Fleschenberg, Kai Kresse, and Rosa Cordillera A. Castillo. ZMO-Studien, 2024.

Baptiste, Brigitte, Miguel Pinedo-Vasquez, Victor H. Gutierrez-Velez, Germán I. Andrade, Pablo Vieira, Lina M. Estupiñán-Suárez, Maria C. Londoño, William Laurance and Tien Ming Lee. "Greening Peace in Colombia." *Nature, Ecology and Evolution* 1 (2017): article no. 0102.

Barria, Lillian and Steven Roper. "How Effective are International Criminal Tribunals? An Analysis of the ICTY and ICTR." *International Journal of Human Rights* 9(3) (2005): 349–368.

Bassiouni, Mahmoud Cherif. "Victims' Rights and Participation in ICC Proceedings and in Emerging Customary International Law." In *Contemporary Issues Facing the International Criminal Court*, ed. Richard Steinberg. Brill Nijhoff, 2020.

Baumann, Matthias and Tobias Kuemmerle. "The Impacts of Warfare and Armed Conflict on Land Systems." *Journal of Land Use Science* 11(6) (2016): 672–688.

Baxi, Upendra. *The Future of Human Rights*. OUP, 2008.

Bebbington, Anthony. *Governing Extractive Industries: Politics, Histories, Ideas*. OUP, 2018.

Beevers, Michael "Forest Governance and Post-Conflict Peace in Liberia: Emerging Contestation and Opportunities for Change?" *The Extractive Industries and Society* 3(2) (2016): 320–328.

Beevers, Michael D. "Forest Governance and Post-Conflict Peace in Liberia: Emerging Contestation and Opportunities for Change." *The Extractive Industries and Society* 3(2) (2016): 320–328.

Bell, Christine. "Transitional Justice, Interdisciplinarity and the State of the 'Field' or 'Non-Field.'" *International Journal of Transitional Justice* 3(1) (2009): 5–27.

Benton, Ted. "Rights and Justice on a Shared Planet: More Rights or New Relations?" *Theoretical Criminology* 2(2) (1998): 149–175.

Benyera, Everisto, ed. *Indigenous, Traditional, and Non-State Transitional Justice in Southern Africa: Zimbabwe and Namibia,* Lexington Books, 2019.

Berhe, Asmeret Asefaw. "The Contribution of Landmines to Land Degradation." *Land Degradation and Development* 18(1) (2007): 1–15.

Bernat, Ignasi and David Whyte. "State-Corporate Crime and the Process of Capital Accumulation: Mapping a Global Regime of Permission from Galicia to Morecambe Bay." *Critical Criminology* 25(1) (2017): 71–86.

Bielefeldt, Heiner. "Moving Beyond Anthropocentrism? Human Rights and the Charge of Speciesism." *Human Rights Quarterly* 43(3) (2021): 515–537.

Bieler, Andreas, Sümercan Bozkurt, Max Crook, Peter S. Cruttenden, Ertan Erol, Adam David Morton, Cemal Burak Tansel and Elif Uzgören. "The Enduring Relevance of Rosa Luxemburg's The Accumulation of Capital." *Journal of International Relations and Development*, 19 (2016): 420–447.

Birch, Kean and Vlad Mykhnenko. "Introduction: A World Turned Right Way Up." *The Rise and Fall of Neoliberalism,* eds. Kean Birch and Vlad Mykhnenko. Bloomsbury Publishing, 2010.

Bisschop, Lieselot CJ, Staci Strobi and Julie S. Viollaz. "Getting Into Deep Water: Coastal Land Loss and State-Corporate Crime in the Louisiana Bayou." *British Journal of Criminology* 58 (2018): 886–905.

Bittle, Steven, Laureen Snider, Steve Tombs and David Whyte. *Revisiting Crimes of the Powerful: Marxism, Crime and Deviance*. Routledge, 2021.

Bliesemann de Guevara, Berit and Roland Kostić. "Knowledge Production In/About Conflict and Intervention: Finding 'Facts', Telling 'Truth.'" *Journal of Intervention and Statebuilding* 11(1) (2017): 1–20.

Boast Richard. "The Waitangi Tribunal and Transitional Justice." *Human Rights Research Journal* 4 (2006): 1–13.

Bobbio, Norberto. *Liberalism and Democracy*. Verso, 1999.

Boege, Volker and Daniel Franks. "Reopening and Developing Mines in Post-Conflict Settings: The Challenge of Company-Community Relations." In *High-Value Natural Resources and Peacebuilding*, eds. Päivi Lujala and Siri Aas Rustad. Routledge, 2012.

Böhm, Maria Laura. *The Crime of Maldevelopment*. Routledge, 2018.

Bojicić-Dzelilović, Vesna. "World Bank, NGOs and the Private Sector in Post-War Reconstruction." *International Peacekeeping* 9(2) (2002): 81–98.

Bond, Patrick. "Sub-Imperial Ecosystem Management in South Africa: Continental Implications of South African Environmental Injustice." In *The Routledge Handbook of Environmental Justice,* eds. Ryan Holifield, Jayajit Chakraborty and Gordon Walke. Routledge, 2018.

Boraine, Alex. "Transitional Justice: A Holistic Interpretation." *Journal of International Affairs* 60(1) (2006): 17–27.

Borda, Aldo Zammit. "History in International Criminal Trials: The 'Crime-Driven Lens' and its Blind Spots." *Journal of International Criminal Justice* 18(3) (2020): 543–566.

Borràs, Susana. "New Transitions from Human Rights to the Environment to the Rights of Nature." *Transnational Environmental Law* 5(1) (2016): 113–143.

Bosselmann, Klaus. "Earth Trusteeship and the Sovereign State." In *The Palgrave Handbook of Environmental Restorative Justice*, eds. Miranda Forsyth, Brunilda Pali, and Felicity Tepper. Palgrave, 2022.

Bourdeau, Ph. "The Man-Nature Relationship and Environmental Ethics." *Journal of Environmental Radioactivity* 72(1) (2004): 9–15.

Bowsher, Josh. "'Omnus et Singulatim': Establishing the Relationship between Transitional Justice and Neoliberalism." *Law Critique* 29(1) (2018): 83–106.

Bowsher, Josh. "The South African TRC as Neoliberal Reconciliation: Victim Subjectivities and the Synchronization of Affects." *Social & Legal Studies* 29(1) (2020): 41–64.

Boyd, David. *The Rights of Nature: A Legal Revolution that Could Save the World*. ECW Press, 2017.

Boyle, Katie. "Reconceptualising Socio-Economic Rights in the Transitional Justice Discipline." *Law, Social Justice & Global Development* 2 (2016): 2–10.

Bradley, Megan. "More than Misfortune: Recognizing Natural Disasters as a Concern for Transitional Justice." *International Journal of Transitional Justice* 11(3) (2017): 400–420.

Braithwaite, John. "Criminology, Peacebuilding and Transitional Justice: Lessons from the Global South." In *The Palgrave Handbook of Criminology and the Global South*, eds. Kerry Carrington, Russell Hogg, John Scott and Máximo Sozzo. Palgrave Macmillan, 2018.

Brankovic, Jasmina. "Transitional and Climate Justice: New Opportunities for Justice in Transition." *International Journal of Transitional Justice* 17(2) (2023): 185–191.

Braverman, Irus. *Settling Nature: The Conservation Regime in Palestine-Israel*. University of Minnesotta Press, 2023.

Brighten, Andrew. "Aboriginal Peoples and the Welfare of Animal Persons: Dissolving the Bill C-10B Conflict." *Indigenous Law Journal* 10(1) (2011): 39–72.

Brisman, Avi and Nigel South. "Resource Wealth, Power, Crime and Conflict." In *Emerging Issues in Green Criminology: Exploring Power, Justice and Harm*, eds. Reece Walters, Diane Solomon Westerhuis and Tanya Wyatt. Palgrave MacMillan, 2013.

Brondízio, Eduardo S., Yildiz Aumeeruddy-Thomas, Peter Bates, Joji Carino, Álvaro Fernández-Llamazares, Maurizio Farhan Ferrari, Kathleen Galvin, Victoria Reyes-García, Pamela McElwee, Zsolt Molnár, Aibek Samakov and Uttam Babu Shrestha. "Locally Based, Regionally Manifested, and Globally Relevant: Indigenous and Local Knowledge, Values, and Practices for Nature." *Annual Review of Environment and Resources* 46(1) (2021): 481–509.

Brooks, Libby. "Indigenous Women Speak Out at Cop26 Rally: 'Femicide is Linked to Ecocide." *The Guardian,* November 11, 2021. https://www.theguardian.com/environment/2021/nov/10/indigenous-women-speak-out-at-cop26-rally-femicide-is-linked-to-ecocide.

Brown, Kris and Fionnuala Ní Aoláin, "Through the Looking Glass: Transitional Justice Futures through the Lens of Nationalism, Feminism and Transformative Change." *International Journal of Transitional Justice* 9(1) (2014): 127–149.

Brown, Wendy. "Neoliberalism and the End of Liberal Democracy." In *Edgework: Critical Essays on Knowledge and Politics,* ed. Wendy Brown. Princeton University Press, 2005.

Bruch, Carl. "Considerations in Framing the Environmental Dimensions of Ius Post Bellum." In *Environmental Protection and Transitions from Conflict to Peace*, eds. Carsten Stahn, Jens Iverson and Jennifer S. Easterday. OUP, 2017.

Bruch, Carl and Akiva Fishman. "Institutionalizing Peacebuilding: The UNCC, Conflict Resources, and the Future of Natural Resources in Transitional Justice." In *Gulf War Reparations and the UN Compensation Commission: Environmental Liability*, eds. Cymie R. Payne and Peter H. Sand. OUP, 2011.

Bruff, Ian. "Neoliberalism and Authoritarianism." In *The Handbook of Neoliberalism*, eds. Simon Springer, Kean Birch and Julia MacLeavy. Routledge, 2016.

Brutt-Griffler, Janina. "Intellectual Culture and Cultural Imperialism: Implications for the Growing Dominance of English in Academia." In *English in Academia: Catalyst or Barrier?* ed. Claus Gnutzmann. Verlag, 2008.

Bukhi Mabele, Mathew, Judith E. Krauss and Wilhelm Kiwango. "Going Back to the Roots: *Ubuntu* and Just Conservation in South Africa." *Conservation and Society* 20(2) (2022): 92–102.

Bullard, Robert, ed. *The Quest for Environmental Justice: Human Rights and the Politics of Pollution*. Sierra Club Books, 2005.

Burdon Peter. "Wild Law: The Philosophy of Earth Jurisprudence." *Alternative Law Journal* 35(2) (2010): 62–65.

Burdon, Peter. "On the Limits of Political Emancipation and Legal Rights." *International Journal for the Semiotics of Law* 34 (2019): 319–339.

Burgis-Kasthala, Michelle and Barrie Sander. "Contemporary International Criminal Law after Critique: Towards Decolonial and Abolitionist (Dis-)Engagement in an Era of Anti-Impunity." *Journal of International Criminal Justice* 22(1) (2024): 127–150.

Burnley, Clementine. "Natural Resources Conflict in the Democratic Republic of Congo: A Question of Governance?" *Sustainable Development Law & Policy* 12(1) (2011): 7–11.

Burns, Ronald."Corporate Crimes and the Problems of Enforcement." In *The Routledge International Handbook of Crimes of the Powerful,* ed. Gregg Barak. Routledge, 2015.

Bustami, Ammar and Marie-Christine Hecken. "Perspectives for a New International Crime against the Environment: International Criminal Responsibility for Environmental Degradation under the Rome Statute." *Goettingen Journal of International Law* 11(1) (2021): 145–190.

Butler, Judith. "Torture and the Ethics of Photography." *Environment and Planning D: Society and Space*, 25 (2007): 951–966.

Butler, Judith. *Frames of War: When is Life Grievable?* Verso Books, 2016.

Butler, Sequoia L. "'I Am the River', the River Is Me": How Environmental Personhood Can Protect Tibal Food Systems." *Wisconsin International Law Journal* 38(1) (2020): 79–107.

Cahill-Ripley, Amanda. "Challenging Neoliberalism: Making Economic and Social Rights Matter in the Peacebuilding Agenda." In *Economic and Social Rights in a Neoliberal World,* eds. Gillian McNaughton and Diane F. Frey. CUP, 2018.

Cahill-Ripley, Amanda. "Foregrounding Socio-Economic Rights in Transitional Justice: Realising Justice for Violations of Economic and Social Rights." *Netherlands Quarterly of Human Rights* 32(2) (2014): 183–213.

Caputi, Jane. *Call Your "Mutha": A Deliberately Dirty-Minded Manifesto for the Earth Mother in the Anthropocene,* OUP (2020).

Carrabine, Eamonn. "Just Images: Aesthetics, Ethics and Visual Criminology." *The British Journal of Criminology* 52(3) (2012): 463–489.

Castelos, Montserrat Abad. "Towards a Holistic Consideration of Crimes against Nature Committed in Times of Armed Conflict: a Critical Approach to the Case of Iraq." *International Journal for Crime, Justice and Social Democracy* 12(3) (2023): 77–92.

Castree, Noel. "Neoliberalism and the Biophysical Environment: A Synthesis and Evaluation of the Research." *Environment and Society* 1(1) (2010): 5–45.

Castro-Sotomayor, José and Paola Minoia. "Cultivating Post-development: Pluriversal Transitions and Radical Spaces of Engagement." In *Challenging Global Development: Towards Decoloniality and Justice,* eds. Henning Melber, Uma Kothari, Laura Camfield and Kees Biekart. Palgrave, 2014.

Castro, Laura Rodríguez. *Decolonial Feminisms, Power and Place: Sentipensando with Rural Women in Colombia*. Palgrave Macmillan, 2021.

Celermajer, Danielle and Anne Therese O'Brien. "Alter-transitional Justice: Transforming Unjust Relations with the More-than-Human." *Journal of Human Rights and the Environment* 12, Special Issue (2021): 125–147.

Celermajer, Danielle, Sria Chatterjee, Alasdair Cochrane, Stefanie Fishel, Astrida Neimanis, Anne O'Brien, Susan Reid, Krithika Srinivasan, David Schlosberg and Anik Waldo. "Justice Through a Multispecies Lens." *Contemporary Political Theory* 19 (2020): 475–512.

Certini, Giacomo, Ricardo Scalenghe and William I. Woods. "The Impact of Warfare on the Soil Environment." *Earth-Science Review* 127 (2013): 1–15.

Césaire, Aimé. *Discourse on Colonialism*. Monthly Review Press, 1972.

Chalmers, Shane and Sundhya Pahuja. "Economic Development and the Rule of Law." In *Cambridge Companion to the Rule of Law,* eds. Jens Meierhenrich and Martin Loughlin. CUP, 2021.

Chandoul, Jihen. *Tunisia and IMF: Transitional Injustice,* September 2017. Policy Brief prepared for Arab NGO Network for Development. https://www.annd.org/uploads/summernote/IMF-TUNISIA-PolicyBrief1612565201.pdf.

Chandran, Rina. "Fears of Evictions as Bangladesh Gives Rivers Legal Rights." *Reuters Asia*, July 5, 2019. https://www.reuters.com/article/us-bangladesh-landrights-rivers/fears-of-evictions-as-bangladesh-gives-rivers-legal-rights-idUSKCN1TZ1ZR.

Charlesworth, Hilary. "International Law: A Discipline of Crisis." *The Modern Law Review* 65(3) (2002): 377–392.

Chauveau, Jean-Pierre. "Question foncière et construction nationale en Côte d'Ivoire. Les enjeux silencieux d'un coup d'Etat." *Politique Africaine* 78 (2000): 94–125.

Chehtman, Alejandro. "A Theory of International Crimes: Conceptual and Normative Issues." In *The Oxford Handbook of International Criminal Law,* eds. Kevin Heller, Jens Ohlin, Darryl Robinson, Frédéric Mégret and Sarah Nouwen. OUP, 2020.

Chiesa, Luis. "Of Persons and the Criminal Law: (Second Tier) Personhood as a Prerequisite for Victimhood." *Pace Law Review* 28(4) (2008): 759–782.

Chimni, B.S. "Third World Approaches to International Law: A Manifesto." *International Commmunity Law Review* 8(1) (2006): 3–28.

Chin, Shirleen. "Lessons Learned from the Adoption of the Crime of Aggression: Ecocide to Charter its Own Path." *An International Crime of Ecocide: New Perspectives.* The Promise Institute for Human Rights, 2023. https://ecocidelaw.com/symposium/.

Choi-Fitzpatrick, Austin. "Disruption and Emergence: How to Think about Human Rights Futures." *Journal of Human Rights* 23(1) (2023): 105–123.

Choudry, Aziz. "Reflections on Academia, Activism, and the Politics of Knowledge and Learning." *International Journal of Human Rights* 24(1) (2020): 28–45.

Christensen, Mikkel Jarle. "The Professional Market of International Criminal Justice: Divisions of Labour and Patterns of Elite Reproduction." *Journal of International Criminal Justice* 19(4) (2021): 783–802.

Christensen, Mikkel. "The Creation of an Ad Hoc Elite and the Value of International Criminal Law Expertise on a Global Market." In *The Oxford Handbook of International Criminal Law*, eds. Kevin Heller, Jens Ohlin, Darryl Robinson, Frédéric Mégret and Sarah Nouwen. OUP, 2020.

Chuji, Mónica, Grimaldo Rengifo and Eduardo Gudynas. "Buen Vivir." In *Pluriverse: A Post-Development Dictionary,* eds. Ashish Kothari, Ariel Salleh, Arturo Escobar, Federico Demaria and Alberto Acosta. Tulika Books, 2019.

Clamp, Kerry. *Restorative Justice in Transitional Settings.* Routledge, 2016.

Clark, Cristy and Beth Goldblatt. "The Right to a Healthy Environment and Social and Economic Rights – Responding to Climate Change in Australia." *Australian Journal of Human Rights* 23(1) (2023): 65–83.

Clark, Cristy, Nia Emmanouil, John Page and Alessandro Pelizzon. "Can You Hear the Rivers Sing? Personhood, Ontology, and the Nitty-Gritty of Governance." *Ecology Law Quarterly* 45(4) (2019): 787–844.

Clark, Janine Natalya. "Are there "Greener" Ways of Doing Transitional Justice? Some Reflections on Srebrenica, Nature and Memorialisation." *International Journal of Human Rights* 20(8) (2016): 1199–1218.

Clark, Janine Natalya. "Harm, Relationality and More-than-Human Worlds: Developing the Field of Transitional Justice in New Posthumanist Directions." *International Journal of Transitional Justice* 17(1) (2023): 15–31.

Clark, Janine Natalya. "The COVID-19 Pandemic and Ecological Connectivity: Implications for International Criminal Law and Transitional Justice." *Journal of International Criminal Justice* 18(5) (2020): 1045–1068.

Clark, Phil and Nicola Palmer. "Challenging Transitional Justice." In *Critical Perspectives in Transitional Justice,* eds. Nicola Palmer, Phil Clark and Danielle Granville. Intersentia, 2012.

Clarke, Kamara Maxine. "Negotiating Racial Injustice: How International Criminal Law Helps Entrench Structural Inequality." *Just Security,* July 24, 2020. https://www.justsecurity.org/71614/negotiating-racial-injustice-how-international-criminal-law-helps-entrench-structural-inequality/.

Clegg, Stewart R. and Mark Haugaard. *The SAGE Handbook of Power.* SAGE, 2009.

Clements, Richard. "Near, Far, Wherever You Are: Distance and Proximity in International Criminal Law." *European Journal of International Law* 32(1) (2021): 327–350.

Code, Lorraine. "Feminist Epistemologies and Women's Lives." In *The Blackwell Guide to Feminist Philosophy*, eds. Linda Martín Alcoff and Eva Feder Kittay. Blackwell Publishing, 2007.

Code, Lorraine. "Ignorance, Injustice and the Politics of Knowledge." *Australian Feminist Studies* 29(80) (2014): 148–160.

Code, Lorraine. *What Can She Know? Feminist Theory and the Construction of Knowledge*. Cornell University Press, 1991.

Colacurci, Marco. "The Draft Convention Ecocide and the Role for Corporate Remediation. Some Insights from the International Monsanto Tribunal and a Recent Research Proposal." *International Criminal Law Review* 21(1) (2021): 154–180.

Collard, Rosemary-Claire, Jessica Dempsey and James Rowe. "Re-Regulating Socioecologies under Neoliberalism." In *The Handbook of Neoliberalism*, eds. Simon Springer, Kean Birch and Julia MacLeavy. Routledge, 2016.

Collins, Toni and Shea Esterling. "Fluid Personality: Indigenous Rights and the Te Awa Tupua (Whanganui River Claims Settlement) Act 2017 in Aotearoa New Zealand." *Melbourne Journal of International Law* 20 (2019): 197–220.

Colquhoun, Heather L. Danielle Levac, Kelly K. O'Brien, Sharon Straus, Andrea C. Tricco, Laure Perrier, Monika Kastner and David Moher, "Scoping Reviews: Time for Clarity in Definition, Methods and Reporting." *Journal of Clinical Epidemiology* 67(12) (2014): 1291–1294.

Comack, Elizabeth. "Corporate Colonialism and the 'Crimes of the Powerful' Committed against the Indigenous Peoples of Canada." *Critical Criminology* 26(4) (2018): 455–471.

Conca, Ken and Jennifer Wallace. "Environment and Peacebuilding in War-Torn Societies: Lessons from the UN Environment Programme's Experience with Post-Conflict Assessment." In *Assessing and Restoring Natural Resources in Post- Conflict Peacebuilding*, eds. David Jensen and Steve Lonergan. Routledge, 2012.

Conca, Ken and Jennifer Wallace. "Environment and Peacebuilding in War-Torn Societies: Lessons from the UN Environment Programme's Experience with Post-Conflict Assessment." *Global Governance* 15(4) (2009): 485–504.

Conca, Ken. "Environmental Peacebuilding: Yesterday, Today and Tomorrow." *The Journal of Social Encounters* 8(1) (2024): Article 3.

Connell, Raewyn and Nour Dados. "Where in the World Does Neoliberalism Come From: The Market Agenda in Southern Perspective." *Theory and Society* 43(2) (2014): 117–138.

Connell, Raewyn. *Southern Theory: The Global Dynamics of Knowledge in Social Science*. Routledge, 2020.

Coolsaet, Brendan and Pierre-Yves Néron. "Recognition and Environmental Justice." In *Environmental Justice*, ed. Brendan Coolsaet. Routledge, 2020.

Costi, Alberto. "Hybrid Tribunals as a Viable Transitional Justice Mechanism to Combat Impunity in Post-Conflict Situations." *New Zealand Universities Law Review* 22(2) (2006): 213–239.

Crawford, Gordon, Zainab Mai-Bornu and Karl Landström. "Decolonising Knowledge Production on Africa: Why it's Still Necessary and What Can be done." *Journal of the British Academy* 9(1) (2021): 21–46.

Crenshaw, Kimberlé. "Demarginalizing the Intersection of Race and Sex: Black Feminist Critique of Antidiscrimination Doctrine, Feminist Theory and Antiracist Politics." *University of Chicago Legal Forum* 1989(1): 139–167.

Crenshaw, Kimberlé. "Mapping the Margins: Intersectionality, Identity Politics and Violence against Women of Color." *Stanford Law Review* 43(6) (1991): 1241–1299.

Crenshaw, Kimberlé. *On Intersectionality: Essential Writings*. The New Press, 2014.

Cribb, Miriama, Elizabeth Macpherson and Axel Borchgrevink. "Beyond Legal Personhood for the Whanganui River: Collaboration and Pluralism in Implementing the Te Awa Tupua Act." *International Journal of Human Rights* (2024): 1–24.

Crook, Martin and Damien Short, eds. *The Genocide-Ecocide Nexus*. Routledge, 2022.

Cryer, Robert. *Prosecuting International Crimes: Selectivity and the International Criminal Law Regime*. CUP, 2005.

Cullen, Pauline, Myra Marx Ferree and Miele Verla. "Introduction to Special Issue: Gender, Knowledge Production and Knowledge Work." *Gender, Work and Organisations* 26 (2019): 765–771.

Cullinan, Cormac. *Wild Law: A Manifesto for Earth Justice*. Bloomsbury, 2002.

Cuppini, Alessandra. "The 'Ideal Victim': A Cage for Victims' Narratives at the International Criminal Court." *Leiden Journal of International Law* 37(2) (2024): 484–505.

Cusato, Eliana. "Back to the Future? Confronting the Role(s) of Natural Resources in Armed Conflict through the Lenses of Truth and Reconciliation Commissions." *International Community Law Review* 19(4–5) (2017): 373–400.

Cusato, Eliana. "Beyond Symbolism: Problems and Prospects with Prosecuting Environmental Destruction before the ICC." *Journal of International Criminal Justice* 15(3) (2017): 491–507.

Cusato, Eliana. "From Ecocide to Voluntary Remediation Projects: Legal Responses to "Environmental Warfare." In: Vietnam and the Spectre of Colonialism." *Melbourne Journal of International Law* 19(2) (2018) 494–520.

Cusato, Eliana. "International Law, the Paradox of Plenty and the Making of Resource-Drive Conflict." *Leiden Journal of International Law* 33(3) (2020): 649–666.

Cusato, Eliana. *The Ecology of War and Peace: Marginalising Slow and Structural Violence in International Law*. CUP, 2021.

D'Eaubonne, Françoise. *Feminism or Death*. Verso, 2022.

Daigle, Michelle and Margaret Marietta Ramírez. "Decolonial Geographies." In *Keywords in Radical Geography: Antipode at 50*, eds. Tariq Jazeel, Andy Kent, Katherine McKittrick, Nik Theodore, Sharad Chari, Paul Chatterton, Vinay Gidwani, Nik Heynen, Wendy Larner, Jamie Peck, Jenny Pickerill, Marion Werner and Melissa W. Wright. *Antipode*, 2019.

Dancy, Geoff and Eric Wiebelhaus-Brahm. "Bridge to Human Development or Vehicle of Inequality? Transitional Justice and Economic Structures." *International Journal of Transitional Justice* 9(1) (2015): 51–69.

Darbyshire, Eoghan. "Deforestation in Conflict Areas in 2020." *Conflict Environment and Observatory,* April 2021. https://ceobs.org/assessment-of-recent-forest-loss-in-conflict-areas/.

Dardot, Pierre and Christian Laval. *The New Way of the World: On Neoliberal Society*. Verso Books, 2014.

Dardot, Pierre and Christian Laval. "Neoliberalism and the Alternative of the Common." In *The Routledge Companion to Theatre of the Oppressed,* eds. Kelly Howe, Julian Boal and José Soeiro. Routledge, 2019.

Davidović, Maja and Catherine Turner. "What Counts as Transitional Justice Scholarship? Citational Recognition and Disciplinary Hierarchies in Theory and Practice." *International Studies Quarterly* 67 (2023): sqad091.

Davies, Margaret. *Law Unlimited: Materialism, Pluralism and Legal Theory*. Routledge, 2017.

Davies, Thom. "Slow Violence and Toxic Geographies: 'Out of Sight' to Whom?" *Environment & Planning C: Politics and Space* 40(2) (2022): 409–427.
Davis Cross, Mai'a K. "Rethinking Epistemically Communities Twenty Years Later." *Review of International Studies* 39(1) (2013): 137–160.
de Greiff, Pablo. "Introduction Repairing the Past: Compensation for Victims of Human Rights Violations." In *The Handbook of Reparations*, ed. Pablo de Greiff. Oxford, 2006.
de Greiff, Pablo. "The Future of the Past: Reflections on the Present State and Prospects of Transitional Justice." *International Journal of Transitional Justice* 14(2) (2020): 251–259.
de Leeuw, Sarah and Sarah Hunt. "Unsettling Decolonizing Geographies." *Geography Compass* 12(7) (2018): 123–76.
de Lucia, Vito. "Competing Narratives and Complex Genealogies: The Ecosystem Approach in International Environmental Law." *Journal of Environmental Law* 27(1) (2015): 91–117.
de Pompignan, Nathalie. "Ecocide." *Mass Violence & Résistance – Research Network,* November 3, 2007, https://www.sciencespo.fr/mass-violence-war-massacre-resistance/en/document/ecocide.html.
De Mijke, Waardt and Sanne Weber. "Beyond Victims' Mere Presence: An Empirical Analysis of Victim Participation in Transitional Justice in Colombia." *Journal of Human Rights Practice* 11(1) (2019): 209–228.
Deckha, Maneesha. *Animals as Legal Beings: Contesting Anthropocentric Legal Orders*. University of Toronto Press, 2021.
DeFalco, Randle C. "Time and the Visibility of Slow Atrocity Violence." *International Criminal Law Review* 21(5) (2021): 905–934.
DeFalco, Randle. *Invisible Atrocities: The Aesthetic Biases of International Criminal Justice*. CUP, 2022.
Delanty, Gerard and Neal Harris. *Capitalism and its Critics*. Routledge, 2023.
Di Chiro, Giovanna. "Mobilizing 'Intersectionality' in Environmental Justice Research and Action in a Time of Crisis." In *Environmental Justice,* ed. Brendan Coolsaet. Routledge, 2020.
Dempster, Lauren. "Northern Ireland: The Right to Life, Victim Mobilisation and the Legacy of Conflict." In *International Conflict and Security Law: A Research Handbook*, eds. Sergey Sayapin, Rustam Atadjanov, Umesh Kadam, Gerhard Kemp, Nicolás Zambrana-Tévar, Noëlle Quénivet. TMC Asser Press/Springer, 2022.
Desierto, Diane. "Environmental Damages, Environmental Reparations, and the Right to a Healthy Environment: The ICJ Compensation Judgment in *Costa Rica v Nicaragua* and the IACtHR Advisory Opinion on Marine Protection for the Greater Caribbean." *Blog of the European Journal of International Law: Talk!* February 14, 2018. https://www.ejiltalk.org/environmental-damages-environmental-reparations-and-the-right-to-a-healthy-environment-the-icj-compensation-judgment-in-costa-rica-v-nicaragua-and-the-iacthr-advisory-opinion-on-marine-protection/.
Dimou, Eleni. "Decolonizing Southern Criminology: What can the 'Decolonial Option' Tell Us About Challenging the Modern/Colonial Foundations of Criminology?" *Critical* Criminology 29(3) (2021): 431–450.
Doak, Jonathan. "The Therapeutic Dimension of Transitional Justice: Emotional Repair and Victim Satisfaction in International Trials and Truth Commissions." *International Criminal Law Review* 11(2) (2011): 263–298.
Doak, Jonathan. *Victims' Rights, Human Rights and Criminal Justice: Reconceiving the Role of Third Parties*. Hart Publishing, 2008.

Domínguez, Rafael, Sara Caria and Mauricio León. "*Buen Vivir:* Praise, Instrumentalization, and Reproductive Pathways of Good Living in Ecuador." *Latin American and Caribbean Ethnic Studies* 12(2) (2017): 133–154.

Dommen, Caroline. "Claiming Environmental Rights: Some Possibilities Offered by the United Nations' Human Rights Mechanisms." *Georgetown International Environmental Law Review* 11(1) (1998): 1–48.

Donais, Timothy. *The Political Economy of Peacebuilding in Post-Dayton Bosnia.* Routledge, 2005.

Donnelly, Jack. "The Concept of Human Rights." In *Universal Human Rights in Theory and Practice*, ed. Jack Donnelly. Cornell University Press, 2013.

Doran, Peter. *A Political Economy of Attention, Mindfulness and Consumerism.* Routledge, 2017.

Doremus, Holly. "The Rhetoric and Reality of Nature Protection: Toward a New Discourse." *Washington and Lee Law Review* 57(1) (Winter 2000): 11–74.

Dorninger, Christian, Alf Hornborg, David J. Abson, Henrik von Wehrden, Anke Schaffartzik, Stefan Giljum, John-Oliver Engler, Robert L. Feller, Klaus Hubacek and Hanspeter Wieland. "Global Patterns of Ecologically Unequal Exchange: Implications for Sustainability in the 21st Century." *Ecological Economics* 179 (2021): 106824.

Doucet, Andrea. "Shorelines, Seashells, and Seeds: Feminist Epistemologies, Ecological Thinking, and Relational Ontologies." In *The Palgrave Handbook of Relational Sociology,* ed. François Dépelteau. Palgrave, 2018.

Draulans, Dirk and Ellen Van Krunkelsven, "The Impact of War on Forest Areas in the Democratic Republic of Congo," *Onyx* 38(1) (2002): 35–40.

Dresse, Anaïs, Itay Fischhendler, Jonas Østergaard Nielsen and Dimitrios Zikos. "Environmental Peacebuilding: Towards a Theoretical Framework." *Cooperation and Conflict* 54(1) (2019): 99–119.

Druliolle, Vincent and Roddy Brett. *The Politics of Victimhood in Post-Conflict Societies.* Springer International Publishing, 2018.

Drumbl, Mark. *Atrocity, Punishment and International Law.* CUP, 2007.

Drumbl, Mark. *Accountability for Property Crimes and Environmental War Crimes: Prosecution, Litigation, and Development.* International Center for Transitional Justice. November 4, 2009. https://www.ictj.org/sites/default/files/ICTJ-Development-PropertyCrimes-FullPaper-2009-English.pdf.

Drumbl, Mark. "Justice Framed: A Genealogy of Transitional Justice." *European Journal of International Law* 30(4) (2019): 1447–1463.

Dudai, Ron. "Transitional Justice as Social Control: Political Transitions, Human Rights Norms and the Reclassification of the Past." *The British Journal of Sociology* 69(3) (2017): 691–711.

Duffy, Aoife. "Bearing Witness to Atrocity Crimes: Photography and International Law." *Human Rights Quarterly* 40(4) (2018): 776–814.

Duggan, Marian. *Revisiting the 'Ideal Victim': Developments in Critical Victimology.* Policy Press, 2018.

Dunlap, Alexander. "The 'Solution' is Now the 'Problem:' Wind Energy, Colonisation and the 'Genocide-Ecocide Nexus' in the Isthmus of Tehuantepec, Oaxaca," *The International Journal of Human Rights* 22(4) (2018): 550–573.

Dunlap, Alexander. "The Politics of Ecocide, Genocide and Megaprojects: Interrogating Natural Resource Extraction, Identify and the Normalization of Erasure." *Journal of Genocide Research* 23(2) (2021): 212–235.

Durbach, Andrea and Louise Chappell. "Leaving Behind the Age of Impunity: Victims of Gender Violence and the Promise of Reparations." *International Feminist Journal of Politics* 16(4) (2014): 543–562.

Durdiyeva, Selbi. "Towards Decolonial Agenda for Transitional Justice: "The Old is Dying and the New Cannot Be Born."" In *The Wretched of the Global South. International Law and the Global South*, eds. Thamil Venthan Ananthavinayagan, and Amritha Viswanath Shenoy. Springer, 2024.

Dusek, Andrew. "Ill Fares the Land: Reparations for Housing, Land, and Property Rights Violations in Myanmar." *Harvard Human Rights Journal* 30 (2017): 129–164.

Duthie, Roger. "Transitional Justice, Development, and Economic Violence." In *Justice and Economic Violence in Transition*, ed. Dustin Sharp. Springer, 2013.

Dutta, Anwesha and Trishant Simlai, "If the Army Cuts Trees, Why Can't We? Resource Extraction, Hunting and the impacts of Militaries on Biodiversity Conservation." *Enforcing Ecocide Power, Policing & Planetary Militarization*, eds. Alexander Dunlap and Andera Brock. Palgrave Macmillan, 2022.

Eagleton-Pierce, Matthew. "Historicizing the Neoliberal Spirit of Capitalism." In *The Handbook of Neoliberalism*, eds. Simon Springer, Kean Birch and Julia MacLeavy. Routledge, 2016.

ECCC, Victims Participation, ECCC Website, n.d., https://www.eccc.gov.kh/en/victims-support/participation#:~:text=Who%20does%20the%20ECCC%20consider,the%20jurisdiction%20of%20the%20ECCC.

Eichler, Lauren J. "Ecocide is Genocide: Decolonizing the Definition of Genocide." *Genocide Studies and Prevention: An International Journal* 14(2) (2020): 104–121.

Elander, Maria. *Figuring Victims in International Criminal Justice: The Case of the Khmer Rouge Tribunal.* Routledge, 2018.

Elden, Stuart. "Reading Schmitt Geopolitically: Nomos, Territory and Großraum." In *Spatiality, Sovereignty and Carl Schmitt: Geographies of the Nomos*, ed. Stephen Legg. Routledge, 2011.

Ellis Erle C, Nicolas Gauthier, Kees Klein Goldewijk, Rebecca Bliege Bird, Nicole Boivin, Sandra Díaz, Dorian Q. Fuller, Jacquelyn L. Gill, Jed O. Kaplan, Naomi Kingston, Harvey Locke, Crystal N. H. McMichael, Darren Ranco, Torben C. Rick, M. Rebecca Shaw, Lucas Stephens, Jens-Christian Svenning and James E. M. Watson. "People have Shaped Most of Terrestrial Nature for at Least 12000 Years," *Proceedings of the National Academy of Sciences* e2023483118 (2021).

Elster, Jon *Closing the Books: Transitional Justice in Historical Perspective.* CUP, 2004.

Emberland, Marius. *The Human Rights of Companies.* OUP, 2006.

England, Kim and Kevin Ward. "Theorizing Neoliberalization." In *The Handbook of Neoliberalism*, eds. Simon Springer, Kean Birch and Julia MacLeavy. Routledge, 2016.

Engle, Karen. "Anti-Impunity and the Turn to Criminal Law in Human Rights." *Cornell Law Review* 100(5) (2015): 1069–1128.

Engle, Karen. "A Genealogy of the Criminal Turn in Human Rights." In *Anti-Impunity and the Human Rights Agenda*, ed. Karen Engle. CUP, 2016.

Escobar, Arturo. "Beyond the Third World: Imperial Globality, Global Coloniality and Anti-Globalisation Social Movements." *Third World Quarterly*, 25(1) (2004): 207–230.

Estes, Nick. *Our History Is the Future: Standing Rock versus Dacota Access Pipeline, and the Long Tradition of Indigenous Resistance.* Verso, 2019.

Evans, Matthew. "Structural Violence, Socioeconomic Rights, and Transformative Justice." *Journal of Human Rights* 15(1) (2016): 1–20.

Evans, Matthew. "Land and the Limits of Liberal Legalism: Property, Transitional Justice and Non-Reformist Reforms in Post-Apartheid South Africa." *Review of African Political Economy* 48(17) (2021): 646–655.

Evans, Matthew. "Beyond Disciplines, Beyond Fields, Beyond Transitional Justice." In *Beyond Transitional Justice: Transformative Justice and the State of the Field (or non-Field),* ed. Matthew Evans. Routledge, 2022.

Evenhuis, Mark. "Developmental Faith, Sacrifice and the Betrayal of Transitional Justice A Bouganvillean Case Study." *State Crime Journal* 6(1) (2017): 102–131.

Ewuoso, C. and S. Hall. "Core Aspects of *Ubuntu*: A Systematic Review." *South African Journal of Bioethics and Law* 12(2) (2019): 93–103.

Falk, Richard A. "Environmental Warfare and Ecocide: Facts, Appraisal, and Proposals." *Security Dialogue* 4(1) (1973): 80–96.

Falk, Richard. "Predicaments of Transformative Justice in a Neoliberal and State-Centric World Order." In *From Transitional to Transformative Justice,* eds. Paul Gready and Simon Robins. CUP, 2019.

Fanon, Franz. *Black Skins, White Masks.* Grove Books, 2008.

Farmer, Paul. "On Suffering and Structural Violence: A View from Below." *Daedalus* 125(1) (1996): 261–283.

Fast, Elizabeth and Margaret Kovach. "Community Relationships within Indigenous Methodologies." *Applying Indigenous Research Methods: Storying with Peoples and Communities* 2 (2019): 21–36.

Fatigato, Maria Chiara. *Buen Vivir*: "An Opportunity to Re-Think the Development and Sustainability Model." Departimento Di Scienze Sociali Ed Economiche Working Papers Series: 2023.

Faure, Michael. "The Development of Environmental Criminal Law in the EU and Its Member States." *Review of European, Comparative & International Environmental Law* 26(2) (2017): 139–146.

Favre, David and Vivien Tsang. "The Development of Anti-Cruelty Laws During the 1800's." *Detroit College of Law Review* 1(1) (1993): 1–35.

Federici, Silvia. *Caliban and the Witch: Women, the Body and Primitive Accumulation.* Penguin, 2004.

Fernandes, Sabrina. "Right-Wing Authoritarianism against Nature: The Latin American Context." *Global Authoritarianism Perspectives and Contestations from the South.* International Research Group on Authoritarianism and Counter-Strategies, De Gryter Brill, 2022.

Firchow, Pamina and Yvette Selim, "Meaningful Engagement from the Bottom-Up? Taking Stock of Participation in Transitional Justice Processes." *International Journal of Transitional Justice* 16(2) (2022): 187–203.

Fletcher, Laurel and Harvey Weinstein. "Violence and Social Repair: Rethinking the Contribution of Justice to Reconciliation." *Human Rights Quarterly* 24(3) (2002): 573–639.

Fletcher, Laurel E. and Harvey M. Weinstein. "How Power Dynamics Influence the North-South Gap in Transitional Justice." *Berkeley Journal of International Law* 37(1) (2018): 1–28.

Foggin, J. Marc. "We Still Need the Wisdom of *Ubuntu* for Successful Nature Conservation." *Ambio* 50(3) (2021): 723–725.

Forde, Susan, Stefanie Kappler and Annija Björkdahl. "Peacebuilding, Structural Violence and Spatial Reparations in Post-Colonial South Africa." *Journal of Intervention and Statebuilding* 15(3) (2021): 327–346.

Forsyth, Miranda. "A Future Agenda for Environmental Restorative Justice?" *International Journal of Restorative Justice* 4(1) (2021): 17–40.

Foster, John Bellamy. "Marx's Theory of Metabolic Rift: Classical Foundations for Environmental Sociology." *American Journal of Sociology* 105(2) (1999): 366–405.

Foster, John Bellamy and Brett Clark. "Ecological Imperialism: The Curse of Capitalism." In *The New Imperial Challenge,* eds. Leo Panitch and Colin Leys. Socialist Register, 2004.

Foucault, Michel. *Discipline and Punish: The Birth of the Prison.* Penguin, 1977.

Foucault, Michel. *Power/Knowledge: Selected Interviews and Other Writings, 1972–1977.* Doubleday Publishing Group, 1980.

Franzki, Hannah and Maria Carolina Olarte. "Understanding the Political Economy of Transitional Justice: A Critical Theory Perspective." In *Transitional Justice Theories,* eds. Susanne Buckley-Zistel, Teresa Koloma Beck, Christian Braun and Friederike Mieth. Routledge, 2014.

Fraser, Nancy. "From Redistribution to Recognition? Dilemmas of Justice in a 'Post-Socialist' Age." *New Left Review* 1(212) (1995): 68–93.

Fraser, Nancy. "Social Justice in the Age of Identity Politics: Redistribution, Recognition, Participation" Discussion Paper, 1998, *NBN-Resolving.* https://nbn-resolving.org/urn:nbn:de:0168-ssoar-126247.

Fraser, Nancy. *Scales of Justice: Reimagining Political Space in a Globalizing World.* Columbia University Press, 2009.

Fraser, Nancy. *Fortunes of Feminism from State-Managed Capitalism to Neoliberal Crisi.* Verso, 2020.

Freeland, Steven. "Human Rights, the Environment and Conflict: Addressing Crimes against the Environment." *International Journal on Human Rights* 2(2) (2005): 113–141.

Freeman, Samuel. *Liberalism and Distributive Justice.* OUP, 2018.

Freidman, Marilyn and Angela Bolte. "Ethics and Feminism." In *The Blackwell Guide to Feminist Philosophy,* eds. Linda Martín Alcoff and Eva Feder Kittay. Blackwell Publishing, 2007.

Fricker, Miranda. *Epistemic Injustice: Power and the Ethics of Knowing.* OUP, 2007.

Friedland, Hadley. "Waniska: Reimagining the Future with Indigenous Legal Traditions." *The Windsor Yearbook of Access to Justice* 33(1): 85–102.

Friedland, Hadley and Val Napoleon. "Gathering Threads: Developing a Methodology for Researching and Rebuilding Indigenous Legal Traditions." *Lakehead Law Journal,* 1(1) (2015): 16–44.

Fulfer, Katy. "The Capabilities Approach to Justice and the Flourishing of Nonsentient Life." *Ethics and the Environment* 18(1) (2013): 19–42.

Galtung, Johan. "Violence, Peace, and Peace Research." *Journal of Peace Research,* 6(3) (1969): 167–191.

Galtung, Johan and Tord Höivik. "Structural and Direct Violence: A Note on Operationalization." *Journal of Peace Research* 8(1) (1971): 73–76.

Garcés, Diana. "When the Forest Does Not Sing Anymore. Cuerpoterritorio Approach of Amazonian Indigenous Women to the Concepts of Conflict and Violence." *Blanquerna School of Communication and International Relations* 51 (2021): 69–83.

García-Godos, Jemima. "Victim Reparations in the Peruvian Truth Commission and the Challenge of Historical Interpretation." *International Journal of Transitional Justice* 2(1) (2008): 63–82.

García-Godos, Jemima and Knut Andreas O. Lid. "Transitional Justice and Victims' Rights before the End of a Conflict: The Unusual Case of Colombia." *Journal of Latin American Studies* 42(3) (2010): 487–516.

Gauger, Anja, Mai Pouye Rabatel-Fernel, Louise Kulbicki, Damien Short and Polly Higgins. *Ecocide is the Missing 5th Crime against Peace.* Human Rights Consortium, School of Advanced Study, University of London, 2012.

Gaynor, Kaitlyn M, Kathryn J Fiorella, Gillian H Gregory, David J Kurz, Katherine L Seto, Lauren S Withey and Justin S Brashares. "War and Wildlife: Linking Armed Conflict to Conservation." *Frontiers in Ecology and the Environment* 14(1) (2016): 533–542.

Gellers, Joshua C. "An Inconvenient Reflection on Human Rights: Comments on Choi-Fitzpatrick's Article, 'Disruption and Emergence.'" *Journal of Human Rights* 23(3) (2024): 314–319.

Geréby, György. "The Theology of Carl Schmitt." *Poiteja* 72 (2021): 21–49.

Ghimire, Amar Jibi. "Articulating the Linkages between Human Rights and Environmental Rights: The Perspective of Transitional Justice." *NJA Law Journal* 5(1) (2011): 85–106.

Gieseken, Helen Obregón, and Vanessa Murphy. "The Protection of the Natural Environment under International Humanitarian Law: The ICRC's 2020 Guidelines." *International Review of the Red Cross* 105(924) (2023): 1180–1207.

Gilbert, Jérémie and Kanyinke Sena. "Litigating Indigenous Peoples' Cultural Rights: Comparative Analysis of Kenya and Uganda." *African Studies* 77(2) (2018): 204–222.

Gillett, Matthew. "Eco-Struggles—Using International Criminal Law to Protect the Environment During and after Non-International Armed Conflict." In *Environmental Protection and Transitions from Conflict to Peace: Clarifying Norms, Principles, and Practices*, eds. Carsten Stahn, Jens Iverson, and Jennifer Easterday. OUP, 2017.

Gillett, Matthew. "Victim Participation and Reparations for Environmental Harm at the International Criminal Court." In *Prosecuting Environmental Harm before the International Criminal Court*, ed. Matthew Gillett. CUP, 2022.

Gilman, Ryan. "Expanding Environmental Justice after War: The Need for Universal Jurisdiction over Environmental War Crimes." *Colorado Journal of International Environmental Law and Policy* 22(3) (2011): 447–471.

Gissel, Line Engbo. "The Standardisation of Transitional Justice." *European Journal of International Relations* 28(4) (2022): 859–884.

Givens, Jennifer E., Xiaorui Huang and Andrew K. Jorgenson. "Ecologically Unequal Exchange: A Theory of Global Environmental Injustice." *Sociology Compass* 13(5) (2019): e12693.

Glasius, Marlies. "Gramsci for the Twenty-First Century: Dialectics and Translatability." *International Studies Review* 14(4) (2012): 666–686.

Goh, Bee Chen. "An Idea for a Better World: Human Rightsponsibility." *Scholarship, Practice and Education in Comparative Law: A Festschrift in Honour of Mary Hiscock* (2019): 69–80.

Gómez Correal, Diana, Pascha Bueno-Hansen and Julissa Mantilla Falcón. "Feminist Trajectories from Peru to Colombia: Taking Violence Experienced by Women into Account in Truth Commissions." *International Feminist Journal of Politics* 25(3) (2023): 482–505.

Gomez-Betancur, Luisa. "The Rights of Nature in the Colombian Amazon: Examining Challenges and Opportunities in a Transitional Justice Setting." *UCLA Journal of International Law and Foreign Affairs* 25(1) (2020): 41–84.

González-Ayala, Sofía N. and Alejandro Camargo. "Voices of Water and Violence: Exhibition Making and the Blue Humanities for Transitional Justice." *Curator: The Museum Journal* 64 (10) (2021): 183–204.

González, Pablo Alonso and Alfredo Macías Vázquez. "An Ontological Turn in the Debate on *Buen Vivir - Sumak Kawsay* in Ecuador: Ideology, Knowledge and the Common." *Latin American and Caribbean Ethnic Studies* 10(3) (2015): 315–334.

Goralnik, Lissy and Michael Nelson. "Anthropocentrism." *Encyclopedia of Applied Ethics*, ed. Ruth Chadwick. Academic Press, 2012.

Gordon, Gregory. "The Trial of Peter von Hagenbach: Reconciling History, Historiography and International Criminal Law." In *The Hidden Histories of War Crimes Trials*, eds. Kevin Jon Heller and Gerry Simpson. OUP, 2013.

Goyes, David, Nigel South, Mireya Astroina Abaibira, Pablo Baicué, Angie Cuchimba and Deisy Tatiana Ramos Ñeñetofe. "Genocide and Ecocide in Four Colombian Indigenous Communities: The Erosion of a Way of Life and Memory." *British Journal of Criminology* 61(4) (2021): 965–984.

Grasten, Maj and Ntina Tzouvala. "The Political Economy of International Transitional Administration: Regulating Food and Farming in Kosovo and Iraq." *Contemporary Politics* 24(5) (2018): 588–606.

Gray, John. *Liberalism*. Open University Press, 1995.

Gray, Mark Allan. "The International Crime of Ecocide." *California Western International Law Journal* 26(2) (1996): 215–272.

Gready, Paul and Simon Robins. *From Transitional to Transformative Justice*. CUP, 2019.

Gready, Simeon. "The Case for Transformative Reparations: Pursuit of Structural Socio-Economic Reform in Post-Conflict Societies." *Journal of Intervention and Statebuilding* 16(2) (2022): 182–201.

Grear, Anna. "Law's Entities: Complexity, Plasticity and Justice." *Jurisprudence* 4(1) (2013): 76–101.

Grear, Anna. "The Closures of Legal Subjectivity: Why Examining 'Law's Person' is Critical to an Understanding of Injustice in an Age of Climate Crisis." In *Research Handbook on Human Rights and the Environment*, ed. Anna Grear. Elgar, 2015.

Green, Joyce, ed. *Making Space for Indigenous Feminism*. Fernwood Publishing, 2017.

Greene, Anastacia. "The Campaign to Make Ecocide an International Crime: Quixotic Quest or Moral Imperative?" *Fordham Environmental Law Review* 30(3) (2019): 1–48.

Grewal, Kiran Kaur. "The Epistemic Violence of Transitional Justice: A View from Sri Lanka." *International Journal of Transitional Justice*, 17(2) (2023): 322–338.

Grinde, Donald A. and Bruce E. Johansen. *Ecocide of Native America: Environmental Destruction of Indian Lands and Peoples*. Clear Light Publishers, 1995.

Guimarães, Verônica Maria Bezerra. "Ecofeminism, Rights of Nature and Climate Justice: Relational Webs and Planetary Restoration." *Simbiótica. Revista Eletrônica* 10(3) (2023). 15–30.

Gutiérrez-Rodríguez, Carlos Arturo. "Beyond Liberal Justice? Decolonising Colombian Transitional Justice through Victims' Participation and Indigenous Rights," *International Journal of Human Rights* 28(10) (2024): 1569–1591.

Haas, Peter. "Introduction: Epistemic Communities and International Policy Co-ordination." *International Organization* 46(1) (1992): 1–35.

Haastrup, Toni and Jamie J. Hagen. "Racial Hierarchies of Knowledge Production in the Women, Peace and Security Agenda." *Critical Studies on Security*, 9(1) (2021), 27–30.

Haesbaert, Rogerio. "Del Cuerpo-Territorio al Territorio-Cuerpo (de la Tierra): Contribuciones Decoloniales." *Cultura y Representaciones Sociales* 15(29) (2020): 267–301.

Haldemann, Frank. "Another Kind of Justice: Transitional Justice as Recognition." *Cornell International Law Journal* 41(3) (2008): 675–738.

Haldemann, Frank and Rachelle Kouassi. "Transitional Justice without Economic, Social, and Cultural Rights?" In *Economic, Social, and Cultural Rights in*

International Law: Contemporary Issues and Challenges, eds. Eibe Riedel, Gilles Giacca, and Christophe Golay. OUP, 2014.

Hall, Matthew. "Environmental Harm and Environmental Victims: Scoping Out a 'Green Victimology'." *International Review of Victimology* 20(1) (2013): 129–143.

Hall, Matthew. *Victims of Environmental Harm: Rights, Recognition and Redress under National and International Law*. Routledge, 2013.

Hall, Stuart. "Foucault." In *Discourse Theory and Practice: A Reader*, eds. Margaret Wetherell, Stephanie Taylor and Simeon J. Yates. SAGE, 2001.

Haluska, Anne. "Restorative Justice and the Rights of Nature: Using Indigenous Legal Traditions to Influence Cultural Change and Promote Environmental Protection." *Mitchell Hamline Law Review* 49(1) (January 2023): 92–125.

Hameiri, Shahar. *Regulating Statehood: State Building and the Transformation of the Global Order*. Springer, 2010.

Hamilton, Mark. *Environmental Crime and Restorative Justice: Justice as Meaningful Involvement*. Palgrave, 2021.

Han, Saerom. "Transitional Justice for Whom? Contention over Human Rights and Justice in Tunisia." *Social Movement Studies* 21(6) (2022): 816–832.

Hanson, Thor, Thomas M. Brooks, Gustavo A. B. Da Fonseca, Michael Hoffmann, John F. Lamoreux, Gary Machlis, Cristina G. Mittermeier, Russell A. Mittermeier and John D. Pilgrim. "Warfare in Biodiversity Hotspots." *Conservation Biology* 23(3) (2009): 578–587.

Haraway, Donna. *Simians, Cyborgs and Women*. Free Association Books, 1991.

Harding, Sandra and Brent Mendoza. "Latin American Decolonial Feminist Philosophy of Knowledge Production." In *The Routledge Handbook of Feminist Philosophy of Science*, eds. Sharon Crasnow and Kristen Intemann. Routledge, 2021.

Harvey, David. *A Brief History of Neoliberalism*. OUP, 2007.

Harvey, Fiona. "Pacific Islands Submit Court Proposal for Recognition of Ecocide as a Crime." *The Guardian*, September 10, 2024. https://www.theguardian.com/law/article/2024/sep/09/pacific-islands-ecocide-crime-icc-proposal.

Hayner, Priscilla. "International Center for Transitional Justice (ICTJ)." In *Encyclopedia of Human Rights*, ed. David Forsythe, OUP, 2009.

Hazan, Pierre. *Judging War, Judging History: Behind Truth and Reconciliation*. Stanford University Press, 2010.

Hearty, Kevin. "Victims of Human Rights Abuses in Transitional Justice: Hierarchies, Perpetrators and the Struggle for Peace." *International Journal of Human Rights* 22(7) (2018): 888–909.

Height, Tatiana, Katherine Martin and Zakiya Leggett. "Call for Environmental Justice Amplification Among Ecology Scholars and Practitioners: A Black Ecology Perspective." *The Bulletin of the Ecological Society of America* 104(1) (2022): e02039.

Hellsten, Sirkku K. "Transitional Justice as a Philosophical and Practical Challenge: Critical Notes on Colleen Murphy's New Theory of the 'Conceptual Foundations of Transitional Justice.'" In *Reconciliation, Transitional and Indigenous Justice*, eds. Krushil Watene and Eric Palmer. Routledge, 2020.

Herremans, Brigitte and Tine Destrooper. "Moving Beyond Formal Truth Practices and Forensic Truth in the Syrian Conflict: How Informal Truth Practices Contribute to Thicker Understandings of Truth." *Social & Legal Studies* 32(4) (2022): 1–21.

Hickel, Jason. "Neoliberalism and the End of Democracy." In *The Handbook of Neoliberalism*, eds. Simon Springer, Kean Birch and Julia MacLeavy. Routledge, 2016.

Higgins, Polly, Damien Short and Nigel South. "Protecting the Planet: A Proposal for a Law of Ecocid." *Crime, Law and Social Change* 59(Special issue) (2023): 251–266.

Hikido, Annie and Susan B. Murray. "Whitened Rainbows: How White College Students Protect Whiteness Through Diversity Discourses." *Race, Ethnicity and Education*, 19(2) (2016): 389–411.

Hinley, Matthew. "Geographies of Environmental Governance: The Nexus of Nature and Neoliberalism." *Geography Compass* 2(2) (2008): 433–451.

Hirschmann, Nancy J. "Feminist Political Philosophy." In *The Blackwell Guide to Feminist Philosophy,* eds. Linda Martín Alcoff and Eva Feder Kittay. Blackwell Publishing, 2007.

Hobbs, Angela. "Physis and Nomos." In *The Routledge Encyclopaedia of Philosophy,* ed. Edward Craig. Routledge, 1998.

Hobbs, Harry. "Locating the Logic of Transitional Justice in Liberal Democracies: Native Title in Australia." *The University of New South Wales Law Journal* 39(2) (2016): 512–552.

Holifield, Ryan, Jayajit Chakraborty and Gordon Walker. "Introduction: The Worlds of Environmental Justice." In *The Routledge Handbook of Environmental Justice,* eds. Ryan Holifield, Jayajit Chakraborty and Gordon Walker. Routledge, 2018.

Holley, Cameron, Neil Gunningham and Clifford Shearing. *The New Environmental Governance.* Routledge, 2012.

Hollo, Tim. "Uncomfortable with Power: Strategies, Policies and Approaches of the Green Part of Aotearoa NZ in Government." *Green Agenda Journal* No. 1 (2022). https://greenagenda.org.au/2022/04/uncomfortable-with-power/.

Horáková, Hana. "Knowledge Production in and on Africa: Knowledge Gatekeepers, De-colonization, Alternative Representations." In *Knowledge Production in and on Africa*, eds. Hanah Horáková and Katerina Werkman. Lit Verlag, 2016.

Horne, Cynthia M, "Transitional Justice and Temporal Parameters: Built-In Expiration Dates?" *International Journal of Transitional Justice* 14(3) (2021): 544–565.

Hossain, Mohammad Pizuar. "The Rohingya Refugee Crisis: Analysing the International Law Implications of its Environmental Impacts on Bangladesh." *International Journal of Human Rights* 27(2) (2023): 238–257.

Houck, Oliver A., "Noah's Second Voyage: The Rights of Nature as Law." *Tulane Environmental Law Journal* 31(1) (2017): 1–50.

Huisman, Wim and Daniel Sidoli. "Corporations, Human Rights and the Environmental Degradation-Corruption Nexus." *Asia Pacific Journal of Environmental Law* 22(1) (2019): 66–92.

Hulme, Karen. "Using a Framework of Human Rights and Transitional Justice for Post-conflict Environmental Protection and Remediation." In *Environmental Protection and Transitions from Conflict to Peace: Clarifying Norms, Principles, and Practices*, eds. Carsten Stahn, Jens Iverson and Jennifer S. Easterday. OUP, 2017.

Humphrey, Michael. "From Victim to Victimhood: Truth Commissions and Trials as Rituals of Political Transition and Individual Healing." *The Australian Journal of Anthropology* 14(2) (2003): 171–187.

Humphreys, Rebekah. "Dignity and its Violation Examined within the Context of Animal Ethics." *Ethics and the Environment* 21(2) (2016): 143–162.

Huneeus, Alexandra, "Territory as a Victim of Colombia's War" *Blog of the European Journal of International Law Talk!* May 7, 2020. www.ejiltalk.org/territory-as

-a-victim-of-colombias-war/#:~:text=In%20two%20recent%20resolutions%2C%20Colombia's,Colombia's%2050%2Dyear%20civil%20war.

Huneeus, Alexandra and Pablo Rueda Saiz. "Territory as a Victim of Armed Conflict." *International Journal of Transitional Justice* 15(1) (2021): 210–229.

Hunt, Lynn. *Inventing Human Rights: A History*. W.W. Norton & Company, 2008.

Huntington, Samuel. *The Third Wave: Democratization in the Late 20th Century*. University of Oklahoma Press, 1991.

Huseman, Jennifer and Damien Short. '"A Slow Industrial Genocide': Tar Sands and the Indigenous People of Northern Alberta." *International Journal of Human Rights* 16(1) (2012): 216–237.

Hwang, Juneseo. "The Political Economy of the Mubuoy Dump in Northern Ireland: A Green Criminology Perspective." *International Journal for Crime, Justice and Social Democracy*, doi: 10.5204/ijcjsd.2842.

Ibañez, Ana Maria. "Forced Displacement in Colombia: Magnitude and Causes." *The Economics of Peace and Security Journal* 4(1) (2009): 48–54.

ICC, The Office of the Prosecutor Launches Public Consultation on a New Policy Initiative to Advance Accountability for Environmental Crimes under the Rome Statute, ICC Website, February 16, 2024, https://www.icc-cpi.int/news/office-prosecutor-launches-public-consultation-new-policy-initiative-advance-accountability-0.

ICTJ. "What is Transitional Justice." n.d., https://www.ictj.org/what-transitional-justice.

Ide, Tobias, Carl Bruch, Alexander Carius, Ken Conca, Geoffrey D. Dabelko, Richard Matthew and Erika Weinthal. "The Past and Future(s) of Environmental Peacebuilding." *International Affairs* 97(1) (2021): 1–16.

Ignatieff, Michael. *Human Rights as Politics and Idolatry*. Princeton University Press, 2001.

Ikubaje, John G. and Usani Odum. "Envisioning a Transitional Justice-Based Approach to Climate-Induced Conflicts in Africa." *Horn of Africa Bulletin*, February 14, 2023. https://life-peace.org/hab-bulletin/envisioning-a-transitional-justice-based-approach-to-climate-induced-Conflicts-in-Africa/.

Ince, Onur Ulas. Colonial Capitalism and the Dilemmas of Liberalism. OUP, 2018.

Independent Expert Panel for the Legal Definition of Ecocide. *Commentary and Core Text*, *Stop Ecocide,* June 2021. www.stopecocide.earth/legal-definition.

Interfax. "Prosecutor General: Investigation into Ecocide in Connection with Attack of Russian troops on Zaporizhia NPP launched." *InterFax*, March 4, 2022. https://interfax.com.ua/news/general/807113.html.

Internal Displacement Monitoring Centre. *Grid 2023: Internal Displacement and Food Security*. Norwegian Refugee Council, 2023.

Iverson, Jens. "Transitional Justice, *Just Post Bellum* and International Criminal Law: Differentiating the Usages, History and Dynamics." *International Journal of Transitional Justice* 7(3) (2013): 413–433.

Iverson, Jens. "Managing the Tensions between a Maximalist Approach to Environmental Protection and Anthropocentric Peacebuilding." In *Research Handbook on International Law and Environmental Peacebuilding,* eds. Daniëlla Dam-de Jong and Britta Sjöstedt. Elgar, 2023.

Izquierdo, Belkis and Lieselotte Viaene. "Decolonizing Transitional Justice from Indigenous Territories." *Peace in Progress* 34 (2018): 11–19.

Jaber, Dina Abu. "Settler Colonialism and Ecocide: Case Study of Al-Khader, Palestine." *Settler Colonial Studies* 9(1) (2019): 135–154.

Jamar, Astrid. "The Crusade of Transitional Justice: Tracing the Journeys of Hegemonic Claims." *Violence and Democracy*. The British Academy, September 2019. https://www.thebritishacademy.ac.uk/documents/242/Violence-and-Democracy.pdf.

Jankowitz, Sarah. "The 'Hierarchy of Victims' in Northern Ireland: A Framework for Critical Analysis." *International Journal of Transitional Justice* 12(2) (2018): 216–236.

Jara, Daniela, Manuela Badilla, Ana Figueiredo, Marcela Cornejo and Victoria Riveros. "Tracing Mapuche Exclusion from Post-Dictatorial Truth Commissions in Chile: Official and Grassroots Initiatives." *International Journal of Transitional Justice* 12(3) (2018): 479–498.

John, Kelsey. "Animal Colonialism: Illustrating Intersections between Animal Studies and Settler Colonial Studies through Diné Horsemanship." *Humanalia: A Journal of Human/Animal Interface Studies* 10(2) (2019): 42–68.

Johnson, Caitlyn. "The ICC and Environmental Protection: Prosecuting Environmental War Crimes in Ukraine." *Journal of National Security Law and Policy* 14(2) (2023): 287–311.

Jones, Briony. "The Performance and Persistence of Transitional Justice and its Ways of Knowing Atrocity," *Cooperation and Conflict* 56(2) (2021): 163–180.

Jones, Briony and Ulrike Lühe, eds. *Knowledge for Peace: Transitional Justice and the Politics of Knowledge in Theory and Practice*. Elgar, 2021.

Jones, Briony and Ulrike Lühe. "Knowledge for Peace: Transitional Justice and the Politics of Knowledge in Theory and Practice." In *Knowledge for Peace: Transitional Justice and the Politics of Knowledge in Theory and Practice*, eds. Briony Jones and Ulrike Lühe. Elgar, 2021.

Jones, Briony, Ulrike Lühe, Gilbert Fokou, Kuyang Harriet Logo, Leben Nelson Moro and Serge-Alain Yao N'Da. "Producing Knowledge on and for Transitional Justice: Reflections on a Collaborative Research Project." In *Knowledge for Peace: Transitional Justice and the Politics of Knowledge in Theory and Practice*, eds. Briony Jones and Ulrike Lühe. Elgar, 2021.

Jones, Stephanie and Stewart Motha. "A New Nomos Offshore and Bodies as their Own Signs." *Law and Literature* 27(2) (2015): 253–278.

Kaapama, Phanuel. "The Enduring Colonial Legacies of Land Dispossessions and the Evolving Property Rights Legal Discourse: Whither Transitional Justice." *Human Rights & International Legal Discourse* 11(1) (2017): 108–119.

Kamolane-Kgadima, Busisiwe and Thandeka Kathi. "The Mpumalanga Highveld Air Pollution Crisis: A South African Reparations Framework for Environmental State–Corporate Harm." *International Journal for Crime, Justice and Social Democracy* 13(1) (2024): 1–13.

Kandic, Natasa. "The ICTY Trials and Transitional Justice in Former Yugoslavia." *Cornell International Law Journal* 38(3) (2005): 789–792.

Kant, Immanuel. "Groundwork of the Metaphysics of Morals." In *Practical Philosophy*, ed. Mary Gregor. CUP, 1996.

Karstedt, Susanne. "From Absence to Presence, From Silence to Voice: Victims in International and Transitional Justice since the Nuremberg Trials." *International Review of Victimology* 17(1) (2010): 9–30.

Kastner, Philipp. "A Resilience Approach to Transitional Justice?" *Journal of Intervention and Statebuilding* 14(3) (2020): 368–388.

Katz, Eric. "Nature's Presence and the Technology of Death: Reflections on Healing and Domination." *Bulletin of Science, Technology and Society* 17(1) (1997): 3–7.

Kauffman, Craig M. "Managing People for the Benefit of the Land: Practising Earth Jurisprudence in Te Urewera, New Zealand." *ISLE: Interdisciplinary Studies in Literature and Environment* 27(3) (2020): 578–595.

Kauffman, Craig M. and Pamela L. Martin. "How Courts Are Developing River Rights Jurisprudence: Comparing Guardianship in New Zealand, Colombia, and India." *Vermont Journal of Environmental Law* 20(3) (2019): 260–289.

Kauffman, Craig M. and Pamela L. Martin. "How Ecuador's Courts are Giving Form and Force to Rights of Nature Norms." *Transnational Environmental Law* 12(2) (2023): 366–395.

Kauffman, Craig M. and Pamela L. Martin. *The Politics of Rights of Nature: Strategies for Building a More Sustainable Future*. MIT Press, 2021.

Kauzlarich, David and Ronald Kramer. "State-corporate Crime in the US Nuclear Weapons Production Complex." *Journal of Human Justice*, 5(1) (1993): 4–28.

Kelsen, Hans. *General Theory of Law and State*. Transaction, 2006.

Kendall, Sara and Sarah Nouwen. "Representational Practices at the International Criminal Court: The Gap between Juridified and Abstract Victimhood." *Law & Contemporary Problems* 76(3–4) (2013): 235–262.

Kenney-Lazar, Miles. "Neoliberalizing Authoritarian Environmental Governance in (Post) Socialist Laos." *Annals of the American Association of Geographers* 109(2) (2019): 338–348.

Kent, Lia. "Local Memory Practices in East Timor: Disrupting Transitional Justice Narratives." *International Journal of Transitional Justice* 5(3) (2011): 434–355.

Kerremans, Sarah and Tine Destrooper. "Exploring the Nexus between Transitional Justice and Ecoterritorial Conflict Resolution: Time for an Ecoterritorial Turn in Transformative Transitional Justice?" *International Journal of Transitional Justice* 17(1) (2023): 54–70.

Kesaieva, Yulia. "Ukraine Launches "Ecocide" and War Crimes Probe into Nova Kakhovka Dam Incident." *CNN*, June 7, 2023. https://edition.cnn.com/europe/live-news/russia-ukraine-war-news-06-07 23/h_36848cd5abb76e0ddd522cd78f 4f5f43 1/12.

Khoury, Stefanie and David Whyte. *Corporate Human Rights Violations*. Routledge, 2017.

Killean, Rachel. "Constructing Victimhood at the Khmer Rouge Tribunal: Visibility, Selectivity and Participation." *International Review of Victimology* 24(3) (2018): 273–296.

Killean, Rachel. *Victims, Atrocity and International Criminal Justice*. Routledge, 2018.

Killean, Rachel. "From Ecocide to Eco-sensitivity: 'Greening' Reparations at the International Criminal Court." *International Journal of Human Rights* 25(2) (2021): 323–347.

Killean, Rachel. "Environmental Restorative Justice in Transitional Settings." In *The Palgrave Handbook of Environmental Restorative Justice*, eds. Brunilda Pali, Miranda Forsyth and Felicity Tepper. Palgrave Macmillan, 2022.

Killean, Rachel. "Imagining Future Reparations for Environmental Destruction." In *Futures of International Criminal Justice*, eds. Emma Palmer, Edwin Bikundo, Susan Harris Rimmer and Martin Clark. Routledge, 2022.

Killean, Rachel. "Ecocide in the International Criminal Court: The Prosecutor v Mr X (Reparations Order)." In *UK Earth Judgments Project*, eds. Helen Dancer, Bonnie Holligan and Helena Howe. Hart, 2024.

Killean, Rachel and Damien Short. *Scoping a Domestic Legal Framework for Ecocide in Scotland*. Environmental Rights Centre for Scotland, 2024. https://www.ercs.scot/wp/wp-content/uploads/2024/04/Scoping-a-Domestic-Legal-Framework-for-Ecocide-in-Scotland_April24_online.pdf.

Killean, Rachel and Elizabeth Newton. "From Ecocide to Ecocentrism: Conceptualising Environmental Victimhood at the International Criminal Court." *International Review of Victimology* (31(2) (2025): 238–264), online access, https://doi.org/10.1177/026975802412694.

Killean, Rachel and Lauren Dempster. "'Greening' Transitional justice?" In *Beyond Transitional Justice: Transformative Justice and the State of the Field (or Non-field)*, ed. Matthew Evans. Routledge, 2022.

Killean, Rachel and Lauren Dempster. "Mass Violence, Environmental Harm and the Limits of Transitional Justice." *Genocide Studies and Prevention* 16(1) (2022): 11–39.

Killean, Rachel and Luke Moffett. "Victim Legal Representation before the ICC and ECCC." *Journal of International Criminal Justice* 15(4) (2017): 713–740.

Killean, Rachel and Luke Moffett. "What's in a Name? Reparations at the Extraordinary Chambers in the Courts of Cambodia." *Melbourne Journal of International Law* 21(1) (2020): 1–29.

Killoran-McKibbin, Sonja and Anna Zalik. "Rethinking the Extractive/Productive Binary under Neoliberalism." In *The Handbook of Neoliberalism*, eds. Simon Springer, Kean Birch and Julia MacLeavy. Routledge, 2016.

Kilomba, Grada. *Plantation Memories: Episodes of Everyday Racism*. Unrast Verlag, 2008.

Kirchengast, Tyrone. "The Expressive Function of #VictimsLaw: Developing a Substantive and Enforceable Framework of Rights and Remedies in Response to Local Need and the Emerging Forms of Victimization." *Journal of Victimology and Victim Justice* 4(2) (2021): 103–118.

Kirchengast, Tyrone. *Victimology and Victim Rights: International Comparative Perspectives*. Routledge, 2017.

Kiyani, Asad. "International Crime and the Politics of Criminal Theory: Voices and Conduct of Exclusion." *New York University Journal of International Law and Politics* 48(1) (2015): 129–208.

Klinsky, Sonja. "Transitional Justice for Climate Change: Transformation Through Solidarity." In *Research Handbook on Transitional Justice*, eds. Cheryl Lawther, Luke Moffett and Dov Jacobs. Elgar, 2023.

Klinsky, Sonja and Jasmina Brankovic. *The Global Climate Regime and Transitional Justice*. Routledge, 2018.

Kochanski, Adam. "The "Local Turn" in Transitional Justice: Curb the Enthusiasm." *International Studies Review* 22(1) (2020): 26–50.

Koleth, Elsa and Linda Peake. "Decolonising Feminist Knowledge." In *Doing Feminist Urban Research*, eds. Linda Peake, Nasya S Razavi and Araby Smyth. Routledge, 2024.

Kolieb, Jonathan. "Through the Looking-Glass: Nuremberg's Confusing Legacy on Corporate Accountability under International Law." *American University International Law Review* 32(2) (2015): 570–602.

Kolpak, Gabriela. "From ENMOD to Geoengineering: The Environment as a Weapon of War." *Conflict and Environment Observatory,* April 7, 2020. https://ceobs.org/from-enmod-to-geoengineering-the-environment-as-a-weapon-of-war/.

Kong, Lingjie and Yuqing Zhao. "Remedying the Environmental Impacts of War: Challenges and Perspectives for Full Reparation." *International Review of the Red Cross* 105(924) (2023): 1441–1462.

Kooijman, Merle. "From Anthropos to Oikos in International Criminal Law: A Critical-Theoretical Exploration of Ecocide as an 'Ecocentric' Amendment to the Rome Statute." In *Netherlands Yearbook of International Law 2021: A Greener International Law—International Legal Responses to the Global Environmental Crisis,* eds. Daniëlla Dam-de Jong and Fabian Amtenbrink. T.M.C. Asser Press, 2023.

Koons, Judith E. "What is Earth Jurisprudence? Key Principles to Transform Law for the Health of the Planet." *Penn State Environmental Law Review* 18 (2009): 47–68.

Kopnina, Helen, Haydn Washington, Bron Taylor and John J Piccolo. "Anthropocentrism: More than Just a Misunderstood Problem." *Journal of Agricultural and Environmental Ethics* 31 (2018): 109–127.

Kortetmäki, Teea. "Anthropocentrism versus Ecocentrism Revisited: Theoretical Confusions and Practical Conclusions." *SATS: Northern European Journal of Philosophy* 14(1) (2013): 21–37.

Koskenniemi, Martti. "Between Impunity and Show Trials." *Max Planck Yearbook of United Nations Law* 6(1) (2002): 1–35.

Kothari, Ashish. "Search of Alternatives to Development: Learning from Grounded Initiatives." In *Challenging Global Development: Towards Decoloniality*, eds. Henning Melber, Uma Kothari, Laura Camfield, Kees Biekart. Springer, 2024.

Kothari, Ashish, Ariel Salleh, Arturo Escobar, Federico Demaria and Alberto Acosta, "Introduction: Finding Pluriversal Paths." *Pluriverse: A Post-Development Dictionary,* eds. Ashish Kothari, Ariel Salleh, Arturo Escobar, Federico Demaria and Alberto Acosta. Tulika Books, 2019.

Kothari, Ashish, Ariel Salleh, Arturo Escobar, Federico Demaria and Alberto Acosta. "Postscript: The Global Tapestry of Alternatives." In *Pluriverse: A Post-Development Dictionary,* eds. Ashish Kothari, Ariel Salleh, Arturo Escobar, Federico Demaria and Alberto Acosta. Tulika Books, 2019.

Kothari, Ashish, Federico Demaria and Alberto Acosta. "Buen Vivir, Degrowth and Ecological Swaraj: Alternatives to Sustainable Development and the Green Economy." *Development* 57(3–4) (2014): 362–375.

Koulagi, Sumanas. *Development as Swaraj: Towards a Sustainable and Equitable Future.* Routledge, 2022.

Kovras, Iosif. *Grassroots Activism and the Evolution of Transitional Justice: The Families of the Disappeared.* CUP, 2017.

Krakoff, Sarah. "Mountains without Handrails ... Wilderness Without Cellphones." *Harvard Environmental Law Review* 27(2) (2003): 417–470.

Kramer, Ronald C., Raymond J. Michalowski and David Kauzlarich. "The Origins and Development of the Concept and Theory of State-Corporate Crime." *Crime and Delinquency* 48(2) (2002): 263–282.

Krever, Tor. "International Criminal Law: An Ideology Critique." *Leiden Journal of International Law* 26(3) (2013): 701–723.

Kurki, Visa A.J. "Animals, Slaves and Corporations: Analyzing Legal Thinghood." *German Law Journal* 18(5) (2017): 1069–1090.

Kurki, Visa A.J. *Legal Personhood.* CUP, 2023.

Kyriakakis, Joanna. *Corporations, Accountability and International Criminal Law: Industry and Atrocity.* Edward Elgar, 2021.

Lähteenmäki, Lisa and Anne Alvesalo-Kuush. "The Imaginary Social Order of Corporate Criminal Liability." In *Revisiting Crimes of the Powerful: Marxism, Crime and Deviance,* eds. Steven Bittle, Laureen Snider, Steve Tombs and David Whyte. Routledge, 2018.

Lai, Daniela. "Transitional Justice and its Discontents: Socioeconomic Justice in Bosnia and Herzegovina and the Limits of International Intervention." *Journal of Intervention and Statebuilding* 10(3) (2016): 361–381.

Lai, Daniela. *Socioeconomic Justice: International Intervention and Transition in Post-War Bosnia and Herzegovina.* CUP, 2020.

Lambourne, Wendy. "Power Struggles and the Politics of Knowledge Production in the Burundian Transitional Justice Process." In *Knowledge for Peace: Transitional Justice and the Politics of Knowledge in Theory and Practice,* eds. Briony Jones and Ulrike Lühe. Elgar, 2021.

Lambourne, Wendy. "Transitional Justice and Peacebuilding after Mass Violence." *International Journal of Transitional Justice* 3(1) (2009): 28–48.

Lamy, Guilluame. "Ecocide à Grézieu-la-Varenne: l'ancien maire, candidat àl'élection du bâtonnat du barreau Lyon." *Lyon Capitale,* November 13, 2022. https://www.lyoncapitale.fr/actualite/ecocide-a-grezieu-la-varenne-l-ancien-maire-candidat-a-l-election-du-batonnat-du-barreau-lyon.

Lang, Miriam. "Buen Vivir as a Territorial Practice. Building a More Just and Sustainable Life through Interculturality." *Sustainability Science* 17 (2022): 1287–1299.

Lang, Valentin. "The Economics of the Democratic Deficit: The Effect of IMF Programs on Inequality." *The Review of International Organisations* 16 (2020): 599–623.

Laslett, Kristian. "Marx Reloaded for the 21st Century: Capitalism, Agency and the Crimes of the Powerful." In *Revisiting Crimes of the Powerful: Marxism, Crime and Deviance,* eds. Steven Bittle, Laureen Snider, Steve Tombs and David Whyte. Routledge, 2021.

Lauren, Paul Gordon. *The Evolution of International Human Rights: Visions Seen.* University of Pennsylvania Press, 1998.

Lawrence, Jessica and Kevin Heller. "The First Ecocentric Environmental War Crime: The Limits of Article 8 (2)(b)(Iv) of the Rome Statute." *Georgetown International Environmental Law Review* 20(1) (2007): 61–96.

Lawrence, Michael J, Holly L.J. Stemberger, Aaron J. Zoldero, Daniel P. Struthers and Steven J. Cooke. "The Effects of Modern War and Military Activities on Biodiversity and the Environment." *Environmental Review* 23(4) (2015): 443–460.

Lawry-White, Merryl. "Victims of Environmental Harm during Conflict: The Potential for 'Justice'." In *Environmental Protection and Transitions from Conflict to Peace*, eds. Stahn Carsten, Jens Iverson and Jennifer S. Easterday. OUP, 2017.

Lawther, Cheryl. "The Construction and Politicisation of Victimhood." In *Victims of Terrorism: A Comparative and Interdisciplinary Study,* eds. Orla Lynch and Javier Argomaniz. Taylor and Francis, 2014.

Lawther, Cheryl, Rachel Killean and Lauren Dempster. "Working with Others: Reflections on Fieldwork in Postconflict Societies." *International Journal of Transitional Justice,* 13(2) (2019): 387–397.

Lazreg, Marina. "Women's Experience and Feminist Epistemology." In *Knowing the Difference: Feminist Perspectives in Epistemology*, eds. Kathleen Lennon and Margaret Whitford. Routledge, 1994.

Le Billon, Philippe. "The Political Ecology of War: Natural Resources and Armed Conflict." *Political Geography* 20(5) (2001): 561–584.

Le Grange, Lesley. "Ubuntu." In *Pluriverse: A Post-Development Dictionary,* eds. Ashish Kothari, Ariel Salleh, Arturo Escobar, Federico Demaria and Alberto Acosta. Tulika Books, 2019.

Lee, George. "Rosa Luxembourg and the Impact of Imperialism." *The Economic Journal* 81(324) (1971): 847–848.

Lee, Roy. *The International Criminal Court: The Making of the Rome Statute.* Kluwer Law International, 1999.

Leebaw, Bronwyn. "The Irreconcilable Goals of Transitional Justice." *Human Rights Quarterly* 30(1) (2008): 95–118.

Lehman, Paul-Jacques. *Liberalism and Capitalism Today.* Wiley, 2021.

Lemaitre, Julieta. "Legal Fetishism: Law, Violence, and Social Movements in Columbia." *Revista Juridica Universidad de Puerto Rico* 77(2) (2008): 331–344.

Lemay-Hébert, Nicolas and Rosa Freedman. "Appraising the Socio-Economic Turn in Reparations: Transitional Justice for Cholera Victims in Haiti." *International Journal of Transitional Justice* 15(3) (2021): 533–552.

Lennon, Kathleen and Margaret Whitford, eds. *Knowing the Difference: Feminist Perspectives in Epistemology*. Routledge, 1994.

Lenta, Patrick. "Transitional Justice and Retributive Justice." *Ethic Theory and Moral Practice* 22(2) (2019): 385–398.

Levi, Michael and Nicholas Lord. "White-Collar and Corporate Crime." In *The Oxford Handbook of Criminology*, eds. Alison Liebling, Shadd Maruna and Lesley McAra, 6th Edition. OUP, 2017.

Levitt, Lacey, David Rosengard and Jessica Rubin. *Animals as Crime Victims*. Elgar, 2024.

Lewis, Simon L. and Mark A. Maslin. "Defining the Anthropocene." *Nature* 519 (2015): 171–180.

Leyh, Brianne McGonigle. "Nuremberg's Legacy within Transitional Justice: Prosecutions Are Here to Stay." *Washington University Global Studies Law Review* 15(4) (2016): 559–574.

Liang, Olivia, "Governing Globalization: Labour Economic Paradigms and International Labour Standards at the International Labour Organization, 1919–1998" Interactions: Regional Studies, Global Processes, and Historical Analysis, 28 February-3 March 2001, https://webdoc.sub.gwdg.de/ebook/p/2005/history_cooperative/www.historycooperative.org/proceedings/interactions/index.html.

Lindgren, Tim. "Ecocide, Genocide and the Disregard of Alternative Life-Systems," *The International Journal of Human Rights* 22(4) (2018): 525–549.

Lindner, Evelin Gerda. "Humiliation and Human rights: Mapping a Minefield." *Human Rights Review* 2(2) (2001): 46–46.

Lindroos-Hovinheimo, Susanna. *Private Selves: Legal Personhood in European Privacy Protection*. CUP, 2021.

Linke, Kai. "Keeping Academia White: A Case Study." In *Who Can Speak and Who Is Heard/Hurt? Facing Problems of Race, Racism, and Ethnic Diversity in the Humanities in Germany*, eds. Mahmoud Arghavan, Nicole Hirschfelder, Luvena Kopp and Katharina Motyl. Verlag, 2019.

Llewellyn, Leonard. "Mining Corporations, Democratic Meddling, and Environmental Justice in South Africa." *Social Sciences* 7(12) (2018): article 259.

Locke, John. *Two Treaties of Government, from the Works of John Locke*. Yale University Press, 2003.

Lomas, Tim, Pablo Diego-Rosell, Koichiro Shiba, Priscilla Standridge, Matthew T. Lee, Brendan Case, Alden Yuanhong Lai and Tyler J. VanderWeele. "Complexifying Individualism versus Collectivism and West versus East: Exploring Global Diversity in Perspectives on Self and Other in the Gallup World Poll." *Journal of Cross-Cultural Psychology* 54(1) (2023): 61–89.

London, Leslie, T.K. Joshi, Eugene Cairncross and Luz. Claudio. "Environmental Justice: An International Perspective." In *The Encyclopaedia of Environmental Health*, ed. J. O. Nriagu. Elsevier, 2011.

Long, Michael A., Paul B. Stretesky and Michael J. Lynch. "Foreign Direct Investment, Ecological Withdrawals, and Natural-Resource-Dependent Economies." *Society & Natural Resources* 30(1) (2017): 1261–1276.

Lopez, Aurelie. "Criminal Liability for Environmental Damage Occurring in Times of Non-International Armed Conflict: Rights and Remedies." *Fordham Environmental Law Review* 18(2) (2007): 231–271.

López Zamora, Luis. "The Recognition of the Rights of Nature in Latin America–The Lost Linkage with the Rights of Future Generations." In *Representing the Absent*, eds. Hélène Ruiz Fabri, Valérie Rosoux and Alessandra Donati. Nomos Verlag, 2023.

Lorde, Audre. *The Master's Tools will Never Dismantle the Master's House.* Penguin Classics, 2018.

Lossau, Julia. "Postcolonialism." In *Spatiality, Sovereignty and Carl Schmitt: Geographies of the Nomos*, ed. Stephen Legg. Routledge, 2011.

Lostal, Marina. "De-Objectifying Animals: Could they Qualify as Victims before the International Criminal Court?" *Journal of International Criminal Justice* 19(3) (2021): 583–610.

Luban, David. "The Enemy of All Humanity." In *The Oxford Handbook of International Criminal Law*, eds. Kevin Heller, Jens Ohlin, Darryl Robinson, Frédéric Mégret and Sarah Nouwen. OUP, 2020.

Lühe, Ulrike. "Developing the African Union Transitional Justice Policy: An Assemblage Perspective." In *Knowledge for Peace: Transitional Justice and the Politics of Knowledge in Theory and Practice*, eds. Briony Jones and Ulrike Lühe. Elgar, 2021.

Lujala, Paivi and Siri Aas Rustad. "High-value Natural Resources: A Blessing or a Curse for Peace?" *Sustainable Development Law & Policy* 12(1) (2011): 19–22.

Lukes, Steven. *Power: A Radical View*. MacMillan, 1974.

Luna, Maritza Felices. "The Pacification of Peru and the Production of a Neoliberal Populist Order." *State Crime* 6(1) (2017): 156–174.

Lundy, Patricia and Mark McGovern. "Whose Justice? Rethinking Transitional Justice from the Bottom Up." *Journal of Law and Society* 35(2) (2008): 265–292.

Luoma, Colin. "Reckoning with Conservation Violence on Indigenous Territories: Possibilities and Limitations of a Transitional Justice Response." *International Journal of Transitional Justice* 17(1) (2023): 89–106.

Lutz, Ellen and Kathryn Sikkink. "The Justice Cascade: The Evolution and Impact of Foreign Human Rights Trials in Latin America." *Chicago Journal of International Law* 2(1) (2001): Article 3.

Luxembourg, Rosa. *The Accumulation of Capital*. Reprinted by Routledge, 2003.

Lykes, M. Brinton and Colleen Murphy. "Decolonizing Transitional Justice: Soft, Radical or Beyond Reform." *International Journal of Transitional Justice* 17(3) (2023): 361–369.

Lykes, M. Brinton and Hugo van der Merwe. "Critical Reflexivity and Transitional Justice Praxis: Solidarity, Accompaniment and Intermediarity." *International Journal of Transitional Justice* 13(3) (2019): 411–416.

Lynch, Kathleen and Manolis Kalaitzake, "Affective and Calculative Solidarity: The Impact of Individualism and Neoliberal Capitalism." *European Journal of Social Theory* 23(2) (2020): 238–257.

Lynch, Michael J., Averi Fegadel and Michael A. Long. "Green Criminology and State-Corporate Crime: The Ecocide-Genocide Nexus with Examples from Nigeria." *Journal of Genocide Research* 23(2) (2021): 236–256.

Lynch, Michael J., Michael A. Long and Paul B. Stretesky. *Green Criminology and Green Theories of Justice: An Introduction to a Political Economic View of Eco-Justice*. Palgrave, 2019.

Lynch, Michael J., Paul B Stretesky and Michael A. Long. "Green Criminology and Native Peoples: The Treadmill of Production and the Killing of Indigenous Environmental Activists." *Theoretical Criminology* 22(3) (2018): 318–341.

Lynch, Michael J., Paul B. Stretesky and Michael A. Long. "The Treadmill of Production and the Treadmill of Law: Propositions for Analyzing Law, Ecological Disorganization and Crime." *Capitalism Nature Socialism* 31(1) (2020): 107–122.

Lyons, Kristina. "'Nature' and Territories as Victims: Decolonizing Colombia's Transitional Justice Process." *American Anthropologist* 125(1) (2023): 63–76.

MacGinty, Roger. "Indigenous Peace-Making Versus the Liberal Peace." *Cooperation and Conflict* 43 (2008): 139–163.

Mack-Canty, Colleen. "Third-Wave Feminism and the Need to Reweave the Nature/Culture Duality." *NWSA Journal* 16(3) (Autumn, 2004): 154–179.

Macpherson, Elizabeth, Cristy Clark, Pía Weber Salazar, Natalie Baird, Afshin Akhtar-Khavari and Edward Challies. "Evolving Rights to (and of) Water in Chile: A Case for Relationship-Based Water Law and Governance." *International Journal of Human Rights* (2023): 1–26.

Macpherson, Elizabeth, and Felipe Clavijo Ospina. "The Pluralism of River Rights in Aotearoa, New Zealand and Colombia." *Journal of Water Law* 25(6) (2018): 283–293.

Macpherson, Elizabeth, Julia Torres Ventura and Felipe Clavijo Ospina. "Constitutional Law, Ecosystems and Indigenous Peoples in Colombia: Biocultural Rights and Legal Subjects." *Transnational Environmental Law* 9(3) (2020): 521–540.

Maddison, Sarah and Laura J. Shepherd, "Peacebuilding and the Postcolonial Politics of Transitional Justice." *Peacebuilding* 2(3) (2014): 253–369.

Madlingozi, Tshepo. "On Transitional Justice Entrepreneurs and the Production of Victims." *Journal of Human Rights Practice* 2(2) (2010): 208–228.

Madlingozi, Tshepo. "Social Justice in a Time of Neo-Apartheid Constitutionalism: Critiquing the Anti-Black Economy of Recognition, Incorporation and Distribution." *Stellenbosch Law Review* 28(1) (2017): 123–147.

Madlingozi, Tshepo, "There is Neither Truth nor Reconciliation in So-Called 'South Africa' in conversation with Léopold Lambert." *The Funambulist*, June 29, 2020. https://thefunambulist.net/magazine/reparations/there-is-neither-truth-nor-reconciliation-in-so-called-south-africa-a-conversation-with-tshepo-madlingozi.

Mailey, Richard. "The Role of the Person in Modern Constitutional Law: How State-inflicted Harms Become Personal." In *Interrupting the Legal Person*, eds. Austin Sarat, George Pavlich and Richard Mailey. Emerald Publishing Limited, 2022.

Makey, Leane, Meg Parsons, Karen Fisher, Alyssce Te Huna, Mina Henare, Vicky Miru, Millan Ruka and Mikaera Miru. "(Un)Heard Voices of Ecosystem Degradation: Stories from the Nexus of Settler-Colonialism and Slow Violence." *Sustainability* 14(22) (2022): 14672.

Maldonado-Torres, Nelson. "On the Coloniality of Being: Contributions to the Development of a Concept." *Cultural Studies*, 21(2–3) (2007): 240–270.

Mallinder, Louise. "Can Amnesties and International Justice be Reconciled?" *International Journal of Transitional Justice* 1(2) (2007): 208–230.

Mallinder, Louise and Kieran McEvoy. "Rethinking Amnesties: Atrocity, Accountability and Impunity in Post-Conflict Societies." *Contemporary Social Science* 6(1) (2011): 107–128.

Maloney, Michelle. "Earth Jurisprudence and Sustainable Consumption." *Southern Cross University Law Review* 14(1) (2011): 119–148.

Maloney, Michelle and Peter Burdon, eds. *Wild Law - Practice*. Routledge, 2014.

Mamdani, Mahmood. "Beyond Nuremberg: The Historical Significance of the Post-Apartheid Transition in South Africa." *Politics and Society* 43(1) (2015): 61–88.

Mangena, Oshadi. "Against Fragmentation: The Need for Holism." In *Knowing the Difference: Feminist Perspectives in Epistemology*, eds. Kathleen Lennon and Margaret Whitford. Routledge, 1994.

Mani, Rama. *Beyond Retribution: Seeking Justice in the Shadow of War*. Polity Press, 2002.

Mani, Rama. "Editorial: Dilemmas of Expanding Transitional Justice, or Forging the Nexus between Transitional Justice and Development." *International Journal of Transitional Justice* 2(3) (2008): 253–265.

Manning, Peter, Jordan Tchilingirian, Somaly Kum and Tudor Nedelcu. "Transitional Justice Networks and the Role of 'Local' Actors in Cambodia." *Journal of Peacebuilding & Development* 18(2) (2023): 158–176.

Marceau, Justin. "Animal Rights and the Victimhood Trap." *Arizona Law Review* 63(3) (2021): 731–788.

Marks, Susan. *The Riddle of All Constitutions. International Law, Democracy and The Critique of Ideology*. OUP, 2000.

Marshall, Virginia. "Removing the Veil from the 'Rights of Nature': The Dichotomy between First Nations Customary Rights and Environmental Legal Personhood." *Australian Feminist Law Journal* 45(2) (2019): 233–248.

Martín, Laura Garciá. "Challenging the Transitional Justice Paradigm: Addressing ESRs Violations in Transitional Justice Processes." *Anuario Espanol de Derecho Internacional* 35(4) (2019): 655–680.

Martini, Pauline, Joe Holt and Maud Sarliève. "Mass Deforestation as a Crime against Humanity." *The International and Comparative Law Quarterly* 72(4) (2023): 1013–1046.

Martini, Pauline and Maud Sarliève. "Fighting Deforestation in Non-International Armed Conflicts: The Relevance of the Rome Statute for Rosewood Trafficking in Senegal." *Transnational Environmental Law* 11(1) (2021): 95–117.

Maruf, Shah. "Environmental Damage in Ukraine as Environmental War Crime under the Rome Statute: The Kakhovka Dam Breach in Context." *Journal of International Criminal Justice* 22(1) (2024): 99–126.

Marx, Karl. *Capital: A Critique of Political Economy, Volume III*, ed. Friedrich Engels. International Publishers, 1894.

Mason, Rebecca. "Two Kinds of Unknowing." *Hypatia* 26(2) (2011): 294–307.

Matsunaga, Jennifer. "Two Faces of Transitional Justice: Theorizing the Incommensurability of Transitional Justice and Decolonization in Canada." *Decolonization: Indigeneity, Education and Society* 5(1) (2016): 24–44.

Matua, Makau W. "A Problem of Utopia: Human Rights and Transitional Justice." In *The Oxford Handbook of Transitional Justice,* eds. Jens Meierhenrich, Alexander L. Hinton and Lawrence Douglas. OUP, 2023.

Mayrand, Hélène. "From Classical Liberalism to Neoliberalism: Explaining the Contradictions in the International Environmental Law Project." In *Locating Nature: Making and Unmaking International Law,* eds. Usha Natarajan and Julia Dehm. CUP, 2022.

Mbembe, Achille Joseph. *On the Postcolony,* University of California Press, 2001.

Mbembe, Achille Joseph. "Decolonizing the University: New Directions." *Arts and Humanities in Higher Education* 15(1) (2016): 29–45.

McAuliffe, Padraig. "Dividing the Spoils: The Impact of Power Sharing on Possibilities for Socioeconomic Transformation in Postconflict States." *International Journal of Transitional Justice* 11(2) (2017): 197–217.

McAuliffe, Padraig. "Rhetoric and Realpolitik: Interrogating the Relationship between Transitional Justice and Socio-Economic Justice." *Finnish Yearbook of International Law* 23 (2013): 239–307.

McAuliffe, Padraig. *Transformative Transitional Justice and the Malleability of Post-Conflict States*. Elgar, 2017.

McAuliffe, Padraig. "Programmatic Approaches to Realising Socio-Economic Rights: Debates, Definitions and Trends." *Melbourne Journal of International Law* 22(1) (2021): 24–56.

McClanahan, Bill, Tatiana Sanchez Parra and Avi Brisman. "Conflict, Environment and Transition: Colombia, Ecology and Tourism after Demobilisation." *International Journal for Crime, Justice and Social Democracy* 8(3) (2019): 74–88.

McCrudden, Christopher. "Human Dignity and Judicial Interpretation of Human Rights." *European Journal of International Law* 19(4) (2008): 655–724.

McEvoy, Kieran. "Beyond Legalism: Towards a Thicker Understanding of Transitional Justice." *Journal of Law and Society* 34(4) (2007): 411–440.

McEvoy, Kieran and Kirsten McConnachie. "Victimology in Transitional Justice: Victimhood, Innocence and Hierarchy." *European Journal of Criminology* 9(5) (2012): 527–538.

McEvoy, Kieran and Kirsten McConnachie. "Victims and Transitional Justice: Voice, Agency and Blame." *Social & Legal Studies* 22(4) (2013): 489–513.

McEvoy, Kieran and Lorna McGregor, eds. *Transitional Justice from Below: Grassroots Activism and the Struggle for Change*. Hart 2008.

McEvoy, Kieran and Lorna McGregor. "Transitional Justice from Below: An Agenda for Research, Policy and Praxis." In *Transitional Justice from Below: Grassroots Activism and the Struggle for Change*, eds. Kieran McEvoy and Lorna McGregor. Hart, 2008.

McEvoy, Kieran, Ron Dudai and Cheryl Lawther. "Criminology and Transitional Justice." In *The Oxford Handbook of Criminology,* eds. Alison Liebling, Shadd Maruna and Lesley McAra. OUP, 2017.

McGill, Daire. "Different Violence, Different Justice? Taking Structural Violence Seriously in Post-Conflict and Transitional Justice Processes." *State Crime Journal* 6(1) (2017): 79–101.

McKane, Rachel G., Patrick Trent Greiner and David Pellow. "Mutual Aid as a Praxis for Critical Environmental Justice: Lessons from W.E.B. Du Bois, Critical Theoretical Perspectives, and Mobilising Collective Care in Disasters." *Antipode* 56(2) (2023): 581–602.

McKinnon, Rachel. "Epistemic Injustice." *Philosophy Compass* 11(8) (2016): 437–446.

McMillan, Mark and Sophie Rigney. "Race, Reconciliation, and Justice in Australia: From Denial to Acknowledgment." *Ethnic and Racial Studies* 41(4) (2017): 759–777.

Mégret, Frédéric. "The Problem of an International Criminal Law of the Environment." *Columbia Journal of Environmental Law* 36(2) (2011): 195–258.

Melaku, Tsedale M. and Angie Beeman. "Academia Isn't a Safe Haven for Conversations About Race and Racism." *Harvard Business Review*, June 25, 2020. https://hbr.org/2020/06/academia-isnt-a-safe-haven-for-conversations-about-race-and-racism.

Mendel, Lulia. '4,000 Children Flee Pollution Disaster on Ukraine-Crimea Border' *New York Times*, September 14, 2018. https://www.nytimes.com/2018/09/14/world/europe/crimea-ukraine-pollution.html.

Mendeloff, David. "Trauma and Vengeance: Assessing the Psychological and Emotional Effects of Post-Conflict Justice." *Human Rights Quarterly* 31(3) (2009): 592–623.

Mentis, Mike. "Environmental Rehabilitation of Damaged Land." *Forest Ecosystems* 7(19) (2020): 7–19.

Merchant, Carolyn. *Radical Ecology: The Search for a Livable World*. Routledge, 1992.

Merino, Roger. "An Alternative to 'Alternative Development'?: *Buen Vivir* and Human Development in Andean Countries." *Oxford Development Studies* 44(3) (2016): 271–286.

Merry, Sally Engle. "Introduction." In *The Practice of Human Rights: Tracking Law Between the Global and the Local,* eds. Mark Goodale and Sally Engle Merry. CUP, 2007.

Merwe Van der, Hugo and M. Brinton Lykes. "Racism and Transitional Justice." *International Journal of Transitional Justice* 14(3) (2021): 415–422.

Metz, Thaddeus. "The Role of Economic Goods in National Reconciliation: Evaluating South Africa and Colombia." In *Transitional Justice, Distributive Justice and Transformative Constitutionalism*, eds. David Bilchitz and Raisa Cachalia with Magdalena Inés Correa Henao and Nathalia Bautista Pizarro. OUP, 2023.

Michalowski, Sabine, ed. *Corporate Accountability in the Context of Transitional Justice.* Routledge, 2013.

Mies, Maria and Vandana Shiva, *Ecofeminism.* Zed Books, 1993.

Mignolo, Walter D. "Epistemic Disobedience and the Decolonial Option: A Manifesto." *Transmodernity* 1(2) (2011): 44–66.

Miller, Zinaida. "Effects of Invisibility: Search of the "Economic" in Transitional Justice." *International Journal of Transitional Justice* 2(3) (2008): 266–291.

Miller, Zinaida. "Embedded Ambivalence: Ungoverning Global Justice." *Transnational Legal Theory* 11(3) (2020): 353–381.

Miller, Zinaida. "Transitional Justice Temporalities." In *The Oxford Handbook of Transitional Justice,* eds. Jens Meierhenrich, Alexander Laban Hinton and Lawrence Douglas. OUP, 2023.

Minha, Donna. "The Possibility of Prosecuting Corporations for Climate Crimes before the International Criminal Court: All Roads Lead to the Rome Statute?" *Michigan Journal of International Law* 41(3) (2020): 491–539.

Mistura, Alessandra. "Is There Space for Environmental Crimes under International Criminal Law? The Impact of the Office of the Prosecutor Policy Paper on Case Selection and Prioritisation on the Current Legal Framework." *Colombian Journal of Environmental Law* 43(1) (2018): 181–225.

Moffett, Luke. *Reparations and War: Finding Balance in Repairing the Past.* OUP, 2022.

Moffett, Luke, Cheryl Lawther and Kevin Hearty. "Redressing Displacement in Northern Ireland: Identity, Land and Dealing with the Past." *Political Geography* 106(10) (2023): 102941.

Molavi, Shourideh C. and Eyal Weizman. *Environmental Warfare in Gaza: Colonial Violence and New Landscapes of Resistance.* Pluto Press, 2024.

Molloy, Sean. "Conceptualising the Transformative Justice Potential of Peace Processes." *International Journal of Human Rights* 27(2) (2023): 307–334.

Monk, Daniel Bertrand and Jacob Mundy. *The Post-Conflict Environment: Investigation and Critique.* University of Michigan Press, 2014.

Monni, Salvatore and Massimo Pallottino. "A New Agenda for International Development Cooperation: Lessons Learnt From the *Buen Vivir* Experience." *Development* 58(1) (2015): 49–57.

Moore, Andrew Ireland. "Defining Animals as Crime Victims." *Journal of Animal Law* 1(1) (2005): 91–108.

Morrow, Karen. "The Anthropocene and Human Rights: A New Context and the Need to Revisit Collective Human Concerns." In *The Routledge Handbook of Law and the Anthropocene*, eds. Peter Burdon and James Martel. Routledge, 2023.

Moyo, Khanyisela. "Mimicry, Transitional Justice and the Land Question in Racially Divided Former Settler Colonies." *International Journal of Transitional Justice* 9 (2015): 70–89.

Mudge, Stephanie. "The State of the Art: What is Neo-Liberalism?" *Socio-Economic Review* 6(4) (2008): 703–731.

Mukherji, Ambarish. "Gandhi's Views on Environment: The Search for an Alternative." *Bulletin of the Ramakirshna Mission Instiute of Culture* (July 2022), 22–27.

Mullan, Matthew. "Reassessing the Focus of Transitional Justice: The Need to Move Structural and Cultural Violence to the Centre." *Cambridge Review of International Affairs* 28(3) (2015): 462–479.

Mungwini, Pascah. ""African Know Thyself": Epistemic Injustice and the Quest for Liberative Knowledge." *International Journal of African Renaissance Studies — Multi-, Inter- and Transdisciplinarity* 12(2) (2017): 5–8.

Murdock, Esme G. "Storied With Land: 'Transitional Justice' on Indigenous Lands." *Journal of Global Ethics* 14(2) (2018): 232–239.

Murdock, Esme G. "A History of Environmental Justice: Foundations, Narratives, and Perspectives." In *Environmental Justice,* ed. Brendan Coolsaet. Routledge, 2020.

Murillo-Sandoval, Paulo J., Kristina Van Dexter, Jamon Van Den Hoek, David Wrathall and Robert Kennedy. "The End of Gunpoint Conservation: Forest Disturbance after the Colombian Peace Agreement." *Environmental Research Letters* 15(3) (2020): 034033.

Murphy, Colleen. *The Conceptual Foundations of Transitional Justice.* CUP, 2017.

Murphy, Colleen. "On Principled Compromise: When Does A Process of Transitional Justice Qualify as Just?" *Proceedings of the Aristotelian Society* 120(1) (2020): 47–70.

Murphy, Michael Warren, George Weddington and AJ Rio-Glick. "Black Ecology and Critical Environmental Justice." *Environmental Justice* 14(6) (2021): 393–397.

Mutu, Margaret. "Behind the Smoke and Mirrors of the Treaty of Waitangi Claims Settlement Process in New Zealand: No Prospect for Justice and Reconciliation for Māori without Constitutional Transformation." *Journal of Global Ethics* 14(2) (2018): 208–221.

Mutua, Makau. "The Ideology of Human Rights." *Virginia Journal of International Law* 36(3) (1996): 589–659.

Mutua, Makua. "What is the Future of Transitional Justice." *International Journal of Human Rights* 9(1) (2015): 1–9.

Mutua, Makau "A Critique of Rights in Transitional Justice: The African Experience." In *Rethinking Transitions: Equality and Social Justice in Societies Emerging from Conflict*, eds. Gaby Oré Aguilar and Gómez Isa. Intersentia, 2020.

Muvingi, Ismael. "Sitting on Powder Kegs: Socioeconomic Rights in Transitional Societies." *International Journal of Transitional Justice* 3(2) (2009): 163–182.

Muvingi, Ismael. "Donor-Driven Transitional Justice and Peacebuilding." *Journal of Peacebuilding and Development* 11(1) (2016): 10–25.

N'Da, Serge-Alain Yao and Gilbert Fokou. "Knowledge Asymmetry and Transitional Justice in Côte d'Ivoire." In *Knowledge for Peace: Transitional Justice and the Politics of Knowledge in Theory and Practice,* eds. Briony Jones and Ulrike Lühe. Elgar, 2021.

Nader, Laura. *Naked Science: Anthropological inquiry into Boundaries, Power, and Knowledge.* Routledge, 1996.

Naffine, Ngaire. *Law's Meaning of Life: Philosophy, Religion, Darwin and the Legal Person.* Hart Publishing, 2009.

Nagy, Rosemary. "Transitional Justice as Global Project: Critical Reflections." *Third World Quarterly* 29(2) (2008): 275–289.

Nagy, Rosemary. "Transformative Justice in a Settler Colonial Transition: Implementing the UN Declaration on the Rights of Indigenous Peoples in Canada." *International Journal of Human Rights* 26(2) (2022): 191–216.

Napoleon, Val. "Thinking About Indigenous Legal Orders." In *Dialogues on Human Rights and Legal Pluralism. Ius Gentium: Comparative Perspectives on Law and Justice,* eds. René Provost and Colleen Sheppard. Springer, 2013.

Naqvi, Zainab Batul, Ruth Fletcher, Diamond Ahiagbor, Katie Cruz and Yvette Russell. "Back at the Kitchen Table: Reflections on Decolonising and Internationalising with the Global South Socio-Legal Writing Workshops." *Feminist Legal Studies* 27 (2019): 123–137.

Narsiah, Sagie. "Neoliberalism and Privatisation in South Africa." *GeoJournal* 57(1/2) (2002): 3–13.

Natarajan, Usha. "Climate, Conflict, and International Law in the Middle East and Beyond." *Proceedings of the ASIL Annual Meeting* 114 (2020): 160–164.

Natarajan, Usha. "Who do We Think We Are? Human Rights in a Time of Ecological Change." In *Locating Nature: Making and Unmaking International Law*, eds. Usha Natarajan and Julia Dehm. CUP, 2022.

Natarajan, Usha and Julia Dehm. "Where is the Environment? Locating Nature in International Law." *TWAILR Reflections* 3, August 30, 2019. https://twailr.com/where-is-the-environment-locating-nature-in-international-law/.

Natarajan, Usha and Julia Dehm, eds. *Locating Nature: Making and Unmaking International Law*. CUP, 2022.

Natarajan, Usha and Kishan Khoday. "Locating Nature: Making and Unmaking International Law." *Leiden Journal of International Law* 27(3) (2014): 573–593.

Natarajan, Usha and Kishan Khoday. "Locating Nature: Making and Unmaking International Law." In *Locating Nature: Making and Unmaking International Law*, eds. Usha Natarajan and Julia Dehm, 21–44. CUP, 2022.

Native Land Information System. *Data Sovereignty*. https://nativeland.info/about/data-sovereignty/.

Ndlovu-Gatsheni, Sabelo J. *Coloniality of Power in Postcolonial Africa: Myths of Decolonization*. Conseil pour le Developpement de la Recherche Economique et Sociale en Afrique, 2013.

Ndlovu-Gatsheni, Sabelo J. *Epistemic Freedom in Africa: Deprovincialization and Decolonization*. Routledge, 2018.

Neimanis, Astrida. "No Representation without Colonisation? (Or, Nature Represents Itself)." *Somatechnics* 5(2) (2015): 135–153.

Nesiah, Vasuki. "Theories of Transitional Justice: Cashing in the Blue Chips." In *The Oxford Handbook of the Theory of International Law*, eds. Anne Orford and Florian Hoffman. OUP, 2016.

Nesiah, Vasuki. "Transitional Justice and Development: Governance at the End of History." In *The Oxford Handbook of International Law and Development*, eds. Ruth Buchanan, Luis Eslava and Sundhya Pahuja. OUP, 2023.

Newton, Elizabeth and Rachel Killean. "Global Rights of Nature Movements." In *The Palgrave Handbook of Environmental Policy and Law*, eds. Robert C. Brears and Jade Lindley. Palgrave Macmillan, 2024.

Ní Aoláin, Fionnuala. "Advancing Feminist Positioning in the Field of Transitional Justice." *International Journal of Transitional Justice* 6(2) (2012): 205–228.

Nichols, Sandra S. "Reimagining Transitional Justice for an Enduring Peace: Accounting for Natural Resources in Conflict." In *Justice and Economic Violence in Transition*, ed. Dustin Sharp. Springer, 2014.

Nickson, Ray and John Braithwaite. "Deeper, Broader, Longer Transitional Justice." *European Journal of Criminology* 11(4) (2014): 445–463.
Nifosi-Sutton, Ingrid. *The Protection of Vulnerable Groups under International Human Rights Law*. Routledge, 2017.
Nixon, Rob. *Slow Violence and the Environmentalism of the Poor*. Harvard University Press, 2011.
Njeru, Shastry and Tyanai Masiya, "The Politics of Knowledge in the Emergence of the Transitional Justice Industry in Zimbabwe: The Case of the 'Taking Transitional Justice to the People Programme', 2009–10." In *Knowledge for Peace: Transitional Justice and the Politics of Knowledge in Theory and Practice*, eds. Briony Jones and Ulrike Lühe. Elgar, 2021.
Nonhuman Rights Project. www.nonhumanrights.org.
Norman, Jana. *Posthuman Legal Subjectivity: Reimagining the Human in the Anthropocene*. Routledge, 2022.
Nouwen, Sarah. "As You Set Out for Ithaka: Practical, Epistemological, Ethical and Existential Questions about Socio-Legal Empirical Research in Conflict." *Leiden Journal of International Law* 27(1) (2014): 227–260.
Nouwen, Sarah and Wouter Werner. "Monopolizing Global Justice: International Criminal Law as Challenge to Human Diversity." *Journal of International Criminal Justice* 13(1) (2015): 157–176.
O'Donnell, Erin. "Repairing our Relationship with Rivers: Water Law and Legal Personhood." In *Research Agenda for Water Law*, eds. Vanessa Casado Pérez and Rhett Larson. Elgar, 2023.
O'Donnell, Erin and Anna Arstein-Kerslake. "Recognising Personhood: the Evolving Relationship between the Legal Person and the State." *Griffith Law Review* 30(3) (2021): 339–347.
O'Donnell, Erin, Anne Poelina, Alessandro Pelizzon and Cristy Clark. "Stop Burying the Lede: The Essential Role of Indigenous Law(s) in Creating Rights of Nature." *Transnational Environmental Law* 9(3) (2020): 403–427.
O'Donnell, Erin, Cristy Clark and Rachel Killean. "Rights and Relationality: Competing Discourses in Water Regulation." *Water Alternatives* 17(2) (2024): 207–238.
O'Donnell, Erin L, Julia Talbot-Jones and Julia Talbot-Jones. "Creating Legal Rights for Rivers: Lessons from Australia, New Zealand, and India." *Ecology and Society* 23(1) (2018): 49–62.
O'Lear, Shannon. "Geographies of Slow Violence: An Introduction." In *A Research Agenda for Geographies of Slow Violence*, ed. Shannon O'Lear. Edward Elgar, 2021.
Obi, Cyril. "Oil as the "Curse" of Conflict in Africa: Peering Through the Smoke and Mirrors." *Review of African Political Economy* 37(126): 483–495.
Obradovic-Wochnik, Jelena. "Hidden Politics of Power and Governmentality in Transitional Justice and Peacebuilding: The Problem of 'Bringing the Local Back In.'" *Journal of International Relations and Development* 23 (2020): 117–138.
OHCHR, Transitional Justice and Human Rights, n.d., https://www.ohchr.org/en/transitional-justice.
Ohdedar, Birsha. "Loss and Damage from the Impacts of Climate Change: A Framework for Implementation." *Nordic Journal of International Law* 85(1) (2016): 1–36.
Ojakangas, Mika. "Carl Scmitt and the Sacred Origins of Law." *Telos* 147 (2009): 34–54.
Okafor, Obiora Chinedu and Uchechukwu Ngwaba. "The International Criminal Court as a 'Transitional Justice' Mechanism in Africa: Some Critical Reflections." *International Journal of Transitional Justice* 9(1) (2015): 90–108.

Olarte-Olarte, María Carolina. "From Territorial Peace to Territorial Pacification: Anti-Riot Police Powers and Socio-Environmental Dissent in the Implementation of Colombia's Peace Agreement." *Revista de Estudios Sociales* 67 (2019): 26–39.

Olsen, Tricia, Leigh Payne and Andrew Reiter. *Transitional Justice in Balance – Comparing Processes, Weighing Efficacy*. US Institute of Peace Press, 2010.

Ombati, Omwanza "Repossession of Illegally Acquired Public Land in Kenya: Limits of Law and the Prospects for Transnational Justice in Redress." *The East African Journal of Human Rights & Democracy* 2(3) (2004): 46–57.

Omeje, Kenneth. *High Stakes and Stakeholders: Oil Conflict and Security in Nigeria*. Routledge, 2006.

Ong, David. "Prospects for Transitional Environmental Justice in the Socio-Economic Reconstruction of Kosovo." *Tulane Environmental Law Journal* 30(2) (2017): 217–272.

Ordóñez, María Fernanda, Kelly Shannon and Viviana d'Auria. "The Materialization of the *Buen Vivir* and the Rights of Nature: Rhetoric and Realities of *Guayaquil Ecológico* Urban Regeneration Project." *City, Territory and Architecture* 9(1) (2022).

Ordóñez-Vargas, Laura, L C Peralta Gonzalez and Enrique Prieto-Rios. "An Ecocentric Turn in the Transitional Restorative Justice Process in Colombia." *International Journal of Transitional Justice* 17(1) (2023): 107–122.

Orentlicher, Diane. "'Settling Accounts' Revisited: Reconciling Global Norms with Local Agency." *International Journal of Transitional Justice* 1(1) (2007): 10–22.

Owiye Asaala, Evelyne. "The Politics of Transitional Justice and Corporate Accountability for Atrocities: Options under International Law." *International Journal of Transitional Justice* 16(3) (2022): 467–477.

Oyeniyi, Abe. "Conflict Resolution in the Extractives: A Consideration of Traditional Conflict Resolution Paradigms in Post-Colonial Africa." *Willamette Journal of International Law and Dispute Resolution* 25(1) (2017): 56–77.

Pahuja, Sundhya. *Decolonizing International Law: Development, Economic Growth and the Politics of Universality*. CUP, 2011.

Pain, Rachel and Caitlin Cahill. "Critical Political Geographies of Slow Violence and Resistance." *Environment & Planning C: Politics and Space* 40(2) (2022): 357–372.

Pali, Brunilda and Ivo Aersten. "Inhabiting a Vulnerable and Wounded Earth: Restoring Response-ability." *International Journal of Restorative Justice* 4(1) (2021): 3–16.

Park, Augustine S. J. "Settler Colonialism, Decolonization and Radicalizing Transitional Justice." *International Journal of Transitional Justice* 14(2) (2020): 260–279.

Park, Augustine S. J. "Transitional Justice and Decolonization." In *The Routledge International Handbook on Decolonizing Justice,* eds. Chris Cuneen, Antje Deckert, Amanda Porter, Juan Tauri and Robert Webb. Routledge, 2023.

Pasipanodya, Tafadzwa. "A Deeper Justice: Economic and Social Justice as Transitional Justice in Nepal." *International Journal of Transitional Justice* 2(3) (2008): 378–397.

Pastor, Lejandrina and Angela Santamaria. "Experiences of Spiritual Advocacy for Land and Territorial Itineraries for the Defense of Wiwa Women's Rights in Postconflict Colombia." *International Journal of Transitional Justice* 15(1) (2021): 86–107.

Pattnayak, Kishen. "Visions of Development: the Inevitable Need for Alternatives." *Futures: The Journal of Policy, Planning and Futures Studies* 36(6) (2004): 671–678.

Paulose, Regine. *Green Crimes and International Criminal Law*. Vernon Press, 2021.
Pavlich, George. "Reframing Colonial Law's Criminally Accused Persons." In *Interrupting the Legal Person*, eds. Austin Sarat, George Pavlich and Richard Mailey. Emerald Publishing Limited, 2022.
Payne, Cymie R. "Defining the Environment: Environmental Integrity." In *Environmental Protection and Transitions from Conflict to Peace*, eds. Carsten Stahn, Jens Iverson and Jennifer S. Easterday. OUP, 2017.
Payne, Leigh A., Gabriel Pereira and Laura Bernal-Bermúdez. *Transitional Justice and Corporate Accountability from Below*. CUP, 2020.
Payne, Leigh A., Gabriel Pereira and Laura Bernal-Bermúdez. "The Business of Transitional Justice." In *The Oxford Handbook of Transitional Justice*, eds. Jens Meierhenrich, Alexander Laban Hinton and Lawrence Douglas. OUP, 2023.
Peacock, Richard. "Institutional and Structural Victimisation: Apartheid South Africa." In *Towards a Victimology of State Crime*, eds. Dawn Rothe and David Kauzlarich. Routledge, 2014.
Pelizzon, Alessandro. "Transitional Justice and Ecological Jurisprudence in the Midst of an Ever-Changing Climate." In *Current Issues in Transitional Justice*, eds. Natalia Szablewska and Sacha-Dominik Bachmann. Springer, 2015.
Pellow, David. "Toward a Critical Environmental Justice Studies." *Du Bois Review* 13(2) (2016): 221–236.
Pellow, David. *What is Critical Environmental Justice*. Polity Press, 2018.
Pellow, David. "Critical Environmental Justice Studies." In *Environmental Justice*, ed. Brendan Coolsaet. Routledge, 2020.
Pendas, Devin. *Democracy, Nazi Trials, and Transitional Justice in Germany, 1945–1950*. CUP, 2020.
Pereira, Maria do Mar. *Power, Knowledge and Feminist Scholarship: An Ethnography of Academia*. Routledge, 2017.
Pereira, Ricardo. "After the ICC Office of the Prosecutor's 2016 Policy Paper on Case Selection and Prioritisation: Towards an International Crime of Ecocide?" *Criminal Law Forum* 31(2) (2020): 179–224.
Perreault, Thomas and Patricia Martin. "Geographies of Neoliberalism in Latin America." *Environment and Planning A* 37(2) (2005): 191–201.
Petersmann, Marie-Catherine. "Narcissus' Reflection in the Lake: Untold Narratives in Environmental Law beyond the Anthropocentric Frame." *Journal of Environmental Law* 30(7) (2018): 235–259.
Peterson, Ines. "The Natural Environment in Times of Armed Conflict: A Concern for International War Crimes Law?" *Leiden Journal of International Law* 22(2) (2009): 325–343.
Pietropaoli. Irene. *Business, Human Rights and Transitional Justice*. Routledge, 2020.
Pinto, Mattia. "Historical Trends of Human Rights Gone Criminal." *Human Rights Quarterly* 42(4) (2020): 729–761.
Piquard, Brigitte. "What Knowledge Counts? Local Humanitarian Knowledge Production in Protracted Conflicts. A Central African Republic Case Study." *Peacebuilding* 10(1): 85–100.
Plumwood, Val. "Beyond the Dualistic Assumptions of Women, Men, Nature." *The Ecologists* 22(1) (1992): 8–13.
Plumwood, Val. *Feminism and the Mastery of Nature*. Routledge, 1993.
Plumwood, Val. *Environmental Culture: The Ecological Crisis of Reason*. Routledge, 2002.
Plumwood, Val. "Decolonizing Relationships with Nature." In *Decolonizing Nature*, eds. William M Adams and Martin Mulligan. Routledge, 2012.

Polizzi, Marc. "Transitional Justice." In *Oxford Research Encyclopedia of International Studies*, ed. Nukhet Sandal. OUP, 2022.

Polizzi, Marc and Jeffrey King. "Aid for Justice? Analysing the Impact of Foreign Aid on Recipient Transitional Justice Implementation." *International Journal of Human Rights* 26(4) (2022): 611–633.

Ponomarenko, Illia. "Ecological Disaster Feared in Donbas as Russian-led Forces Inundate Infamous 'Nuclear Pit.'" *Kyiv Post,* April 13, 2018. https://archive.kyivpost.com/ukraine-politics/ecological-disaster-feared-donbas-russian-led-forces-inundate-infamous-nuclear-pit.html.

Posner, Eric. *The Perils of Global Legalism.* University of Chicago Press, 2009.

Preston, Brian, "The Use of Restorative Justice for Environmental Crime." A paper presented to EPA Victoria Seminar on Restorative Environmental Justice, March 22, 2011. https://lec.nsw.gov.au/documents/speeches-and-papers/preston_use%20of%20restorative%20justice%20for%20environmental%20crime.pdf.

Preston, Brian. "The Use of Restorative Justice for Environmental Crime." *Criminal Law Journal* 35(3) (2011): 136–145.

Pugliese, Joseph. *Biopolitics of the More-than-Human: Forensic Ecologies of Violence.* Duke University Press, 2020.

Putzer, Alex, Tineke Lambooy, Ronald Jeurissen and Eunsu Kim. "Putting the Rights of Nature on the Map. A Quantitative Analysis of Rights of Nature Initiatives across the World." *Journal of Maps* 18(1) (2022): 89–96.

Quan-Baffour, Kofi, Norma R. A. Romm and Janet McIntyre-Mills, "Ubuntu: A Dialogue on Connectedness, Environmental Protection and Education." In *Mixed Methods and Cross-Disciplinary Research*, eds. Janet McIntyre-Mills and Norma R. A. Romm. Springer, 2019.

Quijano, Anibal. "Coloniality of Power, Eurocentrism and Latin America." *Nepantla: Views from South* 1(3) (2011): 533–580.

Quinn, Joanna R. "Whither the 'Transition' of Transitional Justice?" *Interdisciplinary Journal of Human Rights* 8(1) (2014): 63–79.

Quinn, Joanna, Dov Jacobs, Luke Moffett and Cheryl Lawther. "The Development of Transitional Justice." In *Research Handbook on Transitional Justice*, eds. Cheryl Lawther, Luke Moffett and Dov Jacobs. Elgar, 2017.

Ramirez Gutierrez, Camilo and A. Sebastian Saavedra Eslava, "Protection of the Natural Environment under International Humanitarian Law and International Criminal Law." *UCLA Journal of International Law and Foreign Affairs* 25(1) (2020): 123–158.

Ranta, Eija. "Alternative Development Approaches: Utopias, Co-Options, Transitions." In *The Routledge Handbook on the History of Development*, eds. Corinna R. Unger, Iris Borowy, Corinne A. Pernet. Routledge, 2022.

Rawls, John. *A Theory of Justice.* OUP, 1973.

Rawls, John. *The Law of Peoples.* Harvard University Press, 1999.

Repez, Filofteia and Mirela Atanasiu. "The Environment: A "Silent Victim" of Armed Conflicts."" *Acta Universitatis Danubius: Relationes Internationales* 12(2) (2019): 123–133.

Reydams, Luc. "The Rise and Fall of Universal Jurisdiction." In *Routledge Handbook of International Criminal Law*, eds. William Schabas and Nadia Bernaz. Routledge, 2011.

Reynolds, Annika. "A Coloniser's View: On Healing and Native Title Reform." *Alternative Law Journal* 47(4) (2022): 291–295.

Rigney, Sophie. "Building an Abolition Movement for International Criminal Law?" *Journal of International Criminal Justice* 22(1) (2024): 211–233.

Ríos, Jerónimo, Julio González and Mariano García de las Heras. "Environment and Armed Conflict in Colombia: Terrorist Attacks against Water Resources and Oil Infrastructure in Norte de Santander (2010–2020)." *Small Wars & Insurgencies* 34(8) (2023): 1429–1457.

RiverOfLife, Martuwarra, Alessandro Pelizzon, Anne Poelina, Afshin Akhtar-Khavari, Cristy Clark, Sarah Laborde, Elizabeth Macpherson, Katie O'Bryan, Erin O'Donnell and John Page. "Yoongoorrookoo: The Emergence of Ancestral Personhood." *Griffith Law Review* 30(3) (2023): 505–529.

Rivers, Liz. "Shareholder Return: A Nuremberg Defence?" *Environmental Law & Management* 24(1) (2012): 17–19.

Robins, Simon. "Whose Voices? Understanding Victims' Needs in Transition: Nepali Voices: Perceptions of Truth, Justice, Reconciliation, Reparations and the Transition in Nepal by the International Centre for Transitional Justice and the Advocacy Forum, March 2008." *Journal of Human Rights Practice* 1(2) (2009): 320–331.

Robins, Simon. "Towards Victim-Centred Transitional Justice: Understanding the Needs of Families of the Disappeared in Postconflict Nepal." *International Journal of Transitional Justice* 5(1) (2011): 75–98.

Robins, Simon. "Failing Victims: The Limits of Transitional Justice in Addressing the Needs of Victims of Violations." *Human Rights & International Legal Discourse* 11 (2017): 41–58.

Robinson, Darryl. "Ecocide – Puzzles and Possibilities. *Journal of International Criminal Justice* 20(2) (2022): 313–347.

Robinson, Margaret. "Animal Personhood in Mi'kmaq Perspective." *Societies* 4(4) (2014): 672–688.

Rodeiro, Manuel. "Responding to Ecocide through Transitional Justice." *Dialogo* 55(113) (2024): 47–79.

Rodgers, Christopher. "A New Approach to Protecting Ecosystems: The Te Awa Tupua (Whanganui River Claims Settlement) Act 2017." *Environmental Law Review* 19(4) (2017): 266–279.

Rodríguez-Garavito, César. "The Future of Human Rights: From Gatekeeping to Symbiosis." *Sur: International Journal on Human Rights* 11(20) (2014): 499–509.

Rodriguez, Patrical M. "Charting a New Human Rights Discourse "From the Territories": Social Movements and Peace in Cauca, Colombia." Rapoport Center Human Rights Working Paper Series, 5/2018.

Rogers, Richard, Kate Mackintosh and Maksym Popov. "No Longer the Silent Victim: How Ukrainian Prosecutors are Revitalising Environmental War Crime Law." *Just Security*, January 23, 2024. https://www.justsecurity.org/91357/no-longer-the-silent-victim-how-ukrainian-prosecutors-are-revitalizing-environmental-war-crime-law/.

Roht-Arriaza, Naomi. "The New Landscape of Transitional Justice." In *Transitional Justice in the Twenty-First Century: Beyond Truth Versus Justice*, eds. Naomi Roht-Arriaza and Javier Mariezcurrena. CUP, 2006.

Roht-Arriaza, Naomi. "Reparations and Economic, Social, and Cultural Rights." In *Justice and Economic Violence in Transition*, ed. Dustin Sharp. Springer, 2014.

Roht-Arriaza, Naomi. "Natural Resources, Transitional States and Grand Corruption." In *Research Handbook on International Law and Environmental Peacebuilding*, eds. Daniëlla Dam-de Jong and Britta Sjöstedt. Elgar, 2023.

Rojas-Páez, Gustavo. "Resisting Colonial State Crime: The Experience of the Peace Community of San José de Apartadó." *Oñati Socio-Legal Series* 14(1) (2024): 119–144.

Rolston, Bill and Fionnuala Ní Aoláin. "Colonialism, Redress and Transitional Justice: Ireland and Beyond." *State Crime Journal* 7(2) (2018): 329–348.

Rooney, Eilish and Fionnuala Ni Aolaín. 'Underenforcement and Intersectionality: Gendered Aspects of Transition for Women." *International Journal of Transitional Justice* 1(3) (2007): 338–354.

Rosalind, Shaw and Lars Waldorf with Pierre Hazan, eds. *Localizing Transitional Justice*. Stanford University Press, 2010.

Ross, Michael L. "What Have We Learned About the Resource Curse?" *Annual Review of Political Science* 18(1) (2015): 239–256.

Roth, Benita. "Second Wave Black Feminism in the African Diaspora: News from New Scholarship." *Agenda: Empowering Women for Gender Equity* 58 (2003): 46–58.

Rothe, Dawn and David Kauzlarich. *Crimes of the Powerful: An Introduction*. Routledge, 2016.

Rothe, Dawn and David Kauzlarich. *Crimes of the Powerful: White-Collar Crime and Beyond,* 2nd Edition. Routledge, 2022.

Rouse, Joseph. "Power-Knowledge." In *The Cambridge Companion to Foucault*, ed. Garry Gutting. CUP, 1994.

Rožič, Peter and Yuliy A. Nisnevich. "Lustration Matters: A Radical Approach to the Problem of Corruption." *Studies in Comparative International Development* 51 (2016): 257–285.

Ruggiero, Vincenzo and Nigel South. "Toxic State-Corporate Crimes, Neo-liberalism and Green Criminology: The Hazards and Legacies of the Oil, Chemical and Mineral Industries." *International Journal for Crime, Justice and Social Democracy* 2(2) (2013): 12–26.

Ruiz Serna, Daniel. "Territory as Victim. Political Ontology and the Laws for Victims of Indigenous and Afrodescendant Communities in Colombia." *Revista Colombian Journal of Anthropology* 53(2) (2017): 85–113.

Ruiz-Serna, Daniel. "Transitional Justice beyond the Human: Indigenous Cosmopolitics and the Realm of Law in Colombia." *Cultural Politics* 19(1) (2023): 57–76.

Ruiz-Serna, Daniel. *When Forests Run Amok: War and Its Afterlives in Indigenous and Afro-Colombian Territories*. Duke University Press, 2023.

Ruru, Jacinta. "First Laws: Tikanga Māori in/and the Law." *Victoria University of Wellington Law Review* 49(2) (2018): 211–228.

Saad-Diniz, Eduardo. "The Idea of Corporate Justice: Paths to Corporate Criminology in Brazil." *Criminal Justice Review* 46(4) (2021): 435–449.

Saeed, Huma. *Transitional Justice and Socio-Economic Harm: Land Grabbing in Afghanistan*. Routledge, 2022.

Said, Edward. "Identity, Negation and Violence." *New Left Review* 1(171) (1988): 46–60.

Said, Edward. "Orientalism." In *Colonial Discourse and Post-Colonial Theory: A Reader*, eds. Patrick Williams and Laura Chrisman. Harvester Wheatsheaf, 1994.

Salehi, Mariam. "Trying Just Enough or Promising Too Much? The Problem-Capacity-Nexus in Tunisia's Transitional Justice Process." *Journal of Intervention and Statebuilding* 16(1) (2021): 98–116.

Sandoval-Villalba, Clara. "The Concepts of 'Injured Party' and 'Victim' of Gross Human Rights Violations in the Jurisprudence of the Inter-American Court of Human Rights: A Commentary on their Implications for Reparations." In *Reparations for Victims of Genocide, War Crimes and Crimes against Humanity*, eds. Carla Ferstman and Mariana Goetz. Brill Nijhoff, 2009.

Sandoval, Clara. "Transitional Justice and Social Change." *Sur: International Journal on Human Rights* 11(20) (2014): 180–189.

Sandoval, Clara, Leonardo Filippini and Roberto Vidal. "Linking Transitional Justice and Corporate Accountability." In *Corporate Accountability in the Context of Transitional Justice*, eds. Sabine Michalowski. Routledge, 2014.

Santamaría, Angela, Dunen Muelas, Paula Caceres, Wendi Kuetguaje and Julian Villegas. "Decolonial Sketches and Intercultural Approaches to Truth: Corporeal Experiences and Testimonies of Indigenous Women in Colombia." *International Journal of Transitional Justice* 14(1) (2020): 56–79.

Santamaria, Angela, Paula Cáceres, Morgana D'amico, Roxana Sefair, Fabián Rosas, Laura Restrepo, Laura Carianil and Gabriel Moreno. "To Pay, Heal, and Repair Mother Earth in the Sierra Nevada de Santa Marta: Experiences of Indigenous Women's Reparation in the Implementation of the Colombian Peace Accord." *International Review of Victimology* 29(2) (2023): 170–198.

Sarkin, Jeremy, Julian and Ines Pereira Lopes. "Reaching for Both Justice and Peace in Colombia: Understanding the Special Jurisdiction for Peace's Mixed Approach (Using Both Retributive and Restorative Justice) to Deal with International Crimes." *Contemporary Justice Review*, 26(2) (2023): 123–144.

Scheffer, David. "Genocide and Atrocity Crimes." *Genocide Studies and Prevention* 1(3) (2006): 229–250.

Schindler, Stefanie. "The Animal's Dignity in Swiss Animal Welfare Legislation – Challenges and Opportunities." *European Journal of Pharmaceutics and Biopharmaceutics* 84(2) (2013): 251–254.

Schlosberg, David. "Reconceiving Environmental Justice: Global Movements and Political Theories." *Environmental Politics* 13(3) (2004): 517–540.

Schlosberg, David. *Defining Environmental Justice: Theories, Movements and Nature*. OUP, 2009.

Schlosberg, David. "Justice, Ecological Integrity, and Climate Change." In *Ethical Adaptation to Climate Change*, eds. Allen Thompson and Jeremy Bendik-Keymer. MIT Press, 2012.

Schmid, Evelyne and Aoife Nolan. "Do No Harm? Exploring the Scope of Economic and Social Rights in Transitional Justice." *International Journal of Transitional Justice* 8(3) (2014): 362–382.

Schmitt, Carl. *The Nomos of the Earth in the International Law of the Jus Publicum Europseum,* translated: G. L. Ulmen. Telos Press Publishing, 2003.

Scholtz, Werner and Gerrit Ferreira. "Climate Change Negotiations and Transitional Justice: The Advent of a Carbon Truth Reconciliation Commission." *Comparative and International Law Journal of Southern Africa* 48(1) (2015): 42–88.

Schulz, Karsten A. "Decolonising the Anthropocene: The Mytho-Politics of Human Mastery." In *Critical Epistemologies of Global Politics,* eds. Marc Woons and Sebastian Weber. E-International Relations Publishing, 2017.

Schwöbel-Patel, Christine. "Spectacle in International Criminal Law: The Fundraising Image of Victimhood." *London Review of International Law* 4(2) (2016): 247–274.

Schwöbel-Patel, Christine. "The 'Ideal' Victim of International Criminal Law." *The European Journal of International Law* 29(3) (2018): 703–724.

Schwöbel-Patel, Christine. "The Core Crimes of International Criminal Law." In *The Oxford Handbook of International Criminal Law*, eds. Kevin Heller, Jens Ohlin, Darryl Robinson, Frédéric Mégret and Sarah Nouwen. OUP, 2020.

Schwöbel-Patel, Christine. *Marketing Global Justice*. CUP, 2021.

Schwöbel-Patel, Christine. "Real (E)State: Valuing a Nation under Imperial Rentier Capitalism." In *Constitutions of Value: Law, Governance, and Political Ecology,* eds. Isabel Feichtner and Geoff Gordon. Routledge, 2023.

Scott, Colin. "Science for the West, Myth for the Rest?" In *Naked Science: Anthropological inquiry into Boundaries, Power, and Knowledge*, ed. Laura Nader. Routledge, 1996.

Sesay, Mohamed. "Decolonization of Postcolonial Africa: A Structural Justice Project More Radical than Transitional Justice." *International Journal of Transitional Justice* 16(2) (2022): 254–271.

Sessions, George. "The Deep Ecology Movement: A Review." *Environmental Review* 11(2) (1987): 105–125.

Shakya, Prabindra. "Indigenous Peoples: Expanding the Realm of Justice." *Peace Insight,* March 26, 2014. https://www.peaceinsight.org/en/articles/indigenous-peoples-expanding-realm-justice/?location=&theme=human-rights.

Shala, Nita. *Guarantees of Non-Repetition in International Human Rights Law and Transitional Justice: Building Peace after Conflict.* Routledge, 2024.

Sharp, Dustin N. "Addressing Economic Violence in Times of Transition: Toward a Positive-Peace Paradigm for Transitional Justice." *Fordham International Law Journal* 35(3) (2012): 780–814.

Sharp, Dustin N. "Economic Violence in the Practice of African Truth Commissions and Beyond." In *Justice and Economic Violence in Transition,* ed. Dustin N. Sharp. Springer, 2014.

Sharp, Dustin N. "Introduction: Addressing Economic Violence in Times of Transition." In *Justice and Economic Violence in Transition,* ed. Dustin N. Sharp. Springer, 2014.

Sharp, Dustin N. "Emancipating Transitional Justice from the Bonds of the Paradigmatic Transition." *International Journal of Transitional Justice* 9(1) (2015): 150–169.

Sharp, Dustin N, "Transitional Justice and 'Local' Justice." In *Research Handbook on Transitional Justice*, eds. Cheryl Lawther, Luke Moffett and Dov Jacobs. Routledge, 2017.

Sharp, Dustin N. "What Would Satisfy Us? Taking Stock of Critical Approaches to Transitional Justice." *International Journal of Transitional Justice* 13(3) (2019): 570–589.

Sharp, Dustin N. "Crisis, Faith, and Transformation in Transitional Justice." In *Beyond Transitional Justice,* ed. Matthew Evans. Routledge, 2022.

Shaw, Rosalind and Lars Waldorf. "Introduction." In *Localizing Transitional Justice: Interventions and Priorities after Mass Violence*, eds. Rosalind Shaw, and Lars Waldorf with Pierre Hazan. Stanford University Press, 2010.

Shiva, Vandana. *Staying Alive: Women, Ecology and Development.* Southend Press, 2010.

Shiva, Vandana. "Reductionism and Regeneration: A Crisis in Science." In *Ecofeminism,* eds. Maria Mies and Vandana Shiva. Zed Books, 2014.

Shklar, Judith. *Legalism.* Harvard University Press, 1964.

Shklar, Judith. "The Liberalism of Fear." In *Liberalism and the Moral Life,* ed. Nancy L. Rosenbaum. Harvard University Press, 1989.

Short, Damien and Martin Crook. *The Genocide-Ecocide Nexus.* Routledge, 2022.

Shqair, Manal, Hamza Hamouchene and Hafawa Rabhi. "How Arab Eco-Normalisation of Israel Covers Up Its Crimes." *Al Jazeera,* December 12, 2023. https://www.aljazeera.com/opinions/2023/12/12/how-arab-eco-normalisation-of-israel-covers-up-its-crimes.

Sikkink, Kathryn. *The Justice Cascade: How Human Rights Prosecutions are Changing World Politics.* W. W. Norton, 2011.

Sikkink, Kathryn. "Latin American Countries as Norm Protagonists of the Idea of International Human Rights." *Global Governance* 20(3) (2014): 389–404.

Sikkink, Kathryn and Carrie Booth Walling. "Argentina's Contribution to Global Trends in Transitional Justice." In *Transitional Justice in the Twenty-First Century,* eds. Naomi Roht-Arriaza and Javier Mariezcurrena. CUP, 2006.

Sikor, Thomas and Peter Newell. "Globalizing Environmental Justice?" *Geoforum* 54 (2014): 151–157.

Silvers, Anita. "Feminism and Disability." In *The Blackwell Guide to Feminist Philosophy,* eds. Linda Martín Alcoff and Eva Feder Kittay. Blackwell Publishing, 2007.

Singer, Peter. *Animal Liberation Now.* Random House, 2023.

Smart, Carol. *Feminism and the Power of Law.* Taylor and Francis, 1989.

Smith, Chad, Gregory Hooks and Michael Lengefield. "The War on Drugs in Colombia: The Environment, the Treadmill of Destruction and Risk-Transfer Militarism." *Journal of World-Systems Research* 20(2) (2014): 185–206.

Smith, Linda Tuhiwai. *Decolonizing Methodologies: Research and Indigenous Peoples.* Zed Books, 1999.

Smith, Tara. "Creating a Framework for the Prosecution of Environmental Crimes in International Criminal Law." In *The Ashgate Research Companion to International Criminal Law*, eds. William Schabas, Yvonne McDermott and Niamh Hayes. Routledge, 2013.

Snyder, Jack and Leslie Vinjamuri. "Trials and Errors: Principle and Pragmatism in Strategies of International Justice." *International Security* 28(3) (2004): 5–44.

South, Nigel. "The 'Corporate Colonisation of Nature': Bio-Prospecting, Bio-Piracy and the Development of Green Criminology." In *Transnational Environmental Crime,* ed. Rob White. Routledge, 2016.

Spade, Dean. *Mutual Aid: Building Solidarity during This Crisis (and the Next).* Verso, 2020.

Sperfeldt, Christoph. *Practices of Reparations in International Criminal Justice.* OUP, 2022.

Spivak, Gayatri Chakravorty. "Can the Subaltern Speak?" In *Imperialism,* ed. Peter H. Cain and Mark Harrison. Routledge, 2004.

Sprenger, Guido. "Buddhism and Coffee: The Transformation of Locality and Non-Human Personhood in Southern Laos." *Sojourn: Journal of Social Issues in Southeast Asia* 33(2) (2018): 265–290.

Springer, Simon, Kean Birch and Julie MacLeavy, eds. "An Introduction to Neoliberalism." In *The Handbook of Neoliberalism*, eds. Simon Springer, Kean Birch and Julia MacLeavy. Routledge, 2016.

Sriram, Chandra Lekha and Amy Ross. "Geographies of Crime and Justice: Contemporary Transitional Justice and the Creation of 'Zones of Impunity.'" *International Journal of Transitional Justice* 1(1) (2007): 45–65.

Sriram, Chandra Lekha. "Justice as Peace? Liberal Peacebuilding and Strategies of Transitional Justice." *Global Society* 21(4) (2007): 579–591.

Stahn, Carsten, Jens Iverson and Jennifer Easterday. "Protection of the Environment and Jus Post Bellum: Some Preliminary Reflections." In *Environmental Protection and Transitions from Conflict to Peace*: eds. Carsten Stahn, Jens Iverson and Jennifer Easterday. OUP, 2017.

Stahn, Carsten, Jens Iverson and Jennifer S. Easterday, eds. *Environmental Protection and Transitions from Conflict to Peace: Clarifying Norms, Principles, and Practices.* OUP, 2017.

Stahn, Carsten. *A Critical Introduction to International Criminal Law.* CUP, 2018.

Stahn, Carsten. "Confronting Colonial Amnesia: Towards New Relational Engagement with Colonial Injustice and Cultural Colonial Objects." *Journal of International Criminal Justice* 18(4) (2020): 793–824.

Stan, Lavinia. "Transitional justice in Central and Eastern Europe." In *Research Handbook on Transitional Justice,* eds. Cheryl Lawther, Luke Moffett and Dov Jacobs. Elgar, 2017.

Stark, Barbara. "Economic Rights in the United States and International Human Rights Law: Toward an "Entirely New Strategy."" *The Hastings Law Journal* 44(1) (1992): 79–130.

Stegerm, Tamara, Richard Filčák and Krista Harper. "Environmental Justice in Central and Eastern Europe: Mobilization, Stagnation and Detraction." In *The Routledge Handbook of Environmental Justice,* eds. Ryan Holifield, Jayajit Chakraborty and Gordon Walker. Routledge, 2018.

Steiner, Gary and Marc Lucht. "Law and Nature: Human, Non-Human, and Ecosystem Rights." In *Speciesism in Biology and Culture*, eds. Brian Swartz and Brent D. Mishler. Springer, 2022.

Stewart, Mia. "The Revolution Does not Happen Overnight': Philippe Sands on Ecocide and its Links to Nuremberg." *Al Jazeera,* June 29, 2021. https://liberties.aljazeera.com/en/the-revolution-does-not-happen-overnight-aj-speaks-to-phillipe-sands-on-ecocide-and-a-life-in-environmental-lawyering/.

Steyn, Phia. "The Lingering Environmental Impact of Repressive Governance: The Environmental Legacy of the Apartheid Era for the New South Africa." *Globalizations* 2(3) (2005): 391–402.

Stone, Christopher D. "Should Trees Have Standing? Towards Legal Rights for Natural Objects." *Southern California Law Review* 45 (1972): 450–501.

Strang, Veronica. "Justice For All: Inconvenient Truths and Reconciliation in Human–Non-Human Relations." In *Routledge Handbook of Environmental Anthropology*, eds. Helen Kopnina and Eleanor Shoreman-Ouimet. Routledge, 2016.

Stretesky, Paul B., Michael A. Long and Michael J. Lynch. *The Treadmill of Crime: Political Economy and Green Criminology*. Routledge, 2014.

Strickland, Susan. "Feminism, Postmodernism and Difference." In *Knowing the Difference: Feminist Perspectives in Epistemology*, eds. Kathleen Lennon and Margaret Whitford. Routledge, 1994.

Stull, Valerie, Michael M. Bell and Mpumelelo Ncwadi. "Environmental Apartheid: Eco-Health and Rural Marginalisation in South Africa." *Journal of Rural Studies* 47 (2016): 369–390.

Stutzin, Godofredo. "Un Imperativo Ecológico: Reconocer los Derechos de la Naturaleza." *Ambiente y Desarrollo* 1(1) (1984): 97–114.

Suarez, Andres, Paola Andrea Árias-Arévalo and Eliana Martínez-Mera. "Environmental Sustainability in Post-Conflict Countries: Insights for Rural Colombia." *Environment, Development and Sustainability* 20(3) (2018): 997–1015.

Suárez Vargas, Daniela and Rachel Killean. "Women's Experiences of Environmental Harm in Colombia: Learning from Black, Decolonial and Indigenous Feminisms." In *Gendering Green Criminology,* eds. Emma Milne, Pamela Davies, James Heydon, Kay Peggs and Tanya Wyatt. Bristol University Press, 2023.

Subotić, Jelena. "The Transformation of International Transitional Justice Advocacy." *International Journal of Transitional Justice* 6(1) (2012): 106–125.

Sullivan, Shannon. "Pragmatism." In *The Blackwell Guide to Feminist Philosophy,* eds. Linda Martín Alcoff and Eva Feder Kittay. Blackwell Publishing, 2007.

Surma, Katie. "Indigenous Leaders and Human Rights Groups in Brazil Want Bolsonaro Prosecuted for Crimes against Humanity." *Inside Climate News*, June 24, 2021, https://insideclimatenews.org/news/24062021/bolsonaro-amazon-brazil-deforestaiton-climate-change-indigenous-rights-ecocide/.

Sweet, Elizabeth L. and Sara Ortiz Escalante. "Engaging Territorio Cuerpo-Tierra through Body and Community Mapping: A Methodology for Making Communities Safer." *Gender, Place & Culture* 24 (2017): 1–13.

Sweezy, Paul M. "The Accumulation of Capital." *Science and Society* 31(4) (1967): 474–485.

Szablewska, Natalia and Sascha-Dominik Bachmann, "Current Issues and Future Challenges in Transitional Justice." In *Current Issues in Transitional Justice: Towards a More Holistic Approach*, eds. Natalia Szablewska and Sascha-Dominik Bachmann. Springer, 2015.

Szoke-Burke, Sam. "Not Only Context: Why Transitional Justice Programs Can No Longer Ignore Violations of Economic and Social Rights." *Texas International Law Journal* 50 (2–3)(2015): 465–494.

Tallgren, Immi. "The Voice of the International: Who is Speaking?" *Journal of International Criminal Justice* 13(1) (2015): 135–155.

Tamanaha, Brian Z. "Functions of the Rule of Law." In *Cambridge Companion to the Rule of Law*, eds. Jens Meierhenrich and Martin Loughlin. CUP, 2021.

Tamayo-Gomez, Camilo. "Recognition as Transitional Justice 'From Below': Analysing Victims' Grassroots Activism in Postconflict Colombia." *International Journal of Transitional Justice* 16 (2022): 314–330.

Tauri, Juan Marcellus. "Restorative Justice as a Colonial Project in the Disempowerment of Indigenous Peoples." In *Routledge International Handbook of Restorative Justice*, ed. Theo Gavrielides. Routledge, 2018.

Teitel, Ruti G. *Transitional Justice*. OUP, 2000.

Teitel, Ruti. "Transitional Justice Genealogy." *Harvard Human Rights Journal* 16(4) (2003): 69–94.

Teitel, Ruti. "Transitional Justice: Postwar Legacies." *Cardozo Law Review* 27(4) (2005): 1615–1632.

Teitel, Ruti. *Globalizing Transitional Justice: Contemporary Essays*. OUP, 2014.

Teló, Fabricio, Alessandra Gasparotto, Leonilde Servolo de Medeiros and Regina Coelly Fernandes Saraiva. "Land and Transitional Justice in Brazil." *International Journal of Transitional Justice* 15(1) (2021): 190–209.

Temper, Leah. "Blocking Pipelines, Unsettling Environmental Justice: From Rights of Nature to Responsibility to Territory." *Local Environmental* 24(2) (2019): 94–112.

Theidon, Kimberley. "Editorial Note." *International Journal of Transitional Justice* 3(3) (2009): 295–300.

Theriault, Henry C. "Reparations for Genocide: Group Harm and the Limits of Liberal Individualism." *International Criminal Law Review* 14, Special Issue: Armenian Genocide Reparations (2014): 441–469.

Thiong'o, Ngũgĩ wa. *Decolonising the Mind: The Politics of Language in African Literature*. Heinemann Education, 1986.

Thompson, Suzanne Gagnon and Michelle Barton. "Ecocentric and Anthropocentric Attitudes toward the Environment." *Journal of Environmental Psychology* 14(2) (1994): 149–157.

Thomson, Susan and Rosemary Nagy. "Law, Power and Justice: What Legalism Fails to Address in the Functioning of Rwanda's Gacaca Courts." *International Journal of Transitional Justice* 5(1) (2011): 11–30.

Tibori-Szabó, Kinga and Megan Hirst. *Victim Participation in International Criminal Justice: Practitioners Guide*. Springer, 2017.

Tombs, Steve and David Whyte. "The Shifting Imaginaries of Corporate Crime." *Journal of White Collar and Corporate Crime* 1(1) (2020): 16–23.

Torpey, John. *Politics and the Past: On Repairing Historical Injustices*. Rowman and Littlefield, 2003.

Torres, Felix E. "On Deserving Victims and the Undeserving Poor: Exploring the Scope of Distributive Justice in Transitional Justice Theory and Practice." *Human Rights Quarterly* 45(2) (2023): 306–334.

Tovar-Restrepo, Marcela and Clara Irazábal. "Indigenous Women and Violence in Colombia: Agency, Autonomy, and Territoriality." *Latin American Perspectives* 41(1) (2014): 39–58.

Truong, Kiem N. and Khuong V. Dinh. "Agent Orange: Haft-Century Effects on the Vietnamese Wildlife Have Been Ignored." *Environmental Science and Technology* 55(22) (2021):15007–15009.

Tuck, Eve and K Wayne Yang. "Decolonization is Not a Metaphor." *Decolonization: Indigeneity, Education & Society* 1(1) (2012): 1–40.

Turner, Catherine. "Deconstructing Transitional Justice." *Law and Critique* 24(2) (2013): 193–209.

Turner, Rachel A. and Jane Wills. "Downscaling Doughnut Economics for Sustainability Governance." *Current Opinion in Environmental Sustainability Governance* 56 (2022): 1–10.

Tutu, Desmond. *No Future without Forgiveness*. Doubleday, 1999.

Tzouvala, Ntina. *Capitalism as Civilisation: A History of International Law*. CUP, 2020.

Uhlmann, David. "Environmental Crime Comes of Age: The Evolution of Criminal Enforcement in the Environmental Regulatory Scheme." *Utah Law Review* 4 (2009): 1223–1252.

Umukoro, Nathaniel. "Human Rights Violations and Transitional Justice in Nigeria's Niger Delta during Civilian Rule." *Journal of Global South Studies* 35(1) (2018): 87–103.

United Nations Climate Change. "Conflict and Climate." July 12, 2022. https://unfccc.int/news/conflict-and-climate#:~:text=The%20evidence%20is%20clear%20that,climate%20change%20into%20conflict%20risks.

Unruh, Jon D. and Musa Adam Abdul-Jalil, "Housing, Land and Property Rights in Transitional Justice." *International Journal of Transitional Justice* 15(1) (2021): 1–6.

Urueña, René and María Angélica Prada-Uribe. "Transitional Justice and Economic Policy." *Annual Review of Law and Social Science* 14(1) (2018): 397–410.

Urzola, Natalia and María Paula González. "Gender-Based Environmental Violence in Colombia: Problematising Dominant Notions of Gender-Based Violence during Peacebuilding." *Australian Feminist Law Journal* 48(2) (2022): 245–264.

van ben Berge, Lukas. "Ancient Greek Nomos and Modern Legal Theory: A Reappraisal." *Netherlands Journal of Legal Philosophy* 51(2) (2022): 264–276.

van den Herik, Larissa. "Historical Inquiry as a Form of Colonial Reparation?" *Harvard International Law Journal Online* 59 (2018): 1–5.

van den Wyngaert, Christine. "Victims before International Criminal Courts: Some views and concerns of an ICC trial judge." *Case Western Reserve Journal of International Law* 44 (1–2) (2011): 475–496.

van der Merwe, Hugo and M. Brinton Lykes. "Racism and Transitional Justice." *International Journal of Transitional Justice* 14(3) (2021): 415–422.

van der Merwe, Hugo and M. Brinton Lykes. "Transitional Justice and Corporate Accountability: Introducing New Players and New Theoretical Challenges." *International Journal of Transitional Justice* 16(3) (2022): 291–297.

van Houten, Pieter. "The World Bank's (Post-)Conflict Agenda: The Challenge of Integrating Development and Security." *Cambridge Review of International Affairs* 20(4) (2007): 639–657.

van Norren, Dorine E. "African Ubuntu and Sustainable Development Goals: Seeking Human Mutual Relations and Service in Development." *Third World Quarterly* 43(12) (2022): 2791–2810.

van Norren, Dorine E. "The Sustainable Development Goals Viewed through Gross National Happiness, Ubuntu, and Buen Vivir." *International Environmental Agreements* 20 (2020): 431–458.

van Sliedregt, Elies. "One Rule for Them: Selectivity in International Criminal Law." *Leiden Journal of International Law* 34(2) (2021): 283–290.

Van Uhm, Daan P. "Atrocity Crimes and Ecocide: Interrelations between Armed Conflict, Violence and Harm to the Environment." In *The Oxford Handbook on Atrocity Crimes*, eds. Barbora Holá, Hollie Nyseth Nzitatira and Maartje Weerdesteijn. OUP, 2022.

van Wijk, Joris. "Who is the 'Little Old Lady' of International Crimes? Nils Christie's Concept of the Ideal Victim Reinterpreted" *International Review of Victimology* 19(2) (2013): 159–179.

Varona, Gema. "Restorative Pathways after Mass Environmental Victimisation: Walking in the Landscapes of Past Ecocides." *Oñati Socio-Legal Series* 10(3) (2020): 664–685.

Varona, Gema. "Why an Atmosphere of Transhumanism Undermines Green Restorative Justice Concepts and Tenets." *International Journal of Restorative Justice* 4(1) (2021): 41–59.

Vázquez Guevara, Valeria. "Crafting the Lawful Truth: Chile's 1990 Truth Commission, International Human Rights and the Museum of Memory." *London Review of International Law* 7(2) (2019): 253–280.

Velez, Emma D and Nancy Tuana. "Toward Decolonial Feminisms: Tracing the Lineages of Decolonial Thinking through Latin American/Latinx Feminist Philosophy." *Hypatia* 35(3) (2020): 366–372.

Vergès, François. *A Decolonial Feminism*. Pluto Press, 2021.

Viaene, Lieselotte. "Can Rights of Nature Save Us From the Anthropocene Catastrophe? Some Critical Reflections from the Field." *Asian Journal of Law and Society* 9(2) (2022): 187–206.

Viaene, Lieselotte and Eva Brems. "Transitional Justice and Cultural Contexts: Learning from the Universality Debate." *Netherlands Quarterly of Human Rights* 28(2) (2010):199– 224.

Viaene, Lieselotte, Peter Doran and Jonathan Liljeblad. "Editorial Special Section: 'Transitional Justice and Nature: A Curious Silence.'" *International Journal of Transitional Justice* 17(1) (2023): 1–14.

Vielle, Stephanie. "Transitional Justice: A Colonizing Field?" *Amsterdam Law Forum* 4(3) (2012): 58–68.

Vogel, Birte. "Everyday Economic Experiences and Peace Processes." In *Contemporary Peacemaking: Peace Processes, Peacebuilding and Conflict*, eds. Roger MacGinty and Anthony Wanis-St John. Palgrave, 2022.

Waldorf, Lars. "Anticipating the Past: Transitional Justice and Socio-Economic Wrongs." *Social & Legal Studies* 21(2) (2012): 171–186.

Waldron, Jeremy. *Liberal Rights: Collected Papers 1981*–1991. CUP, 1993.

Walker, Gordon. "Beyond Distribution and Proximity: Exploring the Multiple Spatialities of Environmental Justice." *Antipode* 41(4) (2009): 614–636.

Walters, Reece, Diane Westerhuis and Tanya Wyatt. *Emerging Issues in Green Criminology*. Palgrave, 2013.

Warren, Karen J. "The Power and Promise of Ecological Feminism." *Environmental Ethics*, 12(2) (1990): 125–146.

Warren, Karen J. *Ecofeminist Philosophy: A Western Perspective on What It Is and Why It Matters*. Rowman and Littlefield, 2000.

Watson, Irene. "Re-Centring First Nations Knowledge and Places in a Terra Nullius Space." *AlterNative: An International Journal of Indigenous* Peoples 10(5) (2014): 508–520.

Watson, Irene. "Aboriginal Relationships to the Natural World: Colonial 'Protection' of Human Rights and the Environment." *Journal of Human Rights and the Environment* 9(2) (2018): 119–140.

Watts, Michael. "Oil, Development, and the Politics of the Bottom Billion." *Macalester International* 24 (2009)

Watts, Vanessa. "Indigenous Place-Thought & Agency Amongst Humans and Non-Humans (First Woman and Sky Woman go on a European World Tour!)." *Decolonization, Indigeneity, Education and Society* 2(1) (2013): 20–34.

Weinstein, Tara. "Prosecuting Attacks that Destroy the Environment: Environmental Crimes or Humanitarian Atrocities." *Georgetown International Environmental Law Review* 17(4) (2005): 697–722.

Wellman, Kathleen. *Hijacking History: How the Christian Right Teaches History and Why it Matters*. OUP, 2019.

Wengraf, Lee. "The Pillage Continues: Debunking the Resource Curse." *Review of African Political Economy*, January 24, 2017. https://roape.net/2017/01/24/pillage-continues-debunking-resource-curse/.

Werrell, Caitlin E. and Francesco Femia. "Climate Change Raises Conflict Concerns." *The UNESCO Courier,* March 29, 2018. https://en.unesco.org/courier/2018-2/climate-change-raises-conflict-concerns.

Wesche, Philipp. "Rights of Nature in Practice: A Case Study on the Impacts of the Colombian Atrato River Decision." *Journal of Environmental Law* 33(3) (2021): 531–555.

Wessels, Hercules. "Nature's Rights and Developing Remedies: Enabling Substantive and Restorative Relief in Civil Litigation." In *The Palgrave Handbook of Environmental Restorative Justice*, eds. Brunilda Pali, Miranda Forsyth and Felicity Tepper. Palgrave, 2022.

Westberg, Megan. "Rwanda's Use of Transitional Justice after Genocide: The Gacaca Courts and the ICTR." *University of Kansas Law Review* 59(2) (2010): 331–367.

White, Lynn. "The Historical Roots of our Ecologic Crisis." *Science*, New Series, 155(3767) (1967): 1203–1207.

White, Rob. *Climate Change from a Criminological Perspective*. Springer, 2012.

White, Rob. "The Conceptual Contours of Green Criminology." In *Emerging Issues in Green Criminology: Exploring Power, Justice and Harm,* eds. Reece Walters, Diane Solomon Westerhuis and Tanya Wyatt. Palgrave MacMillan, 2013.

White, Rob. *Environmental Harm: An Eco-Justice Perspective*. Bristol University Press, 2013.

White, Rob. "Climate Change, Ecocide and the Crimes of the Powerful." In *The Routledge International Handbook of Crimes of the Powerful,* ed. Gregg Barak. Routledge, 2015.

White, Rob. "Environmental Victimology and Ecological Justice." In *Crime, Victims and Policy: International Contexts, Local Experiences*, eds. Stuart Ross and Dean Wilson. Palgrave, 2015.

White, Rob. "The Four Ways of Eco-Global Criminology." *International Journal for Crime, Justice and Social Democracy* 6(1) (2017): 8–22.

White, Rob. "Ecocentrism and Criminal Justice." *Theoretical Criminology* 22(3) (2018): 342–362.

White, Rob. "Green Victimology and Non-Human Victims." *International Review of Victimology* 24(2) (2018): 239–255.

White, Rob. "Critical Green Criminology." In *Theorising Green Criminology: Selected Essays,* ed. Rob White. Routledge, 2022.

White, Rob. "Ecocentrism and Criminal Justice." In *Theorising Green Criminology: Selected Essays,* ed. Rob White. Routledge, 2022.

Whyte, David. "Regimes of Permission and State-Corporate Crime." *State Crime Journal* 3(2) (2014): 237–246.

Whyte, David. *Ecocide: Kill the Corporation before it Kills Us.* Manchester University Press, 2020.

Whyte, Jessica. *The Morals of the Market: Human Rights and the Rise of Neoliberalism.* Verso, 2019.

Whyte, Kyle. "The Recognition Paradigm of Environmental Injustice." In *The Routledge Handbook of Environmental Justice,* eds. Ryan Holifield, Jayajit Chakraborty and Gordon Walke. Routledge, 2018.

Wijdekop, Femke. "Against Ecocide: Legal Protection for Earth." *Great Transition Initiative*, August 2016. https://www.greattransition.org/images/Against-Ecocide.pdf.

Wijdekop, Femke. "Restorative Justice Responses to Environmental Harm." *An IUCN Report* (2019): 79–80. http://files.harmonywithnatureun.org/uploads/upload864.pdf.

Wijdekop, Femke and Anneke van Hoek. "Green Criminology and Restorative Justice: Natural Allies?" In *Environmental Justice Restoring the Future*, eds. Emanuela Biffi and Brunilda Pali. European Forum for Restorative Justice, 2019.

Williams, Melissa. S. and Rosemary Nagy, "Introduction." In *Transitional Justice*, eds. Melissa S. Williams, Rosemary Nagy and Jon Elster. New York University Press, 2012.

Williams, Paul and Ian Taylor. "Neoliberalism and the Political Economy of the 'New' South Africa." *New Political Economy* 5(1) (2000): 21–40.

Williams, Paul and Milena Sterio. *Research Handbook on Post-Conflict State Building*. Elgar, 2020.

Williams, Sarah and Emma Palmer. "Transformative Reparations for Women and Girls at the Extraordinary Chambers in the Courts of Cambodia." *International Journal of Transitional Justice* 10(2) (2016): 311–331.

Winter, Stephen. "Towards a Unified Theory of Transitional Justice." *International Journal of Transitional Justice* 7(2) (2013): 224–244.

Wolfe, Patrick. "Settler Colonialism and the Elimination of the Native." *Journal of Genocide Research* 8(4) (2006): 387–409.

Woolford, Andrew and Wanda Hounslow. "Symbiotic Victimisation and Destruction: Law and Human/Other-than-human Relationality in Genocide." In *Genocide and Victimology*, ed. Yarin Eski. Routledge, 2020.

Ximena, Sierra Camargo. "The Ecocentric Turn of Environmental Justice in Colombia." *King's Law Journal* 30(2) (2019): 224–33.

Yaka, Özge. "Rethinking Justice: Struggles for Environmental Commons and the Notion of Socio-Ecological Justice." *Antipode* 51(1) (2019): 353–372.

Yankah, Kwesi. "Displaced Academies and the Quest for a New World Academic Order." *Africa Today* 42(3) (1995): 7–25.

Yefet, Bosmat. "Egypt after the 2011 Uprising: The Implications of Transitional Justice in a Non-Liberal Transition." *The Journal of North African Studies* 29(2) (2024): 332–358.

Yusuf, Hakeem O. "Colonialism and the Dilemmas of Transitional Justice in Nigeria." *International Journal of Transitional Justice* 12(2) (2018): 257–276.

Zaitch, Damián and Laura Gutiérrez Gómez. "Mining as State-Corporate Crime: The Case of AngloGold Ashanti in Colombia." In *The Routledge International Handbook of Crimes of the Powerful*, ed. Gregg Barak. Routledge, 2015.

Zaragocin, Sofia and Martina Angela Caretta. "Cuerpo-Territorio: A Decolonial Feminist Geographical Method for the Study of Embodiment." *Annals of the American Association of Geographers* 111(5) (2020): 1503–1518.

Zartner, Dana. "The Culture of Law: Understanding the Influence of Legal Tradition on Transitional Justice in Post-Conflict Societies." *Indiana International & Comparative Law Review* 22(2) (2012): 297–316.

Zukas, Alex. "Terra Incognita/Terra Nullius: Modern Imperalism, Maps, and Deception." In *Lived Topographies and Their Mediational Forces*, eds. Gary Backhaus and John Murungi. Lexington Books, 2005.

Zunino, Marcus. *Justice Framed: A Genealogy of Transitional Justice*. CUP, 2019.

Legal Documents

African Union. *Transitional Justice Policy: An Integrated, Prosperous and Peaceful Africa*. Adopted 12 February 2019.

Association of Southeast Asian Nations (ASEAN). *Human Rights Declaration*, 19 November 2012.

Auckland District Court. *Auckland City Council v 12 Carlton Gore Road Ltd and Mary-Anne Catherine McKay Lowe*, McElrea DCJ, 11 April 2005.

Auckland District Court. *Canterbury Regional Council v Interflow (NZ) Ltd*, McElrea DCJ, 2 March 2006.

Auckland District Court, *Rodney District Council v Sam Wong and Josh Topou*, JP Doogue DCJ, 28 February 2005.

Auckland District Court. *Waikato Regional Council v Huntly Quarries Ltd*, McElrea DCJ, 30 July 2003 and 28 October 2003.

CAVR. *Chega! The Final Report of the Timor-Leste Commission for Reception, Truth and Reconciliation (CAVR)*. KPG in cooperation with STP-CAVR, 2013.

Colombia. *Final Agreement to End the Armed Conflict and Build a Stable and Lasting Peace*. Colombia-FARC-EP, 24 November 2016.

Colombian Congress. *Decree-Law 4633*. 2011.

Commission of Truth and Friendship. *Per Memoriam ad Spem: Final Report of the Commission of Truth and Friendship (CTF) Indonesia – Timor-Leste*. 2008.

Commission on the Truth for El Salvador. *From Madness to Hope: the 12-Year War in El Salvador: Report of the Commission on the Truth for El Salvador*, https://www.usip.org/sites/default/files/file/ElSalvador-Report.pdf.

Council of Europe. *European Convention for the Protection of Human Rights and Fundamental Freedoms*, as amended by Protocols Nos. 11 and 14, ETS 5, 4 November 1950.

Ecuador. *Constitution of Ecuador, Republic of Ecuador*. Entered into force 20 October 2008.

European Court of Human Rights. *Aksoy v. Turkey*, Judgment, App. No. 21987/93, 18 December 1996.

European Court of Human Rights. *Aydin v. Turkey*, Judgment, App. No. 23178/94, 25 September 1997.

European Court of Human Rights. *Bazorkina v. Russia*, App. No. 69481/01, 27 June 2006.

European Court of Human Rights. *Jordan v. United Kingdom*, App. No. 24746/94, 4 May 2001.

European Parliament. *Legislative Resolution of 27 February 2024 on the Proposal for a Directive of the European Parliament and of the Council on the Protection of the Environment Through Criminal Law and Replacing Directive 2008/99/ EC (COM (2021)0851 – C9-0466/2021 – 2021/0422(COD))*. 27 February 2024.

European Union. *The EU's Policy Framework on Support to Transitional Justice*. 2015.

Government of Sri Lanka, *The Report of the Commission of Inquiry on Lessons Learnt and Reconciliation*. December 16, 2011. https://reliefweb.int/report/sri-lanka/report-commission-inquiry-lessons-learnt-and-reconciliation.

Guatemala. *Memory of Silence: Report of the Commission for Historical Clarification Conclusions and Recommendations*. February 2019.

Inter-American Court of Human Rights. *Blake v. Guatemala*, Judgment (Merits), 24 January 1998.

Inter-American Court of Human Rights. *Velasquez-Rodriguez v. Honduras*, Judgment (Merits), 29 July 1988.

Inter-American Court of Human Rights. *Moiwana Community v. Suriname*, Preliminary Objections, Merits, Reparations and Costs, 15 June 2005.

Inter-American Court of Human Rights. *Case of the Saramaka People v Suriname*, Preliminary Objections, Merits, Reparations, Costs. Series C, No. 172. 28 November 2007.

Inter-American Court of Human Rights. *Rules of Procedure*. Approved by the Court during its LXXXV Regular Period of Sessions, held from 16 to 28 November 2009.

International Committee of the Red Cross. *Guidelines on Protection of Natural Environment in Armed Conflict*. 2020. https://www.icrc.org/en/document/guidelines-protection-natural-environment-armed-conflict-rules-and-recommendations-relating%20/.

International Criminal Court. *Rules of Procedure and Evidence*. Official Records of the Assembly of States Parties to the Rome Statute of the International Criminal Court, First session, New York, 3–10 September 2002.

International Criminal Court. *Decision on the Application for Participation in the Proceedings VPRS 1, VPRS 2, VPRS 3, VPRS 4, VPRS 5 and VPRS 6 (Public Redacted Version), Situation in the Democratic Republic of the Congo* (ICC-01/04-101-tEN-Corr) Pre-Trial Chamber I, 16 January 2006.

International Criminal Court. *Situation in Darfur, The Sudan, Summary of Prosecution's Application under Article 58*. ICC- 02/ 05- 152, 14 July 2008.

International Criminal Court. Order for Reparations, *The Prosecutor v. Thomas Lubanga Dyilo*, (ICC-01/04-01/06-3129-AnxA) Appeals Chamber, 3 March 2015.

International Criminal Court. *The Prosecutor v Dominic Ongwen*, ICC-02/04-01/15, Witness UGA-PCV-0003, Open Session. 23 May 2018. https://www.icc-cpi.int/sites/default/files/Transcripts/CR2018_02682.PDF.

International Law Commission. Report of the International Law Commission on the work of its forty-third session (29 April-19 July 1991) (A/46/10). *Yearbook of the International Law Commission* 2(2) (1991).

International Law Commission. *Summaries of the Work of the International Law Commission: Protection of the Environment in Relation to Armed Conflicts*. 2021. https://legal.un.org/ilc/guide/8_7.shtml.

Jurisdicción Especial para la Paz. *Case 002. Auto SRVBIT 079/19*, 12 November 2019.

Jurisdicción Especial para la Paz. *Caso 002. Auto 094*. 10 June 2020.

Jurisdicción Especial para la Paz. *Caso 002. Auto SRVBIT 079*. 12 November 2019.

Jurisdicción Especial para la Paz. *Caso 002. Resolución SRVBIT*. Auto 018. 24 January 2020.

Jurisdicción Especial para la Paz. *Caso 005. Auto 002*. 17 January 2020.

Jurisdicción Especial para la Paz. *Caso 009. Ruling SRVBIT-XCBM-NNHC-JJCP-ACHP- 01.* 11 July 2024.
Jurisdicción Especial para la Paz. *Caso 05. Auto SRVR 226.* 11 July 2023.
Kosovo Specialist Chambers. *Rules of Procedure and Evidence.* Adopted on 17 March 2017, revised on 29 May 2017, entered into force on 5 July 2017, KSC-BD-03/Rev2/2020/1.
League of Arab States. *Arab Charter on Human Rights*, adopted 22 May 2004, entered into force 15 March 2008.
New Zealand Parliament. *Te Urewera Act 2014.* Public Act 2014 No 51.
New Zealand Parliament. *Te Awa Tupua (Whanganui River Claims Settlement) Act 2017.* Public Act 2017 No 7.
Organisation of African Unity (OAU). *African Charter on Human and Peoples' Rights* ("Banjul Charter"), CAB/LEG/67/3 rev. 5, 21 I.L.M. 58 (1982), 27 June 1981.
Organisation of American States (OAS), *American Convention on Human Rights*, ("Pact of San Jose"), Costa Rica, 22 November 1969.
Organisation of American States (OAS). *Additional Protocol to the American Convention on Human Rights in the Area of Economic, Social and Cultural Rights (Protocol of San Salvador)*, entered into force 16 November 1999 OAS Treaty Series No 69 (1988).
Republic of Korea. Truth and Reconciliation Commission, *Activities of the Past Three Years.* March 2009.
Republic of Liberia, Truth and Reconciliation Commission. *Volume Three: Appendices, Title III: Economic Crimes and the Conflict, Exploitation and Abuse.*
South Africa. *Promotion of National Unity and Reconciliation Act 1995.*
Special Tribunal for Lebanon, *Rules of Procedure and Evidence, STL-BD-2009-01-Rev.10*, adopted on 20 March 2009.
UN Compensation Commission. *Governing Council, Report and Recommendations made by the Panel of Commissioners Concerning the Fifth Instalment of 'F4' Claims.* S/AC.26/2005/10. 4 April 2005.
UN Economic and Social Council Official Records. *Revised and Updated Report on the Question of the Prevention and Punishment of the Crime of Genocide.* Human Rights Sub-Commission on the Prevention of Discrimination and Protection of Minorities, 38th Sess., UN Doc. E/CN.4/Sub.2/1985/6. 1985.
UN General Assembly. *Basic Principles and Guidelines on the Right to a Remedy and Reparation for Victims of Gross Violations of International Human Rights Law and Serious Violations of International Humanitarian Law*, UNGA Res 60/147. 15 December 2005.
UN General Assembly. *Universal Declaration of Human Rights*, A/RES/217(III). 10 December 1948.
UN General Assembly. *International Covenant on Civil and Political Rights.* United Nations Treaty Series, vol. 999, p. 171. 16 December 1966.
UN General Assembly. *International Covenant on Economic, Social and Cultural Rights.* United Nations Treaty Series, vol. 993, p. 3. 16 December 1966.
UN General Assembly. *Declaration of Basic Principles of Justice for Victims of Crime and Abuse of Power*, UNGA Res 40/34. 29 November 1985.
UN General Assembly. *Rome Statute of the International Criminal Court* (last amended 2010), ISBN No. 92-9227-227-6. 17 July 1998.
UN General Assembly. *Declaration on the Rights of Indigenous Peoples, A/RES/61/295.* 2 October 2007.
UN Security Council. *The Rule of Law and Transitional Justice in Conflict and Post-Conflict Societies: Report of the Secretary General, S/2004/616.* 23 August 2004.

UN Environment Programme. *From Conflict To Peacebuilding: The Role Of Natural Resources And The Environment*. U.N. Doc. DEP/1079/GE, U.N. Sales No. 09.III.D.14. 2009.

UN Environment Programme. *Protecting the Environment During Armed Conflict: An Inventory and Analysis of International Law*. United Nations Environment Programme, 2009.

UN Secretary-General. *The Rule of Law and Transitional Justice in Conflict and Post-Conflict Societies*. UN Doc. S/2004/616. 23 August 2004.

UN Secretary-General. *Promotion of Truth, Justice, Reparation and Guarantees of Non-Recurrence*. UN Doc. No. A/76/180. 19 July 2021.

UN Security Council. *Statute of the International Criminal Tribunal for the Prosecution of Persons Responsible for Genocide and Other Serious Violations of International Humanitarian Law Committed in the Territory of Rwanda and Rwandan Citizens Responsible for Genocide and Other Such Violations Committed in the Territory of Neighbouring States, between 1 January 1994 and 31 December 1994*. UNSC Res. 955 (1994). 8 November 1994.

UN Security Council, 8372nd Meeting, SC/13540, 16 October 2018.

UN Security Council. *Final Report of the Panel of Experts on the Illegal Exploitation of Natural Resources and Other Forms of Wealth of the Democratic Republic of Congo*, S/2002/1. 16 October 2002.

UN Security Council. *Report of the Secretary-General on the Rule of Law and Transitional Justice in Conflict and Post-Conflict Societies*. UN Doc S/2004/616 (2004). 23 August 2004.

UN War Crimes Commission, *Destruction of Polish Forests as a War Crime' Examination of Cases and Listing of War Criminals,* 1948 History of the United Nations War Crimes Commission and the Development of the Laws of War.

INDEX

'This is an exceptional book. It meets the vital need for transitional justice to acknowledge harms to Nature as simultaneously antecedent and connected to the harms of mass violence. The book is prescient in its demand to revolutionize transitional justice by decolonizing and greening the field, and by providing a multifaceted roadmap on how to do it. It allows us to think beyond anthropocentric transitional justice and confront the field's visible fault lines. It makes an outstanding contribution to the field.'

Fionnuala Ní Aoláin KC (Hons), *Professor of Law, Queens University Belfast and Robina Chair in Law, Public Policy and Society at the University of Minnesota Law School*

'This book is exhaustively researched and exhilaratingly novel; it is precise and probative while also bursting with panache. The authors identify the shortcomings of neo-liberalist transitional justice, and ... inspire with their engagement with alternate paths forward.'

Mark Drumbl, *Director, Transnational Law Institute, Washington and Lee University, USA*

'This brilliant book provides a thought-provoking argument for including harms against Nature and ecological restoration alongside human reparation in the transitional justice process. Critical, compassionate, and challenging, it will stimulate significant reflection about greening transitional justice now and into the future. A must-read.'

Rob White, *Emeritus Distinguished Professor, University of Tasmania, Australia*

'This book is a groundbreaking call to expand the scope of transitional justice by embracing ecological inclusivity. The vision of a 'green' transitional justice presented here is ambitious and inspiring ... a must-read for students, scholars, or anyone committed to sustainable, inclusive justice.'

Damien Short, *Co-Director, Environmental Humanities Research Hub, University of London, UK*

9781032206202